Comparative Economic Development

Internationally written and refereed, *Butterworths Advanced Economics Texts* seek to inform students and professional economists by providing clarity and rigour in economic analysis.

General Editor

Bruce Herrick
Department of Economics,
Washington and Lee University, USA

Consulting Editors

John Enos
Magdalen College,
University of Oxford, UK

Michael Roemer
Harvard Institute for International
   Development,
Harvard University, USA

Gerald Helleiner
Department of Political Economy,
University of Toronto, Canada

Pan Yotopoulos
Food Research Institute,
Stanford University, USA

Published titles

Cases in Economic Development by M. Roemer and J. Stern

Other titles are under consideration

Butterworths Advanced Economics Texts

Comparative Economic Development

David K. Whynes
University of Nottingham

Butterworths
London Boston Durban Singapore Sydney Toronto Wellington

First published 1983

© Butterworth & Co (Publishers) Ltd 1983

British Library Cataloguing in Publication Data

Whynes, David K.
   Comparative economic development. – (Butterworths
   advanced economics texts)
   I. Title
   330.9   HD82

   ISBN 0-408-10683-2
   ISBN 0-408-10682-4 Pbk

Filmset by Northumberland Press Ltd, Gateshead.
Printed and bound in Great Britain by
The Thetford Press Ltd, Thetford, Norfolk.

For Sandra

Preface

Remarking upon the disputes between the followers of Confucius and those of Lao Tzu in the first century BC, the Chinese historian Ssu-ma Ch'ien observed that 'people who follow different ways never have anything helpful to say to one another'. As an empirical observation, this statement has a sad validity. The fabric of human history is interwoven with both individuals and societies either disagreeing with one another about what should be done in particular sets of circumstances or contesting the appropriate methods of reaching a desired end. More often than not, such disputes have had bloody resolutions; the continuum of history is not so much punctuated by international warfare, political revolution and religious persecution as made up of them. I see no reason, however, to take Ssu-ma Ch'ien's remark as a methodological principle, asserting that the followers of one particular way cannot learn anything from the followers of another. In fact, I should prefer to argue the opposite for two reasons. In the first place, irrespective of the objectives and methods that we ourselves choose, the ways of others are instructive. They provide information to us and also serve as a bench-mark against which we can appraise and evaluate our own concepts and preconceptions. Second, and most important for a world that is now capable of obliterating itself almost instantaneously, an appreciation of others' values is vital for an understanding of others' actions and their implications for ourselves.

This book is about 'different ways' in a quite specific sense. It examines alternative conceptions of the goals of economic activity and, *pari passu*, alternative economic structures and institutions that might be devised to allow such goals to be attained. As the title implies, the theme is the comparison of different ways of operating an economy and the assessment of the outcomes that these ways have, both for the society concerned and for other coexisting societies. Should prospective readers insist on some form of classification, they might like to treat this book as a study of 'comparative economic systems' set in the context of 'economic development'. By the end of the book, I hope to have persuaded them that they would be equally entitled to treat it as the exact opposite.

Broadly speaking, the argument proceeds from the purely abstract, through the theoretical, to the empirical. Part I explores the concept of economic progress, a concept central to the entire book. Although I shall define progress in detail at a later stage, we may think of it for the moment as a movement from a less-preferred to a more-preferred state of affairs. Indeed, Chapter 1 sets the scene by discussing such fundamental ideas. Chapter 2 considers the variety of ways in which individuals and societies actually look at and interpret the economic world, emphasizing the sorts of objectives that they seek for their economic systems. It also discusses the difficulties involved in translating abstract or metaphysical objectives into operational policy goals. Chapter 3 reviews and appraises some of the theories of economic progess that have been developed by successive generations of economists, although the wide scope of the enquiry requires us to consider also the views of theorists not generally considered 'economists'. Such theories attempt to identify the basic cause or engine of progressive change. We shall see, however, that certain individuals have expressed doubts about the extent to which this engine can continue to function satisfactorily. The Appendix to Part I is a more technical discussion of the methods currently employed in the measurement of progress.

Irrespective of the means or ends that a particular society chooses in designing its economic structures, it will be obliged to provide answers to a range of questions common to all societies. These questions relate to the nature of economic institutions, consumption, production and external relationships. Part II considers six broad issues in policy formulation that all societies confront. To begin with, all societies are clearly composed of more than one individual. There will therefore exist the problem of designing the method of collective decision making to select policy goals and instruments. Chapter 4 considers the problem of how societies make up their minds. Chapter 5 develops this theme by examining the sorts of 'ground rules' that could be established to serve as a basis for economic behaviour. Not surprisingly, different conceptions of the appropriate social choice procedures and legal constraints or obligations give rise to a range of quite distinct possible outcomes. Chapters 6–8 discuss the basic economic concepts of consumption and production – Chapter 6 considers consumers in terms of the demands they make upon their productive systems, whilst Chapters 7 and 8 analyse the productive inputs of labour and capital respectively. Because no society exists in complete isolation from others, Chapter 9 explores the variety of forms of international economic interrelationships and discusses the implications of different relationships for the parties concerned.

Part III focusses upon empirical experience, by analysing the ways in which particular economies have approached the problem of generating economic progress. It examines the fortunes of countries that either hold similar views of the proper objectives of economic policy (in spite of institutional differences) or confront a similar range of economic problems by virtue of sharing the same type of economic structure. Thus Chapter 10 appraises the progress of two high-growth economies – the Soviet Union and Japan – whilst Chapter 11 deals with the recent experiences of the Western 'mixed economies'. Economic policy in Sweden, and the provision of health care, come in for particular attention. Chapter 12 looks at the specific problems of those economies that share the common characteristic of low levels of material welfare – India and China are case studies here. Chapter 13 parallels the concern of Chapter 9, namely, economic policy in a multinational world. It explores the extent to which the economic strategy of one nation might be constrained by the strategy of another, and goes on to discuss how such a constraint might be overcome. The alternatives open to nations in this respect are, broadly, conflict or cooperation. In keeping with the best traditions of expository writing, I have reserved the final chapter for the more controversial of my personal reflections and speculations.

As with any other book of this kind, the more the readers know about economics, politics and sociology, the more profound will be their insights upon reading it. Nevertheless, the exposition aims squarely at undergraduate students who have completed courses in the principles of economics. It does not require that they have gone on to more specialized studies in comparative systems or economic development. Whilst the target audience therefore consists largely of economists in training, I have taken pains to make the work accessible to students of other social science disciplines. I hope they will profit by reading it, in part because it reveals how economists approach the very broadest problems in economics. The level of discourse is rigorous but non-mathematical; graphs supplement the analysis on occasions.

Any book of less than encyclopaedic proportions must balance breadth and depth, 'forest' and 'trees'. The present volume tries to assay the Big Picture. I feel that the function of any book that aspires to instruct is to raise the most important questions and, hopefully, to stimulate critical minds into exploring the variety of possible answers which the world has to offer. To this end, I have appended a brief Summary to each chapter, to remind readers of the nodes of substantial enquiry. The Further Reading section at the end of each chapter not only lists works that I have found useful in the formulation of my arguments, but also suggests points of departure for those wishing to develop their own individual answers.

Although the words of this book are mine, it goes without saying that a great many of the ideas originate from others. The Bibliography is a catalogue of my most obvious intellectual debts. I have been fortunate in securing the assistance of many people during the writing of this book, and I should like to express my gratitude to the following in particular.

Peter Richardson, of Butterworths, offered enthusiasm and encouragement throughout. Bruce Herrick subjected the entire manuscript to rigorous scrutiny and the results of his perceptive suggestions can be found on every page. My colleagues at Nottingham graciously permitted their expertise in particular areas to be ruthlessly pillaged, thus allowing me to feign knowledge of a variety of specialisms. The United Nations, the International Labour Office, the World Health Organization, the Organization for Economic Cooperation and Development, and the General Agreement on Tariffs and Trade kindly allowed me to reproduce copyright statistical material. Although they had no direct influence on the present volume, I should also like to thank Jack Wiseman, for helping to make me into an economist, and Roger Bowles, for helping to ensure that I remained one. Needless to say, the remaining deficiencies and errors within the book are attributable to myself alone. Finally, I thank my parents for their faith and support, and Sandra, for her continual reminders that I am, after all, only human. Incidentally, on a point of style, it is to be regretted that the English language does not contain a non-specific gender. I have therefore followed the convention of referring to individuals in general by means of the masculine pronoun although, except where the context clearly implies the contrary, no gender discrimination is implied.

Contents

List of Tables and Figures

The Concept of Progress

Chapter One

Background to Progress

In evolutionary terms, *homo sapiens* is a new and remarkably successful animal. Having emerged only within the past few hundred thousand years, the species has spread to all corners of the globe and is currently represented by some 4000 million individuals. No other animal of comparable size has yet managed to match such a number nor has it been able to survive in such diverse habitats as has mankind – jungles, swamps, deserts, high in the air, on and beneath the sea and even (albeit for a brief period) on the surface of the moon. Furthermore, although the individual members of the human species are extremely similar from the biological point of view, they exhibit tremendous behavioural diversity. They are observed to live, for example, under many different regimes of social organization – families, tribes, communes, nations and federations and also, on rare occasions, as hermits. Different social groups eat different food, communicate in different languages, worship different gods and think different thoughts. Such groups have adopted a variety of methods for obtaining the material necessities of life – some hunt and eat other animals, some cultivate crops, whilst others depend upon the creation and operation of complex machinery. This being the case, the question that immediately presents itself is how have these circumstances of numerical proliferation and geographical diversity arisen in such a short space of time? We can approach an answer to this by examining our origins.

1.1 The descent of man

Our knowledge of the greater part of mankind's history is lamentably thin. In particular, our understanding of the remote past is determined by the archaeological record and very few remains from the dawn of human history have so far been unearthed. Even this handful of bones

3

and skull fragments is the subject of considerable controversy and it is quite probable that the future discovery of new remains will necessitate further amendments to the human story. Mankind's closest living relatives are the great apes and it appears that man and ape shared a common evolutionary line until some 30 million years ago. At this time, the hominoid and pongoid lines (producing man and gorilla respectively) began their divergence. Whilst a number of evolutionary similarities continued and are in evidence today (for example, manual dexterity, the refinement of the visual sense and the development of the social grouping), evolutionary divergence resulted primarily from differential environmental adaption. Although apes remained, and continue to be, forest dwellers, the hominoid line took to the plains and this resulted in profound changes in hominoid physiology. The fore and hind limbs became increasingly specialized for manipulation and locomotion respectively and the upright posture was gradually adopted. The hominoid diet also appears to have changed from predominantly herbivorous to predominantly carnivorous.

Anthropologists recognize a number of distinct evolutionary stages through which the hominoid line passed, but the first representative to which the designation *homo* is given emerged, at most, one million years ago. *Homo erectus* (upright man) differed from his hominoid ancestors and his pongoid relatives in several respects, possibly the most significant being his possession of an enlarged brain and fully developed bipedal locomotion. Indeed, in this latter respect, *homo erectus* differed little from modern man, subsequent changes taking place in the areas of brain size and cranial anatomy. The eventual arrival of modern *homo sapiens* (thinking or wise man) remains the subject of much speculation. It seems unlikely that the transition from *erectus* to *sapiens* could have occurred much earlier than 250 000 years before the present, although it is clear that the modern species was globally established by 35 000 years ago. During the intervening period, those characteristics that we term 'racial' probably emerged (for example, differential skin pigmentation and differential physical size) as a result of adaption to various climatic and other environmental conditions. We are still uncertain, however, whether this evolution was strictly unilinear or whether the present human stock has resulted from competition and/or interbreeding between a number of distinct *sapiens* lines.

In spite of these many uncertainties, we can be quite confident when it comes to identifying early man's mode of subsistence. Indeed, this mode was common to all members of the human race from the time of its emergence until approximately 10 000 years ago. Early *homo sapiens* was a hunter; he survived by killing and eating other species of animal (and often, it would appear, his fellows), supplementing this diet with fruit, bulbs and such like, gathered from freely growing plants. We have two sources for this information: first, the archaeological record and, second, observations of the few hundred thousand hunters who have survived to this day, living a life that appears to have changed little since the emergence of our species.

As far as man is concerned, the pure hunting mode of subsistence is simply consumption. Resources are taken out of the ecological system in the form of animal or plant species and this system is then left to replenish itself by means of the reproductive tendencies of the species that are hunted. In such a case, man's survival depends not upon his production, for there is none, but upon the implicit reproductive potential of the environment. Accordingly, there exists a strict ecological balance whereby excessive consumption on the part of man would lead to a decline in the number of animals and plants available for reproduction and thus to the limitation of human population by virtue of starvation.

Evidence from contemporary hunting societies tells us that, in the more abundant environments, the ecologically stable population density for hunters is of the order of 1–2 individuals per square mile; densities higher than this would lead to environmental depletion and a check on population. However, in more hostile climates such as the Arctic or the African deserts, the stable density would be perhaps one individual per 100–200 square miles. Given this sort of information, coupled with our knowledge of the geographical distribution of mankind 10 000 years ago, we can infer that, at that time, the theoretical maximum for world population was around 30 million individuals although, in all probability, the actual figure was of the order of 5–10 millions. We must conclude, therefore, that the growth of human population to its present size is a product of only the most recent past, a mere instant in geological time. Further, this growth was sustained by the increasing ability of mankind to control the environment and, in particular, to produce consumption goods from it. Although a limited amount of production certainly occurred during mankind's hunting phase – the manufacture of flint tools, for instance – the particular form of production that had the most profound impact upon population dynamics was agriculture.

The transition from a hunting way of life to an agricultural one, whereby subsistence was obtained from the cultivation of crops and the domestication of animals, was both protracted and specific to different regions of the world. In Europe, the extinction of the hunting lifestyle took some 3000 years to complete (approximately 4000 to 1000 BC). Although agriculture appeared earlier in parts of Asia and America (6000 BC) and later in Africa (3000 BC), in neither of these cases has the supercession of the hunting mode of subsistence been fully accomplished. In Australasia, non-hunting modes of subsistence were unknown until only a few centuries ago.

At first sight, it is difficult to see why any self-respecting hunter would wish to bother with agriculture. There is, after all, nothing particularly arduous about the hunting lifestyle in that, hunting in a band, each individual is obliged to put in only a few hours' work per day to provide his basic needs. Indeed, the overall impression that one gets of present-day hunters is that they lead an uncomplicated life of leisure whilst present-day agriculturalists appear to spend most of their waking hours in tending their herds and crops. Why, therefore, did the agricultural revolution take place?

It seems likely that the development of agriculture was the product of both conscious decision and necessity. It is clear that 'hunting man' possessed the technology of agricultural production at an early stage; dogs, for example, had long been domesticated and it would not require a great deal of ingenuity on the part of our ancestors to appreciate that other animals might similarly be domesticated for specific uses as food sources. The necessity aspect undoubtedly arose from the diminution of hunting possibilities in certain areas. Some 10000 years ago many large mammal species such as the mammoth, steppe bison and giant elk became extinct and it is suspected that this resulted both from over-hunting and from the substantial climatic changes of the period. Diversification of the means of subsistence thus became necessary for survival.

The earliest agriculture was almost certainly nomadic and was probably still supplemented by hunting. Agricultural styles differed, depending upon the prevailing conditions. Inhabitants of those regions still populated by herd animals, for example, became pastoralists, following their now-domesticated herds from one pasture to the next. Forest-dwellers developed the 'slash-and-burn' arable technique that is widely practised in such areas today. Under this system, an area is cleared by means of axe and fire and crops are grown for several years until the soil's natural fertility is exhausted. The site is then abandoned and the process is repeated elsewhere. Although 'slash-and-burn' is a relatively unsophisticated technique, it nevertheless permits a far higher population density than does the pure hunting lifestyle. The precise figure naturally depends upon climate and soil fertility, but the typical order of magnitude is ten or even a hundred times the density obtainable by means of hunting alone. This being the case, agricultural developments clearly paved the way for population growth. After some time, this nomadic life began to give way to existence within permanent agricultural settlements; such a transition was both voluntary and coerced – more efficient agricultural techniques permitted the feeding of a static population on a fixed area of land. Mobility was, in many cases, hampered by local population growth that increased the pressure on resources.

The establishment of settled agricultural communities marks the appearance of many basic economic and social institutions that exist today and will concern us at later stages of our enquiry. We begin to recognize concepts such as 'property', 'government' and even 'slavery' as taking on the same significance that we in the present confer upon them. Naturally, the particular forms of these institutions were specific to different communities. In some cases, societies emerged that were run along decentralized lines, composed of a number of local tribal or family units that were largely responsible for their own affairs. At the opposite extreme, we observe highly centralized societies in which a small group of individuals retained the political power to direct the efforts of the mass of the subject population. Such a system of authority contributed to the rise of the great agriculture-based civilizations of Rome, Egypt and India.

Coincident with the development of agriculture were advances in productive technology. These included many of contemporary significance such as the crafts of weaving, pottery and the smelting and working of metals. That most famous of early inventions – the wheel – first appeared some 5000 years ago. Many of these discoveries were of particular use in increasing agricultural production still further; the ox-drawn plough, for example, made its first appearance at the same time as the wheel. Indeed, fundamental to the existence of the early settlements were innovations in agriculture itself, such as irrigation and manuring.

The agricultural revolution effectively represented the possibility of production based upon the control of organic sources of energy. The management of animals and plants increased the availability and reliability of food supply whilst the use of animals and slaves as motive power increased the physical inputs into production. As a consequence, the transition to agriculture greatly raised the ecological ceiling for population growth. The early hunting cultures maintained a population equilibrium via high birth and death rates but agriculture served generally to lower such death rates. From around 10 000 years ago we accordingly observe a gradual increase in human numbers, reaching perhaps 100 million individuals by the start of the Christian era and at least 500 million by AD 1700. With the exception of localized shocks such as famines caused by crop failure, or epidemic disease, this increase seems to have been fairly regular and of the order of one-quarter to one-half of a percentage point each year. Since around AD 1700, however, the annual growth rate of world population has increased and, at present, stands at some two percentage points per annum. This explosion in population growth may be accounted for by a second revolution in the means of subsistence, namely, industrialization.

1.1.1 THE IMPACT OF INDUSTRIALIZATION

Cipolla (1965) has remarked that the central characteristic of industrialization is that it represents the harnessing of a new source of energy. The development of agriculture permitted mankind to exercise far more control over the animate energy sources – plants and animals – and this control facilitated an increase in the consumable output available. Correspondingly, the industrial revolution can be seen as an equivalent process concerned with the harnessing of inanimate forms of energy.

Historically, the earliest such role was played by wind and water power but it was the introduction of steam power, based upon coal, that paved the way for the major increases in production in eighteenth-century Western Europe where industrialization first appeared. Since that time newer energy forms have been exploited: natural and manufactured gas, electricity, petroleum and, most recently, nuclear energy.

The industrial revolution has differed from its agricultural predecessor in at least two fundamental respects. In the first place, the movement towards agriculture appears to have been initiated independently in several regions of the world. By contrast, industrialization really emerged in just one region – Western Europe – and was then transmitted via a variety of mechanisms to other continents. Second, the industrial revolution has been a far less protracted affair for, whilst European agriculturalization required three millenniums, European industrialization has been accomplished in less than three centuries. Why industrialization should have begun in Europe, and in England and France in particular, is a complex question; the following answer is accordingly suggestive and not definitive.

The economic organization of medieval England was quite different from that characterizing, say, the earlier great agricultural empires of Rome and India. Within these empires, the ruling group of king and nobility came to own all the territory and had formed an homogeneous bloc of interest that dictated the affairs of society as a whole. Indeed, Wittfogel (1957) has suggested that the centralized bureaucratic structure of these civilizations was intimately intertwined with their productive efficiency, which was based upon large-scale irrigation networks, and this centralized control permitted the channelling of productive effort into the development of what we recognize as the hallmarks of such civilizations – highways, communications systems, monuments and defences.

In contrast, power within the English feudal system was far more decentralized. In the fourteenth and fifteenth centuries, this feudal regime came under pressure as a succession of plagues eliminated perhaps 50 per cent of the population. Coincidentally, the monetarization of production emerged. Formerly, individual farmers had held their land from the local landlord in return for the provision of labour services but, from this time, we observe the beginnings of cash payments, i.e. rent. In addition, the post-plague labour shortages obliged landlords to attempt to attract workers to their estates and this too was accomplished by payment, i.e. we observe the emergence of wage-labour.

The urban centres of England in the later medieval period were quite unlike towns in other regions of the world. Although their social composition was not dissimilar – merchants, craftsmen, servants and so forth – they remained to a large extent beyond the control either of the feudal aristocracy or of any centralized government. Individual holders of wealth accordingly possessed a great deal of autonomy in the use of this wealth and one of the uses to which such wealth could be put was manufacture – the purchase of capital equipment, the hire of wage-labour and the sale of production at a profit.

The massive expansion of production in eighteenth-century England thus resulted from a combination of three factors. First, substantial capital accumulation began to occur and, second, wage-labour became available to be used alongside such capital. Finally, the effect of this increase in potential factor inputs was magnified by the rapid technological progress of the period, which had the effect of increasing the output/input ratio in manufacturing industry. In these terms, the major innovations took place in the textile industry, which, during the eighteenth century, saw the introduction of steam-powered machines for spinning and weaving. At the same time, the technology of iron and steel manufacture was advanced, as was the technology of motive power itself. As industrialization advanced, the ripples on the pond moved outwards. Technical progress, for example, was applied back into agriculture to stimulate the production of foodstuffs, thus permitting a rise in the feasible level of population and the accumulation of more wealth to be used as capital investment. Transport networks were developed that oiled the wheels of commerce by facilitating exchange and factor mobility. The development of such markets further advanced the trend towards specialization and increased production.

As industrialization continued, the total output of consumable items increased rapidly. The main dynamic of this increase was competition. Factories, machines and sources of energy were in the hands of many thousands of individuals who, in order to survive, had to use their holdings to produce commodities exchangeable for the necessities of life. This involved producing goods of sufficient cheapness and/or novelty to encourage purchase by the rest of the population. Similarly, the industrial labour force, which was growing in size as a result of natural increase and gradual alienation from the land as labour-saving agricultural techniques were developed, had to offer its services to the owners of capital in return for wages with which purchases might be made. Although philosophers have delighted in describing the condition of man the hunter as the state of nature – the war of all against all – this description is far more applicable to the early period of English industrialization. One consequence was rapid innovation, cost reduction and the substantial growth of material output.

The harnessing of new energy sources and the control of productive potential was not confined to England alone for, although it was certainly the first to emerge as an industrialized economy, similar transitions were also occurring in the neighbouring states of Western Europe. During the nineteenth century, however, industrialization was to break out of this geographical confinement with great rapidity. Although the European states had established contact with other regions of the world at an earlier stage in their histories, competition for resource inputs, the search for new markets in which to sell their products and the desire to find living space for growing populations all resulted in the extension of European influence on such regions. Within a very short space of time, vast tracts of land including the continents and subcontinents of India, Africa and South America – areas where little indigenous industrialization had thus far occurred – were brought into the European orbit. In the majority of cases, this influence was exerted by physical conquest.

If it is hard to assess the global impact of agriculturalization, it is even more difficult to formulate generalizations about the overall impact of industrialization. From a world point of view, this particular revolution is still in its infancy. Only in a handful of modern states – the USA, Japan, Western Europe – do we find a significant proportion of the population engaged in non-agricultural pursuits. On the other hand, it would be foolish to understate the profound influence of industrialization and its consequences for human history over the past few centuries. As our understanding of the present is contingent upon our conceptions of the past, we must attempt to unravel some of the strands that have contributed to the current state of affairs. For our present purpose, the following would seem to be of the greatest significance.

For the inhabitant of an industrialized economy, the process of industrialization brought about a dramatic change in the style of living. From the point of view of consumption, the range of available goods and services, and hence the potential choice open to the consumer, has been gradually extended, both by virtue of increasing material wealth and because of invention and innovation. Modern man (at least modern Western man) is truly 'modern', for his property largely consists of products of the 'modern' era – telephones, television sets, automobiles, refrigerators, air-conditioning – often constructed from 'modern' materials – plastics, nylon and fibreglass. From the production point of view, the relative contribution of labour has been drastically reduced owing to the increasing use of capital equipment. The entire scale of operation in industrialized economies has also been altered: many single factories in present-day Italy or England employ more workers than the total population of medieval Rome. Furthermore, the urban communities in which modern industrial man presently lives are out of all proportion to the size of the hunting band or the agricultural village.

As we have said, only a small fraction of the world is totally industrialized. However, a second vital feature of the industrialization tendency was the internationalization of knowledge and influence. Social intercourse is not, of course, a new phenomenon; agricultural communities had always traded with one another to diversify their consumption opportunities and we have ample archaeological evidence of early trade-based communities that specialized in particular activities such as fishing or flint-mining. War too was common between pre-industrial societies, either for the purpose of gaining control of territory or for the winning of slaves. The international impact of industrialization, however, was both quantitatively and qualitatively different. In the first place, the sheer physical power of the industrialized nations was so great that entire agriculture-based continents were overrun in a matter of years. Furthermore, the social system imposed as a result was usually totally unfamiliar to the conquered peoples and it resulted in a traumatic dislocation of their mode of living. Relatively autarkic agricultural societies were rapidly remodelled to serve the interests of the industrial nations. This spread of industrialization gave rise to the twentieth-century international economy in which whole regions, as never before, have become enmeshed in a nexus of economic interdependency. In the same way as industrialization had been accompanied by individual specialization within the productive process, internationalization gave rise to regional specialization. Broadly speaking, the industrial nations found themselves at the centre of a network of international trade, taking in primary products and exporting manufactures.

Of equal importance was the diffusion of knowledge. As a result of this cultural interaction, and also as a consequence of developments in transport and communication, new technologies were able to spread rapidly across the globe. Innovations in production quickly became common property. Such diffusion, however, was not restricted to the methods of production, for internationalization has had a marked impact upon aspirations. The contact between societies with differing styles of living, and the increased availability of information as a result of the rapid advances in communications technology, have permitted each society to appraise its own particular mode of life with reference to an increasingly wide range of practical and theoretical alternatives. We have only to open a book or turn on our television sets to be instantly acquainted with the philosophy of thinker A or the political beliefs of country B, both of which provide a datum on which to base an assessment of our own particular circumstances. The initial industrialization of nineteenth-century Russia, or even that of post-war Japan, for example, were classic cases of observation and imitation.

A third salient feature of industrialization has been its demographic impact. The demographic profile of the purely agricultural community of the past was characterized by a long-run decline in the death rate owing, amongst other things, to the increased supply of subsistence. The general upward trend in population growth was only occasionally interrupted by famine or pestilence, which reduced numbers often by a substantial proportion. In the industrializing countries, the increase in material wellbeing and improvements in medicine and hygiene precipitated a major decline in long-term mortality and especially in infant mortality, which, historically, has always been the single most important element in the determination of death rates. Accordingly, the population of Europe, where industrialization was concentrated at the time, doubled between 1750 and 1850. However, because of the internationalization of industrialization, the belief in the possibility of, and the necessary economic conditions for, reductions in mortality spread to the pre-industrialized areas of the world. By the end of the nineteenth century, therefore, the death rates in the non-industrialized economies also began to decline and the doubling of population that took place in Europe during the eighteenth and nineteenth centuries occurred in regions such as Africa, Asia and Latin America in the late nineteenth and twentieth centuries, up to the present day.

A fourth facet of industrialization is the concomitant evolution of the modern form of macropolitical organization, the nation state. Mankind has, of course, always pursued a social existence, even before it received the designation *homo*, for collaboration proved to be an effective survival mechanism. In this respect, man differs little from many other social animals. Prior to industrialization, however, the basic social and political unit appears to have been small and often with a relatively informal structure. The industrialization process, which entailed increasing specialization, mechanization and the technical sophistication of war-fare, redefined the optimum size of the economic unit. The simplest form of human socio-economic organization – the hunting band – obeys fairly precise rules in terms of size; a number less than about 25 does not constitute an efficient hunting team, whilst a number in excess of 100 constitutes too many mouths for the hands to feed successfully. The mass production of industrial society does not comply with such simple rules; from the material point of view, bigger is distinctly better. Industrialization accordingly saw the coalition of individuals into 'bands' of ever-increasing size. Indeed, we might in retrospect detect a certain inevitability about the rise of the nation state for, once a conglomerate has formed, generally the only way in which smaller individuals can compete against this coalition, in terms of the acquisition of resources and military strength, is to form a rival coalition amongst themselves. The geo-political subdivision of the world into nation states is now well entrenched in the human imagination and most contemporary social investigations, at least those at the world level, take the nation state, or the 'government' or 'economy' thereof, as the basic unit of analysis. Throughout the present study we shall follow this convention, although this will not deter us, especially at later stages of our discussions, from pointing out some of its implications and limitations.

1.2 History and progress

The preceding whistle-stop tour of 30 million years of human history has now brought us to the starting point of our enquiry proper – the present time or, more specifically, the future. This tour has been under-taken not only for reasons of completeness and, possibly, entertainment but also to introduce and support some very fundamental propositions about the present circumstances of the world and the historical path or paths that lead to such circumstances. To begin with, however, let us not consider the world in actuality but rather our conception of that world.

The historical record is a record of change, of contingency and of control. Depending upon their predilections, different stereotypes of social analyst might draw out different themes from the transitions in mankind's history. Whilst the economist, for instance, might be intrigued by the changing mode of subsistence as described earlier, the military strategist might concern himself with the changing style of conflict, from stone axes to ballistic missiles. Anthropologists and political scientists might wish to home in on the structure of kinship and the formation of governments. Much time and effort has been expended in the past in discussing such apparently profound changes as man's attitude to his gods and such apparently trivial changes as fashions in headgear. Historical analysis, however, is not simply a catalogue of facts about religion or hats. Rather, it is an attempt to discover the causal connection between temporal events, to explain why such events occurred and the extent to which one was contingent upon another. One extremely important conclusion that might be drawn from such an appraisal is the extent to which human control over historical events appeared feasible. From the point of view of biological accuracy, Marx was wrong in asserting that the feature that distinguishes man from other animals is his ability to produce his means of subsistence – certain species of ants discovered this a long time ago – but, if we interpret production in a wider sense, it certainly seems correct to assert that no other animal species possesses so much potential power over its environment. It is accordingly likely that any analysis of events will yield the conclusion that conscious human interference was at least partially responsible for the historical sequence.

The historical record is also a record of diversity. The contemporary world drama is not played by an homogeneous troupe of actors and the roles of these actors, individuals or societies, are circumscribed by their histories. Put simply, people are different, and this difference is entailed by their differing historical experiences. Different societies, for example, have access to different volumes of resources, in both quantitative and qualitative terms. Most importantly, different societies have different aspirations for the future. Paradoxically, these very differences imply an essential similarity in consequences, for what we are saying is the following.

Each individual can be taken to possess a set of desires, wants or needs, manifested in terms of a state of affairs that would be preferred: I like peanut butter and I should like to have more peanut butter. The wider world can be regarded as a repository of resources available for the satisfaction of such desires. Now, if it were the case that the sum total of available resources always exceeded the sum total of human desire then the world would indeed be a fortunate place, if only because the discipline of economics would not then exist. Economics does exist, however, and is founded upon the contrary principle that the sum total of human wants always exceeds the means available to satisfy such wants. The subject of economics is human welfare, that is, the satisfaction of human wants, and its task is to devise methods to satisfy wants as well as possible, to increase welfare as much as possible. To give a neat textbook definition, economics is the maximization of welfare subject to the constraint of resource availability.

The above is a statement of the economic problem, a problem common to all societies and to all individuals. For analytical purposes, we can break it down into three elements. First, there exists a set of desires or preferences that individuals hold and defines what they regard as welfare. Psychologists tell us that humans manifest many varieties of need, from the physiological (food, sleep, sex) to the economic (material plenty) to the sociological (social approval, status and security). Second, there exists the bundle of resources available for the satisfaction of these needs – natural resources such as coal and timber, productive power such as labour and machinery, plus the more intangible resources of the social network. The final element is the organizational or technological form that translates resources into satisfactions – systems of resource allocation, techniques of production, methods of exchange and control and so forth. In its 'pure' form (if that description is appropriate), economics is most immediately concerned with this final element, with the evaluation of alternative forms with a view to determining which one might give rise to the highest welfare level.

Accepting these propositions, we immediately see that economics has two specific inclinations. First, it is future-oriented, that is, it is concerned with the adjustment of present circumstances to yield an outcome at some point in the future. Second, it is inevitably progress-oriented, defining progress as a movement from a state of lower welfare to one of higher welfare. However, the essential point is that, whilst all individuals and/or societies will be attempting to solve this common economic problem, that is, they will be trying to progress, there is absolutely no *a priori* reason whatsoever to assume that they will adopt identical solutions. We have no grounds for believing, for example, that the particular aspirations of each and every individual in the world will be identical. Because of the subjective nature of preferences, it is quite logical for the same chain of historical events to be evaluated differently by different individuals. Consider the following example. Suppose Britain decided to automate its textile industry, with the anticipated effect of doubling textile output, of halving costs and prices, and of making half the labour force redundant. Is such automation therefore a 'progressive' move? It seems likely that we should receive different answers to this question depending upon whether we posed it to, say, a textile consumer, a now-redundant loom operator, a textile factory owner, a foreign competitor in textiles or the 'British people' (the answers being, respectively, 'yes', 'no', 'yes', 'no' and 'maybe'). The example is somewhat facetious. Questions of this nature nevertheless require an answer and the purpose of the present study is to attempt to understand the manner in which individuals, or more accurately societies, devise strategies or policies in order to bring about progress. Before embarking upon our quest, a further word or two on progress itself.

As the criterion for what constitutes a progressive change in human welfare levels is subjective, we can be fairly confident that we shall be unlikely to be able to produce a universal theory of progress. If individuals' notions of desirable ends are going to differ then it is also likely that they will not agree upon the most appropriate means of realizing such ends. However, if we remove ourselves to the realm of meta-theory (the theory of theory) we can, in fact, abstract elements that all theories of progress will possess. Indeed, the two necessary conditions for a concept of progress have already been established – a perception of changing states of the world and the possibility of associating welfare or preference levels with these states.

These two conditions merely tell us what progress is; they do not tell us how progress is to be realized. The second element of the meta-theory that gives rise to variations amongst the theories of progress is the particular theorist's answer to the general question of the causation of historical change and, in particular, the influence of human action. The reason for this variation is that the past, like the future, is uncertain. Depending upon the evidence available and the subjective weighting of that evidence in the theorist's mind, it might be suggested that the historical continuum (embracing past, present and future) is in fact a sequence of random events or, at the opposite extreme, that it operates according to strict and definable rules. As neither of these possibilities leaves a great deal of scope for independent human action we shall favour the interpretation of change as an admixture of accident, tendency and conscious direction although, as we shall shortly see, the variable balance of these ingredients produces diverse recipes. When we therefore talk about strategies for progress we have in mind three related ideas. First, we have a subjective, specific and *ex ante* conception of what we should like the world to look like in the future. Second, we are conscious of our starting point – the present – which is, of course, some function of the past. Third, we have an idea of the process via which our aspirations might be realized. The remaining chapters of this section of the book explore these ideas in more detail.

Summary

Throughout most of his time on this planet, man has been a hunter. As a hunter, he acted purely as a consumer, obtaining his means of subsistence from the natural environment. The agricultural revolution, which heralded the arrival of man the producer, began independently in many regions of the world, some 10 000 years ago. In the earliest forms of agriculture, man remained nomadic. As a pastoralist, he followed his herds from one pasture to the next. Forest-dwellers practised 'slash-and-burn' cultivation, which involved clearing a site, planting crops and migrating to a new site once the soil's fertility had become exhausted. Eventually, agricultural communities became settled and new forms of production activity emerged, e.g. commerce, pottery-making, weaving. The increased availability and reliability of the food supply paved the way for population growth.

Some two centuries ago, large-scale industrialization began in Western Europe, notably in England and France. Industrialization in England was the product of the coincidence of a number of factors, important ones being the beginnings of capital accumulation, the existence of a labour force willing to work for a wage, invention and innovation, and the ability to harness new sources of energy. Once started, industrialization spread out from Europe to other parts of the world. Although the industrial revolution remains in its infancy, several of its major effects can be identified. Industrialization has brought about a dramatic transition in way of life and has led to the internationalization of knowledge. It has been partly responsible for the formation of the modern nation state and is a major factor in explaining the high rate of world population growth over the past two centuries.

Irrespective of their specific histories, all societies face a common economic problem. This involves deciding upon the best way of using their scarce resources to satisfy the desires and preferences of their members. Any change that leads to a better allocation of resources amongst competing ends will be deemed 'progressive' by the society in question. Economic policy is explicitly future- and progress-oriented.

Further reading

The brief introduction to human prehistory follows Weiner (1971) and Clark (1978), although the latter author, in common with a number of palaeoanthropologists, uses the general term *homo habilis* to categorize the transformation of earlier hominoid forms to *homo erectus*. The discussion of the origins of agriculture and industry follows Carrington (1963) and the stimulating work of M. Harris (1978). The economic systems of agricultural peoples are analysed by Viljoen (1936) and Sahlins (1974). Coon (1972) examines the lifestyles of present-day hunting peoples. Socio-economic transitions over time in pre-industrial economies are dealt with by Pryor (1977) and by Hobhouse, Wheeler and Ginsberg (1930), the latter being a correlation of earlier anthropological research. The characteristics of feudal Europe derive from Hilton (1973), whilst the account of European industrialization follows Dobb (1946). Population estimates come from Cipolla (1965) and Petersen (1975).

Chapter Two

Economic Ideology

The range of objectives of human activity and the norms for the evaluation of socio-economic change are limited, in the same way as the potential range of human desires is limited, only by the extent of the human imagination. Accordingly, the number of possible candidates for inclusion within an individual's or a society's set of aspirations, as well as the number of permutations that place different weights on different objectives, can effectively be regarded as infinite. Each desire of the individual or the society cannot, however, be considered in isolation, for together they form a part of a body of interrelated concepts that we term an *ideology*. In simple terms, an ideology is a way of looking at the world or, in the words of Robinson (1964), society's view of the 'proper way of conducting its affairs'. A more precise definition is provided by Dobb (1975) who sees an ideology as

a whole system of thought, or coordinated set of beliefs and ideas, which form a framework, or higher-level group of related concepts, for more specific and particular notions, analyses, applications and conclusions ... At its most general an ideology implies a philosophical standpoint, in our present context a social philosophy (pp. 1–2).

The essential feature of an ideology is that it is a set of metaphysical propositions; it is *not* a set of scientific propositions in the sense that it admits to verification or falsification by reference to empirical evidence. Suppose I were to assert that 'all men are equal'. From a scientific point of view, this could be construed as meaning that I think that all men are of equal height, weight, intelligence, ability at brain surgery and so forth. Clearly, such a hypothesis would take little time to refute. However, if I make the assertion as a component of my ideology, it could be taken to imply that I believe that all men should be treated equally in terms of their dealings with society, for example with reference

17

to access to welfare services or the ability to participate in collective decision making. Even the fact that it might be observed that my society does not currently practise such equality does not invalidate my claim to hold this particular normative criterion. This being the case, the criterion for the acceptance of this ideological proposition is simply ethical acceptability, as it is for equivalent propositions such as 'our society should treat fat men better than thin men' or 'people who write economics texts should be incarcerated'.

If we can therefore possess a wide variety of metaphysical statements, the logical statuses of which are equivalent, what is the economist, as social scientist, to make of them? We appear to have no scientific criterion for discriminating between, say, the two propositions 'all men should be treated equally' and 'all men should be treated unequally'. In fact, the problem may not be as great as might be supposed for, as was suggested above, it is from the ideological presuppositions that society's practical notions about the conduct of affairs are derived and it is these notions that have scientific form. At this level, the economist can pursue his enquiries at three levels: he can test the consistency, the feasibility and the implications of the specific ideological position. Before we explore these ideas, however, let us get some impression of what real-world ideologies look like. Throughout the following we shall be concerned primarily with social or collective, rather than individual, views of the world although, as we shall see, the latter is inevitably intertwined with the former.

2.1   Components of ideology

The identification of a society's ideology is fraught with problems. Humanity has a great facility for acting in an irrational manner, from the scientific point of view, by simultaneously purporting to hold one point of view whilst following a policy that appears to be based upon another. States that enshrine in their constitutions such ideological principles as sexual equality or religious tolerance are frequently observed to practise sexual discrimination or religious persecution. Analysis from the behavioural point of view is also problematic, for the arrival of a society at a certain position does not necessarily mean that this was the outcome originally desired – Columbus, it will be recalled, found America whilst looking for India. Indeed, the economist is a cause for concern in his own right. He will have his own private ideological views and might thus interpret the consequences of unfamiliar ideologies 'incorrectly'. This being the case, we must tread rather warily.

We noted above that the potential scope for an ideological position was very wide. This should not be taken to imply, however, that different societies always adopt different positions along every possible dimension. One very common feature, for example, is the attitude to risk. Indeed, we can fairly generalize by saying that individuals and societies prefer certainty to uncertainty, other things remaining equal. This is really an established axiom of economics, for a certain increase of X welfare units may be expected to yield at least as much and probably more than an increase of X units with a less-than-unity probability factor attached. There is evidence, of course, that the running of risks *per se* actually generates welfare but we should suggest that this will occur only in cases where the risky choice might possibly yield higher benefits than the certain option.

Looking at ideology purely from an economic point of view, we can isolate three principal issues, that is, three principal dimensions along which a society will adopt a position. These are, first, the appropriate relationship between the individual and the aggregation of individuals that we term society, second, the appropriate level of material welfare and, third, the appropriate distribution of welfare benefits amongst the individuals within society. We shall examine each in turn.

2.1.1   INDIVIDUAL AND SOCIETY

Man is a social animal and the individual cannot be divorced from the society in which he lives. However, we may gain an idea of the sorts of social organizations that might be favoured by mankind if we employ the trick used by political philosophers. Let us consider a set of individuals who are contemplating the establishment of a society or state in order to secure such benefits as security or enhanced material welfare. What type of society might such individuals form?

Let us assume that what is important to the individual is the attainment of his own private ends. It is clear that a social existence might imply either the enhancement or the prevention of these ends being realized; as far as one individual is concerned, his fellows might be helpful or harmful. It seems reasonable to suppose that the greater the freedom that each individual has to pursue his own objectives without hindrance from others then the happier he will be. In addition, let us also assume that, before the society is formed, each individual has a certain basic right to control his own person and a set of material resources considered to constitute his property. Given these postulates, the appropriate form of social organization is the following.

In the first place, the only legitimate interaction that can take place between individuals is the product of the voluntary entry of such individuals into a binding agreement or contract, constituted to further their own ends. Second, the freedom of the individual in such an overall system of contracts can legitimately be constrained only by the necessity of securing equivalent freedoms for all other individuals in society. Each individual's claim to freedom is, in other words, regarded as being equally valid. Finally, we deduce that society as such exists as a facilitator and maintainer of contracts between individuals, and for the purpose of resolving disputes on the basis of some agreed procedure, disputes that might arise from a clash of individual wills.

The basic right of freedom of the individual is, in fact, a composite bundle and it possesses many facets. Machlup (1969) suggests that the following aspects of freedom will be included in the whole. First, the individual must be entitled to moral or intellectual freedom, such as the freedom to hold opinions of any persuasion and the freedom to behave in a manner not necessarily coincident with the precepts of his fellows. Second, there exists a class of political freedoms, including the freedom to participate in collective decision making, the freedom of expression and the right of privacy. Finally, economic freedoms should be secured, such as the freedom of contract between individuals in terms of, for example, the production and exchange of goods and services, the freedom of mobility and the freedom of choice of occupation.

The ideology described above is commonly referred to as 'liberalism'. The acceptance of such an ideology has a number of implications for the practical form of social and economic institutions. Amongst other things, the liberal society is likely to be one in which private property rights are defined and maintained, although such rights will be exhangeable by means of inter-individual contract. Within such a society, it is likely to be the individual who initiates economic activity with a view to enhancing his own particular welfare level. Even so, we should not necessarily anticipate that the market mechanism will be the sole form of such activity; it is quite feasible that individuals would agree to create a supra-individual agency to handle certain affairs such as collective defence. Such an agency might be empowered to tax individuals in return for the provision of benefits (in this case, security). As we shall see later, there are in fact many areas of economic activity that might be operated via either a market mechanism or a collective agency and liberal societies will accordingly be concerned to assess the superiority of alternative methods, the selection criteria being the resource cost relative to benefit and the impact upon individual freedom.

In this liberal view of the world it is held that certain rights of the individual exist at a point logically prior to the formation of the society. This being a metaphysical proposition, we have no necessary reason for accepting it. We could contrarily assert that when individuals form a society it is this society that should dictate, via the medium of its decision-making process, exactly which rights and freedoms are to be made available to the individual. The existence of a particular facet of freedom, say the freedom of speech, does not therefore exist as an *a priori* inalienable right but rather as one that society might grant to individuals if it is felt to be in the collective interest. This view of the world is more characteristic of the ideology of 'socialism' and it is likely to give rise to some significant differences in socio-economic organization from that encountered under the liberal ideology. Economic activity will generally be initiated by the collectivity (as represented by the government or appointed bodies) although, just as liberal societies might entrust activity to their governments, so socialist societies might entrust activities to particular individuals if this is deemed appropriate. Because the ownership of private property implies individual discretion over its use, socialist societies are more likely to favour collective ownership, especially of property concerned with the production of material output (the means of production). It should be noted that, in socialist societies, the form of the social decision-making structure is particularly crucial, for it is social decisions that direct activity.

The liberal philosophy is essentially that of the *preservation* of individual human rights against the encroachment of society. Although we should not expect any empirical society to conform precisely to the ideal-types discussed above, we can see evidence of this view in the constitutional documents of those modern societies, such as Britain and the United States, that purport to espouse certain liberal values. The Great Charter of 1215, for example, put specific constraints upon the power of the British monarchy, whilst the 1776 Declaration of Independence, holding that the inalienable right of liberty was a 'self-evident truth', repudiated the particular form of government that was being imposed at the time. By contrast, the socialist ideology concerns itself with the *creation* of rights and freedoms that, in the case of, say, China and the USSR, were regarded as non-existent (both theoretically and empirically) prior to the revolutionary formation of these modern states.

The liberal and the socialist models discussed above are of only recent origin. In their modern form they emerged in parallel with industrialization, and the works of the seventeenth-century theorists, such as Hobbes and Locke, are conventionally taken as the starting point for a movement away from an earlier 'traditional' ideology. From our point of view, this traditional ideology is of interest because there are certain residual elements of it in the ideologies of many modern states to which we might want to give the label 'liberal' or 'socialist', and also because of its perpetuation, in specific variants, in many regions of the contemporary pre-industrial world.

Both liberalism and socialism are based upon the concepts of individuality and, to an extent, the moral equality of individuals in terms of available rights and obligations. The distinguishing feature of the traditional ideology, in contrast, is its definition of the individual by virtue of his specific position in a network of established social rights and obligations. Each individual, in other words, is a functionary in a set order of things. In pre-industrial Europe, this established order was supported by a 'theocentric conception of authority' (Bluhm, 1974, p. 30), typically manifested as a rigid hierarchy of power and status and surmounted by a 'divinely ordained' monarch. The roles of individuals in such a system were therefore the playing of parts in accordance with the perceived wishes of the celestial scriptwriter, parts that were generally cast by accident of birth. The traditional ideology is pre-rational in the specific sense that it concerns itself with the maintenance of a network of relationships that has evolved historically and it does not seek to question the validity of the evolution.

As Gluckman (1965) has shown, different forms of traditional ideology have had different implications for rights structures. The part played by the monarch in pre-colonial Africa, for example, appears to have been exceptionally subtle. Whilst the king in African tribal society typically owned all the land (in the sense that he was able to control rights of usage), he was also obliged to make such land available to his subjects for cultivation on demand. Such reciprocity was uncommon, however, in medieval Europe where the nobility was far more advantaged in the allocation of traditional rights, to the extent that it was permitted (unlike the African king) to indulge in a style of living greatly different from that enjoyed by the mass of the population (pp. 36–43). The central point is that a traditional ideology may permit certain allocations of rights and obligations amongst individuals, depending upon their position in the social network, in a way that the liberal or the socialist society would regard as manifestly 'unfair', that is, in such a way for some groups to appear to gain at the expense of others. Given the realization of the metaphysical nature of ideology, such a claim may not be logically supportable.

2.1.2   STANDARD OF LIVING

An individual's standard of living is the level of welfare that he enjoys as a result of the consumption of resources or the product of such resources. Whilst this definition conveys the flavour of the concept, it is not very helpful for analytical purposes, as the welfare criterion is, of course, subjective. In order to make the standard of living into an operational concept, economists generally make a number of simplifying assumptions along the following lines.

In the first place, whilst the level of individual welfare is not observable or measurable, the level of consumption certainly is, for it consists of a physical bundle of goods and services. We therefore assume that there exists a one-for-one correspondence between the level of consumption and the level of welfare induced by such consumption (in mathematical terms, we are assuming that the welfare function is a monotonic transformation of the consumption function). Second, the individual's consumption bundle is bound to be heterogeneous, being composed of such items as housing, food, various manufactured goods and so forth. The aggregation of these different physical amounts is impossible unless we make the assumption that, within the society, any one item is potentially exchangeable for any other between individuals. The observation of the terms under which items are exchanged gives us a range of values for all consumption items relative to any one item, which we may term 'money'. Using money as a numeraire we may thus derive a single total for the value of consumption.

Over the longer term, welfare cannot be considered to be dependent solely upon immediate consumption for it is generally the case that resources must be forgone in one period in order to generate consumption in the next. Long-term living standards are therefore dependent upon both present period and future period consumption, that is, upon consumption now and upon investment for consumption in the future. If we now assume that the source of such consumption and investment is the production of the society concerned, we might now equate a society's standard of living with its aggregate production. The economist's label for aggregate production is gross domestic product (GDP) and the individual's standard of living may be considered to be equal to the average GDP (total product per head of population).

The economist's homomorphism for the standard of living is thus the monetary valuation of total social product per capita. Clearly the correspondence is only rough and ready, by virtue of the necessary assumptions. The nature of the measurement problem with respect to the standard of living (and with respect to progress in general) is discussed in the Appendix to Part I of this book. Granted the imprecision, however, it is still the case that a statement to the effect that the standard of living of country X is $\$Y$ per head is fairly meaningless. The figure Y cannot be equated directly to any particular level of welfare. GDP figures are therefore employed in a relative sense, either in terms of comparisons between countries or in terms of comparisons of the standard of living in the same country at different points in time. Thus, within the confines of our assumptions, it becomes reasonable to make statements to the effect that country A is richer than country B (i.e. the individual inhabitants have a higher standard of living) or that country C is poorer than it was ten years ago (i.e. its per capita GDP has fallen).

The distribution of living standards across the globe is extremely uneven and we may gain a general idea of this by considering the average GDPs of the various regions. By far the richest area is North America (the USA and Canada) whose 1976 living standard was estimated to be $7940 per capita. In a listing of 'rich-to-poor' regions, Australasia and Western Europe appear next with figures of $5450 and $5140 respectively, followed by the Middle East ($1870) and Central and South America ($1220). Finally, the poorest regions of the world are Africa ($470) and South East Asia ($230). The 'average' North American is therefore more than thirty times richer than the 'average' South East Asian. However, even within these regions there are wide variations in standards of living – Table 2.1 provides data for 45 countries in five regions.

Obvious omissions from the list are China, the Soviet Union and the states of Eastern Europe. The principal reason for this is that, as very little exchange takes place between these countries and the rest of the

TABLE 2.1 GDP per capita in selected countries, by region, 1978 (in $US)

Country	Per capita GDP ($US)	Country	Per capita GDP ($US)
Africa		*Middle East*	
Malawi	184	Jordan	842
Madagascar	253	Syria	959
Tanzania	263	Turkey	1159
Kenya	370	Iraq	1620*
Senegal	407	Cyprus	2224
Liberia	427	Israel	3913
Zambia	513		
Morocco	654	*South East Asia*	
Nigeria	717*	Burma	133
Tunisia	988	India	159*
Ivory Coast	1014	Sri Lanka	183
South Africa	1594	Pakistan	257
Libya	7262	Indonesia	340
		Thailand	484
Central/South America		Philippines	506
Haiti	278		
Peru	665	*Western Europe*	
El Salvador	679	Portugal	1816
Bolivia	790	Greece	3375
Ecuador	958	Spain	3999
Panama	1260	UK	5545
Mexico	1413	France	8851
Brazil	1635	West Germany	10419
Uruguay	1713	Switzerland	13335
Barbados	1931		
Venezuela	3024		

* 1977 figure.
Source: United Nations (1980), *Monthly Bulletin of Statistics*, **34–6**, pp. xxxi–xxxii.

world, it is difficult to evaluate these countries' production in terms of a common currency unit. However, much research has been undertaken to derive comparable estimates – for example, Wiles (1971) – and such research suggests that China would probably appear in the middle of the South East Asia spectrum of *Table 2.1*, whilst the USSR and the rest of Eastern Europe would be grouped in the lower half of the Western Europe range. Czechoslovakia and the German Democratic Republic would probably figure as the two richest nations in the socialist bloc.

Irrespective of the position that a society occupies in this 'rich-to-poor' scale, and irrespective of its attitude towards the proper relationship between individual and society as discussed above, it is invariably the case that the desire to increase its standard of living, or level of material wellbeing, is a cornerstone of its ideology. Indeed, the economic discipline, irrespective of its ideological foundations, takes the preference for greater material welfare, other things remaining equal, as axiomatic.

For certain societies, the objective of increasing living standards appears to be so basic that it has become enshrined in the constitution of the society in question; Article 11 of the Constitution of the USSR notes, for example, that

> The economic life of the USSR is determined and guided by the state economic plan for the purpose of increasing the wealth of society [and] steadily raising the material and cultural standards of the working people ... (Wolf-Phillips, 1968, p. 171).

Article 15 of the Constitution of the People's Republic of China expresses almost identical sentiments.

Not all states, of course, possess formal constitutions and, of those that do, not all feel the need to use them to specify their objectives. However, we can also gain an idea of social goals by examining government statements of economic policy. The following example – from the French government's directive to the architects of the Fourth Five-Year Plan – clearly demonstrates the concern for improving living standards:

> In spite of the 40 per cent increase experienced during the last ten years, the present standard of living in France cannot be considered adequate ... [It] follows that one of the fundamental results of the Fourth plan must be to assure the full employment of the coming generations and to increase individual consumption by providing more and better food and clothing, by improving housing and by increasing the purchase of industrial goods that add to the comfort of the home and the ease of life (Hackett and Hackett, 1963, p. 372).

This passage, incidentally, highlights a likely implication of the belief in the desirability of higher living standards. As the volume of consumption is dependent upon production, in turn a function of the volume of resources put into the production process, societies concerned to maximize the standard of living will accordingly be concerned to maximize the employment of available resources.

Perhaps the nearest we can get to a general demonstration of the desirability of material plenty is the fact that this goal is included in the Charter of the United Nations. This organization currently possesses a membership in excess of 130 states that, between them, comprise the great majority of the world's population. Although experience suggests that UN members do not always coexist in the harmony that was hoped for at the outset, one of the least tendentious areas of debate has been the socio-economic field. Article 55 of the UN Charter notes that 'the United Nations shall promote ... higher standards of living, full employment and conditions for economic and social progress' (UN, 1945, p. 345) whilst Article 56 pledges each individual UN member to undertake the joint or separate actions necessary to achieve the goals of Article 55.

Whilst we might therefore be willing to accept that increases in living standards are likely to represent a theme common to most ideologies, we must not forget that the material wealth that we are concerned with is an aggregate concept. The material production of a modern industrial economy is in fact made up of the production of tens of thousands of qualitatively different outputs – food, electricity, health care, coal, motor cars and so on – with the result that, whilst all societies might agree that more production is preferable to less, they might well disagree about the relative importance to be attached to the particular components of aggregate production. Indeed, they do disagree. Differences in tastes and preferences between individuals, and between societies, are widely established and have entered popular mythology. The national stereotype of the Englishman, for example, portrays him drinking a cup of tea, whilst his European and American colleagues are all said to prefer coffee. The data of *Table 2.2* suggest that this popular stereotype has some factual basis. Differences between national strategies are therefore likely to be revealed not in the pursuit of plenty *per se* but in the pursuit of particular types of plenty.

TABLE 2.2 Per capita consumption of tea and coffee for selected countries, 1977 (in grams)

	Tea	*Coffee*
France	113	5010
Sweden	363	8600
UK	3457	1740
USA	381	4330
West Germany	186	5710

Source: United Nations (1979), *Statistical Yearbook 1978*. New York, UN, Tables 168–9.

2.1.3   DISTRIBUTIVE JUSTICE

Let us for the moment think of society as an organization for the production of welfare-generating consumption items. Each individual in this society contributes to production in some particular way by, say, working in a factory or on a farm. In general, we might think of such individuals as being involved in the 'baking of the national cake'. However, once the cake has been baked, the question arises as to the appropriate size of share to be apportioned to each of the individuals involved in its production. Again, the answer to this question depends upon the nature of the metaphysical premises adopted. Possibly the most straightforward ideological starting point is our earlier example – all men are equal. Taken at face value, this proposition might be seen to imply that every individual in society should be entitled to an equal share of the total product. Simple as this position is, however, it appears to have found little favour in real-world societies, with the exception of those cultures that we regard as remnants of the earlier hunting mode of subsistence.

If we were to accept the liberal ideology outlined earlier, the belief in the legitimacy of the private ownership of material resources and the freedom of inter-individual contract could also generate a distributional criterion. We might simply assert that the distribution of benefits resulting from the process of free contract is the one that society thinks is the best or 'just' solution. Here we encounter an interesting problem because the nature of the contract drawn up between individuals is likely to be a function of the *ex ante* distribution of property. The consequence of this is a redistribution in favour of those with the greater bargaining strength, partially determined by initial property endowment. As Marx demonstrated for nineteenth-century Britain, it was the ownership of scarce productive capital that permitted the capital-owners to cream off the major share of net product from the productive process because such ownership placed the owners in a position of bargaining strength vis-à-vis the owners of labour, the supply of which was relatively abundant. If it is believed, therefore, that distribution in period $t + 1$ is likely to be a function of distribution in period t and before, the society in question has two options available. First, it might borrow an aspect of the traditional ideology and assert that the distribution of property, wealth or other benefits that has evolved historically is the 'correct' one and therefore any consequent distribution is 'just'. Alternatively, it might, at any one time, regard the *ex ante* distribution as arbitrary and simply alter it in a manner found acceptable. 'Just' contracts may now be made, following from the 'just' distribution created.

It was, of course, the belief that inter-individual contracts with an imbalance of property rights would lead to a manifestly 'unfair' distribution of benefits in liberal-type societies that prompted Marx and those countries that follow his doctrines to reject rights of private property and to advance alternative distributional criteria. In fact, such countries have adopted the Aristotelian notion of 'reciprocal proportion' – the belief that individuals should receive benefits in proportion to their contribution towards the creation of those benefits. Indeed, this principle is clearly spelled out in Article 12 of the Soviet Constitution:

> Work in the USSR is a duty and a matter of honour for every able-bodied citizen, in accordance with the principle: 'He who does not work, neither shall he eat'. The principle applied in the USSR is that of socialism: 'From each according to his ability, to each according to his work' (Wolf-Phillips, 1968, p. 171).

Expanding slightly, we may presumably interpret the second principle as meaning that society expects each individual to contribute to production in the way best facilitated by his natural endowments and aptitudes. He is correspondingly rewarded by society in proportion to the amount of value that his work contributes to that society.

The principle of reciprocal proportion is not, of course, confined to societies upholding socialist ideology. It is also applicable in an economy characterized by markets and individual enterprise, for neoclassical economic theory suggests that an entrepreneur will reward factors of production in proportion to the marginal addition to the value of output that their employment generates. Note that, in such a society, the value of the contribution will be private rather than social.

On reflection, we see that the above principle offers only one possible conception of an ethically acceptable distribution criterion. It maintains that only those who work 'ought' to be able to eat. As such, the principle can really be considered as an incentive system. An equally reasonable candidate might be, to continue the metaphor, the principle that those who are hungry should be able to eat. This principle argues that resources should be distributed so as to benefit those who wish to consume them rather than those who help produce them, there being no necessary correspondence between the two. This, of course, is Marx's principle of communism: 'from each according to his ability, to each according to his needs'. Whilst there are at present no real-world societies that even purport to follow Marx's doctrine to the letter, the principle of distribution according to need is nevertheless popular. Many economies, for example, run public health services under which the population permits itself to be taxed so that health care resources are available for all those deemed to be in 'need' of medical treatment. Such a system represents a net transfer of resources from those not needing treatment to those who do, a transfer not necessarily related to the extent to which the patient might be able to contribute towards the provision of medical care. In a more general sense, many societies accept the existence of a 'poverty line' or minimum subsistence level and they believe that all individuals should have the right to a share in total product of at least this amount, irrespective of the individuals' contribution to production. Redistribution measures to effect this are accordingly considered legitimate.

Actually, the list of possible distribution criteria outlined above is really quite modest. Pen (1971) has drawn up his own list of 21 defendable ethical criteria that might be used to serve as a guide for distribution within a particular society. Pen notes that he was struck by the length of his list, especially in view of its incompleteness (p. 293). In addition to the criteria mentioned above, he includes such ideas as legitimate and illegitimate inequality (i.e. societies might favour egalitarianism in some areas but not in others), the possibilities of discrimination (i.e. not treating equals equally), rewards for special efforts, and the notion that individual income could be related not to production but to contribution to potential production.

2.2   Ideology and policy

An ideology is an abstraction, truly an idea. As such, it is constrained by nothing except logic (although not necessarily by that). This is not the case, however, for the economic policy decisions that individuals and societies make in order to realize the objectives implicit within these ideologies. There seems no reason, for example, why I should not believe that the abrupt termination of the earth's spin would be of inestimable benefit to mankind. You might choose to agree or disagree with me. However, as I am not H. G. Wells's man who could work miracles, the contemplation of this as a possible policy appears somewhat futile in view of the physical constraints that oppose me. The real world, in other words, imposes limitations that the metaphysical world does not, and a role for the economist, as scientist, is to determine the constraints that might influence the extent to which a particular ideological aspiration may be realized. Of these constraints, it is the physical that are the most obvious. At any moment in time, we live in a world of fixed resources and a fixed stock of knowledge. Although an element of our policy may be to increase the level of both, we cannot possibly produce at a level in excess of that corresponding to the currently most efficient use of all available resources. Economists also recognize the important fact of opportunity cost: in a finite world, resources employed in one manner preclude their use in any other. In addition to this general principle, however, there are one or two additional problems in policy formation.

2.2.1   CONFLICT BETWEEN GOALS

If we were to ask a society at random what its ideological goals were, it might well reply along the lines of 'We believe in individual freedom, high living standards and egalitarian distribution'. Indeed, such sentiments would probably be considered as quite noble in many modern states. However, in practical terms, it might be the case that the more one pursues goal A then the further one departs from goal B; the simultaneous achievement of goals may not be technically feasible. Let us consider some examples.

First, consider individual freedom. Suppose our society were to assert that every individual was to be completely free, i.e. beyond collective control, in every respect. This statement immediately presents us with a contradiction, for it presumably requires that you should be free to annihilate me whilst I should possess freedom from annihilation by you. At a less extreme level, it also implies that I should be free to drive my automobile at vast speeds under the influence of considerable quantities of alcohol if I so wish. This freedom, however, would be a cause of concern to you, as a pedestrian, for it would increase your chances of being run down, i.e. it contradicts your freedom to walk unscathed. We infer from these instances that a universal concept of freedom is likely to imply conflicts between particular facets of freedom. It will accordingly be necessary for our society to establish a hierarchy of freedoms, to establish whose activities should take precedence. Incidentally, most societies seem to accept that my right to life takes precedence over your right to murder, whilst your freedom to walk down the street unharmed is superior to my right to drive drunkenly.

All real-world societies possess at least a rudimentary form of legal structure that specifies the hierarchy of legal rights of individuals. There is, however, no reason to suppose that the same hierarchy would prove acceptable to all. Two eminent modern liberal theorists, Rowley and Peacock (1975), assert that *their* particular values place political freedoms above economic freedoms and intellectual freedoms above both. In other words, if we could imagine a circumstance where the choice had to be made between the freedom to practise one's religion and the freedom to choose one's occupation, Rowley and Peacock's society might be expected to choose the former in preference to the latter. As these authors state, however, the choice is a personal one – there is no reason why a specific society should not choose to reverse these priorities. It should be noted that societies would not encounter many of these problems if they were to reject the concept of fundamental *ex ante* individual rights.

Whilst there is likely to be conflict within the goal of freedom itself, the goal of freedom may also be in conflict with other objectives. Consider the following case. Most societies accept that education makes a significant contribution to the raising of living standards. Not only will there be a private benefit to the educated individual but society as a whole is likely to benefit from the qualitative and/or quantitative change in production that educated labour can engender. If only for this reason, therefore, most modern societies are willing to subsidize an individual's education to a greater or a lesser extent. Suppose, however, we permit the individual the freedom to migrate. Having acquired his skill he will now wish to live in the society that can offer him the greatest reward in return for the use of his abilities and there is no reason to expect this to be the society that trained him. From the point of view of the individual's home country, this movement is potentially undesirable for, having paid for the education, the society is faced with the prospect of being denied its benefits. The receiving country, on the other hand, will view the arrangement favourably for it obtains the benefits without having incurred the training costs. This example is by no means hypothetical for, since the late 1950s, we have observed regular mobilizations of skilled labour. The migration of scientists and engineers to the USA, which offered the individuals more economic opportunities, became a source of public concern in the UK during the late 1960s – the so-called 'brain drain' – whilst the flow of skilled labour from the poorer countries of Asia to the USA and the UK has been steady for the past two or three decades. Different countries have reacted to the problems posed by such emigration in different ways. Those that place a high premium on freedom are willing to accept the loss of potential output; others more concerned with production have introduced legal or fiscal sanctions to induce labour to remain.

The potential conflict between raised material output and maintaining an egalitarian distribution of consumption opportunities is a well-known one in economics. The point is simply that, in the words of Holesovsky (1977), 'inequality may be good for us'. The essential argument is that the ability to increase the rewards of production that come in an individual's direction as a result of contributing to production acts as an incentive to that individual to increase his input. The promise of material gain is therefore a 'carrot' to increase effort. Suppose I were to offer you an increased proportional share of the national cake in return for your working harder, thus enabling us both to produce more. The national cake now becomes bigger. Although I am now left with a smaller proportion of the total, it could well be the case that the absolute value of my share has increased, although I personally have put in no extra effort. Accordingly, if the incentive assumption is correct, I, as the relatively poorer partner, might be quite happy to live in this two-person inegalitarian society for I should prefer, say, 20 per cent of 500 production units to, say, 50 per cent of 100 units. This idea of inequality possibly representing a net benefit to society, by virtue of its stimulus to effort, is implicit in several modern liberal conceptions of distributive justice, notably that of Rawls (1972), and this gives rise to the view that there might exist an optimum degree of inequality within society in order to attain the goal of material plenty.

2.2.2   INTERNATIONAL CONSTRAINTS

By living in society, it is clear that the realization of the aspirations of any one individual might be facilitated, hampered or generally influenced by other individuals. It is equally clear that the same is true for any one society, living as it does in a world made up of a large number of nation states. A state's ideology is therefore likely to contain attitudes and views not only regarding its internal welfare criteria, such as freedom, wealth and justice, but also about the appropriate relationships between itself and other states. If we accept the existence of independent sovereignties, any one state's policies may be constrained or at least affected by the policies of others.

Consider the case of a state that wants to increase its standard of living. Now, the geo-political structure of the world limits it to the use of those resources that the collection of states in general accept are legitimately owned by that state in particular. The value or utility of these resources may be raised, nevertheless, with the compliance of other states. First, state A could agree to exchange resources or products with state B. It could give up resources that it deems less valuable in exchange for resources that it deems more valuable, always assuming that a reciprocal attitude is held by state B. This international exchange model is, of course, the macroeconomic equivalent of the model of exchange between individuals in an economy characterized by private property rights, and exchange occurs for equivalent reasons. Second, state A would benefit if it could persuade others to pool resources in a project of mutual advantage characterized by increasing returns to scale since, individually, no one state acting in isolation would possess sufficient resources to gain as much as a conglomerate (assuming acceptable distributional criteria were agreed). Examples of this practice are the current collaborations of Western European states in aircraft manufacture and in nuclear and space research.

In the above cases, the objectives of our states 'mesh together' as it were, for the exchange or production relationship established is simultaneously beneficial to all parties. In such cases, the societies' objectives are not at all in conflict. Unfortunately, not all real-world objectives are of this nature; it is quite likely that we shall find that state A wishes to pursue policies that state B finds positively unpleasant. In the simplest case, A might wish to obtain something from B that B refuses to give up. Again, A might wish to pursue an internal policy that has negative external effects from B's point of view: A might, for example, decide to experiment with bacterial warfare, which could have undesirable effects upon its neighbours should it permit the bacteria to get out of control. In such circumstances, state B really has two alternatives – it can go along with whatever A has in mind, or it can attempt to persuade A to change its plans. Clearly, it would prefer the latter to the former and the extent to which its attempt will be effective is determined by the relative powers of the states in question. Jenkins (1970) has argued that if we rank the contemporary nation states of the world along a variety of power dimensions – geographical size, population, production, military strength – we tend to find that nations ranking high on one dimension also rank high along others. Each nation can accordingly be considered as having a power position, power being defined as the ability to influence others and being determined by the above factors. It follows that state B has a much greater chance of persuading A to change its mind if B is powerful and A is weak and much less chance, other things being equal, if the positions are reversed. The power position of interested parties therefore acts as a constraint upon the objectives of any one state and, $de\ facto$, determines their feasibility. Indeed, we could work out specific probabilities for a variety of power relativities. Clearly, this issue will be of some importance in identifying optimal strategies for progress and we shall devote some time to it at a later stage, for the central point is vital. In a world characterized by international relationships, the appropriate strategy can be designed only if account is taken of the reciprocal action anticipated from other states. Whilst this admits the possibility of cooperative drives towards progress, it also admits the possibility of a state progressing via the deliberate imposed regression or 'underdevelopment' of another. Under many circumstances, economics may be a positive-sum game, but we have no $a\ priori$ knowledge of the likely distribution of gains.

2.2.3   ECONOMIC CONTROL

In the previous sections we suggested that the realization of objectives was conditioned by a variety of internal and external constraints. In addition, such realization is also constrained by the scope of economic control that the decision maker possesses. In fact, economic control is influenced by two factors – information and ideology. In the first place, the effectiveness of an individual decision is constrained by the extent of knowledge of cause and effect, of interactions between events; only by understanding that X causes Y can we be said to have controlled event Y by policy X. Second, the extent of control over activities exercised by individuals or governments is limited by the amount of power that the citizens who make up the state are prepared to give to such individuals or governments.

The occurrence of a future desired event may be associated with several possible types of controls. The first of these we have already mentioned; this is the case of zero control, which clearly leaves no room for manoeuvre. However, where a finite degree of control may be considered to exist, we have two potential options, namely direct or indirect control. In the former instance, we aim at our objective directly (as the name implies) whilst, for the latter, we proceed by a more circuitous route. We may demonstrate these alternatives by the following example.

Consider an industrialized economy that is experiencing inflation. Suppose everyone agrees that less inflation would be more desirable from his own point of view but that he nevertheless wishes to spend his money as fast as possible before prices rise still further and depress the value of his purchasing power. Abundant purchasing power chasing a limited supply of goods will naturally generate further inflationary pressure. How can we stop this inflation? Although no individual can alter the circumstances, the government can, depending upon the power that it is permitted and its understanding of the economy. The mechanism of this simple model is purchasing power pushing up prices. A direct control response would be for the government to dictate to producers that prices must be fixed at a constant level. Assuming we define inflation as producer price rises, we have, by definition, no more inflation. However, the government might reason that, as purchasing power causes price rises, the contraction of such power would bring about price stabilization. An indirect policy would therefore be to attack price rises by limiting purchasing power by means of, say, increased taxation.

Which policy should the government of our hypothetical economy employ? The direct alternative is initially appealing for, of itself, it requires no knowledge of the workings of the system; it is simply a case of setting a zero inflation level by fiat. Citizens of this economy might, however, regard such a high-handed approach on the part of the government as illegitimate; they might well accept individual freedom of contract as part of their ideology. Furthermore, the direct policy might have undesirable economic consequences that the government was unable to foresee as a result of its ignorance of the economic mechanism. With fixed prices, a 'black market' could easily become established, initiated by the few who were fortunate enough to purchase at the fixed price reselling their purchases at a higher price. Such gains from speculation might well be considered unfair and, in addition, the policy simply has the effect of driving inflation underground. The indirect policy also has complications. It clearly requires a very precise understanding of the functional interaction of prices and purchasing power to enable the government to set the exact tax rate necessary to maintain zero inflation. It also entails knowledge of wider economic issues. Consumers, for example, might well make up the purchasing power paid in taxation by withdrawals from their savings, resulting in no net decrease in purchasing power as the government had hoped. Indeed, just as the producers above might have thought it wrong for the government to fix prices, so our consumers might consider it wrong for the government to tax away purchasing power without necessarily providing services in return.

In selecting its policy instrument, a society must accordingly decide whether (i) the instrument will actually work, purely from a technical point of view, (ii) the implications of the instrument are desirable from an ideological point of view. These criteria for the selection of policy instruments will be implicit within most of the chapters that follow, because all strategies for progress entail a decision about the most appropriate means for the realization of ends. We might argue, for example, that the standard of living of us all would be raised if every individual was engaged in production. Do we regard it as legitimate, however, to coerce those individuals who do not wish to work into undertaking productive activity? Should we simply allow the government to offer them suitable inducements or, indeed, should we actively subsidize those wishing to remain idle? It is suggested that humanity will not return unanimous answers to such questions.

Summary

All societies have ideologies, which are subjective criteria against which they assess the implications of economic policy. Ideologies are metaphysical statements about the proper conduct of economic affairs and there is no reason to suppose that one economy's ideology will be shared by another. An economy's ideology will have many components. Three important issues on which modern states express an opinion are the proper relationship between the individual and society, the appropriate level of living standards and the acceptable distribution of economic benefits between the members of the society.

Liberal ideology holds that members of society are endowed with certain fundamental freedoms and rights that may only be infringed by other individuals under specific circumstances. Amongst such rights are the right to own private property and the right of contract. In contrast, socialist ideology tends to the view that individual rights cannot exist in isolation from society. Rather, they are products of social decisions.

Contemporary societies are unanimous in agreeing that a higher standard of living is preferable to a lower one. The economist finds it convenient to equate living standards with total economic output per head of population. Evidence suggests that standards of living vary considerably between countries. In certain cases, the policy goal of raising living standards is incorporated into a state's formal constitution.

There are many possible criteria for a 'just' distribution of economic rewards. One version of liberal ideology would suggest that the just distribution is the one that results from the making of contracts between individuals. Other criteria might be that individuals should be rewarded in proportion to their productive contribution or that all individuals should have an equal share in collective output.

When attempting to translate desires into practical policies, societies may encounter a number of problems. First, the goals of policy may be in conflict. Owing to the structure of the economic system it may be impossible, for example, to generate a high rate of economic growth whilst maintaining an egalitarian income distribution. Second, the economic policy of one nation may be in conflict with, and thus constrained by, the policy of another. Third, policy makers might not possess sufficient control over their economy to effect a desired change. Economic control can be either direct or indirect. The selection of instruments is determined by their feasibility and their acceptability.

Further reading

A useful introduction to ideologies and belief systems is Plamenatz (1970). More comprehensive studies of theory and experience are N. Harris (1968), Groth (1971) and Bluhm (1974). Hunt (1972) provides a basic history of economic ideologies. Probably the best account of the development of the 'liberal' conception of socio-economic organization is Macpherson (1962). Rowley and Peacock (1975) explore some implications of the modern liberal view. Socialist ideology appears in a number of manifestations; Wilson (1977) is a helpful overview of Maoist thought whilst Lane (1981) examines Leninist ideology. D. Tucker (1980) is an excellent treatment of contemporary theories of individualism.

The data for GDP per capita by region are derived from UN (1979), Table 192.

Chapter Three

Approaches to Progress

Having identified the sorts of objectives that societies might conceivably aim at, our next task is to decide how they might get there. We need now an understanding of the mechanism of progress, of the processes by which our goals may be realized. In this chapter we shall examine the mechanism of progress as a variety of general principles that have been put forward by theorists. For convenience of exposition we shall examine the causes of progress under two headings: material and social. By material progress we mean increases in total national economic output for, as we have seen, such increases are usually regarded as progressive. Social progress is accordingly a label for virtually everything else although, as we shall see, the two concepts are not always easily distinguished in practice.

Sidney Pollard (1971) opens his historical account of the subject with the assertion that 'the world today believes in progress' (p. 9). Were we to conduct some sort of global survey, asking everyone whether or not the world could be made a better place, then it seems probable that Pollard's assertion would be validated. However, it is unfortunate that what is believed possible is not always so in reality; the belief, widely held at one time, that the world was flat did absolutely nothing to alter its essential roundness. At this stage, therefore, we must at least admit to the logical possibility that we are in pursuit of a chimera, for it is conceivable that our hopes for an improvement in the lot of mankind are fanciful.

In fact, the great majority of theorists of the past have conceded that progress is possible; they differ, rather, in their belief in the extent to which it is likely. After examining the general causation of progress we must accordingly review some of these reservations. Specifically, these are of three types. First, some analysts argue that, whilst human progress is certainly possible, its potential is strictly finite and limited. Second, there exists a body of thought that suggests that the fortunes of mankind follow a cyclical pattern of progress and regression, a pattern that is largely impervious to human interference. Finally, several theorists have argued, somewhat depressingly, that the human future may take only one direction and that that direction is distinctly downhill. Let us begin, however, on an optimistic note.

3.1   Material progress

The European Enlightenment marks something of a watershed in intellectual history for it was a turbulent period in both a mental and a physical sense. The nascent industrialization of the European economies was beginning to reveal its potential for increasing material output and there was a growth in the expansion, and hence the accumulation, of scientific knowledge. Such knowledge not only fuelled the industrialization movement still further but it provided a new intellectual position from which to view the affairs of the world, a position that was in active competition with that engendered by the traditional religious orthodoxies. The historical structure of political power, authority and property was increasingly called into question and was, in a number of cases, amended violently and drastically. Not surprisingly, these were 'boom years' for social philosophy and many of the ideas that were developed at the time remain the basis of contemporary ideological positions.

The French *philosophes*, and especially Turgot (1727–81), were perhaps the first to appreciate the practical consequences of mechanization and the advance of scientific knowledge and innovation. Turgot regarded these factors as progressive for, not only did they generate increases in economic output, but they served to liberate mankind from the full-time task of simple survival. The establishment of such freedom permitted man to divert still more energy to the pursuit of knowledge that could then be applied back to the productive process. Progress for Turgot thus became self-perpetuating; as material progress occurred and man's mastery of nature developed so he became freer to engage in those pursuits that would generate still more progress.

Significant as Turgot's realization was, it was left to the Scottish economist, Adam Smith (1723–90), to formalize the idea into the first theoretical analysis of the creation of economic progress in his *Inquiry into the Nature and Causes of the Wealth of Nations*, first published in 1776. Indeed, it is hard to overstate the significance of Smith's view of the causation of economic prosperity, for it has been a major influence upon twentieth-century conceptions. Smith identified three specific features that, in combination, were the key to increases in output. First, he argued that a regime of production organization characterized by the division of labour – that is, labour specialization in particular tasks – had the effect of raising output per man. Smith demonstrates this point in his famous passage about pin-making:

> ... a workman not educated to this business ... could scarce, perhaps, with his utmost industry, make one pin in a day, and could certainly not make twenty. But in the way in which this business is now carried on, not only is the whole work a peculiar trade, but it is divided into a number of branches of which the greater part are likewise peculiar trades. One man draws out the wire; another straights it; a third cuts it; a fourth points it; a fifth points it at the top for receiving the head; to make the head requires two or three distinct operations; to put it on is a peculiar business ... (Smith, 1873, p. 3).

From this observation of business practice Smith concluded that ten men working under a regime of specialization could produce 'upwards of forty eight thousand pins a day' (a productivity increase of at least 2000 per cent!).

The appropriate form of industrial organization, however, was only an epiphenomenon of the root cause of economic growth; this cause was the use of capital as a complement to labour power in production. Smith defined capital (strictly, fixed capital) as 'all useful machines and instruments of trade which facilitate and abridge labour', industrial buildings, improved agricultural land and also 'the acquired and useful abilities of all the inhabitants and members of society' (p. 113). Increases in material output were accordingly consequences of the increased application of labour with capital:

> Every increase or diminution of capital, therefore, tends to increase or diminish the real quantity of industry, the number of productive hands and consequently the exchange value of the annual produce of the land and labour of the country, the real wealth and revenue of all its inhabitants (p. 138).

As to the source of this capital:

> Whatever a person saves from his revenue he adds to his capital ... so the capital of a society, which is the same with that of all individuals who compose it, can be increased only in the same manner (p. 138).

Smith was therefore suggesting that resources saved in one period could be transformed into capital and used, in combination with labour, to generate further production in the next period. It further followed that the more that was saved in the first period the more capital would be available in, and the more output would result from, the second period. Smith's penetrating insight remains implicit in many of our modern formulations of economic growth. One of the simplest is the one that Myrdal (1968) has called the 'master model', which derives an expression for the growth rate (g) of total output (Y). If we assume that all resource savings (S) are used as investment (I) to increase the capital stock (i.e. $S = I$), and if we define the savings/output ratio

$(S/Y = s)$ and the technologically determined incremental capital/output ratio $(I/dY = v$, where dY is the per period change in $Y)$, we may write the proportionate change in output as

$$\frac{dY}{Y} = \frac{dY}{I} \cdot \frac{S}{Y}$$

i.e. $g = \dfrac{s}{v}.$

Assuming a fixed technology, the growth of our economy is proportional to the relative level of savings, although technical change that increases the efficiency of capital will naturally have a positive effect upon the growth rate.

Unfortunately, this model is a little oversimplified, for we have ignored the productive contribution of labour. If we assume that the labour/capital ratio is also technologically fixed then increases in the amount of capital will require increasing availability of labour to operate such capital. The overall growth of output is therefore constrained by the smaller of two growth rates – the capital growth and the labour supply growth. As the increase in economic output entails an increase in population to produce it, it follows that under our assumptions the average standard of living remains constant: more output is being produced by and is being distributed amongst more people. However, it is quite reasonable at this stage for us to follow Smith's assumption that capital will act as a labour substitute, i.e. the capital/labour ratio is variable and is likely to increase. In general, this has indeed been the case in the industrialized economies over the past few centuries; output growth has outstripped labour growth leading to a net rise in living standards. Given this possibility, growth can therefore occur under conditions of a stationary or even a declining population.

If it were free to choose, we might reasonably expect an output-maximizing society to opt for the highest available output/capital ratio. Would it also opt for the highest possible savings ratio? As with most questions in economics, the answer is 'not necessarily' and we shall now see why. First, let us rewrite our earlier model as a difference equation that describes changes over discrete time periods. It becomes

$$\frac{Y_{(t+1)} - Y_t}{Y_t} = \frac{S_t}{Y_t} \cdot \frac{Y_{(t+1)} - Y_t}{I_t}$$

or $$\frac{Y_{(t+1)} - Y_t}{Y_t} = sk$$

where k is the output/capital ratio. In turn, this equation may be re-written as

$$Y_{(t+1)} = Y_t(1 + sk),$$

which gives us the generalized difference equation

$$Y_t = Y_0(1 + sk)^t.$$

In any one period this product is allocated to two ends – present consumption to promote welfare now and savings to be invested for the production of output, and welfare, in the future. From the above equation we may derive the expression for consumption at any period (C_t), which is

$$C_t = (1 - s) Y_0(1 + sk)^t.$$

From this formulation it seems probable that there exists a conflict between present consumption and savings – between consumption now and consumption in the future. We can demonstrate this fact by a simple numerical example. *Figure 3.1* shows the consumption paths over time derived from the above equations for three values of the savings ratio: 0.1, 0.2 and 0.3. For simplicity, we assume a constant output/capital ratio of 0.3, identical starting points ($Y_0 = 1000$) and labour substitution such that population may be considered constant. Recorded consumption changes are therefore real standard of living changes. Consider the extreme options, $s = 0.1$ and $s = 0.3$. By choosing $s = 0.3$ our society deliberately lowers its earlier period consumption relative to what might be obtained from $s = 0.1$ and it is not until the end of period 5 that the consumption benefits of the two strategies become equal. The option $s = 0.3$ has therefore cost us consumption benefits to the value of the area *ABC*. Thereafter, however, $s = 0.3$ begins to pay clear dividends and, by around period 10, the earlier losses have been recouped. For all subsequent time periods, $s = 0.3$ always provides a superior consumption outcome to the lower savings strategy.

Viewed over the longer term, it is clear that we should prefer high savings strategies to high consumption strategies, other things remaining equal. However, viewed from the present, our decision will be influenced by our time preference – our valuation of the relative welfare gains from consumption in different periods. Clearly an important factor in our decision will be the time elapsing before the high-sacrifice strategy begins to produce equivalent rewards to the high-consumption strategy. If the ten periods of our example were equivalent to 50 years in real time, it appears that, with $s = 0.3$, I am being asked to make sacrifices for a welfare gain in which I am most unlikely to share. Accordingly, I am equally unlikely to be willing to sanction such an option unless I am particularly concerned about the welfare of my grandchildren. In addition, suppose that the material welfare level of our hypothetical society was currently extremely low, with a subsistence minimum at, say, 900 consumption units. Although we might be well disposed to a high-growth strategy for whatever reason, this is logically precluded, since any increase in the savings ratio above 0.1 would, for our model economy, lead to the eventual starvation of the population. Sacrifices

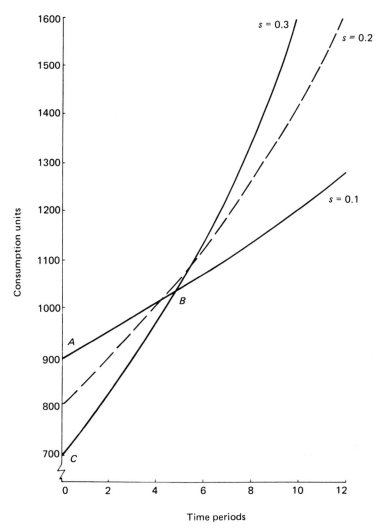

Figure 3.1 Alternative consumption patterns

in consumption below the minimum necessary for physical survival are non-feasible, except in cases where societies are willing to make, literally, human sacrifices.

Such objections do not invalidate the central proposition that capital causes growth; rather, they simply show that the decision about the optimal growth path will be somewhat complex. We still lack, however, a mechanism to explain how capitalization takes place; this mechanism was the third feature of Smith's analysis. Division of labour and capitalization only became viable, Smith argued, with the establishment and expansion of markets. It was only when society could purchase its own production that it became worthwhile for the individual to specialize in a certain area of economic activity to the exclusion of others, and for specialist capital equipment to be installed for production. Once these three factors coexisted, their interaction was cumulative, as Turgot suggested. Given an embryonic market and a certain amount of capital too, labour division would occur to raise output. The consequent rise in incomes would widen the scope of the market, permit increased saving to provide capital and thus further enhance the possibilities for specialized production. In particular, Smith argued that the driving force behind the whole process was the pursuit of private interest, for the pursuit of such interest was bound to produce a cumulative effect upon economic output. In one of his most famous passages he observes:

> As every individual, therefore, endeavours as much as he can, both to employ his capital in support of domestic industry, and so to direct that industry that its pro-duce may be of the greatest value; every individual necessarily labours to render the annual value of the society as great as he can. He generally, indeed, neither intends to promote the public interest, nor knows how much he is promoting it.... he is in this, as in many other cases, led by an invisible hand to promote an end which was no part of his intention (Smith, 1873, p. 184).

From our point of view, the significance of Adam Smith's work is its isolation of the causes of material progress – specialization, exchange, innovation and accumulation. Since Smith's time, there appears to have been very little disagreement as regards the contents of this list; the modern development economist, W. A. Lewis, noted in his *Theory of Economic Growth* (1955) that the 'three proximate causes of economic growth ... are economic activity, increasing knowledge and increasing capital' (p. 23) and this analysis is clearly in the Smithian tradition. In this particular respect, so too is that of Marx and Engels. Engels appreciated that the realization of his goal of communism was only feasible in a capitalizing epoch. It had only been legitimate to con-template the goal, he argued,

> since machinery and other innovations made it possible to hold out the prospect of an all-sided development, a happy existence for all members of society. Communism is a theory of liberation which was not possible for the slaves, the serfs, or the handicraftsmen ... (Engels, 1847, p. 101).

For all these authors, then, the basic problem was not so much whether progress was possible (for they were all convinced that it was), but rather the discovery of the best way of mobilizing the basic causes of progress.

3.2 Social progress

Increases in material production were not the sole concern of the Enlightenment thinkers. The contemporaries of Smith – for example, David Hume and Adam Ferguson – devoted much attention to the development of democratic government, which was to be regarded both as a facilitator of material progress, in the manner described by Smith, and as a constituent of progress in some wider sense in its own right. Even so, it was really left to the nineteenth-century theorists to develop a synthetic view of progress that related simple economic growth to other dimensions.

In a century of intellectual giants it is hard to discover just who is the tallest. Auguste Comte (1798–1857), certainly the inventor of sociology, can probably also be credited with the first holistic conception of progress. For Comte, human history was a story of man's intellectual development from theological, or mythical, belief, through the stage of abstraction, to the present state of positive understanding. This increasing control of his own mind, and consequently the possibilities of the control of his material existence to establish a true civilization, represented an iron law of evolution that was, of course, to be approved.

Civilisation develops, to an enormous degree, the action of man upon his environment ... It is unquestionable that civilisation leads us on to a further and further development of our noblest dispositions and our most generous feelings, which are the only possible basis of human association ... The influence of civilisation in perpetually improving the intellectual is even more unquestionable than its effect on moral relations (in Thompson, 1976, pp. 153–4).

This view of the individual's mental development exercising a mutually reinforcing effect upon society in general is a distinct echo of Turgot's more scientific observations. In turn, Comte's views were to influence other nineteenth-century thinkers, notably John Stuart Mill and Herbert Spencer. However, his almost mechanistic positivism provided a thesis to which modern theorists, such as Talcott Parsons and von Hayek, have developed their own antithetical interpretations of human actions.

As an appraisal of all the nineteenth-century paradigms of progress constitutes a book in itself, we shall restrict our discussions to a few of the major theorists. The first of these paradigms, important if only because of its subsequent impact upon the formation of contemporary ideology, derives from the work of Karl Marx (1818–83) and his collaborator, Friedrich Engels (1820–95).

In common with his precursors – Adam Smith and the economists of the classical school – Marx was appreciative of the enormous productive potential of industrialization. However, he believed that the full analysis of the process required that it be set in its proper historical context – the development of productive forces within the European economies. Marx saw the industrial growth of the eighteenth and nineteenth centuries as the result of a transition towards a new mode of production, or system of economic organization. The earlier modes were slavery, feudalism and small-scale handicrafts production. The new mode – capitalism – had a number of distinguishing features. First, capitalist technology made use of capital equipment inputs, i.e. machinery, in combination with specialized labour inputs. In purely technical terms, this made the capitalist technology far more efficient than the technologies that had prevailed earlier, when the division of labour and capital formation were absent. Second, the trend towards labour specialization meant that each individual labourer became less and less self-sufficient as his activities became concentrated into a narrow area of production. Individuals therefore came to produce primarily for the purpose of exchange, rather than for personal consumption or the use of their output. Finally, capitalism was characterized by the existence of private ownership rights. Individuals were permitted to hold, and exercise control over the use of, the means of production – essentially labour power and capital equipment. It was these features amongst others that, Marx argued, made capitalism the engine of economic growth. Of interest in our present context, however, is Marx's contention that these very conditions that mobilized the expansion of material wealth must prove, in the long run, to be inimical to the realization of a progressive society in the wider sense.

From his observations of the European experience, Marx came to the conclusion that capital formation implied the concentration of ownership. The simple cost-effectiveness of capital-intensive production in the earliest stages of industrialization drove out the small-scale producers owing to the latter's inability to compete. Naturally, it was only the rich who could afford to acquire productive capital. Thus, society became polarized into two classes: a relatively small group of capital-owners, and the bulk of the population, which owned no productive property save labour power. In Engels' words:

The machines thus delivered industry entirely into the hands of the big capitalists and rendered the workers' scanty property which consisted mainly of their tools, looms, etc., quite worthless, so that the capitalist was left with everything, the worker with nothing (Engels, 1847, p. 99).

As production required that capital and labour be combined, Marx acknowledged that some bargain would have to be struck between capitalists and workers. However, Marx saw the bargaining strengths of the two parties as being quite unequal. The scarcity of capital, and the inability of the individual worker to produce effectively without capital, placed the capitalists in a strong position. The individual capitalist could rely upon competition amongst the workers to ensure that wage rates remained low. Further, Marx believed that the economic power of the capitalist class could be translated into political power, and thus the advantageous position of the class could be further entrenched. Overall, capitalists were in a position to exploit the workers and to expropriate a disproportionate share of the rewards from production.

Whilst, for Marx, capitalism was manifestly unfair, he also took the view that it gave rise to the moral and social immiseration of all those involved in it. Capitalism implied the 'alienation' of the individual from himself, from his product and from society. One of the most obvious forms of alienation under capitalism was the worker's inability to own the result of his own labour. The concept of alienation was fundamental to Marx's work. Indeed, it was the transcendence of the conditions of alienation that constituted Marx's vision of eventual progress. The paradox of industrialization, Marx argued, was that, whilst it generally represented the increased control of man over his environment, it locked the individual into a system of productive relationships from which he was powerless to escape. What made a man human, Marx suggested, was his powers of creativity in production. Under capitalism, however, labour was obliged to hire itself out to capital, not to satisfy its need to create but to gain resources to satisfy other needs. Creativity was therefore being transformed into labour for physical survival. In asking 'what constitutes the alienation of labour' under the capitalist system, Marx arrived at the following conclusion:

As a result, therefore, man (the worker) only feels himself freely active in his animal functions – eating, drinking, procreating, or at most in his dwelling and in dressing-up, etc.; and in his human functions he no longer feels himself to be anything but an animal. What is animal becomes human and what is human becomes animal (Marx, 1844, pp. 274–5).

Marx's prognosis of the human condition was optimistic, not in the sense that he believed that the downfall of capitalism was inevitable, but in the sense that his analysis of historical dynamics led him to believe that it was likely. Recognizing that capitalism was inherently progressive in providing the potential for human liberation (i.e. via industrialization), he believed that the socio-economic structure carried within itself contradictions. In the long run, it must eventually collapse. Marx marshalled a number of arguments to support this belief, some of which we shall meet at later stages of this book. He suggested, for example, that the individualistic investment behaviour of capitalists would lead to cyclical fluctuations in the level of economic activity. These fluctuations would have a tendency to become more severe as time went on. Stagnation was also possible if the bargaining strength of the capitalists was such that the workers received insufficient income to purchase industrial output. Active political participation and the expansion of human awareness and consciousness would also assist in securing the demise of capitalism. 'Higher' forms of society could then emerge in which private property, the root cause of the internal contradictions, would cease to be defined. The individual would then be unfettered from his obligation to be involved in alienating industrial production since technological advances would, by then, have reduced necessary labour time to the bare minimum.

As is the case for all theorists, Marx and Engels did not write in a vacuum; they were aware of the work and ideas being developed by their contemporaries. One of the ideas that inflamed the nineteenth-century intellectual imagination was the implications of the newly dis-covered theory of evolution. In particular, it appeared that the biological world pursued an upward path by virtue of some innate logic, in the same way as the fortunes of mankind were believed to follow an upward trend. A discussion of the evolutionary view is complicated because, contrary to popular belief, there was no one single theory that all the evolutionists accepted. Instead, different theorists chose to emphasize different aspects and, not surprisingly, reached different conclusions. There was, however, a basic agreement on what the evolutionary principle stated: as circumstances change, individuals, institutions and societies change in reaction and those that survive are those that are best adapted for survival. Clearly, to merge a theory of progress with this principle we must attach some superior welfare level to the ability to survive.

In relating progress and evolution we arrive at a number of possible positions. In the first place, we might assert that what evolves is *de facto* progressive; because something has happened it must necessarily have been for the better. In the past, this view of the world has been used to justify certain forms of economic behaviour that, under alternative criteria of progress, might appear somewhat dubious – the gradual imperialist expansion of Western Europe might be held to have been 'natural' and hence progressive from the point of view both of Europe and also of those countries forming the empire. Second, we might assert the reverse of the first proposition, namely, that what is progressive will 'naturally' evolve. We should suppose that countries adopting this view would be likely to favour 'laissez-faire' economic policies, believing that nothing should be done to interfere with the smoothly working machine producing progress. A variant of this view would be a deterministic attitude that, as the world naturally evolves progressively, nothing can be done to interfere with its outcomes. Such a view would place humanity in a position of glorious irresponsibility.

One particular version of the evolution/progress interaction has had, in the words of Gellner (1964), 'enormous and almost irresistible appeal' and its influence upon contemporary thinking is still very strong. Gellner calls it the 'World-growth Story' (p. 12). In its extreme view, the story asserts that, first, all social change is inherently progressive, second, all societies follow a common evolutionary path and therefore, third, 'advanced' societies are simply blueprints for the future for 'less advanced' societies. A modern example of this view has followed from W. W. Rostow's *Stages of Economic Growth*, which was published in 1960. Rostow presented an historical generalization of empirical economic growth as a series of stages, from traditional civilization, via the 'take-off' into industrialization and leading to the period of 'high mass consumption'. Although Rostow himself urged caution in making this unilinear stage approach into a general theory of development, his followers have been far less concerned. As Varma (1980) has shown, the Rostovian model, which demonstrates the necessity of the less advanced economies following the same lines (in social, political and economic terms) as the advanced nations, has been widely used as a criterion for economic and social policy in those countries that are believed to be at the beginnings of the development spectrum. Such countries have been urged to adopt Western political institutions and Western economic practices; in the words of Galbraith (1964), they are 'beads being moved along a string' (p. 50). We should add, incidentally, that the socialist bloc of nations, led by the USSR, had already elaborated the thoughts of Marx into a stage theory of progress that, from their own point of view, provided the appropriate guide for economies at the beginnings of the Marxist spectrum.

Although the Rostovian position enjoyed a brief vogue during the 1960s, and despite the ideological strength of the Soviet view, the modern theories of progress have undergone certain further amendments. Before we consider the most up-to-date views, let us examine some of the reservations about the possibilities of progress that we mentioned earlier.

3.3   The stationary state

As we have seen, the late eighteenth-century writers were generally optimistic about the progress of mankind by virtue of the increases in material output that were being realized. They were also aware, however, of one possible pitfall. If material progress was to increase the welfare of the population, what would be the consequences for the size of the population itself? The theorists were unanimous in their response to this question – as man's standard of living increased, so the possibilities of the survival of more people would increase, owing to man's reproductive proclivities. If short-term prosperity were to be matched by short-term population growth the long-run effect must be the reaching of an equilibrium level of prosperity, a balance between population and output at the subsistence level. The proposition was put most forcibly by Thomas Malthus (1766–1834):

Must it not then be acknowledged by an attentive examiner of the histories of mankind, that in every age and in every State in which man has existed, or does now exist,
That the increase of population is necessarily limited by the means of subsistence,
That population does invariably increase when the means of subsistence increase, And,
That the superior power of population is repressed, and the actual population kept equal to the means of subsistence, by misery and vice (Malthus, 1895, p. 45).

If the earlier theorists were so convinced of the inevitability of production causing reproduction, entailing stationary living standards, why were they still so progress-oriented? Quite simply, evidence was beginning to suggest that the Malthusian spectre of perpetual poverty could be avoided. Indeed, Malthus published six versions of his population theory over some 30 years and became less alarmist with each new edition. The evidence was of three types. First, the Malthusian model depended upon the assumption of fixed supplies of land. The production of foodstuffs could therefore be increased only in a strict arithmetical ratio and would be subject to diminishing returns eventually. However, throughout the nineteenth century, virgin agricultural land was continually being exploited throughout the world, giving a potential source of subsistence goods in excess of immediate demand. Second, developments in productive technology were taking place such that the expansions of output, even from given inputs, appeared to be more than capable of keeping pace with population increases. Finally, it had become evident that the conscious control of the birth rate might not be the impossibility that Malthus's original theory had suggested. In his later editions, Malthus himself became an enthusiastic advocate of control in the form, for example, of the postponement of marriage.

In fact, the Malthusian prognosis is probably more a cause for concern at the present time. Recent ideas in this vein have tended to follow two lines of thinking, the first of which we might term the 'global ecological' view. An example is the work of Culbertson (1971). Although the world is finite, he suggested, the earlier conditions of mankind's existence made it appear infinite. Now its limitations are being appreciated at an increasing rate. The accumulating effect of population growth and technical developments is rapidly draining away the fixed stock of natural resources and the nineteenth-century options are no longer open to us. Culbertson was accordingly concerned to develop policies for rational environmental usage and such policies will concern us in later chapters.

Using the contributions of Leibenstein (1954) and Nelson (1956) we may derive a more formal model of the Malthusian position. By making certain assumptions about the responses of population growth and production growth to increases in prosperity we can demonstrate that, under certain conditions, economies might find themselves locked in an equilibrium state, a position that is difficult to ameliorate.

Consider a 'typical' pre-industrial economy that is producing at a level close to the subsistence minimum. High birth rates are being counterbalanced by equally high death rates. We might reasonably suppose that the output of this economy is some function of the available capital stock and the population or labour input. As capital will be formed out of savings from the production of previous periods, we must anticipate low levels of capital formation at low levels of per capita output. This is because most of the output will be needed for immediate consumption. If, however, we were able to engineer increases in living standards, we might expect more savings to be forthcoming. More capital could then be created. In turn, increased capital formation should lead to the generation of more output. Overall, therefore, output growth will be positively associated with increases in per capita output. From the population point of view, the effect of an increase in living standards will be associated, in the short run at least, with a decline in the death rate. Prosperity should reduce the incidence of malnutrition and poverty-related disease. Because of its more complex socio-cultural determinants, the birth rate is likely to be influenced only in the longer term.

On the basis of these broad assumptions we can map out the relationships between population and production growth and per capita output. The exact nature of these relationships will depend upon factors exogenous to the assumptions made above. The relationship between output growth and living standards, for example, will depend upon the economy's propensity to reinvest savings and the nature of the available productive technology. Similarly, population growth will respond to mortality-reducing medical technology and household decisions about family size. For ease of exposition, let us take as our starting point a standard of living at the minimum subsistence level with zero growth in the capital stock. At this point, population growth and production growth both equal zero. From our initial assumptions we know that, above this minimum, both population growth and output growth rise as living standards increase. The minimum level is represented by the point T in *Figure 3.2*. The figure also illustrates two possible output relationships $(Q_1$ and $Q_2)$ and two possible population relationships $(P_1$ and $P_2)$.

Suppose that the relationships appropriate to our economy were Q_1 and P_1. In this case, any increase in per capita output above T has the effect of increasing output growth by more than it increases population growth. Once it has moved from T, our economy therefore encounters cumulative prosperity: increases in per capita output generate further

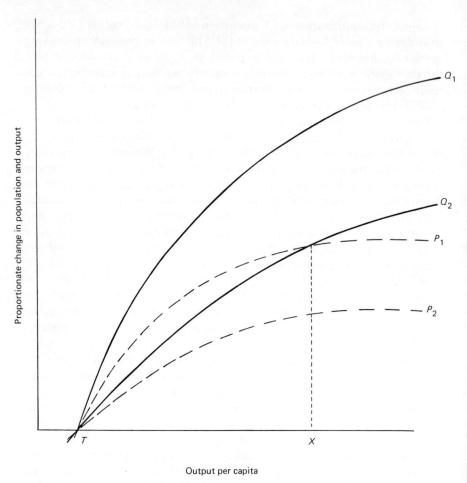

Figure 3.2 Conditions for low-level equilibrium

increases in per capita output because output growth exceeds population growth. This conclusion would also be true if the functions for our economy were to be Q_2 and P_2, or Q_1 and P_2. However, the interesting case in our present context occurs when our economy finds itself faced with the functions Q_2 and P_1. In this instance, a movement to the right of T has the effect of increasing population growth by more than it increases output growth. The net effect will accordingly be to lower per capita output; the system will return to T. Indeed, all per capita output levels between T and X display the same property. They are all unstable positions and will lead to a return to the equilibrium at T. It is only when our economy lies at a point beyond X that the cumulative changes of the previous instances can occur.

Nelson (1956) referred to economies characterized by functions such as Q_2 and P_1, and occupying positions between T and X, as being in a 'low-level equilibrium trap'. An economy finding itself in such a trap has, in general, two policy alternatives. First, it might attempt a population control policy, i.e. it might attempt to make its population grow along P_2 rather than P_1. Second, it could aim for an output expansion policy, i.e. shift the output function from Q_2 to Q_1. Conceivably, it might also contemplate some mixture of the two. It should be noted that these policy implications are revolutionary rather than evolutionary. Marginal 'tinkering' with the economy is likely to produce no long-term benefit owing to the stability of the low-level equilibrium. Leibenstein (1963) advanced the 'critical-minimum-effort' thesis, which argues that in order to escape from the trap the economy will require some substantial internal or external stimulus to lift it bodily, as it were, away from the equilibrium position. Once it has so escaped, it will then be able to progress under its own steam.

So far, we have discussed the low-level trap only as a theoretical possibility. We should therefore enquire into the empirical conditions necessary for its occurrence. Clearly, the trap is more likely to be experienced if (i) the economy has a low propensity to save and invest, (ii) productive technology is inefficient, (iii) the economy has no access to unemployed internal resources or resources from external sources, (iv) population growth is particularly responsive to changes in living standards. This view of the world is much in line with the Rostovian evolutionary model, for it suggests that, whilst some economies might easily clear the 'take-off' hurdle and go on to attain cumulative economic expansion, institutional factors may exist in others to prevent long-term growth. Whether certain contemporary poor economies are indeed in such a trap remains a moot point. Nelson believed that the conditions necessary for the trap do exist in 'many underdeveloped countries' although the empirical work necessary to substantiate such a generalization is lacking. One factor that complicates a present-day application of the model is the international transfer of mortality-reducing technology from the rich to the poor economies. This has served to diminish the impact of increases in living standards on population growth, at least from the point of view of reducing the death rate. However, we should note that exogenous reductions in the death rate would have the effect of making the occurrence of the trap more, rather than less, likely as far as the abstract model is concerned.

The preceding variant of the Malthusian proposition – that rises in living standards encourage reproduction, the effect of which is to depress living standards – is not dependent upon the system of economic organization that a country might adopt. We might imagine Malthusian population growth taking place under either a capitalist or a socialist economic system. However, there are a number of theories that suggest that specifically capitalist societies, by virtue of their particular system of economic organization, possess inherent tendencies towards an equilibrium or stationary state. Such theories are termed 'underconsumptionist' and suggest that economic progress in the long run will be prohibited by insufficient demand for consumption goods.

In addition to his work on population dynamics, Malthus also had a view on this issue. In any one period, the theory goes, total income (which is equivalent to total production cost) is divided between consumption and savings. Suppose these savings are now invested; the effect is to create both more income and more productive capacity. If the levels of consumption and investment remain unchanged in the subsequent period, excess capacity must appear and this has the effect of discouraging capitalists from investing, for they are able to meet demand from the available plant. A surplus of savings over investment precipitates a depression, which will only be ameliorated when the excess capacity has been used up. Even so, the depressionary tendencies will reappear in future periods for similar reasons. The only solution to the problem of increasing productive potential is increasing consumer demand, but here's the rub – whilst savings liberates investment resources, it both cuts down demand for output and enhances the supply of output. For the economy to grow at all it must grow exponentially; investment must increase at a constant rate each year.

This is really a restatement of the 'master model' mentioned in section 3.1 of this chapter. What the Malthusians were suggesting was not that exponential growth was impossible but that self-interested investors would be unlikely to find sufficient investment opportunities to increase their allocation each time period. In certain respects, this view was echoed by John Maynard Keynes (1883–1946), who emphasized the declining rate of return on investment as an influence upon capitalists' expectations and who pointed out that the problem would be exacerbated if we anticipated an increasing marginal propensity to save as living standards increased. An alternative view of the underconsumption problem suggests a different mechanism however. Originating with the work of Sisimondi, this view is implicit in the analyses of modern neo-Marxists such as Paul Baran and Paul Sweezy.

In simple terms, this line of reasoning runs as follows. As capitalism evolves and population increases, the bargaining position between the owners of capital and the owners of labour power is such that income and wealth become redistributed in favour of the former, a relatively small section of the population. With the advance of technology, the economic surplus (the difference between the output and the costs of production, which accrues to the capitalists) tends to increase. As the bulk of consumer demand comes from the labour force it is clear that, in relative terms, demand will decrease. In the face of this, capitalists will be reluctant to invest and, even though they might engage in luxurious private consumption, the total effect will be insufficient to channel the surplus back into the economy. The result is stagnation.

These theories are specific to capitalist economies because the stagnation problem arises when individual decision makers act independently in their own interests (as opposed to the collective interest). In both cases, investors simply do not wish to invest. Although this is not the place to appraise these theories or to make policy prescriptions, we might note that both of the above models seem to imply that stagnation in the purely capitalist economy is only avoidable with government interventions of the Keynesian type.

3.4   Decline and fall

We have seen that, grafted onto the theory of the biological evolutionary process, the principle of human progress has a certain intuitive appeal. However, if we pursue the metaphor to its biological conclusion, we arrive at somewhat more pessimistic results. Individual organisms do not simply appear and progress forever; rather, they eventually deteriorate and die. In the same manner, is it not possible that the allotted span of a society or economy is finite; will progress inevitably give way to decline? In fact this more sombre view of the human condition has at least as long a pedigree as the view of the optimists and there are two distinct strands to the approach. The first of these we might term 'the fall from grace' and it is exemplified by the work of Jean-Jacques Rousseau (1712–78).

For Rousseau, the state of grace occurred near the very dawn of mankind's history when small family or village units became established. Thereafter the long decline began. The agricultural revolution was the first disruptive force, for it led to the creation of private property, the division of labour, specialization and exchange, and thus competition. Emerging from this structural change came a political revolution, government being initially established by the strong and used by them to further their own powers. Rather than oppose this system, the average individual is forced to work within it, competing to survive and accepting the prevailing form of government. Rousseau therefore saw human history as the sacrifice of individual independence for a world of competition for power, property and esteem. Starting in a competitive, animal and pre-social 'state of nature', man finally finds himself back where he started except that his position is now made inferior by virtue of his loss of natural independence from other individuals.

With the benefit of hindsight, it is a simple task to criticize Rousseau's views. We might, for instance, suggest that his 'Golden Age' is ahistorical and we might also wish to dispute the virtues of a small-scale pre-agricultural existence. Even if we do accept that the organization of contemporary economies has decreased man's natural independence, we might also point out that, since Rousseau's day, it seems to be factors such as competition and the division of labour that have given rise to substantial increases in material welfare. There is no necessity to agree with Rousseau that liberty is the sole element in the human objective function – perhaps we might prefer to be rich slaves rather than free paupers? Such objections do not, however, invalidate the kernel of Rousseau's idea that, as the social machine becomes more complex, there arises the possibility of individual man's submergence within it. Indeed, this theme has been taken up directly by a number of modern Western writers such as Jacques Ellul and Herbert Marcuse. These authors argue that the developments of technology that have led to material prosperity have also dehumanized individuals to the extent that they have become simple technical appendages; we have, in other words, no choice but to become rich slaves and, furthermore, we no longer possess the wit to choose. As Marcuse (1972) observed:

> A comfortably smooth, reasonable, democratic unfreedom prevails in advanced industrial civilisation, a token of technical progress. Indeed, what could be more rational than the suppression of individuality in the mechanisation of socially necessary but powerful performances (p. 16).

We recognize in this view, of course, the influence of Marx; Marcuse too argued that the subject of economic activity – man – has been made the object. Human activity is oriented towards keeping the machine going, not towards enjoying either the process of production or its output. In two respects, however, Marcuse's views differ from those of Marx. First, whilst Marx saw the problem as one of ownership of technology, Marcuse saw it as stemming from the existence of technology *per se*. Second, whilst Marx interpreted the prevailing industrial system as being likely to give way to more progressive forms of organization, Marcuse concluded that there was 'nothing but a chance' of a transition to a happier world (p. 200).

The second strand of the 'decline and fall' approach is perhaps a generalization of the first. This is the concept of the social cycle whose motor is the dialectic. The basic idea is that conditions that give rise to a progressive shift in human affairs also eventually spawn contradictory conditions that operate in direct opposition to such progress. The most famous dialectical view of history is, of course, that of Marx, a view rooted in the work of Hegel. Some of Marx's views have already been considered. It must be borne in mind, however, that the Marxian dialectic operates around a rising trend, i.e. it is implicitly a progressive theory in the long run. Thus, for Marx, whilst the capitalist epoch of progress would eventually be terminated by the internal contradictions of the capitalist mode of production, it would be superseded by a new mode representing a distinct improvement in welfare terms. Similarly, this new mode (socialism) would be replaced by a still higher form. However, for some other social philosophers, no such rising trend exists.

Probably the most famous of these, and certainly the most uncompromising, was Oswald Spengler (1880–1936) whose massive work, *The*

Decline of the West, appeared in the 1920s. Spengler saw the fundamental course of history as the rise and fall of civilizations, guaranteed by immutable historical laws. Just as the civilizations of the past had emerged, flourished and declined via decadence into oblivion, so too, argued Spengler, was the Western industrial civilization inevitably doomed to a similar fate. Indeed, as a prophet of doom, Spengler probably has no equal, for his work consists almost entirely of a catalogue of the symptoms of decline. The English historian, Toynbee, was much influenced by Spengler's volumes and, in his monumental *Study of History* (volumes of which appeared between 1934 and 1954), he chronicled the fortunes of 21 civilizations of the past. Finding the conclusions of his analysis too unpalatable, Toynbee subsequently developed a progressive cycle theory, arguing that the rise and fall of civilizations in the past were a vehicle for man's progress in a spiritual sense.

Spengler's vitriol contains very little analysis of the causation of the cycles of civilization and, as such, we cannot really term his work a true theory. Rather, its importance lies in its opening-up to Western theorists the possibility of non-cumulative developments. In the world at large, however, Spengler was a late arrival in the field of social cycles, for the typical Eastern view of human fortune had long been of this nature. Taoist philosophy, for example, embodied notions of sequential improvements and deteriorations in the human condition, whilst the medieval Arab historian, Ibn Khaldun, had developed a sophisticated vision of endless cycles of barbarism, civilization, decadence and conquest. In fact, one of the most ambitious models of the social cycle is a clear result of the fusion of the Eastern and Western traditions and is of relatively recent origin. This is the theory of the contemporary Indian philosopher, Prabhat Ranjan Sarkar.

Sarkar's view of the dynamics of history may be broken down into three propositions. First, he asserts that every society is composed of four types of individual, each characterized by a different form of mentality. The definition of each mentality is complex but, simplistically, we might think of these individuals as labourers, capitalists or accumulators, intellectuals and warriors or 'heroes'. Second, in the history of a society, any one of these groups of individuals may become politically or economically dominant with the result that the specific characteristics of the society during that epoch mirror the mentality of the dominant group. Third, society moves dialectically – i.e. when one group achieves dominance, the seeds are sown for its downfall and eventual replacement by another group. Moreover, the replacement sequence is immutable and continues to repeat itself indefinitely. History is therefore a cycle of form if not content. In his analysis of Sarkar's theory, Batra (1978) interprets the historical evolution of a number of societies in terms of the cycle theory by examining the specific dialectical transition between epochs. Batra argues that, in all cases, the cycle model can be fitted and the internal tensions within the epoch identified. Furthermore, the pattern having been established, it now becomes possible for Batra to predict the futures of various societies. Western culture, it appears, will go through a period in which 'labourers' will overthrow 'capitalists' thus heralding a Golden Age in which the warriors will eventually achieve dominance, whilst the USSR is heading for an 'intellectual' epoch after its present 'warrior' phase.

From the point of view of breadth of vision, Sarkar's theory must rate as the nearest thing to 'the general theory of the world' that we currently possess. Although it transcends the dynamics set by Marx (which Sarkar would argue are only part of the story), it is clearly influenced by the latter's work to a great extent. The same is true of another theory of cycles, that of Joseph Schumpeter, which was restricted to the analysis of capitalist development.

Schumpeter (1934, 1954a) charted the history of capitalism as the interrelationship between two types of cycle, the first being the various forms of business cycle that had long been known to exist in capitalist economies. In Schumpeter's view, such cycles arise primarily as a result of the existence of individual enterprise and innovation; the mechanism runs as follows. Suppose we start with an economy in economic equilibrium. An innovating firm will destroy this equilibrium by recognizing the opportunities for profit-making and other firms will follow this lead. In terms of total output, economic activity will expand. After some time, new business opportunities will diminish and the economy will restructure itself at a new and higher equilibrium. This primary cycle of expansion and recession will, however, generate a secondary cycle. A boom in one particular sector will lead, for example, to expectations of booms in others and this secondary effect might well enhance the cyclical pattern of activity.

The model of the innovation-induced cycle does not give rise to an economy-wide cyclical fluctuation owing to the specific nature of the cyclical process. Different innovations, for example, take differing lengths of time to be introduced. One innovation might lead to others, all of which will generate cycles of their own. Again, a number of independent innovations might, by chance, occur simultaneously and could produce some net interactive effect. It follows that the economy will follow a path determined as the result of all these innovatory cycles. Schumpeter himself believed that this path would itself be cyclical, being made up of short (3–4 year) and medium (8–10 year) cycles within a long (50 year or 'Kondratiev') cycle.

In material terms, the capitalist economy thus moves forward on a cycle of cycles. Now, however, we have to impose our second form of cycle, which we might term sociological. Schumpeter argued that, as material development takes place, forces are set in motion that erode the motor of material development, namely, innovation and enterprise. He argued, for example, that the increasing scale of enterprise leads to the routinization of innovation and the spontaneity of individual initiative is thereby lost. Further, scale and corporatization diminish the entrepreneur's personal interest in innovation. Schumpeter also felt that this rationalization of capitalism would eventually precipitate antagonistic social or political reactions. Taken together, these two cycles spelled out to Schumpeter the end of the capitalist epoch and he foresaw its replacement by some form of socialism. Significantly, he did not view this as a necessary improvement; indeed, there is evidence that he believed the contrary. For Schumpeter, however, the transition was simply inevitable owing to the cyclical pattern.

We cannot leave our discussions of possible internal contradictions within societies without reference to the recent work of Hirsch (1977). Hirsch was concerned to examine some paradoxical observations arising from the growth of material prosperity amongst the richer, industrialized nations. In particular, he believed that such societies are characterized by certain features that can be represented as three questions. First, why do individuals in affluent societies appear to be disappointed by the supposed fruits of progress; second, why does there appear to exist greater concern for the distribution of benefits, possibly at the expense of increasing those benefits; third, why do liberal societies extol the virtues of individualism at the same time as public provision and government intervention are on the increase? For the sake of argument, let us assume that these questions are factually based. Hirsch then suggested that the problem lies in the inherent conflict between individual and social optimality, for the individual's aspirations have become constrained rather than facilitated by his fellows. The existence of externalities is an obvious example. Although they have always existed within societies, Hirsch felt that their extent had become more magnified in recent years. However, the essential conflict is brought about by inter-individual competition and one of the examples that Hirsch employed was that of education. Better education will, in most societies, lead to the earning of higher incomes. What is important to the individual, however, is not only that he should receive a good education, but that he should receive a better education than others who might otherwise compete for his position and thus threaten his income. If everyone receives an equally good education, his plans for relative superiority are thwarted. The Marxian will not, of course, find anything radically new in Hirsch's position for, to him, it would simply represent a manifestation of the way in which the individual is alienated from society under certain modes of production. However, Hirsch's viewpoint leads to the intriguing possibility that, if we include high welfare levels relative to others in the individual's objective function, many societies will find themselves facing a problem that is, in principle, insoluble.

3.4.1   WHERE DO WE STAND?

Throughout this chapter we have examined the views of a number of theorists who have been concerned both to explain the method of historical progression and to evaluate its consequences. Even so, our examination has been quite limited, for many eminent theorists have been omitted from our survey. We have also paid little attention to political or social models that argue that progress consists of a movement towards popular democracy or from a 'traditional' to a 'modern' culture although, again, such ideas are implicit in our models of industrialization.

The question therefore arises – which of these theories is correct? Do we accept, with Marx, that the contemporary Western economic system will be replaced by a superior organizational form or do we reluctantly acquiesce to Marcuse's view that we are all being steadily impoverished in a spiritual sense by those very forces that enrich us in a material sense? Or do we accept Sarkar's view that we are riding on a roller-coaster that we can barely control and from which we can certainly not get off?

In reply to the question 'where do we stand' – which view of progress do we accept as correct – we shall answer that the asking of it at this juncture is mis-timed. This is not to say, however, that the discussion of theories of progress has been unimportant at this stage, for it has not. Indeed, the very existence of theories of progress has two significant implications. First, these theoretical concepts have the power to lead us to the appraisal of empirical phenomena, just as the theories themselves were generally derived from the theorists' impressions of empirical phenomena. They provide us, in other words, with a set of questions to ask about the real world, and the answers to these questions are likely to be found rooted, not in abstraction, but in the historical experience of that real world. Second, these theories have a powerful ideological impact, for they form a contribution of man's assessment of the appropriate strategy (if any) by which progress is to be achieved. It is only after such enquiries have been undertaken that we can return to answer our original question.

Just as Part I of our study has been principally concerned with the sorts of objectives that societies might set themselves, so Part II will be essentially an examination of the themes of realization. In Part II, we shall appraise a number of 'dimensions' of progress, that is, issues on which a society will be obliged to adopt a specific stance. Clearly, the position along the dimension, or the policy finally chosen by any one society, will be determined by a multitude of factors, possibly the most important being the nature of its objective function and the extent to which a particular policy can be considered as legitimate within the confines of this objective function. However, the ultimate matching of means and ends is left to Part III, Part II's role being the analysis of options that might, in principle, be open to societies in devising their particular strategies for progress.

Summary

There exist a great many views about the possibilities and mechanisms of progress. Adam Smith identified three factors that, in combination, gave rise to sustained increases in material output. These were the division of labour, the use of capital in production, and the expansion of markets in goods and factors of production. In this respect, Smith's work remains a foundation of modern economic thinking. In general, the rate of economic growth depends upon society's willingness to sacrifice present consumption benefits in anticipation of higher future consumption benefits. Smith argued that the driving force behind economic progress was the individual's pursuit of private interest.

Other theorists have examined progress in a wider perspective. Auguste Comte saw progress in terms of mankind's intellectual development. Karl Marx and Friedrich Engels developed a theory in which economic progress played a central role. They argued that the economic structure analysed by Smith was progressive in the sense that it expanded material wealth. However, it also led to the dehumanization of the participants. Marx and Engels believed that the capitalist economic system was inherently unstable and was likely to break down. With its demise, a more progressive form would emerge. Since the development of the theory of evolution in biology, a number of theories have appeared that attempt to relate evolution to progress. One particular variant suggests that there is a common historical pattern of economic and social change to which all societies conform.

The possibility of the existence of long-term progress has been questioned by several theorists. Thomas Malthus devised a simple model to suggest that, owing to the dynamics of population and subsistence, economies would tend towards an equilibrium state. This Malthusian model may be formalized to suggest the possibility of a 'low-level equilibrium trap' in poorer economies. An implication of the analysis is that escape from such a trap requires radical policy measures. Malthus was also one of the first to argue that, as the capitalist economy expanded, investment and consumption would be insufficient to maintain growth. There was, in other words, an inevitable tendency towards stagnation even in industrial economies.

Rousseau is an example of a theorist who has argued that the human condition has regressed rather than progressed, because of the sacrifice of individual independence. His views are echoed by modern writers such as Marcuse, who point to the alienating nature of modern industrial society. Sarkar and Schumpeter have each developed a cyclical theory of progress. Human fortunes are argued to be the subject of bursts of progress followed by periods of regression. Hirsch suggested that there are contradictions in modern society that lead to progress in some respects, whilst entailing regression in others.

Further reading

As the discipline of economics has been intimately concerned with the issue of progress in a specific sense, the history of theories of progress is, to an extent, also the history of economic thought. Many such histories exist, for example Blaug (1968), Barber (1967), Gordon (1975) and Schumpeter (1954b), the latter being widely regarded as a 'classic' in its own right. Van Doren (1967), Sklair (1970) and Nisbet (1980) are historical reviews of philosophies of progress. An overall perspective of progress involves, of course, a grounding in historiography; Carr (1961) and Leff (1969) are useful starting points here.

Three of Turgot's most important works are contained in Meek (1973) which has a helpful introduction. Lundberg (1964) explores a theory about Turgot's influence on Smith. Of Adam Smith's *magnum opus* there exist countless editions; the one edited by Edwin Cannan is usually taken as definitive. Recent commentaries on Smith's views include Hollander (1973), O'Driscoll (1979) and Skinner (1979). Smith's political and philosophical views are analysed by Winch (1978).

Myrdal's 'master model' rests on a series of papers written by Harrod and Domar in the 1940s. Hahn and Matthews (1964) provide a detailed explanation of the model and its subsequent refinement. The other mathematical growth models in this chapter are based on those described by Ghatak (1978).

In common with Smith, Marx has had many commentators, such as Avineri (1968) and the less sympathetic Tucker (1961). It is difficult to point to a single work by Marx that encapsulates his thoughts on progress; possibly his best-known work, *The Communist Manifesto*, comes the closest in this respect. Fine (1975) is a helpful 'reader's guide' to *Capital*. The relationship between Marx's theories and evolutionism is discussed by Schmidt (1971), whilst Meek (1977) contains essays on both Marxian and Smithian thought.

The underconsumptionist argument of Malthus follows Blaug (1968), pp. 166–7. Bleaney (1976) is a comprehensive review and critique of underconsumptionist theories.

Rousseau's view on the progress of the human condition is contained specifically in his 1753 *Discours sur l'origine de l'inégalité*. Helpful commentaries on Rousseau's thought are Broome (1963) and Cobban (1964). Schumpeter's arguments are expounded and appraised by Clemence and Doody (1950). Sievers (1962) considers Schumpeter's contribution in the context of his contemporaries.

In the chapter it was mentioned that our discussions of progress theories had been selective. Two nineteenth-century writers who should also be included in the pantheon of heroes are Ricardo and Hegel; excellent discussions of their views are Hollander (1979) and C. Taylor (1975) respectively. Three important twentieth-century viewpoints are those of Aron (1968), Baran (1973) and Szentes (1976). Soviet thinking on the nature of progress is explored by Clarkson (1979). Varma (1980) is a comprehensive survey of many forms of modern progress theory.

Measuring Progress

This Appendix concerns itself with some of the more technical issues involved in the measurement of progress and perhaps the first question to be asked is why we should wish to measure progress at all. There appear to be three reasons why the establishment of some form of progress index might be considered desirable. First, it is being argued throughout this book that economies will attempt to implement policies that will lead to welfare improvements. We shall therefore need some measurable criterion of progress to assess the efficacy of such policies. Second, a yardstick of progress will be useful to analysts such as ourselves who are concerned to compare the operations of different economies and to assess the outcomes of different strategies. Third, in an international world, the behaviour of any one country has implications for all others. Country A will therefore require information on economic matters, including the extent of progress, in Country B in order to formulate its foreign policy; depending on circumstances, this might range from trade expansion to aid donation to military conquest. It should be noted that, whilst our first response above simply implies that progress should be measured, our second and third imply that it should be measured in an equivalent manner across countries, i.e. it should be internationally commensurable.

We have already decided that progress is likely to mean different things to different people, for not only is one society's list of variables to be included in the 'progress function' likely to differ from another's, but so too will the importance ascribed to each variable. In general, we might write a progress measure as

$$P = a_1 X_1 + a_2 X_2 + \ldots + a_n X_n$$

where P is the progress index, X_1 to X_n are indices measuring a country's performance with respect to particular objectives such as material plenty or the distribution of wealth, and a_1 to a_n is the vector of weights that the country associates with the particular objectives. It follows that, in order to measure progress, we must measure its constituents.

In Chapter 2, we suggested that material welfare was likely to be a significant objective for most, if not all, economies and we introduced the index of living standards – GDP per capita – as a measure of it. As we shall now see, although this measure is widely employed, it is not the only possible index in this respect.

A.1   Standard of living – some alternatives

The GDP per capita index assumes the existence of an exchange economy for, given this, we can derive an equivalence between incomes, expenditures and the value of production. In return for their productive contributions, factors are paid in the form of wages, rents, dividends or profits. As consumers, the individuals who can be considered to own these factors of production spend this income on consumption goods, or spend it directly or indirectly on investment items or via the government sector. In any one time period, then, the value of production is equivalent to the value of expenditure, which, in turn, is identical to the value of income available to purchase that production. As long as such assumptions are met we might reasonably argue that our measure provides a useful index of average material welfare, for it simply defines the amount of material resources available. In reality, however, the accuracy of the index is somewhat more debatable. Let us consider one or two of the problems involved in drawing up a table of GDP estimates such as *Table 2.1*.

The first and most general problem is the availability, collection and accuracy of the primary data necessary for the calculation of an index that really represents a grand sum of almost every area of national economic activity. Whether or not an economy has such records available is really a function of any need that it might have found to record such data. Thus, whilst centralized bureaucratic economies such as the USSR take pains to accumulate primary information as it is of use in the procedures of economic planning, more decentralized economies that give greater economic initiative to individual agents are less likely to feel the need to record their activities. As it is usually the government of a society that takes on the responsibility for data collection, it is generally the case that those economies with proportionately low levels of government involvement possess the least well-established recording systems. Even if records are available, this availability is no guarantee of their accuracy. A number of African and Asian countries, for example, have a significant nomadic population and the physical task of counting them is therefore rather arduous; an error in population figures would, of course, be reflected as an error in the GDP per capita index.

Our second problem for national accounting derives from the nature of the economic system. The logic of the per capita GDP calculation derives essentially from Western economic experience for, in Western market economies, virtually all production is exchanged as commodities and it thus enters fully into the income and expenditure calculus. This is not the case, however, for the so-called subsistence economies of the Southern hemisphere, where agricultural producers either consume their output directly or exchange it by means of barter with other such producers. A substantial volume of output therefore has no explicit value to be incorporated into the GDP statistic – Usher (1968) estimated that over 50 per cent of agricultural production in Thailand was un-traded. In order to make such subsistence economies commensurate with market systems it becomes necessary to impute a valuation of non-traded goods and services and, given that such an imputation is hypothetical, we cannot guarantee its accuracy or even, some would argue, its validity. An exactly analogous problem exists with countries such as the USSR and the Eastern European states. These economies use their own individual form of national accounting, which has to be duly 'modified' to conform with Western practices.

Even supposing that we could logically derive an aggregate value for economic output that meant the same thing in all economies, this aggregate would naturally be expressed in terms of the monetary value of the country concerned. For comparative purposes, we must clearly express all figures in terms of one particular currency; in reality, the US dollar is the most common denominator. If we assume, as we did before, that all commodities are potentially tradable (this time at an international level) then, clearly, we may simply determine all GDP values relative to a single numeraire by conversion via the foreign exchange rate, a surrogate for demand and supply variations at an international level. As Usher (1968) observes, however, this effective price is influenced by three factors – it is restricted to those commodities that are actually traded, and it is influenced by international transport costs, and also by any taxes or subsidies levied on traded goods – and he argues that conventional exchange rate conversions thus overstate the differentials between rich and poor economies measured in GDP terms. Consider the case of services, for example, which are typically non-traded internationally. Rich countries have relative labour shortages and therefore value (and price) labour-intensive services highly. Hence their value contribution to GDP is high. However, poorer countries with a labour surplus find services relatively cheap and their contribution to the GDP sum is thus low. Clearly, this does not necessarily equate with a lower living standard.

The commonly used solution to this problem is the comparison of the consumption or output vectors for various countries by means of a common set of prices. In his comparison of Thailand and the United Kingdom, Usher (1968) found that such a correction lowered the conventional GDP per capita difference measured in exchange rate terms by over 50 per cent. This result is in accordance with earlier findings, such as those of Clark (1951) and Gilbert *et al.* (1958). The exchange rate issue was central to the more recent and extensive study undertaken by Kravis, Heston and Summers (1978). These authors acknowledge that simple conversions of GDPs by means of the exchange rate systematically overstate the differentials between high- and low-income economies, as compared to the method that accounts for parities of purchasing power. After making the necessary adjustments to the conventional GDP figures for over 100 individual countries, the authors draw some conclusions about the global distribution of income. Conventional exchange rate conversions of GDP, for example, suggest that the standard of living of Western industrial economies is some thirteen times greater than that of the non-socialist pre-industrial world. When the adjustment for differential purchasing power is carried out, however, the ratio between the two comes down to approximately six.

There are, nevertheless, at least two alternatives to this solution. It might, for example, be argued that what is important in the material sense is the extent to which an economy lies above the level of bare subsistence. We might therefore express our GDP figures, not as an absolute value, but rather as a ratio to the level of income necessary for subsistence. Such a procedure would, of course, also compensate for price variations between economies. Gleason (1961) used this method to reassess the GDP differential between the United States and Japan and he concluded that the gap suggested by conventional exchange rate conversions was far too large. An alternative modification is to suggest that GDP figures are invalidated not only by international price variations but also by the fact that different societies consume different bundles of goods and services. Several analysts have accordingly argued that we can only compare living standards in terms of certain 'key' items that figure in all societies' consumption functions. Bennett (1951), for example, included calorie intake, textiles production, energy production and medical facilities. Although there is no reason in principle why these alternatives should not provide the basis for any one country's standard of living index, they both retain inherent problems when we come to international comparisons. The determination of the constituents of 'bare subsistence' and 'key consumption commodities' is bound to be subjective.

From the foregoing, it might be thought that the problems for any index of material welfare lie in the necessity to compare economies, the fundamental features of which are essentially dissimilar – consumption patterns differ, prices differ and so forth. However, as Usher's most recent analysis (Usher, 1980) of material prosperity in Canada over a 50-year period suggests, we are still not on particularly safe ground when we examine just one economy. By conventional estimates of GDP, the Canadian standard of living rose by an annual average of 2.45 per cent between 1926 and 1974. Usher argues, however, that this figure ignores some important changes in items pertaining to prosperity. Relative prices of commodities, for example, are likely to have changed over the period, as has the nature of the bundle of goods and services available for consumption – television sets and the opportunities for air travel are obvious innovations. Substantial alterations have been made to the working environment, for example in the factor mix in production and in hours of work. Most importantly, average life expectancy has risen over the period. By making imputations for all these elements, Usher concludes that the simple GDP growth rate may understate annual improvements in material living standards by as much as 1 per cent per annum.

If aggregate output per capita is such a problematic index of material welfare, why does it remain such a popular measure? Indeed, why does every text on economic progress and development (including this one) contain an obligatory listing of GDP figures? There seem to be three major reasons for this. First, of all the possible estimates, the GDP figure is by far the simplest to calculate because virtually all economies prepare national accounts of some description for their own internal purposes. Using these prepared figures, multiplied through by the observable foreign exchange rates, is a far simpler way of proceeding than is the more complex route through imputation, correction and estimation. Second, the data do serve a useful purpose, for they often appear, to a considerable extent, to represent a monotonic transformation of most other conceptions of material prosperity. As Nordhaus and Tobin (1972) remark: 'Although GNP and other national income aggregates are imperfect measures of welfare, the broad picture of secular progress which they convey remains after correction of their most obvious deficiencies' (p. 24). It is significant, for example, that the modifications to the GDP figures outlined above alter the absolute distance between nations but they do not significantly affect the relative ranking of our list of rich-to-poor. Finally, it is a simple fact that such figures are used because they are used! Having been initially developed by Western economists, the national accounts system became the established practice of the large international organizations such as the World Bank and the United Nations. The method having thus achieved a certain legitimacy, it is clearly logical for countries to continue using it. It being easier to swim with the current rather than against it, the effect is to reinforce the usage of the accounting convention.

The figures for per capita GDP are simply statements of the average material living standard; they contain no information about the actual distribution of welfare amongst the various inhabitants of a country. Clearly, we require some form of index for distribution if such an element is to be included in our progress function.

A.2 Distribution

Statistical theory provides us with a number of ways to measure in-equalities in the distribution of income or wealth. One popular method involves the use of the Lorenz curve (*Figure A.1*). This graph records the percentage of income, wealth or any other benefit that accrues to progressively richer percentages of a country's population – in our

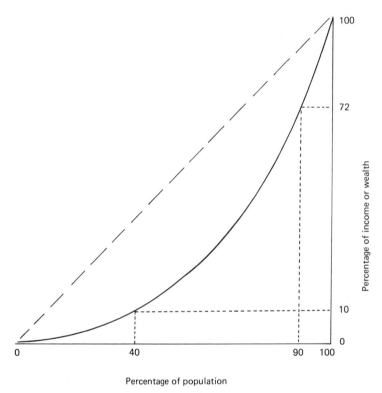

Figure A.1 The Lorenz curve

example, the poorest 40 per cent of the population receive 10 per cent of the total income, whilst the richest 10 per cent receive 28 per cent of income. A purely egalitarian distribution would naturally be represented by the (dotted) 45 degree line and progressive shifts in the curve, away from this line and towards the origin, indicate increases in inequality. In order to give more precision to the graphical measure, we may derive two statistics. First, we might use the Gini coefficient, which is the ratio of the area between the 45 degree line and the Lorenz curve to the total area beneath the 45 degree line. This coefficient can therefore take on any value between 0 (equality) and 1 (total inequality). A second,

TABLE A.1 Distribution of pre-tax incomes for selected countries

Country, and date of survey	Percentage of annual income received by: Poorest 40%	Middle 40%	Richest 20%	Gini coefficient
Africa				
Madagascar (1960)	11.7	29.3	59.0	0.53
Tanzania (1964)	12.6	26.4	61.0	0.54
Senegal (1960)	10.0	26.0	64.0	0.56
Zambia (1959)	15.9	27.0	57.1	0.48
Morocco (1965)	14.5	20.1	65.1	0.50
Nigeria (1959)	14.0	25.1	60.9	0.51
Tunisia (1971)	10.7	24.4	65.0	0.53
Ivory Coast (1959)	18.0	27.0	55.0	0.43
South Africa (1965)	6.1	36.6	57.4	0.58
Central/South America				
Peru (1961)	8.3	23.5	57.6	0.61
El Salvador (1965)	12.0	26.6	61.4	0.53
Bolivia (1968)	11.5	27.5	61.0	0.53
Ecuador (1968)	16.4	39.3	44.2	0.38
Panama (1969)	14.3	29.0	56.7	0.48
Mexico (1963)	10.1	30.4	59.5	0.53
Brazil (1965)	12.5	26.0	61.5	0.54
Venezuela (1962)	13.4	38.9	47.1	0.42
Western Europe				
Greece (1957)	19.3	31.2	49.5	0.38
UK (1964)	15.3	40.5	44.0	0.38
France (1962)	9.5	36.8	53.7	0.50
West Germany (1964)	15.4	31.7	52.9	0.45
Middle East				
Iraq (1956)	8.0	24.0	68.0	0.60
Israel (1957)	20.2	40.4	39.4	0.30
South East Asia				
Burma (1958)	23.0	28.5	48.5	0.35
India (1956–7)	20.0	38.0	42.0	0.33
Sri Lanka (1963)	13.7	34.0	52.3	0.44
Pakistan (1963–4)	17.5	37.5	45.0	0.37
Philippines (1961)	12.7	31.5	55.8	0.48
Others				
USA (1969)	17.9	41.0	41.1	0.34
Japan (1962)	15.3	38.7	46.0	0.39

Source: Compiled from data in F. Paukert (1973), 'Income Distribution at Different Levels of Development: A Survey of Evidence', *International Labour Review* (Geneva, International Labour Organisation), **108**, pp. 114–15.

and related, measure is the 'maximum equalization percentage', which indicates the percentage of total income (or other benefit) that would have to be redistributed in order to produce complete equality.

Those empirical studies that have been undertaken suggest that Gini coefficients tend to vary from country to country in the range 0.3 to 0.6. Put another way, this means that the poorest 60 per cent of a population could receive anything between, say, 20 and 30 per cent of total income, whilst the share of the richest 5 per cent might vary from 15 to as much as 50 per cent. The results of income distribution surveys conducted at various times for a selection of those countries appearing in *Table 2.1* are presented in *Table A.1*. Having analysed data of this nature, Paukert (1973) believes that a hypothesis earlier advanced by Kuznets can be substantiated, namely that inequality of income tends to increase with material prosperity (in per capita GDP terms) up to a certain level and thereafter begins to decline. As a whole, richer economies tend to be more egalitarian than poor ones and the statistical explanation for this lies with the incomes of the very rich, the top 5 per cent. With increases in GDP for the cross-section, the income share of the very rich typically falls from around 30 per cent to less than 20 per cent. Such a generalization must be made with care, for there are, of course, exceptions – France and West Germany are noticeably richer than Britain in GDP terms, but their distributions are significantly more inegalitarian.

Looking at distribution from the time-series rather than the cross-section point of view, the data indicate that trends in the past have been towards a more equal distribution. Paukert (1973) notes, for example, that the proportion of income enjoyed by the richest 20 per cent of the UK population has fallen from nearly 60 per cent to around 40 per cent over the past century; similar trends are observable for West Germany, Sweden, India and the USA, although the time-series for these nations is shorter. Again, however, we must be wary of making all-embracing generalizations – a 1970 survey of Venezuela (Chenery *et al.*, 1974, pp. 8–9) records that the 1962 vector given in *Table A.1* had changed from (13.4 38.9 47.1) to (7.9 27.1 65.0), i.e. there had been a marked shift towards inequality. Indeed, such a trend is quite characteristic of many Latin American economies.

As the appropriate distribution of income and wealth is likely to be an objective in a nation's progress function and therefore a goal of economic policy, it is likely to be fruitful if we analyse particular distributions in terms of economic ideology rather than, say, in terms of levels of material welfare. As some movement towards egalitarianism is an avowed objective of most socialist nations, it is not surprising that Chenery *et al.* (1974) discover that indices of inequality tend to be lower in such countries. By way of a conclusion to this section, it is perhaps sobering to reflect that the distribution of income for the *world* economy gives rise to a Gini coefficient of 0.64, a figure higher than that for any single nation within the world economy. Two-thirds of the world's 4000 million people are currently competing for less than one-fifth of its annual production.

Although the Gini coefficient is widely employed in the measurement of income distribution, we should bear in mind that a number of statistically acceptable alternatives exist. The standard deviation about the mean of a frequency distribution is one such measure of dispersion. Again, the divergence between the arithmetic mean and the geometric mean of incomes could also serve as an index of inequality. There is, in other words, no unique measurement procedure. In his comparison of measures of distribution, Champernowne (1974) notes that the various indices display a 'fairly high degree of agreement'. Given this, however, he also argues that different indices are sensitive to different types of inequality, e.g. cases where the spread of incomes is very wide, or where many incomes are very high or very low. In his tests, the Gini coefficient appeared to be particularly responsive where there was a 'wide spread of the less extreme incomes'. The implication is that, if the type of inequality within an economy changes over time, any one index might over- or understate the magnitude of the distribution change. His comparison, concludes Champernowne:

> ... suggests that the choice of index could quite frequently decide the answer to such questions as whether inequality has increased or decreased in a country over a decade. In making the choice one should accordingly be very clear in what type of inequality one is interested (p. 807).

A.3   Generalized indices

Even if we produce our measures of distribution and an acceptable surrogate for material welfare, we are still some way short of our overall index for progress for, it might be argued, significant constituents of human welfare are still unrepresented. In this section, we shall consider two approaches towards the establishment of a more universal progress index.

The 'measure of economic welfare' (MEW) devised by Nordhaus and Tobin (1972) represents an augmentation of the basic standard of living index derivable from national accounts by other factors that might legitimately be taken to appear within a progress concept. The authors argue that the use of an aggregate such as GDP as a welfare measure is in reality misguided, even from the point of view of material prosperity, simply because it is an output index. Whilst, as has been argued earlier, output might be a useful approximation to consumption, it seems to make greater sense to measure consumption directly. This immediately involves us in a reclassification of the existing system of national accounts into two types of expenditures – consumption and investment for future consumption on the one hand, and 'instrumental expenditures' on the other. Nordhaus and Tobin argue that, although these latter resource commitments appear in the national accounts as positive items, they in fact represent activities 'that are evidently not directly sources of utility themselves but are regrettably necessary inputs to activities that may yield utility' (p. 9). Examples of such instrumental expenditures include government spending on law and order, the maintenance of roads, public amenities such as health care and education and national defence.

However, elements of these 'regrettables' will naturally show up in direct consumption figures, the effects of education and health, for example, being found in changes in household income. Note that the effects are *not* to be found in the level of health or education expenditure, which is an input to the process and not an output.

Furthermore, Nordhaus and Tobin believe that several important aspects of final consumption are ignored by the conventional accounting procedures. First, they wish formally to incorporate the value of non-market activity, which, in the instance of the USA, which is their case study, is essentially 'housework' undertaken largely by females. The value of this activity can be assessed by multiplying the average time spent by women in the activity by the wage rate appropriate to such activities when undertaken on a commercial basis. Second, patterns of leisure change over time owing to unemployment, changes in the length of the working day, legislation regarding the retirement age and the typical number of years of schooling. Valuations of leisure time can be made in a manner equivalent to the valuation of non-market activity. Finally, it is suggested that allowances must be made for the 'disamenities of urbanization' and other externalities; these are calculated from income differentials between rural and urban areas. Higher wages paid in cities, it is argued, represent 'disamenity premia' that compensate for living in 'less pleasant surroundings'. Having augmented the GDP accounts by these imputed valuations, and having made assumptions about the impact of technical progress, Nordhaus and Tobin compare MEW with the conventional estimates of material prosperity in GDP terms. They conclude that, whilst the index of GDP per capita rose from 100 to 187.5 between 1929 and 1965, MEW only rose from 100 to 141.8 over the same period (p. 53).

MEW is presented by the authors not so much as a definitive statement (some of the assumptions appear a little dubious) but simply as an indication of the extent to which the standard of living index is capable of extension. Indeed, they point out two further candidates for inclusion in an extended index that might well appear as policy objectives for many nations. These candidates are natural resource depletion – shadow prices rather than market prices being incorporated if it was felt that the current rate of resource use was incorrect – and population growth – dummy variables might be incorporated to show up the effect of a changing balance between productive and non-productive population.

Our second approach is the one that possibly comes the closest to our earlier formulation of the progress function and is the sort of framework described by Drewnowski (1974) for the measurement of the 'quality of life'. Drewnowski initially argues that the essential problem with the GDP approach to living standards is not that they are necessarily invalid in their own terms but that they are too often taken as *the* index of progress *in toto*. Drewnowski suggests that they should be set in the context of some more general measure of social welfare and he proceeds to establish the basis of such a measure. He believes that welfare can be considered in both a static and a dynamic sense for, in any one time period, an individual can be considered to be in a 'state of welfare' whilst also being the recipient of a 'flow of welfare'. Drewnowski sees the state of welfare as 'the sum total of characteristics of a person or population expressed in quantitative form and referring to the state in which that person or population is found as a result of needs satisfaction' (p. 79).

There are three component elements to this state: physical characteristics (such as nutritional intake, health status and life expectancy), mental characteristics (such as literacy rates, educational attainment and levels of employment) and social characteristics (such as the degree of political participation permitted). All of these elements are to be measured as specific cardinal or ordinal indices although some can, of course, be measured directly, e.g. average life expectancy in years. The 'level of living' index, on the other hand, measures the flow of welfare to the population and contains further elements, such as the quantity and quality of the provision of housing, clothing, leisure and security, as well as indices for the nature of the social and physical environment. These indices having, in principle, been developed, Drewnowski then proceeds to demonstrate that the welfare indices may be combined with the conventional national accounting framework to provide a social accounting matrix, and the system is interactive. First, we can set out the productive relationship between the factors of production – labour, capital and technology – in terms of their contribution to the generation of consumption and investment goods. Second, this consumption allocation contributes to the 'level of living' by providing for the satisfaction of needs. Finally, these changes in level of living induce changes in the state of welfare that feed back into the basic production relationship because of the productivity effect of a changing welfare level on the quantity and quality of labour (and, indirectly, on technology).

Apart from the problems of data accuracy and availability that beset any empirical research, there are two particular worries that we might have about this particular approach to progress measurement. These are, first, the difficulties of measuring certain variables that appear intuitively immeasurable, such as the quality of labour relations or the extent of personal security, and, second, the subjective nature of the list of items to be included in the two overall indices; would all societies, for instance, agree on the importance of a 'beautiful environment'? Drewnowski concedes that the measurement of progress by means of these indices and the weightings given to the various arguments in the overall function will remain a subjective matter – 'the statement of targets in national plans can have only national validity' (p. 31). Perhaps, however, this is not the point. If we are happy to accept that concepts of progress are subjective, what this approach provides is a model (in fact, a generalized input–output model) that not only permits us to set up our own subjective progress function with weightings and measurement scales defined to our own standards, but also serves as a basis for rational planning to realize that function. The technique will therefore measure the progress that we wish to create.

A practical example of the sort of model that Drewnowski proposes is the OECD's Social Indicator Development Program, which was set up in 1970. By 1973, members had agreed on a 'list of common social concerns' and nine 'goal areas' were established. These were taken to be the principal components in the citizen's welfare function and included the following: health status and access to health care, educational levels and opportunities, quality of working life, leisure time, 'personal economic situation', the physical environment, personal safety and the nature of the judicial system, opportunities for political participation and the degree of social inequality. Reporting on the advances of the programme, OECD (1976) notes that these goal areas were to be broken down into a large number of component indices, some 50 of which had already been established. However, the task appears to be far from completion. In the first place, many of the proposed indicators are conceptually new and data are thus not yet available on which they can be practically based. Second, other indicators seem, as yet, to defy measurement (e.g. 'extent of confidence in the administration of civil law'). Finally, it would seem quite possible that, as the OECD delves further and further into the mechanisms of the process, it could well find that, whilst members accept the goal areas, they will disagree about the manner in which they can be measured. These problems should not, however, be taken to imply that the indicator programme is unproductive; OECD (1976) notes that the ability to assess progress is fundamental to the design of strategy and the existence of such problems is thus an invitation to redouble the research effort.

Summary

Problems arise in calculating per capita GDP, and in using it as an index of living standards. Such problems include lack or inaccuracy of data, structural differences between economies and the fact that exchange rates do not reflect the true purchasing power of local currencies. A number of modifications to the conventional system of measurement have been proposed. The majority of these modified methods suggest that income differentials between rich and poor economies have been overstated by the conventional system. Some of these modified methods may not be internationally acceptable owing to their subjective natures.

The Gini coefficient is a popular measure of income and wealth distribution. It may be calculated from Lorenz curve data. Empirical studies suggest that income distribution varies dramatically from country to country.

There have been a number of attempts to devise generalized indices of progress. In addition to economic variables – living standards and distribution – such indices include social and political variables, e.g. leisure time, environmental factors and political participation. The development of generalized indices remains in its infancy.

Part II

Dimensions of Progress

Chapter Four

Making Social Decisions

Society, it has been argued by the classical political philosophers from Plato to Rousseau, comes into existence when human beings become conscious of their individual inadequacies. Many worthwhile objectives appear to be far more easily and effectively attained by individuals agreeing to act in concert rather than by individuals acting in isolation; examples that presumably occurred to our palaeolithic ancestors included the provision of personal security by collective defence and the cooperative hunting of food. Indeed, in this respect as in many others, the human species differs little from the remainder of the animal kingdom. Many other species pursue a social existence in which certain activities are group concerns. This desire to live socially and to indulge in collective action in order to obtain a common goal poses, however, a particular type of problem for the participants, namely the identification of the appropriate method for deciding what the common goal is to be and for determining the optimal strategy for its achievement. Whilst we might reasonably suppose that the individual in isolation has only himself to please, the decision to act within a coherent supra-individual unit requires the members to devise a decision-making procedure for the collectivity that will result in outcomes that conform to the interests of all participating individuals.

We have already discovered that it is possible to discern a variety of metaphysical positions regarding the relationship between the individual and his society and it therefore seems likely that there will exist a corresponding variety of attitudes about the appropriate method for reaching social decisions. A discussion of the appropriate form of social decision making in the context of this examination of progress is important for two reasons. First, it is possible that society will regard the establishment of the 'correct' form of decision making as an objective in its own right, that is, the correct form of decision making will be considered as a legitimate goal within, or constituent of, progress *per se*. Second, it is likely that the specific form of decision structure adopted will have implications for the feasibility of the other goals in the objective function, such as material wealth and its distribution. It might therefore be possible to demonstrate that certain decision structures can perform in a manner considered better than others.

To begin with, let us make a very broad distinction between two types of collective decision. For the first type, which we shall term 'democratic', all individuals within the society will consent to the decision structure employed. In our second type, the 'coercive' system, the decision-making structure is not voluntarily adopted by the individuals within the society and is maintained by force. As we shall see, it is rare for real-world societies to fall exactly into either category.

4.1   Democratic variants

Possibly the simplest form of democratic decision making is that referred to as 'direct democracy'. The approach presumes, first, that social choice (or, rather, society's choice) is the aggregation of individual preferences or the preponderance of individual opinion; put another way, 'society thinks what most individuals think'. Second, it assumes that one individual's opinion should be regarded as being of equal significance or importance as the opinion of any other individual. In practical terms, we might think of individuals formally recording their preferred choice from a range of policy options as a 'vote', the option that gains the highest number of votes being taken as the one that represents the preponderant opinion within society. This decision-making model is widely used throughout the world, although at an infranational rather than at a national level for reasons that we shall examine shortly. How is its use justified?

Clearly, the method will find favour in societies that base their socio-economic organization on the metaphysical presupposition that all individuals are equally endowed with fundamental 'natural' rights. The necessity of each individual to voice his opinion (his private opinion) in the context of deciding on collective policy is frequently seen as a basic constituent of individual freedom in the negative sense, for the 'liberal' conception of society would hold that any constraint to liberty, as might be represented by a binding social decision, is only legitimate if each individual concerned participates in the debate that precedes the imposition of the constraint. We might further argue that the very act of individual participation in the process of decision making carries with it, under this philosophy, positive virtues, for it serves to make individuals sensitive to the desires and opinions of others, thus welding the community into an integrated unit and extending the potential for cooperation. Finally, societies that do not accept the possibility of political absolutes would regard the existence of policy choices, as presupposed by this model, as the best possible safeguard against rigidity and as a facilitator of pragmatism.

Irrespective of the grounds upon which a country justifies the adoption of direct democracy, it is important to appreciate that the mechanism described above is just one possibility amongst a variety of institutional structures permitted by the principles. Let us consider a few of the variables in the context of a hypothetical nation using this system. In the first place, we asserted that all individuals in the society should be permitted to vote; in practice, this is unlikely to be the case. It seems inconceivable that any real-world society would permit day-old infants to register a vote and yet they are presumably individuals in their own right. In general, a society is likely to argue that all individuals should have equal political rights providing that they can fulfil certain conditions. In the past, a great variety of social groups have been explicitly excluded from the social choice process. Classical Greece is a widely cited instance of the use of the direct democratic method, although it should be remembered that the franchise did not extend to women, males below a certain age, and slaves. It is probable, therefore, that society will decide that only a proportion of its population is either entitled to make, or is capable of making, social decisions. It is this proportion that constitutes the electorate.

Having permitted those enfranchised individuals actually to vote for the outcome that they prefer, we shall presumably sum these votes to determine the preponderant opinion. However, we have, as yet, no clear guide as to what determines either preponderance or majority. Consider the following possibility. Suppose the 100 people in our model society cast their votes 60:40 in favour of policy A as opposed to policy B. In a strictly mathematical sense, A is clearly the majority opinion. Now suppose that only 50 per cent of the electorate bothered to vote, but the ratio between the votes cast remained 60:40. In this case, and depending upon whatever assumptions we care to adopt, we could argue either (i) half the population did not vote as they were indifferent between A and B and therefore A is, on the whole, preferred more positively than B, or (ii) policy A is, in fact, not preferred as only 30 per cent of the electorate registered a preference for it.

Neither of these alternatives is, of course, objectively correct. We should note, however, that, given the usual electoral participation rates in most societies, a policy would stand more chance of being approved under criterion (i) than under criterion (ii). Interestingly enough, the two recent instances of direct democracy in the United Kingdom each employed a different criterion. In 1975, a referendum was held to decide whether Britain should maintain its membership of the European Economic Community. In the referendum, the government decided to employ the standard electoral practice of simple majority, i.e. the outcome was to be decided by the majority decision of those actually voting. However, for the 1979 referendum on devolution of political power to the regions of Scotland and Wales, the criterion for the acceptance of such decentralization was the assent of at least 40 per cent of the registered electorate of these regions. In the 1975 case, electoral turnout was 64 per cent, with 67 per cent of voters (i.e. 43 per cent of the electorate) favouring continued EEC membership. In the 1979 case, just over 40 per cent of the Scottish electorate favoured devolution, although the proposal was heavily defeated in Wales.

Such a complication is paralleled in the cases where an electorate is confronted with a non-binary choice amongst policies. If we were automatically to adopt the policy proposal that received the highest number of votes, we might discover that, for a choice amongst a dozen policies, the winning outcome was only supported by perhaps 10 or 20 per cent of the electorate. Again, the implication could be drawn that 90 or 80 per cent of the electorate did not like this alternative! A widely adopted rationalization of this procedure is to reduce all non-binary decisions to binary ones, via successive ballots. After the first ballot, the least successful alternative is withdrawn and voters now choose between the remaining, and more popular, alternatives. This process continues until the position of absolute majority is reached. A procedure of this form is currently used to elect the President of France.

The only position that is completely respectable and unambiguous from an abstract point of view is absolute unanimity. If unanimity were to be required in real-world societies, however, one suspects that they would remain remarkably static places. Just one contrary vote would be sufficient to veto any proposed policy.

In certain cases, we might find that the majority criterion was a variable. The appropriate majority for the overturning of a constitutional principle might be higher than that necessary to make day-to-day social decisions. The former might, for example, require a two-thirds majority whilst the latter might require only a simple majority. Societies might therefore adjust the majority criterion to make certain types of social decision 'harder' to make.

A popular characterization of direct democracy is 'one person, one vote'. Again, however, this is simply a special case of a whole range of possibilities that permit each individual to cast any number of votes. In fact, the availability of a number of votes to the individual confers a distinct advantage, for it permits an extra dimension to be included in the voting calculus, namely the intensity of preferences. Suppose an individual is faced with three policy options, A, B and C. Under the one-vote system, he would give his vote to his most preferred choice, say A, and options B and C would score zero. We may record this as $1:0:0$. If we had analysed his preferences further, however, we might have found the contrast was not so startling as the above preference ordering suggests – whilst he was a supporter of A he also had certain sympathies for B. If we had permitted him to use ten votes rather than one, he might have cast them $6:4:0$. To keep things simple, let us have just one other person voting in our society. We shall suppose he is a *C*-supporter whose preferences are the mirror-image of our first individual. He would therefore vote $0:0:1$ under the one-vote system and $0:4:6$ under the ten-vote system. Which policy should society follow? Under the one-vote method, it appears that society is evenly split between *A* and *C* but does not care at all for *B*; under the ten-vote system, however, the preferred outcome is *B* (with eight votes, as distinct from the six each scored by *A* and *C*)!

The ten-vote system has clearly yielded an outcome in diametric opposition to the one-vote method yet, again, it is just one example of a whole host of possibilities. Rather than ten, we might insist that each member of the electorate be given far more votes to allocate, say 100 or even 1000, and we should presume that the more votes that each is given then the more precisely could the voter tune his voting allocations to match his attitudes to the options. Whilst the one-vote system requires the voter to say 'I like this, I don't like anything else', an *n*-vote system (where *n* is any number we care to pick above 1) permits the voter to register an opinion along the lines of 'I prefer this option *X*-times as much as this other option'. Between these extremes, there exists a third possibility in which a cardinal scale of preference is permitted but is established *ex ante*. Expressed in the same form as above, we might tell each voter: 'Record five votes for your most preferred option, three for your second ...' and so forth. Again, the numbers are arbitrary and any monotonic transformation could be substituted. As has been shown (Whynes and Bowles, 1981), with a specific set of preference intensities, decision rules may be devised to ensure the final acceptance of *any* policy option.

From the foregoing discussion, we must conclude that not one but many methods of operating a direct democracy exist, if only because of permissible variations in the size of the electorate, the concept of majority and the technical methods of vote aggregation. Furthermore, it is difficult to argue objectively about the merits of the alternatives in view of the ideological foundations of some seemingly arbitrary structures: just what sort of people should be excluded from the electorate and just how big does a majority have to be? We can, however, examine the implications of the specific variants of the democratic principle that are currently in use throughout the world. Although direct democracy is frequently employed in small organizations, it does not find much employment in the making of day-to-day decisions at a national level. In Western economies at least, national decision making is based upon a modification of direct democracy known as 'representative democracy'.

4.1.1   REPRESENTATIVE DEMOCRACY

The system of representative democracy operates at two levels. First, the electorate of the society concerned chooses individuals from a range of candidates and these selected individuals constitute a 'legislature'. Second, this legislature now makes social decisions on behalf of the whole society using, usually, the principle of direct democracy. Rather than select their economic policies or strategies directly, as they did in the previous case, the members of society select individual representatives who are responsible for making the binding policy decisions. A society might justify its use of this form of decision-making structure in a number of ways. First, it might be argued that experience suggests that social cooperation is subject to economies of scale (that is, the effectiveness of social units in performing such tasks as the provision of security, the production of commodities and so forth increases with the size of the social unit), but this process of the expansion of membership into national social units of tens of millions of individuals would pose substantial diseconomies for a system of direct democracy – would it be physically possible to consult entire populations on each and every social issue? Second, we might argue that the individual's desire to participate in social decision making is determined by an economic calculus in the same way as is his decision to engage in any other form of activity. Political participation embodies an opportunity cost and individuals might well wish to devote their time and energies to some subjectively profitable activity whilst leaving the job of making decisions to those who prefer it. Just as everyone does not want to be an economist, not everyone will necessarily wish to spend every waking moment making social decisions. Finally, the electorate might feel that, as it regards itself as being incompetent at making collective decisions, it would prefer to choose 'wise men' to make policies on its behalf.

In a study of the workings of representative democracy we can, of course, repeat all the propositions about the characteristics of direct democracy that we encountered earlier. The history of most Western representative democracies, for example, is littered with peculiar notions about the appropriate composition of the electorate. At one time or another the adherents of virtually every major religion have found themselves excluded from the franchise, whilst women did not begin to obtain their 'natural' rights of political equality until around a century ago. Early Western franchise legislation generally included a minimum income or wealth qualification, although this has since been gradually relaxed, and the 'age of majority' is now widely accepted to be 18 years. Most representative democracies elect their legislature via the 'one person, one vote' principle, deciding the outcome in terms of simple majority – i.e. the winner is the candidate polling the highest percentage of votes actually cast.

The workings of representative democracies have been studied by economists for several decades and one of the most influential contributions has been that of Downs (1957). His model explores the implications of those democratic procedures (such as those of Britain and the United States) where candidates forming the legislature are subject to regular popular election. Downs comes to some intriguing conclusions on the basis of two simple assumptions: first, that candidates compete for office with a view to being elected and, second, that each individual voter will vote for the candidate who offers the best chance of having that voter's preferences adopted as the social preference by the legislature. Voters are thus assumed to be self-interested; they will vote for the candidate most likely to make policy of the greatest benefit to that voter. Candidates are clearly those individuals who derive pleasure from the holding of office. We may now predict how such candidates are likely to behave. In order to be elected, the candidate must obtain more votes than his rivals and he can do this in two ways. First, he must formulate policy proposals that the majority of voters will favour and, second, he must convince the electorate that such policies have a good chance of being adopted as the final social decision. These tasks may be accomplished by the formation of a coalition between a number of representatives who agree upon a common policy, i.e. the formation of a political party. The reason for this is that the individual representative in the legislature has only one vote amongst many and in this respect competes on equal terms with fellow representatives. However, if several representatives agree upon a common political platform, their voting power vis-à-vis the remaining individual representatives, and thus their chances of having their views accepted by the legislature, increases. In order to combat such a coalition it will be optimal for other individual representatives to form a rival coalition (or coalitions).

The number of coalitions that finally result within any particular legislature depend upon two factors, the first of which is the mathematical condition for majority. With the simple majority principle, the long-run equilibrium is likely to be at two parties, since, in the case of three or more coalitions, majority could always be secured by two or more of the parties forming a coalition of coalitions. Additionally, binary voting (the one-vote system that obliges voters effectively to vote for one party and against all others) reinforces this tendency. The second factor – the political polarization of the particular electorate – may contradict this, however. The formation of party coalitions amongst representatives and candidates for election will generally require a certain degree of compromise on the part of each, it being unlikely that all would share identical views on every issue. The individual voter therefore discovers that a favoured candidate might offer the best chance of policy implementation by virtue of party membership although this occurs at the cost of commitment to a wide variety of policies in the party 'package', not all of which the voter might agree with. Attitudes to this trade-off will vary from polity to polity – whilst the UK and the US electorates accept the existence of two or three distinct 'packages', countries such as France and Italy support far more political parties grounded in specific sets of ideologies. Multi-party coalitions of the latter type typically lead to instability, for there exist contrary tendencies of a desire for further coalition to secure a majority coupled with a reluctance to compromise in the area of the political platform. Italy's ruling coalitions have broken down at a rate in excess of one per year since the Second World War.

Being particularly interested in the experiences of the UK and the USA, Downs concentrates on the 'duopoly' variant of the model, in which just two parties compete for effective control of the legislature. Following Downs' assumptions, we see that parties formulate policies with a view to attracting votes; they do not seek office with a view to carrying out preconceived programmes. Accordingly, they are highly unlikely to offer the electorate policy packages distinguished by features on which there is substantial consensus. If the parties feel, in other words, that no electoral gain (or even that mutual electoral loss) may be made in a certain area, this area will be 'taken out of politics'. Citizens are therefore effectively denied the option of expressing a view in the area. Actually, the competition between two parties is an extremely subtle affair, as the theory of economic competition between oligopolists demonstrates. In order to attract votes from one's rival, it is necessary to resemble one's rival as much as possible whilst still main-taining a distinctive feature to retain 'consumer loyalty'. In a two-party system, therefore, we should anticipate a growing similarity of electoral platforms, to permit the parties to appeal to as wide a section of the electorate as possible, coupled with the exaggeration of 'cosmetic' distinc-tions between the competitors.

An important question to ask is the extent to which the Downsian model stands up to empirical testing. A certain degree of verification has been achieved but some areas are far more easily tested than others. How do we detect, for example, if party positions on issues are really similar? The fact that the electorate appears divided might simply mean that party advertising has proved particularly effective. One implication that is easily tested is Downs' realization that, under this electoral system, there is very little incentive for the individual citizen either to vote at all (as the single vote has a negligible marginal impact on the final outcome) or to take the time necessary to become informed about the election issues. Most electoral studies support the view that Western electorates display considerable apathy, although there does appear to be some correlation between the 'status' of elections and voter turn-out. Even so, USA presidential, or UK general, elections rarely see more than 60–70 per cent of the electorate voting (i.e. around one-third of the countries' populations), whilst UK local elections (where, paradoxic-ally, the marginal impact of the individual vote is higher owing to the smaller size of local electorates) are often decided on the basis of a 30–40 per cent turn-out. This point is given particular prominence by Dahl (1961) in his famous study of government in New Haven, Connecticut, USA, during the 1940s and 1950s. In his discussion of the use of 'political resources' that people have at their disposal, such as access to relevant information, involvement in campaigns and the use of the vote itself, Dahl notes: 'The first fact, and it overshadows almost everything else, is that most citizens use their political resources scarcely at all. To begin with, a large proportion of the population of New Haven does not even vote' (p. 276, emphasis omitted). Dahl's study also provides some neat examples of party competition through careful selection of candidates and programmes. New Haven possessed a sizeable Italian community and, for the elections at the end of the 1950s, the Republican Party sought to attract votes from this group by nominating a number of candidates of Italian extraction. The Democratic Party immediately countered this strategy by including in its political programme some substantial schemes for the urban redevelopment of several neighbour-hoods whose populations were predominantly Italian (pp. 216–17).

Downs' basic model has been extended by a number of theorists. The views of Breton (1974) are of particular interest because they pursue the question of the political behaviour of voters in more detail. A major problem confronting the economic theory of political behaviour in representative democracies is why individuals bother to participate at all, in view of the marginal impact of each individual's vote. Breton agrees with Downs that the programme of the political party is determined by the expected success of this programme in securing elec-tion, plus any financial or psychological gains that might accrue to the successful candidates. However, Breton sees the decision facing the voter, i.e. the determination of 'effective demand' for the party programme, in a slightly different way. A legislative decision, he argues, will influence the voter's welfare in two ways. First, if the social decision involves the allocation of resources, it is likely that the voter will be either a net recipient of, or net contributor to, public funds. Individuals will therefore consider the net taxation cost of a political package in terms of its impact on themselves. We would presume that a party offering the prospect of low net costs would appear more attractive than a party offering a high net cost. The second influence arises from the 'public goods' nature of government policies. Suppose that a government supplies 100 units of defence expenditure for the protection of its citizens. Each citizen there-fore enjoys security equivalent to the value of 100 units. Now, whilst certain citizens might regard this level of defence provision as being quite appropriate, others who are more security-minded feel it to be insufficient. Other members of the population might feel that 100 units represents too high an allocation to defence. The essential point is that, whatever level the social decision maker chooses, and whatever level the candidate for election promises, it is likely that, for certain voters, it will be the wrong level. Once the government is in power, however, the electorate as a whole has no choice but to accept the level provided. In Breton's words, they will be *coerced* into the acceptance of the level of government provision. When choosing between the party programmes, therefore, each voter will take account of the degree of coercion implied by such programmes. He will assess the divergence between his own subjectively optimal provision level and the level implicit within each programme. Defence provision is, of course, just one example. The logic will also be followed in other public policy areas, e.g. educational provision, health care, pension schemes and so forth.

Breton now suggests that the degree of implied coercion, and the extent of the potential tax costs of policies, will determine not only the manner in which an individual might cast his vote but, more importantly, whether or not it might be preferable to engage in some other form of political activity. Voting for a representative is, after all, only one of a number of ways of influencing the final social decision. Under certain conditions, individuals might find that a more effective way of registering their opinions is to 'lobby' their existing representatives, to organize public demonstrations or to set up alternative provision agencies in cases where parties do not offer enough. *In extremis*, migration or revolution might be contemplated. Clearly, the choice of political technique is determined by the resources, powers and opportunities open to particular individuals. Breton's analysis is thus a complement to the Downsian view in suggesting that there exist more forms of political activity in the representative democracy than the formal system of voting.

4.1.2 PEOPLE'S DEMOCRACY

The democratic models developed above are essentially systems of institutionalized conflict. The 'liberal' conception of the world presupposes the possible existence of a variety of discrete and legitimate positions, about which all individuals may express a formal opinion. The appropriate path for society to follow is taken to be the one for which there exists a preponderance of individual acquiescence. Society is therefore the sum or, more accurately, the majority of its parts. This equation of 'democracy' with 'adding up individuals' votes' is so entrenched in the Western ideology that it is easy to forget that the liberal view is only one approach to the concept of 'government by the people'. Suppose we were to consider the people in a different way, as a group or 'a people'. We might go on to argue that individuals *per se* do not possess discrete wills of their own because, just as each individual is a component of the wider society, so each individual's will is, in reality, one component of an embracing social will. To distinguish them from representative democracies (where no collective consciousness is defined), societies that accept the existence of a conceptually distinct social will, a will of the people as a whole, are termed 'people's democracies'. The conception has a distinguished pedigree dating back to Classical times. Indeed, an Ancient Greek 'democrat' would be unlikely to recognize many Western representative systems as 'democratic', given their lack of concern for the collective will! The more recent manifestations of people's democracy are to be found in the Marx-inspired states of today.

Whilst it is easy to see how social decisions are derived under the earlier democratic models – they come from aggregating individual preferences – it is far harder to discern the social will, given that society, as an aggregate, is difficult to identify with precision. How, then, is the social will to be identified in such cases? There are a number of possibilities. Perhaps the simplest is that favoured by Plato, a theory subsequently refined to a high degree by Stalin. Here it is argued that certain individuals are endowed by nature or socialization with such insight that they are able accurately to discern the 'objective' truths of human affairs, whilst other individuals are able to operate only at the level of private or subjective interests. In *The Republic*, Plato suggests that, just as we should not expect a good shoemaker also to be a good weaver or builder, so we should permit each, including the rulers, to follow that pursuit at which they are the most capable. In Plato's model, the group whose expertise lay in the area of objective decision making was the Guardians; in contemporary states such as the USSR and China, the group is the Communist Party. In such nations, the Party is seen as the vanguard of collective consciousness that identifies and mobilizes resources towards the attainment of the optimal policy. This role is perhaps most clearly identified by Stalin:

The Party cannot be a real party if it limits itself to registering what the masses of the working class feel and think ... The Party must stand at the head of the working class; it must see farther than the working class; it must lead the proletariat, and not follow in the tail of spontaneous movement (in Holden, 1974, p. 44).

Although such an attitude is prevalent in modern socialist societies, it should be noted that it is by no means restricted to them. Certain countries might, for example, wish to base their operational decisions upon religious or transcendental principles, and they would rather leave them to religious officials well versed in the interpretation of such principles.

It may seem something of a paradox that countries such as the USSR stress the importance of popular voting, given that individual decisions have no real meaning in collectivist philosophy. To see this as a paradox, however, is to misunderstand the function of such elections; they serve, not to make collective choices (as in the liberal case), but rather to acclaim and affirm popular solidarity with the views expressed by the Party.

The variant of Marxism developed by Mao Tse-Tung derives from a more subtle interrelationship between the political vanguard and the mass of the population. This may be seen from the following advice that Mao offered to Party members:

> ... take the ideas of the masses (scattered and unsystematic ideas) and
> concentrate them (through study turn them into concentrated and systematic ideas),
> then go to the masses and propagate and explain these ideas until the masses
> embrace them as their own ... Then once again concentrate ideas from the masses
> and once again go to the masses so that the ideas are persevered in and carried
> through. And so on, over and over again in an endless spiral, with the ideas
> becoming more correct, more vital and richer each time (1966, p. 129).

In his study of Chinese political structure from the revolutionary period up to the mid-1960s, Townsend (1967) examined the institutional implications of Maoist ideology. It appears that the mass/Party relationship operated in two dimensions. In the first place, Mao instituted an electoral system that bore a superficial resemblance to those systems operated by the Western democracies. There were, however, two distinct differences. European states, for example, are typically governed at two levels, the national and the local. Citizens elect independent representatives to both bodies although, in cases of conflict, the national legislature is presumed sovereign over the local. In the Chinese model, however, the levels of government were integrated into a hierarchy: citizens elected candidates to local bodies who in turn elected regional bodies, and so forth, the process culminating with the election of the National People's Congress. Furthermore, Chinese ideology insisted that political equality was only meaningful if citizens were also in a state of economic equality; for China as with most socialist states, this can only be obtained with the establishment of collective ownership of productive property. The distinction is perhaps most graphically illustrated by Townsend's observation that the electoral law governing the 1950s' Chinese elections excluded certain private property owners from the franchise (p. 118). We might compare this with the experience of Britain, where the 1832 Reform Act *limited* the franchise to property owners.

The second and perhaps more typical form of political relationship between mass and Party during the Mao Tse-Tung period was the use of mass mobilization. Townsend observes:

> On nearly all major national issues, the Chinese political process culminates in a
> mass movement that coordinates in one general campaign all the organisational and
> educational efforts that prepare the citizen for political action. Mass movements
> are the most characteristic expression of the Chinese style of political participation
> (p. 185).

It was via the mass movement that the policital wisdom of the Party became practically applied, serving simultaneously to realize the policy and to develop popular unity for the policy. Clearly, it was via the mass movement process that the objectivity of the Party was to be tested and it is interesting to note that, whilst the mobilization of support revealed successes in certain policy areas in the Chinese experience (such as the creation of the rural communes), the difficulties encountered in mobilization for other issues (such as the establishment of urban communes and proposals for certain legal reforms) caused the Party to reinterpret its position and amend its policies. By virtue of its own inner logic, the Party was obliged to interpret apathy on the part of the citizens as a *de facto* vote of censure; in Western democracies it can be interpreted as indifference.

Compared to the 'economics of representative democracy', analytical contributions towards an 'economics of people's democracy' are as yet somewhat thin on the ground. A few general observations might nevertheless be made. In the first place, we should anticipate that people's democracies that do operate with some variant of a popular voting system would be responsive to electoral pressure in the same way as purely Downsian systems are. Competition between candidates would now occur, however, with reference to a far narrower variation in political platform. We should suppose that candidates would all share a common ideology as represented by the 'party line'. Candidates would accordingly be limited to competition on relatively peripheral issues for, from this point of view, most of the major issues would have been 'defined out of politics'. Second, in cases where a monolithic party is operating, we might draw the parallel between this state of affairs and that analysed in the 'economics of bureaucracy' literature (discussed in the next chapter), pointing out that such structures could well give rise to technical inefficiencies owing to lack of competitive pressures. Such a criticism could not be made, however, if it were to be accepted that, by definition, the ruling party was the repository of superior wisdom.

4.2   Coercion and political change

In the above discussions of models of decision-making procedures we have managed to avoid mentioning one particular problem common to them all. An example of this problem is the following. Suppose the distribution of income in a society is particularly uneven and the majority of citizens vote (the representative democracy case) or the principal party decides (the people's democracy case) to shift resources from rich to poor. How will the rich react to a prospective decline in their standard of living? A people's democracy could possibly sustain such a shift on the assumption that all individuals (including the rich) accept that the social decision maker is in the best position to assess objective truth – i.e. the rich would in fact agree that their impending poverty is beneficial to society for this is what 'society' says. A representative democracy is in a more difficult position because of the axiomatic belief in the pursuit of subjective self-interest as the determinant of political behaviour. Here the rich minority are presumably going to be most dissatisfied with the social decision, made by the majority of poorer individuals. However, if we admit to the possibility of a few 'deviants' even in a people's democracy, who do not relish the prospect of their own immiseration to further the cause, it is clear that both types of society could find that the rich do not wish to relinquish their property in accordance with the social decision. It will therefore be necessary for the social decision maker to be able to exert power over this minority in order to enforce the implementation of the chosen policy; on this issue, there is almost total unanimity amongst all species of political philosopher. With the exception of societies composed of individuals with identical preference functions (i.e. where unanimity exists), the social decision maker or government must, it is argued, possess coercive power to enforce policy decisions. Most of the social contract theorists, such as Hobbes and Rousseau, view this as 'voluntary coercion', that is, individuals entering into a state of civil society will voluntarily assign coercive power to a sovereign body in return for those benefits that civil society confers.

Logically, this form of coercion can be distinguished from 'non-voluntary coercion' for, in the above case, individuals appear to be accepting the possibility of social coercion simply as part of the social contract; rich people pay taxes 'reluctantly' in representative democracies and 'enthusiastically' in people's democracies! Irrespective of their reluctance or enthusiasm, such individuals might still agree that society ought to continue to be run along existing constitutional lines. They agree with the method of decision making if not with the specific decision. Indeed, Tullock (1976) sees this aspect as a central stabilizing force within representative democracies; individuals attach utility to the decision-making process and its wider implications, whilst accepting that they are unlikely to obtain all their preferences on all issues. The knowledge that each person 'wins some and loses some' is sufficient to ensure popular allegiance to the political system. This position is to be contrasted with a pure coercion system in which individuals might not only disagree with the decisions reached by whatever body happens to possess the coercive (and thus the legislative) power, but they also deny that body's legitimacy in the making of such decisions. Obedience to authority results not, therefore, from voluntary consent, but from fear of physical violence perpetrated by those who wield the power.

In reality, such nice rational distinctions are hard to observe. The sort of question we might frame is 'if left to their own devices would rich people voluntarily pay taxes?' Clearly, if the answer is 'no' then *de facto* such tax payers are coerced. The central problem with the consensus theories discussed earlier is that they are ahistorical in a central respect: individuals do not decide *ex ante* what sort of society they would like to establish and then, having established it, agree to abide by its rules; rather they are born into an existing set of social relationships. Social institutions, in the main, pre-date individuals, who are obliged to operate within the confines of such institutions. The act of supreme rationality in choosing a form of social organization, an act applauded by the political philosophers, is not, in historical terms, a conscious act at all but simply an accident of circumstance. It accordingly follows that the extent to which an existing society can persuade or coerce its new members to follow the existing political rules depends upon its powers of persuasion and coercion. It is likely that the evidence will be ambiguous here. Suppose we were to observe a society with no outward signs of political unrest; social decisions were being made by the government and were being complied with instantly. At a superficial level, such an observation is consistent with any one of three hypotheses: (i) individuals obey the government voluntarily and thus a rational consensus exists; (ii) the government has successfully 'fooled' the individuals into believing that what it does is best for them; (iii) the coercive power of the government is such that individuals dare only obey.

Accepting the mythological nature of the social contract and the fact that society's composition is continually changing (owing to births, deaths and migration), we must accept the possibility, indeed the likelihood, that the decision-making procedure set up in period 1, by whatever method, will come to be regarded as inappropriate by those individuals constituting society in, say, period 100. How, then, will political change come about? We should point out that we are not concerned at this juncture with what may be termed 'normal' political activities, e.g. the replacement of party A by party B in a representative democracy such as might result from a switch in voter preferences. We are concerned to discover the origins of changes in principle rather than changes in the functioning of a particular principle. There appear to be three possible candidates.

First, an existing political structure might decide of its own accord, so to speak, that change is necessary. An early example of this option was the UK parliament's restoration of the office of monarch in 1660, the principle of hereditary monarchy having been abolished some ten years previously after the execution of Charles I. A much more recent instance was Tanzania's decision in 1965 to move from a 'multi-party' to a 'one-party' political system as a result of overwhelming support in the elections for the Tanganyika African National Unity party. It also seems probable that a long-run political objective of Salvador Allende, elected to power in Chile in 1970 via a representative democracy system, was the establishment of a form of people's democracy, although his death in 1973 gave little time for any movement in this, or any other, direction. In spite of these examples, however, there is good reason to believe that a voluntary change of system is unlikely in most cases. History provides little evidence of monarchs, for example, willingly giving up their responsibilities and perquisites in favour of a republican system. Similarly, people's democracies are unlikely to permit voluntaristic change, for, if the Party is to be accepted as the repository of 'objective' truth, how can a superior system be logically identified? The track record of representative democracies is little better, for two reasons. First, many representative democracies permit freedom of political action to all *except* those wishing to undermine or subvert the existing constitutional structure. Parties wishing to change political structures are often forbidden to compete in elections. Second, the movement from an individual-based to a collectivist-based political structure is unlikely to emerge via the ballot box. Supporters of a 'people's democratic party' in a representative democracy would argue that, as individuals are voting for themselves in such a system, and as they are thus unable to perceive their true social interests, it is most unlikely that any party purporting to represent their true interests would ever get elected! Interestingly enough, this outcome has a strong parallel in the theory of the provision of public goods where it can be shown that, acting in isolation, individuals would vote for a sub-optimal level of provision of goods with public characteristics.

A second possibility is political change as the result of external intervention; it is frequently the case that states react to military conquest from without by reforming their political structure once independence is again achieved. An example here was the formal replacement of the 1875 French constitution, which had aimed at 'the creation of a kind of nineteenth century paternalist and corporatist dictatorship' (Pickles, 1965, p. 5), by the 1946 constitution (explicitly republican and democratic); this was facilitated by the defeat of Germany, which had occupied the whole of France since 1942. Similarly, the independence of many African and Asian states between 1945 and 1965 saw the adoption by these countries of forms of decision making radically different from those prevalent at the time of conquest by the imperial powers, and indeed different from the forms employed in these countries by the imperial powers.

In common with many political theorists, Thomas Hobbes distinguished between a commonwealth founded by 'institution' and one founded by 'acquisition'. Although theorists have spent much time on the excessively rational discussion of the institution of civil society, the fact remains that a major explanation of political change is the forcible acquisition of political power from the existing ruling group by another group. Political change, in other words, frequently results from the force of arms rather than the force of argument. Most of the present-day classic models of empirical democracy are the result of revolutionary activity in the past – England (1642–51), the USA (1776) and France (1789) are representative democracy examples, whilst the USSR (1917) and China (1949) are people's democracy instances. Since 1945, at least 50 per cent of the states of Africa, Asia and Latin America have experienced military coups in which the armed forces of the countries involved have forcibly deprived the ruling groups of their legislative power. In the majority of these cases, the military has continued to retain decision-making power after the coup. The present political geography of the globe therefore provides substantial support for Marx's assertion that force is the midwife of history or, alternatively, for Mao's more graphic statement that political power grows out of the barrel of a gun. If only for this reason, the various theories of gradual and peaceful political progress, which have mirrored the models of economic progress, have been intellectually discredited. To some observers, especially those in the poorer regions of the world, it follows that not only will violence be necessary to wrest power from an entrenched elite (which is seen to be using power for its own ends), but also that such violence will have a beneficial cathartic effect upon the population. Whether such a wresting of power is a feasible solution is another matter.

4.3   Nationalism and social objectives

Irrespective of the mechanism of change in political structures, we can affirm quite definitely one particular direction that all political structures have taken over the past century, and that direction is towards the creation of national identity. The emergence of nationalism is, of course, to be predicted from the theory of coalitions mentioned earlier, although the equilibrium conditions in the case of nations are not so unambiguous as they are in the case of political parties. Individuals, we might argue, will find it optimal to collaborate in the production of commodities and to maintain the security of person and material property, the latter to be held either privately or collectively. In the face of the strength of such a coalition, other individuals will react by forming coalitions of their own for similar reasons. However, the position at which coalition-forming ceases to be economic, the position at which economies of scale give way to diseconomies, can only be determined with reference to the technology of production and security. Over the past few centuries, it is fairly clear that the benefits of industrialization and the efficacy of military strategy have both been positive functions of the scale of economic activity and thus the number of notionally sovereign regions of the world has declined to its present figure of a couple of hundred. The process of nation-building is essentially a task for the government generated by a society, the government's role being to integrate individual productive activities into a holistic network and to confer benefits upon those whom it sees fit to benefit. This it will do in a political way – via the definition of laws and rights – as well as in a purely economic manner – by taxation and expenditure.

The nation state need not, however, be an efficient unit in all respects, for it might well be the case that certain decisions are 'better' made at a sub-national level. There are a number of reasons for this. First, the ideology of the society in question might suggest that, as the government has only a limited right to direct individuals' activities, it should correspondingly be restricted to limited areas of decision making. Second, it might well be the case that, even if the government wished to make *all* the decisions, the technical complexity of the direct running of the lives of hundreds of millions of people precludes this possibility. Finally, it might be argued that decisions affecting only a small group of citizens within the nation should be made by those individuals themselves because (i) these people would probably be better informed about the issues than would the national government and (ii) as the decision would not influence the lives of people outside the group, why should outsiders be involved in the decision? It accordingly seems probable that the provision of, say, a facility to be used by the inhabitants of a specific region of the state would be left by the national government to some sub-national authority, whilst the provision of a commodity with marked public good and externality aspects would remain the responsibility of central government. The possibility of the local provision of facilities, via some system of local public finance, leads to the possibility of tax-induced migration, the idea being that individuals will move to areas where local governments offer 'good value for money'. There is abundant evidence that this indeed takes place, at least in Western economies (D. Mueller, 1979, pp. 134–42) and the analysis is clearly applicable at the international level.

Irrespective of the manner in which the nation state came into existence and the level at which it makes its decisions, the fact of its existence in the human imagination is well established. This fact presents sizeable problems for the social analyst. Social science, and especially economics, tends to be inherently nationalistic and, from a behavioural point of view, any analysis in this respect may be considered historically correct in that the objective functions of nations can be treated, *de facto*, as the objective functions of national governments. From a logical point of view, however, this is not a satisfactory position because of the existence of coercion. To a liberal, the ideology of a socialist does not make sense – people's democracies are viewed as 'non-democratic' because political competition is precluded and individual liberal rights may be denied. To a Marxist, on the other hand, a capitalist representative democracy is 'non-democratic' because the political equality of voting is rendered spurious by virtue of the imbalance of economic power amongst the voters. In the words of *The Communist Manifesto*, the machinery of capitalist government is 'but a committee for managing the common affairs of the whole bourgeoisie' and inter-party competition is little but the superficial adjustment of power amongst the property-owning classes. Both liberal and Marxist would probably agree that the exercise of control by a monarch or a military dictator does not represent a social decision at all. It is, rather, the wielding of naked physical power to secure the private ends of those in possession of such power. In universal terms, therefore, all existing practical systems are likely to be found wanting. How, then, are we to proceed? For the purposes of what follows, we shall analyse at the *de facto* rather than at the *de jure* level. The policy preferences considered will be observed and/or revealed government preferences, irrespective of any opinions we might have about the legitimacy of such a government. However, this stance cannot prevent us from remarking upon any effects that specific governmental forms might have on strategies for progress. The essential purpose of this chapter has been to demonstrate that different societies will use different criteria on which to base their social choice processes. This gives each government particular characteristics that cannot help but have implications for the sorts of strategies that they are likely to pursue and the extent to which such strategies are likely to be successful.

In concluding this chapter, let us introduce an idea that we shall meet again at later stages of the argument. Even within the limitations specified above, we are bound to admit the possibility that the objective function of a government, which is a *de facto* national government, might well include non-national elements. It could prove optimal for any given nation state to transcend its existing national conceptions, either by fragmenting into a number of smaller 'nations' or by joining with others to create a larger political entity. One need only turn the pages of an historical atlas to see that fragmentation and unification of states have occurred throughout history on a regular basis. The formerly independent medieval states of Burgundy, Orleans, Anjou and Provence, for example, have long been incorporated in the modern republic of France. In place of the old Turkish Empire we now see modern nation states such as Greece, Albania, Bulgaria and, of course, Turkey itself. If nation states are capable of being combined or broken up, then clearly a simple 'national' analysis will need some extension.

Of particular interest in this respect is the conclusion reached by Myrdal (1965). He argues that the contemporary Western nation states have discovered that the collectively regulated economic structure that we term the 'welfare state' represents a beneficial form of organization. There seems no reason, he argues, why such benefits as are realized by internal cooperation should stop at the existing, purely arbitrary, national frontiers. He concludes:

The plain fact is this: When once the national Welfare State has come into existence and built its moorings firmly in the hearts of the peoples who in the democracies of the Western world have the political power, there is no alternative to international disintegration except to begin, by international cooperation and mutual accommodation, to build the Welfare World. The conclusion from our analysis stands not only, and not primarily, as an expression of a political valuation of what would be desirable, but is presented as a statement of a factual situation. Any other conclusion from my analysis would do violence to logic and to what we know about social reality in the Western countries (pp. 149–50).

We shall return to the theme of constructing the 'welfare world' towards the end of our enquiries.

Summary

In order to undertake collective actions, individuals must make collective decisions. Societies must therefore devise an appropriate form of social decision-making structure. Their choice of structure will be influenced by their ideologies. We can broadly distinguish democratic from coercive structures, the former entailing voluntary compliance on the part of the citizens.

Direct democracy is the simplest variant of the democratic structure. Under this system each individual expresses his opinion by means of a vote and the opinion of the majority is taken to be the social decision. In cases where only a proportion of the population is permitted to vote, the identification of the social preference is open to interpretation. Many different voting procedures may be employed to take account of the intensity of voters' preferences. Voting outcomes are often a function of the particular voting procedure adopted.

Western economies typically make decisions using the method of representative democracy. Individual voters elect representatives who then make decisions on the former's behalf. Representative democracy has been modelled by a number of economists. In such models, candidates are assumed to offer policies to the electorate that give the maximum chance of electoral success. Voting behaviour is assumed to be a function of the net expected tax costs of political programmes and the degree of implied coercion. Amongst other things, these models predict the formation of political parties, limitation of political choice and voter apathy. Under certain conditions, political action outside the formal voting arena may appear an attractive alternative.

Economies such as the Soviet Union and China are people's democracies. Social decisions in such cases are made by individuals or groups that are considered as being able to discern the social will. This social will is conceptually distinct from the will of any, or all, of the individual members of society. Voting in people's democracies has a different function from voting in representative democracies.

In principle, any political system is likely to entail the coercion of some or all of its members. The extent to which such coercion is deemed acceptable will depend upon the ideology of the society in question. Changes in political structure may result from conscious decision, external intervention or internal revolution.

The macropolitical systems of the contemporary world are the nation states. It is necessary to use this framework for subsequent analysis. However, there is no reason to believe that the present nation state structure is either permanent or optimal.

Further reading

Social choice theory has been approached from two academic directions, via traditional political theory and via the more recent 'economics of politics' approach. Barker (1951) and D'Entrèves (1967) are representatives of the former. Democratic theory is described and analysed by Dahl (1956), Sartori (1965) and Holden (1974). The important contributions to the 'economics of politics' literature are surveyed in D. Mueller (1976), a more detailed survey being D. Mueller (1979). Barry (1970) provides a parallel assessment of both approaches.

Useful starting points for the analysis of political change are Wertheim (1974), Macfarlane (1974) and Cohen (1975). The view that the violent seizure of political power is both necessary and beneficial is central to the work of Franz Fanon. His most celebrated work is *Les Damnés de la terre* (1961). An introduction to Fanon's views is provided by Caute (1970). The concept of nationalism is discussed by Kedourie (1960), Kohn (1961) and Cobban (1969).

Many of the issues raised in this chapter are explored in more detail by Whynes and Bowles (1981). Van den Doel (1979) examines some important economic implications of democratic decision making.

Chapter Five

Establishing
the Legal Framework

The previous chapter examined just one half of a two-way relationship between the individual members of a society on the one hand and their decision-making machinery, or legislature, on the other. In particular, we were concerned with the various procedures for the determination and derivation of collective choices that would constitute a policy commitment binding on all individuals. Now we shall focus on the other half of the relationship by examining the way in which collective decisions are implemented or operationalized amongst the members of society. In our earlier models of social formation we used the idea of individuals coming together and reaching agreement about the form of decision process to be employed in their society and we can continue in this vein by asking what sort of rules of procedure are likely to be established in order to govern the citizens' affairs. Such a code of conduct will have relevance in one specific context, namely, where there occurs the possibility of a dispute or conflict between individuals or groups within the society concerned. In this context, the code will act as an arbiter between two or more potentially incompatible modes of conduct. As we have seen, human demands are complex and, in all probability, insatiable at the limit and we must therefore anticipate such disputes occurring even in the best-ordered societies.

Fundamental to any society's rules of behaviour is the assignment of 'rights' to the citizens. Put simply, rights state explicitly who is entitled to do what. More precisely, we may think of a right in the following terms. If we assign a particular right to individual A with respect to individual B, then B is seen to be obliged to perform in the particular manner with respect to the wishes of A. Any failure to comply voluntarily could be considered legitimate grounds for the use of coercion to ensure performance. Although we have just specified rights in terms of individuals it is quite possible for a society to establish rights on a collective basis such that groups of individuals have rights over other such groups. In addition, we might suppose that the social decision maker will retain

98

rights of some description over all other members of society; the armed forces of most nations of the world, for instance, are assigned the right to conscript manpower in times deemed to constitute national emergencies and all citizens accordingly have a duty to oblige in the face of potential coercion.

Possibly the most important right that might be assigned, as far as the economist is concerned, is the right of property or ownership. This involves the specification of a rights relationship between two parties with respect to a 'thing' that may be owned. Whilst it is generally the case that the right-holder and the right-regarder are both either individuals or groups of individuals, the category of 'things' is much wider. First, it might include all inanimate natural resources and goods and services resulting from production – coal, oil, motor-cars and pencils. Second, it might include certain intangible items such as the level of noise or the visual beauty that emanates from a material thing. Third, the category of things could include animate objects – plants and animals such as corn, potatoes, cattle and elephants. Finally, in certain cases, society might agree that human beings can be considered as things for the purpose of the assignment of ownership rights. For party A to be said fully to own a thing, it will be the case that (i) A has the right to enjoy all benefits conferred by the thing and (ii) A has the right to control the destiny of the thing. By implication, any other individual, B, is obliged not to transgress these rights.

Given this basic notion of a property right, there is no reason to expect all societies to agree upon either the things that might be owned or those individuals who might own them. Slavery, for example, whereby one individual has exclusive use of another, is nowadays viewed with disfavour, although it was regarded as morally and economically acceptable by the (non-slave) populations of Greece, Rome and Egypt many centuries ago and, indeed, by the southern states of the USA until little more than a century ago. It is only in the present century that Britain has established citizens' rights to clean air and manufacturers are now generally discouraged from polluting the atmosphere. At the time of writing, most countries of the world accept that they no longer possess any ownership rights over whales, although the earlier view, that whales might legitimately be hunted, is still retained by Japan and the USSR. Turning to the question of the identity of owners, nations that follow the precepts of Marxist theory do not permit individuals to hold full ownership rights over inputs to the productive process (the means of production). It is held that this would permit such individuals to profit unfairly by virtue of their exploitation of those denied such ownership. Productive property, it is argued, should be held by the collectivity instead. In contrast, the capitalistic view of the world accepts that the private ownership of the means of production is not only desirable *per se* but is a necessary condition for economic efficiency.

Even supposing that societies are free to assign ownership rights according to their ideological predilections, there will still exist a common problem. Rights may conflict. Your right to drive your car at any speed and in any manner you choose is likely to conflict with my right to a safe passage along the pavement; my right to burn my house down if I so wish could have a detrimental effect on my neighbour's right to security of property. In order to resolve these conflicts, it will be necessary for society, having established a rights' allocation, to further establish a hierarchy of rights to indicate which has precedence in cases of conflict. In these cases, society might judge, for example, that my right to safety has predominance over your right to drive recklessly, whilst my neighbour's right to security is more important than my right of destroying my own property. Full ownership rights, therefore, are unlikely, at the limit, to be vested in anything; it is likely that the society as a whole will always reserve the right to attenuate them in some way. In most cases, there will be some external limitation imposed upon the owner in respect of his enjoyment of the owned thing or of his control over its destiny.

The allocation of rights to members of society and the establishment of a hierarchy of rights are necessary conditions for the existence of a legal system. They are not sufficient, however; two further elements are required. If the key feature of the rules of social conduct is that they are to be followed or, alternatively, not to be broken, it will be necessary for a society to devise some procedure by which transgressions can be identified. Furthermore, and given that society would attach negative welfare to the breaking of its rules, it will be necessary to establish a system of disincentives to discourage transgression, the coercive power necessary to enforce obedience being vested in the social decision maker. We may accordingly see a legal system as a mechanism for social order via incentives or, more formally, 'A legal system is a coercive order of public rules addressed to rational persons for the purpose of regulating their conduct and providing a framework for social cooperation' (Rawls, 1972, p. 235).

Throughout the preceding exposition, we have made the convenient assumption that, on Day One, a society makes all its decisions regarding the allocation of rights and the appropriate mechanisms for their enforcement. In reality, however, we might suppose that legal systems emerge as a reaction to the sort of conflicts in behaviour that it experiences – if a society is not experiencing pollution, for instance, we should hardly expect it to legislate against it. In this context, Demsetz (1967) provides some interesting evidence relating to the emergence of property rights amongst the Indian population of northwestern America. The property right in question is the right to hunt the indigenous animal species. The records of the early Western explorers suggest that, in the seventeenth century, Indian tribes and families did not demarcate their own hunting areas; rather, anyone was free to hunt wherever they wished. As Demsetz observes, the lack of specified hunting rights posed a general externality problem, in that the hunting of an animal by family *A* reduced the hunting potential for family *B*, although it appears that this cost was not regarded as being particularly high. By the eighteenth century, however, it appears that the division of territory into specific hunting grounds had become rigidly enforced. Demsetz argues that, over the period, Europe increased its demand for the hunting products of northwestern America, especially furs and skins. Animal species therefore became far more valuable than before, when demand had simply reflected the indigenous population's need for food and clothing. Furthermore, the cost of the externality was raised by the increase in hunting activity that resulted from the demand increase. Each tribe therefore found it optimal to exclude others from hunting in particular areas in order to maximize its private gains in the short run and also, via the appropriate conservation strategies, in the long run. Demsetz notes that the contrasting absence of territoriality amongst the plains Indians of southwestern America resulted from the facts that, first, the indigenous animal species were extensive grazers and thus the costs of enforcing rights would have been high and, second, these animals did not have the same degree of economic significance as did the fur-yielding species of the north. Put another way, the costs of private rights structures were high relative to benefits in the southern case but low in the northern.

Although the decision structures of early Indian societies were in-formal as compared to modern nation states, we may nevertheless con-clude that these tribes felt that their interests were better served by a change in the existing rights structure. Other societies provide examples of deliberate rights modifications. Two significant changes in the English legal system occurred in the seventeenth century; these were the 1679 Habeas Corpus Act, which limited the power of governments to in-carcerate individuals indefinitely, and the 1673 Declaration of In-dulgence, which was designed to give adherents of all religions (except the Catholics) equal access to economic and political opportunities. Perhaps the most famous volte-face in this respect is represented by the eighteenth and twenty-first amendments to the US constitution: the former (1919) curtailed the right of citizens to manufacture, sell, transport, or trade in intoxicating liquors 'for beverage purposes', whilst the latter (1933) totally repealed this provision.

In recent years, economists have become interested in the implications of particular forms of rights structure and the appropriate methods of law enforcement. We shall now consider this latter area before turning o an examination of instances of rights allocation.

5.1   Enforcing the law

For the practical functioning of a legal system, a society will find it necessary to develop an agency concerned with legal affairs. Depending upon social attitudes, however, the level of involvement of this agency can vary. In the first place, society must determine the allocation of responsibility for the detection of law-breaking – is the agency actively to seek out all offences on behalf of society, establish guilt and mete out punishment, or is it simply to serve as an arbitrator in instances where individuals make claims regarding rights infringements by others? Conceivably, it could operate at both levels, as determined by the nature of the infringement. Second, society must decide whether all cases of dispute must be handled by that agency or whether it should permit negotiations between injured and injuring party to resolve the dispute privately. Third, society must determine whether it is the agency or the citizen that is to be held responsible for the prevention of illegal activity. Such decisions are important, for they have significant economic implications. As we might reasonably suppose that an enforcement agency will be operated collectively rather than privately by any one individual, the level of involvement chosen by the agency will determine the extent to which enforcement costs are born privately or publicly.

In order to determine how best to enforce the law, it is important to understand why legal disputes between individuals or groups might arise. One clear possibility arises from the structure of the law itself. If the law does not fully specify rights and rights hierarchies, it is possible for two or more parties to contest desirability of a particular course of action. The same will be true if parties are ignorant of legal pronouncements or rights allocations. Indeed, if a law lacks specificity it may well become optimal for individuals to enter into disputes in order to try to gain from a legal decision. We might therefore conclude that the frequency of disputes is a function of the precision of legal formulations, one remedy for 'too many' conflicts being the tightening up of legal codes and entitlements. Whilst there probably exists a case for the revision of legal provisions in most countries, revisions cannot solve all the problems. First, even if it were actually possible to establish rules for each and every possibility in each and every dispute, how could we deal with novelties? Second, as Posner (1977) argues, 'the more precise a rule is, the more likely it is to open up loopholes – to permit by implication conduct that the rule was intended to forbid ...' (p. 425). It might well be the case, therefore, that a reduction in disputes as a result of more formalized rules could be obtained only at a higher level of social cost.

One particular form of dispute that has begun to interest economists is where the breaking of the law is a potentially optimal strategy from the point of view of any one individual. In such a case, the enforcement agency will be concerned to devise a counter-strategy that nullifies the optimality. This counter-strategy will involve the detection of the crime and the prosecution and punishment of the criminal. Let us consider the case of an individual (well versed in economic theory) who is contemplating breaking the law with a view to personal gain. Suppose he is considering stealing someone else's property. The crime (assuming that society defines the act as such) will appear optimal if the expected welfare or utility from normal or 'legal' activity (U_L) is exceeded by the expected utility from 'illegal' activity (U_I), net of any punishment costs (C) that our criminal might expect to incur as a result of detection and prosecution. Crime pays when

$$U_L < U_I (1 - p) - Cp,$$

where p is the probability of the criminal being convicted of the crime. Looked at in this way, we can derive a number of implications for agencies concerned to lower society's crime rates. First, the more effective the detection and prosecution activities of the agency, then the less likely is illegal activity to be optimal (as p is being raised). If the effectiveness of the agency is a function of the resources allocated to it, lowering crime rates necessitates, *ceteris paribus*, increased expenditure allocations to the agency. Second, the punishment meted out to criminals should be related to the criminal's expected benefit from illegal activity, as a fixed-rate penalty is simply an inducement to commit more lucrative crimes. Third, criminal activity should be less prevalent when the benefits that can be derived from legal activity are relatively high. To date, little empirical work has been undertaken to evaluate hypotheses of this nature. A notable exception is the econometric analysis for areas of the USA conducted by Ehrlich (1974). In particular he concludes:

The rate of specific felonies is found to be positively related to estimates of relative gains and negatively related to estimates of costs associated with criminal activity ... Our empirical investigation also indicates that rates of all felonies, particularly crimes against property, are positively related to the degree of a community's income inequality (pp. 111–12).

The latter piece of evidence leads Ehrlich to suggest that an optimal law enforcement strategy might be deterrence, not by increased punishment costs or increased resource allocations to the enforcement agency, but by the equalization of economic opportunity in the community. We might further speculate, on the basis of Ehrlich's conclusion, that increased criminality could be an inevitable consequence of government economic policy under certain circumstances. Increasing taxation, or employing measures that lead to increased unemployment, are likely to make illegal activity more optimal from the criminal's point of view.

The preceding analysis suggests that punishment for criminal activity should be related to the expected utility derived by the criminal from his illegal activities. An alternative approach is to regard punishment as a 'payment' for the costs that such activities impose upon the society. These costs have two elements. First, we might expect that the criminal offence *per se* imposes disutility upon society – the possibility of being murdered in their beds would lower the subjective security levels of most individuals in any society. Second, the criminal imposes costs because of societies' necessary expenditures on detection, prosecution and punishment of the crime. Viewing punishment as a payment for social costs incurred, Becker (1968) makes a case for the use of fines as punishment. Not only does society incur zero punishment costs in this case (as opposed to, say, keeping the felon in prison), but the victims of the crime will be able to gain direct compensation out of the fine revenue. We may add two corollaries to the Becker position. First, if the objective of punishment is social compensation, any form of resource transfer from criminal to society will fit the bill. Enforced community service, whereby convicted criminals are obliged to work without remuneration on social projects, is an obvious alternative and is employed in a number of European countries. Second, the Becker position implies that punishment should fit the crime and not the criminal. The effects of punishment on deterrence are therefore different from those of the model above. For example, the theft of a motor-car by a rich man or a poor man would incur the same fine, although the incentive to steal would be far higher in the latter's case.

Given that crime rates in most contemporary societies are rising, the question of optimal law enforcement is clearly a relevant cause for concern. Using either of the above approaches, society's position is clearly unenviable. If, according to the criminal calculus, the severity of punishment influences criminal activity and if redistribution is not to be contemplated, a society might find itself obliged to devise suitably horrendous fates for miscreants at a time when the concern for the humanitarian treatment of criminals appears to be increasing. Again, if we accept Becker's argument that resource transfers from criminals are an effective form of redress, we encounter the unfortunate problem that the correlation between criminal activity and poverty is generally high. Those people, in other words, who are most likely to impose costs on society are those least able to repay them.

The enforcement of law is costly. Presumably, economies will be concerned to minimize such costs. More accurately, a society will devote resources to law enforcement up to the level where the ratio of marginal benefits to marginal costs is equal to that obtaining in other areas of allocation. Again, little empirical work has so far been undertaken to discover if real-world agencies conform to the economic criterion, although the Ehrlich study suggests that the USA in the 1960s was underspending in this area (pp. 110–12). The objective assessment of the effectiveness of enforcement agencies is, in any case, problematic.

Even if it were argued that expenditure on enforcement was excessive in a particular case, it is difficult to forecast the potential cost increases were expenditure (and presumably therefore deterrence) to be reduced. Furthermore, the 'output' of the law enforcement system is, to some extent, self-defeating. We might, on the one hand, argue that the more disputes that get resolved and the more criminals who are punished, then the better is that agency functioning. However, we could also reason that the laws are better enforced if no one is in dispute or committing a crime. Increasing convictions are thus a sign of failure and not one of success; as Thomas Paine wrote, a country should boast its constitution only when its jails are empty of prisoners.

Interesting developments, with a view to cost reduction, are presently taking place in a number of Western states; these are the use of out-of-court settlements and plea-bargaining. Here litigants and suspected criminals are encouraged to circumvent the formal, and expensive, legal procedures by being given the inducement of a prospective lowering of costs. Such practices produce intriguing consequences for criminal behaviour. For example, the criminal calculus now becomes modified; within the probability of detection factor, the criminal could choose between a relatively light sentence (cost) and a gamble between acquittal or a stiffer penalty. There is also likely to be a wealth effect, since the relatively poor litigant is more likely to agree to a reduced settlement with a relatively rich litigant if (i) he is risk-averse, (ii) he is obliged to bear the costs of trial. In societies where costs of litigation are borne collectively, however, we should anticipate less interest in external settlements. We should add, incidentally, that the cost aspect of criminal activity is not a source of concern for the legal agency alone. Economic theory demonstrates that, amongst firms, collusion to earn monopoly profit is often a superior strategy to individual action. In the same way, we could regard organized crime, or collective criminality, as a possible optimal strategy for those economically alert criminals seeking to reduce the costs of their operations.

This section has examined the approach that an economist might adopt to the question of law enforcement in society. A source of concern is the apparent arbitrariness and irrationality of existing legal systems, which have, in most cases, evolved in an *ad hoc* fashion over the centuries. Stigler (1970) notes some punishment anomalies in the USA case; for example, it appears that the penalty for reducing freight rates at the time could be 'ten times as much for a barge operator as a trucker'. He concludes that the existing United States' 'penalty structure is not well designed for either deterrence or guidance of enforcement' (p. 534). However, economists such as Stigler are not arguing for the operation of legal systems on purely economic criteria; merely that any agency that absorbs a considerable quantity of resources should be appraised in terms of the benefits that the expended resources yield.

In principle, a society could legislate on anything it wished, assuming

that such legislation was enforceable. It is also at liberty to alter legislation or change the rules of conduct deemed acceptable. If the rules were
to be changed we should accordingly expect human behaviour to change.
In the following section, we shall examine the economic implications
of differing sets of rules in the context that we earlier identified as
significant, namely property rights.

5.2   Property rights and the organization of production

An almost universal feature of human productive activity is that it is
conducted by what economists call 'teams'. Alchian and Demsetz (1972)
define team production in the following terms. First, team production
involves the use of not one but several different types of resource input,
e.g. different labour skills or types of capital equipment. Second, the
output of team production is more than the simple sum of the individual
outputs of each resource input employed. Third, it is the case that
ownership rights of inputs do not reside with a single individual but
are distributed in some fashion amongst the team members. Thus each
individual might, for example, own his specific labour power, whilst
some own capital and others the land or raw materials. In certain
instances, society as represented by the government could constitute a
team member. The exact nature of production will obviously be a
specific function of the output to be produced, the technology of production and the particular distribution of ownership rights, but we should
note that even the simplest productive forms (such as the prehistoric
hunting band) all employ team techniques. At the other extreme, the
production of, say, automobiles in an industrialized economy clearly
relies upon team production.

Irrespective of the specific pattern of ownership rights we may safely
assume that team members will only contribute resources in the anticipation of gaining direct consumption, or indirect exchange, benefits from
the team's output. Here, however, we encounter two problems. Individuals are contributing 'their' resources with a view to gain but, if output
emerges from the team as a whole and not from any specific input,
how can we identify that share of the composite output to which each
contributing member is entitled? Furthermore, as all gains are generated
collectively, what incentives will exist for each member of the team to
contribute to his fullest potential? From an individual point of view, it
is surely optimal for each individual to minimize his input contribution
to production and to 'free-ride' on the efforts of his colleagues. Even if
the contribution of each member could be accurately assessed, it seems
likely that the necessity of each individual having perpetually to police
the activities of his fellows would prove expensive.

The establishment of acceptable rewards' distributions and the ensuring of efficient input performance are clearly vital to the maximization

of the welfare level of the team and Alchian and Demsetz suggest that these requirements can be met by the team's appointment of one or more individuals as managers who are to take on responsibilities in such areas. Clearly, the managers too will need some incentive system in order that efficient management will be encouraged. An obvious way to do this is to relate the manager's gains to the level of team performance resulting from his management. We may see how such an incentive system might operate by examining a common form of team production that is employed in very many countries, namely commodity production by firms based upon what Meade (1972) calls the 'entrepreneurial system'.

The operating strategy of the entrepreneurial manager depends upon two flows – the revenue from product sales and the costs incurred in production. Of the two, the total revenue aspect is the less controllable from the manager's point of view; in a free-market economy, total revenue is a function of consumer demand and preferences whilst, in a planned economy, output prices are likely to be fixed by the government or planning agency. Far more flexibility exists, however, on the cost side, for we might assume that the management is free to purchase as many or as few resource inputs as it wishes, either at rates negotiated between it and the resource-owner or at rates established by the planning authorities. At any particular price/output combination, therefore, there exists some relationship between revenues and costs; at some outputs, costs exceed revenues and at others the reverse is true. In terms of the economy, the optimal position for production is where the incremental production cost exactly equals the incremental amount that consumers are willing to pay, i.e. where marginal cost equals marginal revenue. At this point, the difference between total cost and total revenue is at a maximum. If this is the output level we wish our managers to aim for, we may clearly accomplish this by making the remuneration of managers proportional to the size of the residual from revenue after costs have been deducted. In fact, Western economies tend to vest managers with ownership rights in the residual, although Western governments reserve the right to tax away such 'profit' if they so desire. By contrast, certain socialist states, such as the USSR, hold that the residual is rightly owned by society as a whole but that a proportion of it should be redistributed to the managers as a reward for their performance.

The implications of the entrepreneurial system are two-fold. First, it sets an implicit distribution criterion for rewards from activity, for managers will hire factors of production up to the point where the remuneration paid to the factor equals its marginal contribution to the value of output according to the prevailing demand conditions. Second, any inefficient resource use or 'shirking' behaviour on the part of the team members will manifest itself as an increase in costs at a given level of output. As this would result in a fall in the residual at this output (and therefore a fall in managerial remuneration), we should expect managers to be particularly concerned to enforce full resource utilization and also actively to seek out cost-reducing technologies.

Let us now consider managerial behaviour under an alternative system, namely cooperative production. Yugoslavia is a commonly cited example of an economy that operates such a system of production organization in certain sectors. Under the cooperative system, some features of the model remain the same, such as the assumption regarding the determinants of total revenue. Similarly, the cooperative manager is charged with hiring amounts of non-labour inputs. Under the cooperative system, however, labour inputs are treated somewhat differently. The residual is defined as total revenue net of non-labour costs and this residual is owned collectively by the labour force participating in the cooperative. The objective of the team in this case is to maximize the residual per employee. Under these specific conditions, the manager can be considered to be a member of the labour force and his raising of everyone else's remuneration also raises his own. The incentive thus appears in a similar fashion, namely by the manager having a personal interest in the residual. Note, however, that in the cooperative case, the labour force too has an interest in the size of the residual.

These two models effectively represent different forms of rights allocation in terms of benefits from team production. We may now show that this gives rise to differing forms of economic behaviour, in spite of the fact that, as Meade (1972) shows, the long-run equilibria for both systems will be identical, given fixed exogenous demand conditions, fixed technologies and fixed cost conditions. First, how will the two types of systems react to demand increases in the short run? If we consider a demand increase as a prospective change in price (from P to P') then it is clear that the entrepreneurial firm will wish to hire more labour, since this factor's marginal revenue product has risen from MP to MP' (where M is labour's marginal product). The cooperative, however, is more interested in average residual per employee, which we can write as

$$\frac{PQ - K}{N}$$

where Q is the amount of the commodity produced, K is the fixed non-labour costs and N is the number of employees. Whilst the change in the value of the marginal product as a result of the demand increase is $M(P' - P)$, the change in average earnings per worker is

$$\left(\frac{P'Q - K}{N}\right) - \left(\frac{PQ - K}{N}\right) = \left(P' - P\right)\frac{Q}{N}.$$

Since average product (Q/N) always exceeds marginal product (M) for factors experiencing diminishing returns, it is clear that the increase in average earnings exceeds the rise in marginal revenue product as a result of the new demand conditions. It therefore follows that average earnings will rise further if labour is fired rather than hired, for the reduction in the value of output of the marginal worker is less than the share of the residual that that worker received. This conclusion in itself has interesting implications. We should anticipate that the size of firms in cooperative economies would be smaller than in entrepreneurial economies. Also, it should be noted that Keynesian-type demand management policies would have exactly opposite effects in the two cases.

A second possible behavioural constraint is the attitudes of team members to risk. Under the entrepreneurial system, most of the risk involved in production, such as the selection of the appropriate technology, the choice of the appropriate quality and quantity of output to satisfy the consumers and so forth, is borne by the manager. If the correct decision is made, the manager is rewarded with a high level of residual; any management errors are correspondingly penalized. By contrast, owners of resources hired at fixed rates take fewer risks, as their remuneration is not solely a function of the firm's short-run performance. In a cooperative system, on the other hand, risks are borne by the labour force in general and its welfare is a function of its manager's ability. Meade (1972) suggests that cooperatives are therefore not likely to survive in conditions of high risk or in conditions where the residual accruing to labour is a proportionately small element of total revenue.

In the context of these two systems we have made an implicit assumption that the manager's objective is the maximization of his share of the residual and that the ability to appropriate this share is his incentive for efficiency. However, we might reasonably suppose that a manager will have wider interests than the simple increase of private income and wealth. We argued earlier that the policing of the team to ensure efficiency entails a cost and we are assuming that the manager will be willing to incur such cost in return for his share of the residual. What he might do, however, is to trade off increases in remuneration gained via greater efficiency against his increasing costs of policing, i.e. he will opt for 'ease of management' once a satisfactory level of profits has been achieved. Under the assumption of diminishing marginal utility, we should presume that material incentives become less effective as managerial income rises. In planned economies, where target directives relating to future managerial performance are influenced by current levels of output, we should anticipate that managers would have a strong incentive to 'shirk' in order to ease their required performance in future planning periods. In general, the extent to which managers can substitute remuneration for effective leisure is a function of the competitive pressure exerted by other firms in the industry and, especially in the case of cooperatives, the amount of political control that the labour force possesses over its managers.

In making our comparisons between these two organizational forms, we have implicitly assumed that the entrepreneurial or cooperative firm operates within a competitive environment, i.e. there exist a number of such firms within a given industry. However, a problem that confronts both capitalist and socialist economies alike is the development of operational criteria for institutional monopolies. Such monopolies might exist for a number of reasons. There might, for example, be evidence of economies of scale within an industry, implying that industrial concentration could prove economic. Alternatively, it might be felt that a particular industry 'needed' central direction. In many countries throughout the world, goods such as iron, coal, rail transport, health care and education are all supplied by such institutional monopolies.

In most cases, the production of these monopolies could be organized in one of two ways. First, the monopoly could be permitted to trade according to the entrepreneurial or cooperative approach outlined above. Consumers would purchase from the firm on a unit-by-unit basis, and the firm's residual would be appropriated by the firm's management or workforce. Second, and this is a common approach, the monopoly could be organized as a *bureaucracy*. In this case, the consumers (usually via the government) would endow the monopoly with an *ex ante* lump-sum payment or budget, on the understanding that the bureaucracy would supply amounts of the commodity equivalent in value to the budget provided. Note that, for a bureaucracy, a residual (and therefore the right of ownership in the residual) is not defined. Thus, the residual cannot be central to the motivation of managers as it will be in the case of either competitive or monopolistic firms. We should therefore expect a bureaucracy to behave in a different manner from such firms. That this is likely to be the case can be predicted from the following model.

Consider how we might organize the production of a commodity, the demand and cost conditions of which are illustrated in *Figure 5.1*. The demand curve (D) is downward-sloping and total costs (TC) increase with output produced. For simplicity, we shall assume linear relationships and marginal cost (MC) is therefore constant. Suppose, first of all, that production took place in a regime of competitive entrepreneurial firms. Economic theory tells us that the long-run equilibrium will occur where price equals marginal cost, at the price/output combination P_cQ_c. This is because, were price to exceed marginal cost in the short run, new firms would enter the industry and compete for the extra profits available. Price would then be forced down to the equilibrium level. On the other hand, were price to fall below marginal cost in the short run, we might expect some firms to go out of business, again leading to a restoration of the equilibrium.

Let us now permit the commodity to be produced by a single (monopoly) entrepreneurial firm. The manager of this firm will be concerned to maximize his residual from total revenue after total costs

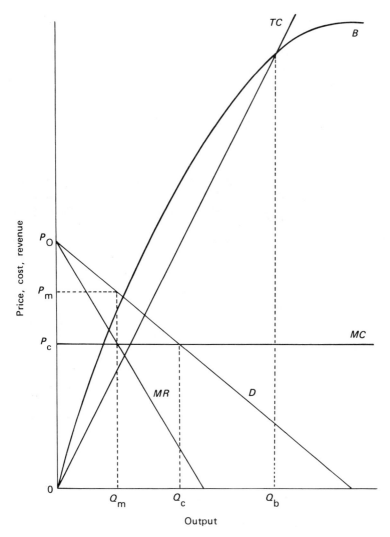

Figure 5.1 Output optima for differing organizational forms

have been met. He will therefore select the price/output combination $P_m Q_m$, where marginal revenue equals marginal cost. Other things remaining equal, we should expect a higher price, and a lower output level, in a monopolistic market than would prevail in a competitive regime.

If we now consider the provision of the same commodity by a bureaucracy, we must introduce two additional factors. The first of these is the nature of the motivations of the bureau's manager. As he will, most likely, be a salaried employee of the organization, he will have no interest in any residual as did his monopoly counterpart; indeed, we have already established that no residual will exist for the bureaucracy. The important variable for the bureaucrat is the size of the bureau's budget. For a number of reasons, we should suggest that he would prefer a higher budget to a lower one. There tends, for example, to be an empirical correlation in most economies between managerial remuneration and the size and prestige of the bureau. We would expect that the manager's desire for power and status would be more readily satisfied if he were to control a larger, rather than smaller, organization. A higher budget would also contribute to the 'ease of management' of the bureau.

The second factor is the determination of the size of the bureau's budget. Clearly, the objective of the bureaucrat – to gain as large a budget as possible – is completely at variance with the interests of the consumers of the bureau's product. Consumers would surely wish to obtain the commodity as cheaply as possible. The final size of the budget will therefore be determined by bargaining and negotiation between the bureau and its sponsors. In this bargaining process, the bureau has a specific advantage because it is in a position to appropriate consumer surplus. The bureau controls the supply of the commodity and can reason as follows. The demand curve (D) suggests that consumers in general are willing to pay a price for P_c for an output Q_c. However, they are also willing to pay a higher price (such as P_m) for a smaller output (Q_m). In other words, at price P_c there must exist consumers who would be prepared to pay a higher price in order to obtain the commodity. The demand curve, in fact, tells the bureau the maximum amount that consumers would be prepared to pay for different outputs. The first unit, for example, would be purchased at a price very close to P_0, whilst the second unit would be purchased at only a slightly lower price. By disaggregating down the demand curve, i.e. by discriminating amongst all the consumers, the bureau can estimate the maximum budget that consumers would be willing to provide for different output levels. This is the curve B in *Figure 5.1*, and it represents the area under the demand curve. Having obtained its budget, the bureaucratic organization will elect to produce at an output level where the total cost of production just equals the budget that the consumers are willing to provide, i.e. at output Q_b. This level clearly represents a higher output than that produced under the competitive regime or by the monopoly firm.

Certain features of this model need underlining. First, it should be noted that differences in output levels result from the differing methods of finance and incentive structures. They do not result from mismanagement, 'shirking' or inefficiencies on the part of managers; we have, of course, assumed the existence of identical cost conditions. Any inefficiencies in production would be represented as upward shifts in the cost curves and these would serve to reduce the output optima in all cases. Second, neither the monopoly firm nor the bureaucracy operates at the strict neoclassical optimum where consumer surplus is maximized (P_cQ_c in *Figure 5.1*). Third, the bureaucratic optimum identified in the model represents the extreme position, in which bureaucrats are able to appropriate all of the consumer surplus. In specific circumstances, for example, where bureaux are the subjects of stringent monitoring and control, we should expect the sponsors to possess greater bargaining strength. In these cases, the budget curve (B) will be lower for all levels of output and the optimum output level will be correspondingly reduced. Finally, price discrimination is not the sole prerogative of bureaucracies. Indeed, it is a common practice amongst monopolistic firms. As long as there exist distinct classes of consumers (defined in terms of differential ability and willingness to pay), and as long as one class cannot resell the commodity to another, price discrimination is likely to prove an optimal strategy for the firm. Railways in many countries, for example, charge different rates for the transportation of different products. Manufacturers frequently sell their goods at different prices on the home and on the overseas market. Such a factor clearly adds complications to our existing simple model.

From the model above, it appears that we can employ a number of organizational structures within an economy, structures that are each defined by the nature of ownership and the specific allocation of property rights within the producing unit. From such models we may develop more specific lines of enquiry to analyse the practical implications of particular structures, with corollaries for changes in such structures. The following examples currently interest economists.

In the first place, the analysis suggests that bureaucracies, as distinct from entrepreneurial firms, have no interest in residuals. This implies that they have no necessary interest in maintaining low cost levels and therefore, if left to their own devices, might be willing to let costs rise in exchange for ease of management. Niskanen (1968) has suggested that this trend might be countered by adopting a property rights structure within bureaucracies, by making managerial remuneration 'a negative function of the budget of the bureau for a given set of outputs' (p. 305). Van den Doel (1979) further shows that a managerial incentive system within a bureaucracy structured as a cooperative will lead to a reduction in employment (and costs) within that bureaucracy (pp. 140–1), as might be predicted from the model above.

Second, there has been a growing interest in the Western capitalist world, and especially in Europe, in extending the influence of firms' workforces by allowing them to participate in decision making. Worker participation has been justified on a number of grounds, such as an appeal to social justice, the belief that it would lead to improved labour relations and the idea that worker motivation must necessarily increase. As Chiplin and Coyne (1977) point out however, the consequences of worker participation depend upon the nature of the property rights reform involved. They argue that the 'half-way house' form of participation (a form widely used in Europe), in which workers are permitted to participate in firms' decisions but are still remunerated by wages representing an element of the firms' costs, is likely to produce curious outcomes. This is because workers are now in a position to influence the residual but, as their remuneration does not depend upon the extent of the residual, they are able to make corporate decisions without necessarily incurring any risks entailed by such decisions. Correspondingly, the power of the manager, who retains the residual as a return for ensuring efficient production, will be reduced and we should therefore conclude that such worker-managed firms are less likely to be efficient (in the technical sense but not necessarily in the social sense) than purely entrepreneurial or cooperative firms.

A third outcome of research has led to the analysis of 'corrupt practices' in institutional monopolies and especially within bureaucracies. 'Corruption' results from the establishment of private property rights on the part of the organization's management or employees from which markets may be created in those circumstances where the established price of the organization's output differs from the private valuations of specific consumers. In such a case, it becomes worthwhile for such consumers to try to purchase 'favours' from members of the organization concerned. The concept of corruption is thus determined by the ideological principles under which an organization is set up. It basically involves the question of whether or not individuals 'ought' to be allowed to create property rights and to use them as a basis for exchange. Consider the case, for example, of the British National Health Service, which uses a system of waiting lists to allocate medical care in a manner deemed socially just. For a particular physician to sell his services and thus allow a patient to avoid the queue would be regarded as a corrupt practice for, under a national service, a physician should not, it is argued, be permitted to establish such a property right. However, in the case of non-national health service physicians in Britain, rationing by price is acceptable and cannot therefore be regarded as corrupt. This is also true for other countries that operate private health care schemes.

Sanchez and Waters (1974) argue that the necessary conditions for corruption to occur are (i) the existence of excess demand at the prevailing price, (ii) the possibility of the creation and exchange of property rights on the part of the members of the organization, and (iii) the belief that, by undertaking corrupt practices, members will not impair their positions in the 'normal' running of the organization. Seen in this light, corruption is essentially a symptom of price rigidity, or an imbalance between supply and demand at the prevailing price. Were the organization to be providing at the 'correct' price and output levels (the levels equivalent to demand and supply equilibrium) there would, presumably, be no market for any quantity supplied 'corruptly'. If we accept that corrupt allocation is undesirable *per se*, society will be obliged to take steps to prevent its occurrence. One alternative might be to remove the purchasing power of the consumers of the 'corrupt' output, by the imposition of taxation. Again, a corrupt organization could be policed by an agency created for the purpose. This does raise the problem, however, of the possibility of the emergence of corruption within this policing agency! Perhaps the most obvious remedy would be the restructuring of incentives for 'non-corrupt' practices within the organization. If doctors within a public health care system were being tempted to devote all their time to private patients willing to pay for their services, then perhaps society might consider increasing the doctors' remuneration that resulted from the treatment of 'public' patients. Clearly, the alternative chosen – indeed, whether an alternative is chosen at all – will depend upon the specific society's social choice process and the power of the decision maker to enforce social decisions.

5.3   The ownership of land

As, during the greater part of human history, land has been a significant material input to production, it is not surprising that the appropriate form of land ownership has been an enduring question. This has led to societies experimenting with land reform, that is, with the redistribution of ownership rights, in an attempt to secure superior levels of welfare. The possibility of beneficial redistribution appears well established and we have evidence of ownership reforms, often on a regular basis, dating back to the great agricultural civilizations of Greece, Rome, China and Africa. In these earlier times, reform frequently meant concentration and consolidation of land-holdings. In recent years, however, land reform has become equated with a rights distribution in the opposite direction, from inegalitarian towards egalitarian.

King (1977) notes three types of ownership pattern in which the need for reform has been identified. First, the latifundian system (particularly characteristic of South America and pre-revolutionary Russia) appears to give rise to problems. This system consists of large estates worked by peasants bound to landowners in a quasi-feudal relationship. King notes that in those countries that have not experienced land reform 'generally about 3–4 per cent of the landowners own 60–80 per cent of the agricultural land' (p. 8). Second, a common Asian land-holding system has involved the renting out of land by large landowners as a great number of smallholdings for private cultivation. Third, often as a consequence of imperialism, much agricultural land in the African, Asian and South American continents has been operated via the plantation system in which land and output have been owned by the imperialist power with labour working for a wage.

Having inherited any one of these forms of ownership, a society might present a number of arguments in favour of land reform. First, it might be argued that such a heavily inegalitarian distribution is 'unfair' on the grounds of some notion of social justice. Second, it might be suggested that the concentration of economic power entailed by such land ownership will give landowners a disproportionate and undesirable strength in the machinations of the political process. Third, it might be argued that this concentration of property rights gives rise to an inefficient outcome, that is, more output could be produced from the same land area if ownership rights were to be redistributed in some fashion, owing to the different motivations of landowner and landworker.

Following Barlowe (1953), we can distinguish three major forms of land reform that governments have employed in the past and that are ranked according to the extent to which they entail a redefinition of ownership rights. First, there is the establishment of agricultural assistance schemes that require no change in ownership patterns, being simply concerned at improving technical efficiency of current owners and cultivators. This method is particularly applicable in circumstances where the land-holdings are small, such that economies of scale cannot be reaped. Examples include the provision of credit and banking facilities by the government, schemes for cooperative marketing of produce, and assistance where, indeed, the consolidation of land-holdings is envisaged. The second level of reform involves positive interference in ownership patterns. A government might feel, for instance, that the tenant's rent should be fixed by statute rather than by the landlord. In this category of 'mild' attenuation of property rights we should also include obligatory land consolidation schemes. Continuing up the scale, we come to a third type more applicable to the cases of large land-holdings. Here we find that the owner will be deprived of his property, which will subsequently be reallocated to, say, former peasants or tenants to farm as their own land. The major collectivization schemes, such as those that occurred in post-revolutionary Russia and China, represent the most severe intervention in the traditional ownership structure.

Given the diversity of historical conditions and of the prevailing ideologies of societies concerned, it is difficult to assess exactly what form of land reform, if any, is likely to prove optimal. The land reforms of the past, however, do provide us with some clues. We know, for example, that the collectivization of Soviet agriculture in the 1930s, in which residual production was expropriated by the state, led to a major decline in both input and output on the part of the agricultural workforce, an outcome to be expected on the basis of the behavioural models that we examined above. Again, it has been suggested that the redistribution of land into smaller, egalitarian land-holdings would lead to a lowering in the rate of accumulation on the grounds that richer, larger owners have a higher marginal propensity to save. Empirical evidence for India suggests, however, that this is probably not the case (Griffin, 1979, pp. 225–33). Indeed, in the majority of cases, the results of a more egalitarian distribution of land have been increases in total output (although, if the society placed a high value on the sanctity of private property, the necessary rights attenuation to produce such gains would invalidate them). Rather than attempt to review all the possibilities, let us consider just one example of the effects of land reform.

5.3.1   LAND REFORM IN MEXICO

The case of Mexican land reform is interesting for at least two reasons. First, it has been a relatively gradual process occurring throughout the twentieth century and, second, the transfer of ownership involved has been substantial. At the turn of the century it has been estimated that 97 per cent of the available agricultural land was owned by just 1 per cent of the population, and this figure surely represents a very high degree of ownership inequality by any standards. Since that time, however, approximately 50 per cent of the total land area has been redistributed, this scale of redistribution only having been exceeded by the USSR and China.

In common with most Latin American economies, Mexico had a long history of ownership concentration on the latifundian principle, dating from the time of the European incursions in the later Middle Ages. What made the Mexican case particularly pronounced, however, was nineteenth-century legislation that prohibited the holding of land on the part of both the Church and the indigenous Indian population. As a result of such laws, vast tracts of land became available for purchase virtually overnight and were taken over by those most able to afford them, i.e. the existing large landowners. By 1900, life had become singularly unpleasant for the majority of the population as the estate owners used their monopsony power to maintain low wage rates, a power enhanced by the increasing number of unemployed and dispossessed rural labourers. In the face of economic depression, which had the impact of raising food prices, the resultant social unrest rapidly manifested itself in the form of revolution during the period 1910–20.

As agriculture was central to the standard of living of the mass of the population, it was naturally also central to the policies of the postrevolutionary governments. It is probably fair to say that the main motivation for this derived from a feeling that concentration of economic power as in pre-revolutionary times was inherently unjust. However, whilst it was agreed that the latifundia (or *hacienda* in the Mexican case) should be broken up, there was some disagreement about the forms of ownership that should replace the latifundian system. In 1922, the *ejido* became established as the basic model for land reform.

This can best be thought of as a form of village commune in which villagers have communal or cooperative rights in land-holding and production. In order to create *ejidos*, latifundian land was simply transferred to villages on a local area basis, although an alternative system – *dotación* – also existed whereby villages could petition for land endowments. The formation of *ejidos* was especially widespread during the 1930s: between 1930 and 1940 the amount of arable land held privately fell from 12.7 to 7.9 million hectares whilst *ejido* holdings rose from 1.9 to 7.0 million hectares. These developments were accompanied by the emergence of a central government interest in agriculture, notably via the construction of irrigation schemes.

During the 1940s, a significant change of direction began to emerge as a role for private ownership came to be defined. Although the enormous latifundia of the pre-revolutionary period were no longer deemed to be justified, a case was made for allocations of land to private owners, particularly in the area of non-arable farming (e.g. cattle ranching) that required extensive land use. Central government interest in agriculture continued, both with respect to the provision of irrigation schemes and in terms of developing previously unused land. Between 1940 and 1960, the total area of land under cultivation increased by 60 per cent and, of the 1960 total, around 45 per cent was held by *ejidos*. Taking agricultural land as a whole (that is, including the extensive area used for forestry and grazing, which was largely held privately), the *ejido* total drops to around 25 per cent.

How successful has the Mexican land reform experiment been? If we see the objective as simply the evening out of the distribution of ownership, then the answer is 'considerably so'. Approximately 25 per cent of the Mexican population currently own and farm *ejidos* on a collective basis. Furthermore, the average size of private land-holdings has decreased, indicating that there are now more private land-holders than before. Looking at success in terms of expansion of output, we might note that Mexico is, at present, one of the few Latin American economies that can make any claim towards being self-sufficient in agricultural products. Putting the village communes on the same footing as a non-monopoly private farm (i.e. giving agricultural labour an interest in the residual) and raising agricultural incomes (i.e. increasing aggregate demand) were two policy factors contributing to a more than two-fold increase in arable output over the period 1940–60. Although, at face value, the growth in private output exceeded the growth of *ejido* production, account must be taken of the fact that, in general, *ejidos* enjoyed poorer soil and irrigation conditions and had relatively less access to credit. Taking such factors into account, M. Mueller (1970) has estimated that *ejidos* actually out-performed the private farms in the 1950s.

Mexico's achievement in meeting its objectives of a fairer distribution of property and increases in output, especially during the middle of the present century, should not be taken to imply that no inherent problems remain. In spite of the radical alteration in tenure patterns, there are still several million landless labourers whose social and economic conditions have been scarcely affected by the land reforms. The size of this group is increasing owing, in part, to rapid population growth. Furthermore, it appears that the development of productive potential has been highly regionalized. Most of the *ejido*-type reform has taken place in central Mexico whilst most of the government assistance has been allocated to the northern region, where private farms predominate and where there is easier access to the important US market. As a result, there exist regional disparities in productivity and such disparities appear to be increasing. In turn, this has lately given rise to a new concentration trend amongst the larger landowners. Clearly, such inherent tendencies could be taken to represent a *prima facie* case for further land reform.

Additional insights into the potential of land reform may be gained if we supplement the empirical observations with some theoretical conclusions. The existing structure of Brazilian agriculture has certain similarities to that of Mexico at its early-reform stage, in that land ownership is highly concentrated. However Brazil, unlike Mexico, has only possessed limited land reform legislation since 1964. Limited reform permitted Cline (1970) to use Brazil as a case-study for a simulation projection of the consequences of land reform in a 'typical' Latin American economy. His results are useful in the interpretation of the Mexican data and serve as an indication of what might be expected from land reform programmes in other economies. Cline argues that the optimum size of land-holding, defined in terms of productive efficiency, should be determined by the extent to which capital equipment can be used efficiently. Whilst this might initially be seen as a justification for the existence of large, rather than smaller, farms, Cline suggests that the relative factor costs in an economy at the early stages of industrialization mean that capital is of only limited relevance in production. This result suggests that returns to scale in the case of Brazilian agriculture are likely to be constant at best; in other words, subdivision of land-holdings would not lower technical efficiency.

Possibly the most significant finding of Cline's study is his conclusion that small farms probably use resources more intensively than do large farms. Cline found a number of influences in this respect. First, large farm-owners often hold land for speculative or prestige, rather than production, purposes. Second, the system of household or family production on small farms produces a different wage pattern from that produced on the larger capitalistic estates where labour is hired for a wage. Whilst the optimum labour force for a capitalistic estate is determined by wage equalling marginal product, the optimum for the family unit (which is essentially a cooperative team) is where effective wage equals average family product. Thus the family producer unit may retain labour that is technically unproductive but that, in fact, still contributes to output in a positive way. Third, large estates are likely to be local monopolies and/or monopsonies, whilst smaller firms will be more competitive. Economic theory suggests that the optimum production and employment levels for a monopoly industry are lower than those for a competitive one. Finally, smaller firms tend to be very much price-takers when it comes to the negotiation of credit and sales; this should lead, other things being equal, to more intensive factor usage than in the case of larger firms with more bargaining power.

Finally, Cline notes that a reduction in average farm size would have the beneficial economic effect of altering the efficient productive technology. With smaller farms, more labour and less capital could be employed. Given the existence of labour unemployment, a change to such a technology would represent a low opportunity cost. On the basis of such conclusions, Cline's simulation suggests that an 'across the board' land redistribution would increase the output of Brazilian agriculture by some 20 per cent, *ceteris paribus*. Although land reform involves issues other than simple productivity increases, such as considerations of ethics and social justice and the pursuit of prosperity over the longer as well as the shorter term, such theoretical findings for Brazil, and the empirical data for Mexico, do indicate the enormous implications for the pursuit of progress entailed by ownership patterns, their distribution and their redistribution.

Summary

The code of conduct that a society will establish to regulate its affairs will include the assignment of rights within the context of a legal system. From the economic point of view, the most important right is the right of ownership. Societies will differ in their judgements about what may be owned, about who is entitled to own, and about the scope of ownership. A hierarchy of rights, or a priority ordering, must be established to resolve possible conflicts between rights.

Legal systems are enforced by legal agencies. There exist several possible operating criteria for such agencies. Under certain circumstances, individuals might find it optimal to break the law. Economists have devised models to explain such behaviour. Because law enforcement involves costs, criteria are required to determine how much should be spent on this activity. These criteria will be related to wider issues of economic policy.

Production is undertaken by teams under managerial supervision. The ownership rights assigned to the manager influence how he and the team behave. Under the entrepreneurial system, the manager hires factors of production and appropriates the residual from revenue after costs have been met. In a cooperative, the manager is concerned to maximize residual per employee. Cooperative and entrepreneurial firms respond differently to risk and short-run demand changes. In either case, managers may also have wider objectives that influence behaviour. Under a bureaucratic system, no residual exists. The bureaucrat can be seen as a budget-maximizer. A bureaucratic monopoly will respond to given demand and cost conditions in a manner different from the response of an entrepreneurial monopoly. Ownership structures have implications for worker self-management and corruption.

Changes in the pattern of land ownership have occurred throughout history. Modern land reform movements have emphasized the need for a more egalitarian distribution of land-holding. Twentieth-century land reforms have included schemes for agricultural cooperation, rent control, land consolidation and collectivization. Land reform in Mexico has been oriented towards the breaking-up of the latifundia and the establishment of village communes. Economic models demonstrate that more egalitarian land distributions could lead to output increases of considerable magnitude.

Further reading

From the point of view of the basic philosophy of law, texts such as Dworkin (1977a) and Hart (1961) will outline the relevant features of legal systems. Dworkin (1977b) considers the specific concept of 'rights'. L. Becker (1977) analyses the nature of property rights from a philosophical standpoint. A number of important contributions relating to the economic consequences of particular rights allocations are collected in Furubotn and Pejovich (1974). These authors have also undertaken a literature survey of the field (1972). At present, the definitive text for the economic analysis of law is Posner (1977). Journal articles relating to law enforcement are collected in G. Becker and Landes (1974). The costs of criminal activity are dealt with in Gray (1979).

The organization of activity via the entrepreneurial model is central to the neoclassical theory of economic behaviour and it is accordingly discussed in all basic economics texts – Hirschleifer (1976) is one example among many. The theory of the cooperative form is laid out by Vanek (1970), this author having also edited a valuable collection of readings (1975) on the subject of worker self-management. Cooperative enterprises in Yugoslavia are examined by Moore (1980). The principal figure in the 'economics of bureaucracy' field is Niskanen (1968, 1971, 1973). Borcherding (1977) surveys the literature. The nature of corruption in Asia is an important theme of Myrdal (1968).

Dorner (1972) is a basic text relating to the role of land reform in the creation of economic progress. Lehmann (1974) and the comprehensive King (1977) provide many case-studies of land reform programmes. Gersovitz (1976) raises some general land reform questions. Bardhan (1979) and Bardhan and Ashok (1980) examine the effects of the structure of land-holding in the Indian context. The principal sources for the Mexican case-study are King (1977) and Barraza Allende (1974). Statistical data are derived from the work of Dovring, quoted by King. Pearse (1975) is a general study of the Latin American peasantry.

Chapter Six

People as Consumers

In general terms, we can consider an economic system or strategy as a means of realizing welfare gains for its participants. From the purely material point of view, strategies will involve the combination of natural resources and factor inputs, such as labour and capital, to produce items for people to consume. If consumption is going to be a primary goal for any strategy, and we argued earlier that it would be, then we must clearly come to terms with the nature of consumption. As a first approach, let us assume that society has undertaken some production. Now, what issues confront any individual who is trying to decide exactly what out of the production bundle he is going to consume? For any one individual, the following factors might be of significance.

First, the feasible consumption set of period t – that is, the bundle of available goods and services from which the individual might make his choice – is naturally constrained by the actual production set of period $t-1$; people cannot, after all, consume goods that have not been produced. The consumption opportunity set will therefore be determined by a variety of factors, such as the quantity and quality of productive inputs available to society and also the latter's ability to trade with other economies. However, although present period consumption must be limited to what is available, evidence of consumer interest in items as yet unproduced might serve as a signal to producers to restructure the composition of output in future periods.

Second, perhaps the most significant, and at the same time the most indefinable, causal factor is what we might term the individual's 'psychological constitution'. This is the subjective manner in which he translates the consumption of items into perceived welfare gains. We noted in Chapter 2, for example, that the 'average' Englishman drinks more tea than the 'average' Frenchman, the latter showing a preference for coffee. Given that both these individuals inhabit relatively rich countries with plentiful trading opportunities, the cost of the items is possibly not a major determining factor in the consumption decision. To explain the difference, we might have to ask the following sorts of question: does the fact that the former British Empire contained regions suited to tea production offer an explanation; has the British public been subjected to persuasive advertising on the part of tea producers; is the biochemistry of the British taste-bud noticeably different from that of the French? The general point to be made is that we should not expect different societies or different individuals to view the same item in the same way in terms of its potential welfare effects.

Third, if consumption goods yield welfare for whatever reason, we might expect each individual to want an infinite amount. As this would not be physically feasible, all societies employ rationing systems to equilibrate aggregate consumer demand with available supply. The most common form of rationing is the allocation of purchasing or consumption power to individuals on the basis of some ethical norm regarding the appropriate distribution of such power; we might, for example, argue that purchasing power should be a function of the individual's contribution to commodity production. In order to consume, individuals give up a portion of purchasing power (i.e. income) in exchange for the item they wish to consume and the stipulation is made that the total value of consumption purchases may not exceed the individual's income in the long, if not the short, run. Of course, the combination of this notion of an income constraint together with the 'psychological constitution' simply involves the basic concept of opportunity cost. With a given amount of consumption power, the individual will derive a rank ordering of consumption priorities based upon the subjective valuations of their welfare benefits relative to welfare costs or opportunities forgone as a result of consuming these, as opposed to alternative, items. Such a ranking determines those items that appear in the actual, as distinct from the feasible, choice set.

Fourth, although consumption choice via the assessment of opportunity costs is the general principle to be applied, an aspect of it merits specific consideration. Given an allocation of purchasing power, consumers will choose not only spatially, i.e. between good A and good B, but also temporally, i.e. whether to consume A or B now or at some time in the future. Consider the consumption of a non-renewable resource such as coal or oil. Depending upon its 'time preference', a nation might choose to deplete its coal stocks rapidly and use some other energy source in the future or, alternatively, it might save the coal and switch to the consumption of alternative energy now. We shall return to these issues in Chapter 8.

Fifth, consumption decisions might also be made with reference to the consumer's, or the whole society's, view of the influence of a particular consumption decision upon others. Again, there is both a spatial and a temporal dimension. If my consumption of a cigar imposes pollution costs upon you, a non-smoker, I might, in deference to your feelings, be persuaded to reduce my cigar consumption. Alternatively, the assessment of such external effects may be made at a social level, legislation being developed to regulate individual consumption that involves externalities; in this case, society might prohibit me from smoking in certain areas inhabited by non-smokers. The inter-temporal externality effect can also be demonstrated with the example of the non-renewable resource: if I and my fellow citizens decide rapidly to deplete oil stocks, all generations following us will be denied any direct benefits that the availability of oil might have conferred upon them. Perhaps a more graphic instance is the case of an indestructible 'resource', nuclear waste. The decision of several real-world societies to consume nuclear energy, generating nuclear waste that remains active for tens of thousands of years, is also a function of the contemporary consumer's concern for his own welfare relative to that of the many generations as yet unborn. Decisions of this nature are particularly difficult to make – the people of the future do not have formal representation in decision-making processes and we are also totally ignorant of what their aspirations, technological abilities and circumstances are likely to be.

All these features can be summarized by saying that the individual's consumption will be determined by what he is permitted to consume (in legal terms, in terms of his income constraint, in terms of practical feasibility), and also by his subjective assessment of opportunity costs in spatial and temporal terms. In this chapter we shall further consider people's consumption behaviour in two ways: first, the behaviour of individual consumers within a society and, second, the effect of aggregate consumption upon the economic system.

6.1   Household behaviour

Given the theoretical determinants of consumption outlined above, a number of empirically based questions immediately present themselves. If the individual's consumption bundle is determined by his available income, how will he react to increases or decreases in his income level: will he consume more of some items and less of others, or simply more or less of everything? Is there any relationship between levels of material welfare and the choice between present and deferred consumption? At an aggregate level, what is the impact on the consumption mix of some redistribution of purchasing power? Answers to such questions are clearly relevant to the design of any strategy for progress that involves consumption, and economists have been investigating the area for a considerable period of time. Perhaps the most famous forerunner in the field was the nineteenth-century Prussian statistician Engel whose insights were developed particularly by C. Clark (1951). A general survey of changes in consumption patterns has been undertaken for the World Bank by

Lluch, Powell and Williams (1977). We shall review this analysis in some detail.

Although we have so far been talking in terms of individual consumption, economists often prefer to use the 'household' as the basic unit in this respect. A household is a group of individuals, usually living together under one roof and bound by kinship ties, who demand commodities collectively on the basis of some form of communal decision procedure. Such a unit, it is argued, is typical of most regions of the world. The World Bank study considers household behaviour for 26 countries with widely differing socio-economic structures, ranging from relatively poor economies such as Taiwan and Thailand to relatively rich nations such as Australia and Sweden.

For the purpose of analysis, household consumption was divided into eight categories – foodstuffs, clothing and housing (which together with foodstuffs were taken to constitute 'subsistence' consumption), durables, personal care, transport, recreation and 'other expenditures'. For all the countries analysed, expenditure on foodstuffs was the single largest proportion of the household budget although aggregate cross-section analysis revealed that (i) the proportion of the budget allocated to 'subsistence' declined with per capita income and (ii) the proportion of expenditure on food within the subsistence category declined with per capita income. Thus it was found, for example, that the budget proportions for food and subsistence in the case of low-income Korea were 60 and 82 per cent, whilst the corresponding figures for the high-income USA were 27 and 59 per cent (p. 40). Put another way, the proportion of the household budget that is allocated to items other than the basic means of subsistence appears to increase with income per head.

Given the importance of food expenditure, it is not surprising to discover that the purchase of foodstuffs has an impact upon household savings behaviour. In particular, savings were found to be sensitive to the price of food (i.e. if food prices rose, households saved less), although this effect was less pronounced at higher income levels. Although some correlation was established between the household's marginal propensity to save and its income, occupation appeared to be the main determining factor. In particular, it was established that farmers in most of the countries surveyed had propensities to save far larger than did urban or even non-farming rural dwellers. Korean farmers, for example, appeared to save over 50 per cent of incremental income, whilst the figure for wage earners in towns was around 20 per cent. The marginal propensity to save in the case of Yugoslavian farmers was even higher (p. 118). Why this should be the case is not at all clear. Lluch *et al.* suggest that farm incomes are prone to higher levels of instability than incomes from other forms of employment. The normal risk-aversion assumption would lead us to predict higher savings levels as 'insurance'. In addition, the tenancy arrangements in many low-income countries require that farmers accumulate reserves to pay to landlords. We might also note that, in the case of such farming enterprises, the household is not only the unit of consumption but also the unit of production. The surplus is accordingly necessary to permit reinvestment to maintain consumption over time. Such an investment allocation would not be required by, say, an urban factory worker receiving wages.

Turning now to consumers' responses to income changes, the World Bank study confirmed the result first developed by Engel and now known as 'Engel's Law' – the elasticity of demand for food with respect to income is positive but less than unity and it falls with increases in the level of household income. By contrast, it was found that the income elasticity of demand for housing and transport increased with income levels, although no distinct relationship emerged for the other consumption categories. With respect to price elasticity, it appeared that demand for all types of consumption item was more responsive at higher income levels.

Although economists typically restrict their analyses of consumption to price and income effects, the World Bank study indicated that other influences exist. Data for Chile suggested, for example, that the age of the household (or rather the age of the 'head' of the household) had an impact on savings behaviour, older households appearing more likely to save larger proportions of income increases than younger households. The actual size of the household appeared to be significant, for 'economies of scale' were observed: per capita subsistence expenditure was frequently lower for large families than for small ones. Finally, consumption behaviour appeared to be influenced by the socio-economic class of the household, as determined by the head's occupation.

If we take data for one particular economy, we can immediately detect the tendencies observed in the World Bank study. Over the period 1958–79, per capita GDP in Britain rose by around 60 per cent and direct consumption expenditure on the part of households (itself some 60 per cent of total domestic expenditure) accordingly rose in line. Over this period, aggregate household expenditure on food as a proportion of the total household budget fell from 33 per cent to 23 per cent, whilst the proportional allocation to both housing and transport rose from 7–8 per cent to 13–14 per cent. Proportional allocations to fuel and clothing displayed fractional declines, whilst consumers' expenditures on services remained constant at around 10 per cent. The same type of phenomena are revealed if we disaggregate the 1979 household expenditure into different household income classes. Whilst the poorest UK households spent 63 per cent of their incomes on basic subsistence (food, housing and fuel in this case), the proportion for the richest households was around 35 per cent.

Up to this point, our evidence has been purely behavioural in that we have been content to consider how people in the recent past have actually consumed at certain levels of income and at different points in time. It is a different question altogether to ask what people might want to consume. Scitovsky (1976) has developed some thought-provoking ideas in this respect. Citing some opinion polls conducted in the USA over a 25-year period, he notes that the proportion of the population that reveals itself to be wholly or partially satisfied with its lot, and indeed the proportion that reveals itself to be positively dissatisfied, remains remarkably constant in spite of a 60 per cent growth in real per capita incomes. Data of this nature suggest that equating consumption of goods and services with the generation of welfare could, to say the least, be suspect. Scitovsky advances four possible explanatory factors.

In the first place, for societies such as the United States where the prevailing ideology is individualistic, it may well be the case that consumer satisfaction is a function not of the absolute level of consumer spending but of the level relative to other individuals or households. People only become conscious of their welfare, in other words, in relation to the manner in which their peers are performing. If economic progress occurs in an even manner, that is, by distributing the gains equally to all parties, the relative ranking will remain unchanged. As in the case of the Hirsch (1977) approach mentioned in Chapter 3, this view leads to an interesting policy implication. Consider a world composed of two similar individuals, one rich and one poor. We assume that interpersonal utility comparisons are possible and that increased consumption is characterized by diminishing marginal utility. Given these assumptions, it is clear that aggregate utility will be enhanced by a more egalitarian distribution of income, because the resulting welfare gains of the previously poor man are likely to exceed the welfare losses of the previously rich man. However, if we follow Scitovsky and suggest that overall utility is also a function of relative consumption utilities, the distribution optimum becomes unclear. The optimum now depends upon the extent to which the rich man gains pleasure from the knowledge of his superior position and also upon the extent to which the poor man feels disadvantaged, not absolutely, but relative to the consumption of the other individual. If it were the case that individuals derived increasing welfare returns from income and consumption differentials, the optimum would be perfect inequality!

Second, Scitovsky implicitly argues that the concentration on consumption satisfaction is misplaced because the individual's act of production also carries with it utility implications. If, in order to earn more income, the worker is obliged to incur more disutility by increasing his productive effort, we should not expect any net change in satisfaction levels.

Scitovsky's third explanation involves 'addiction'. At any level of income, households will make a bundle of purchases that may be defined as a consumption norm. At low income levels, this bundle will consist largely of subsistence items. However, as income rises, people are able to add to the basic bundle and these new purchases become defined within the consumption norm. In contemporary industrial societies, goods once defined as 'luxuries' – automobiles, television sets, refrigerators, central heating and air conditioning – have come to be regarded as necessary ingredients of an acceptable style of living. To understand why a household may not feel its circumstances to be improving, we need only suggest that, as its income rises, it continually redefines its norm, or base of consumption satisfaction, at higher levels and therefore perceives its circumstances, relative to this new level, as unchanged.

The fourth factor, and the one that Scitovsky finds particularly intriguing, is the pursuit of novelty. Scitovsky argues that, up to a point, individuals gain welfare from novelty in terms of both the physical and mental stimulation that the new situation or good generates. Accordingly, a 'progressive' society must be seen as one that caters for the provision of such stimulation. However, if Scitovsky is correct in this belief about the nature of human motivation, there are two related causes for concern when we come to devising strategies for progress. In the first place, the desire for novelty could give rise to a 'grass is greener' paradox – i.e. individuals will always prefer circumstances other than the ones in which they currently find themselves. In this pathological case, no possible outcome can permanently satisfy individual preferences. In less extreme instances, the pursuit of novelty may be accommodated by the introduction of a certain degree of flexibility into the economic system, although it should be borne in mind that flexibility can only be bought at a price. It is generally easier to direct activities towards the attainment of one target than to attempt to align them towards several possible objectives. Second, the awareness of novelty, if coupled with an inability to consume that novelty, may be a source of considerable disutility. This 'demonstration effect' on poor individuals within a society can have unpredictable outcomes; whilst, on the one hand, it might be argued that novelty serves as a goal to encourage the poor 'to increase the productive efforts to reap the possible gains', it is also the case that it serves as a stimulus to the poor to agitate against an economic structure that appears iniquitous. This problem also arises at an international level, for any government of a relatively poor country that is attempting to engineer a growth strategy via austerity runs the risk of alienating the population, who view with envy the consumption opportunities in other, less austere, economies. A by-product of the internationalization process is the common acquisition of aspirations but not the common possession of the resources necessary to realize such aspirations.

6.2   Aggregate consumption and food supply

As we have seen, the typical household consumption bundle is likely to vary from society to society, depending upon tastes and preferences, income, resource availability and so forth. Furthermore, household purchasing patterns within one particular economy also display variability. Any question of whether the 'correct' consumption mix is being achieved can only be assessed subjectively and will have a culturally specific answer. There is, however, one possible exception to this generalization. Irrespective of whether or not a nation derives consumption benefits from such items as aeroplanes, cinemas or washing machines, we can be certain that it will derive welfare from the physical necessities of survival, essentially from food. Indeed, we have already seen that people all over the world spend a sizeable proportion of their incomes on food. Whilst we cannot exclude the logical possibility that a specific society might wish to commit mass suicide, it does seem more reasonable to suppose that the provision of the basic level of foodstuffs necessary for continued physical survival will be a primary objective of all nations. In the previous section, we were concerned with partial analysis, i.e. with the individual household, and we implicitly assumed that households could obtain as much as they wished from an available stock. However, let us now proceed to the general level by considering aggregate food consumption in relation to the supply available to all consumers. We can approach the problem by considering two types of data: (i) the static relationship between the availability of food and the present demand conditions, and (ii) changes in demand and production over time.

Probably the closest we can come to a scientific criterion of the minimum acceptable consumption level is the nutritional requirement necessary to maintain the human body and to prevent physiological deterioration. Such a requirement can be expressed in terms of daily recommended intakes of calories, proteins, fats, carbohydrates, vitamins and so forth. It will be related to the biology of the individual and to the environment in which he lives. A number of such nutritional norms have been devised; here, we shall consider the implications of one devised by the Food and Agriculture Organization (FAO) of the United Nations, in consultation with the World Health Organization, in the early 1970s. If we compare the FAO norms with nutritional data for the 50 African economies for which such data are presently available, we find that, for the period 1972–4, in only 16 of these countries did the individual, on average, consume more than the recommended daily calorie intake. Furthermore, for 19 out of the remaining 34 economies, the average calorie intake was more than 10 per cent below the FAO norm. Similarly, several Asian and Latin American economies fell into the '10 per cent below the minimum' category in the early 1970s. Examples include India, Bangladesh and the Philippines in the former continent and Bolivia, Haiti and El Salvador in the latter. It is clear that nutritional deficiency is a regional problem, for not one European economy during the 1972–4 period fell below the FAO norm. In fact, the country that came the closest in this respect was Albania, where average daily calorie intake was 4 per cent above the FAO minimum. Intakes for the United Kingdom, the United States and the Soviet Union were all approximately 33 per cent above the norm.

Naturally, nutritional experts disagree about the precise identification and measurement of physiological norms of this nature; the FAO minima are not universally accepted. However, even if we believe that the norms are set at too high a level, such evidence at least suggests the possibility of inadequate food supplies in certain parts of the world.

We have so far examined only a slice in time. Let us therefore now consider trends in population growth (i.e. aggregate food demand) and food production. *Table 6.1* presents some relevant data. Again, we get the impression of distinct regional differences. Whilst, for example, the rate of population growth in Western Europe rarely exceeds 1 per cent per annum, rates in Africa all exceed 2 per cent. Furthermore, and this is the vital point, the domestic production of foodstuffs has grown faster than population in Western and Eastern Europe and in the United States during the 1970s. Exactly the reverse tends to be true for the countries of Africa, Asia and Latin America.

TABLE 6.1 Demographic and food production data for selected countries, early 1970s

Country	Birth rate[a]	Death rate[a]	Life expectancy (years)[b]	Population growth rate (per cent)[c]	Food production growth rate (per cent)[d]
Africa					
Algeria	48.7	15.4	53.3	3.2	1.0
Ethiopia	49.4	25.8	38.1	2.4	0.0
Ghana	48.8	21.9	43.5	2.8	0.0
Kenya	48.7	16.0	49.1	3.6	1.2
Mozambique	43.1	20.1	49.1	2.3	0.0
Nigeria	49.3	22.7	37.0	2.8	1.0
Tanzania	47.0	22.0	40.5	2.8	1.2
Zimbabwe	47.9	14.4	51.6	3.5	1.9
Central/South America					
Argentina	22.9	9.4	68.3	1.3	2.3
Bolivia	46.6	18.0	46.8	2.7	2.2
Brazil	37.1	8.8	59.3	2.8	2.1
Chile	23.9	7.8	63.3	1.9	0.0
Cuba	19.8	5.6	70.2	1.7	1.1
Dominican Republic	45.8	11.0	57.9	2.9	1.8
Ecuador	41.8	9.5	56.5	3.4	1.8
Haiti	35.8	16.3	50.0	1.6	0.9
Mexico	42.0	8.6	64.7	3.5	1.9
Nicaragua	48.0	13.9	52.8	3.4	2.5
Paraguay	39.8	8.9	61.9	2.9	2.6
Peru	41.0	11.9	54.1	2.8	0.9
Venezuela	36.1	7.0	64.8	3.1	2.5
Western Europe					
Austria	11.3	12.2	71.5	0.2	1.0
Belgium	12.4	11.4	71.0	0.3	1.0
Denmark	12.2	9.9	73.9	0.5	1.0
France	14.0	10.1	73.0	0.6	1.1

Country	Birth rate[a]	Death rate[a]	Life expectancy (years)[b]	Population growth rate (per cent)[c]	Food production growth rate (per cent)[d]
Greece	15.4	8.9	71.4	0.8	2.2
Italy	13.2	9.6	72.0	0.7	1.0
Netherlands	12.5	7.9	74.8	0.9	2.1
Spain	18.0	7.7	72.3	1.2	2.3
Sweden	11.6	10.7	74.5	0.4	1.4
UK	11.8	11.7	70.8	0.1	0.9
West Germany	9.5	11.5	71.3	0.2	0.9
Middle East					
Egypt	37.7	11.8	52.7	2.2	1.0
Iran	42.5	11.5	57.5	2.6	2.3
Iraq	48.1	14.6	52.7	3.4	0.9
Israel	26.1	6.8	73.0	3.0	2.7
Saudi Arabia	49.5	20.2	45.4	3.0	1.0
Syria	45.4	4.8	56.6	3.3	5.0
Turkey	39.6	14.6	53.7	2.7	2.2
South East Asia					
Afghanistan	43.0	21.0	40.3	2.3	1.4
Burma	39.5	15.8	49.6	2.2	1.2
India	35.2	15.9	40.1	2.2	1.7
Indonesia	42.9	16.9	47.5	2.6	1.6
Malaysia	30.9	6.1	68.8	2.8	2.5
Philippines	43.8	10.5	58.4	2.9	3.0
Sri Lanka	29.9	7.7	65.9	1.6	2.8
Eastern Europe					
Albania	33.3	8.1	66.0	2.9	2.1
Bulgaria	16.1	10.7	71.3	0.5	1.2
Czechoslovakia	18.7	11.5	70.2	0.7	1.9
East Germany	13.3	13.4	71.5	−0.2	2.0
Hungary	16.7	12.4	69.5	0.4	2.4
Romania	19.6	9.6	69.7	1.0	3.3
Yugoslavia	17.7	8.4	67.8	1.0	1.8
USSR	18.1	9.6	69.0	0.9	1.6
USA	15.3	8.8	72.6	0.8	1.6
New Zealand	17.8	8.2	71.6	1.4	1.3

[a] Crude rates per 1000 population.
[b] Simple male/female averages; generally, female life expectancy exceeds male.
[c] Average annual rates for the period 1970–77.
[d] Average annual rates for the period 1970–78.
Source: Derived from United Nations (1979), *Statistical Yearbook 1978*. New York, UN, Tables 18, 19 and 24.

Taking both the static and dynamic data together, we can now locate countries along two dimensions. Countries such as the United Kingdom and the United States we should position at a point corresponding to 'oversatisfied' nutritional requirements with every prospect of a continued upward trend in food supply relative to population, at least in the short run. At a mid-point, we might position countries such as Albania, Argentina and Syria, where 'satisfactory' nutritional levels look likely to be maintained as food output grows in line with consumption demand. However, an alarmingly large number of countries, drawn mainly from the non-industrialized regions of the world, would find themselves in a position corresponding to poor nutritional standards with the prospect of further deterioration as population growth outstrips increases in food production. As we suggested earlier, societies will not contemplate lightly the prospect of impending starvation.

There are, in principle, three courses of action open to such malnourished countries. First, they might attempt to increase their domestic food production in line, at least, with their population increases. Second, they might try to obtain food supplies via trade with other regions. These options we shall consider at a later stage; here, we shall consider the third, a reduction in the rate of population growth. Before exploring population policy, let us first examine the determinants of population growth.

6.2.1   FACTORS IN POPULATION GROWTH

During the process of industrialization, Western Europe went through a 'demographic transition'. In its early agricultural period, birth rates appear to have been high, of the order of 40–50 per 1000, although population growth was held in check by a correspondingly high average death rate, brought about by sporadic and pronounced peaks of famine and disease. In the United Kingdom and France particularly, industrialization and material prosperity removed many of the causes of the death peaks. The early industrial period therefore witnessed the beginnings of sustained population growth. Over the longer term, however, European birth rates have slowly fallen. At the present time, both birth and death rates are of the order of 10–15 per 1000. Accordingly, population growth has now declined to a negligible level. Non-European economies that began their industrialization later (such as the United States) all underwent a similar demographic transition.

Over the same period in which birth and death rates were slowly declining in the industrializing world, the non-industrial regions were also entering a demographic transition. However, the agent of their transition was not industrialization *per se* but rather the impact of the industrializing world. It seems likely that the demographic profiles of countries in Africa, Asia and Latin America a few centuries ago were not too dissimilar to those of the pre-industrial European societies – high birth rates with equivalently high death rates. However, the transition experienced to date by these other pre-industrial societies has been characterized by a considerable fall in the death rate with no corresponding decline in the birth rate. Such an imbalance accounts, of course, for the high population growth rates as indicated in *Table 6.1*. Let us consider the contributing factors in more detail.

The earliest declines in the death rate of pre-industrial societies date from the nineteenth century and may be attributed directly to imperialism. By taking formal control over vast tracts of Asia and Africa, for example, the British helped to reduce inter-tribal warfare and thievery, which had become to a large extent endemic and which had contributed greatly to the insecurity of life. Nor was the morality of the imperialists particularly well disposed to a form of population control that, evidence suggests, has been widely practised by all societies until recently, namely infanticide and simple child neglect. Furthermore, the reorganization of production undertaken by the imperialists generally had a positive effect in the first instance upon aggregate production and material living standards; malnutrition thus became a relatively less significant cause of fatality. However, as Petersen (1975) has pointed out,

Before 1940 the effective operation of most death-control measures depended upon a rise in the general welfare level, which, when it occurred, took place slowly. The crucial difference in the post-1945 period is that this prior link between a rise in the level of living and a decline in mortality has been broken to some degree (p. 602).

It is, therefore, in the relatively brief period since the Second World War that the most significant attack on the death rate seems to have been made. In this respect, the use of science and technology in the control and elimination of diseases has been a major factor. For example, the use of pesticides and the clearance of swamps have considerably reduced the impact of insect-transmitted diseases such as malaria, and the use of antibiotics has proved successful in treating diseases such as yaws and syphilis. Mass immunization programmes have contributed to the eradication of communicable diseases such as smallpox in many areas, whilst the maintenance of standards of hygiene and sanitation have assisted in the control of diseases such as cholera.

Relatively low mortality, brought about by disease control and improvements in living standards, is only one half of the demographic profile; we still have to explain the persistence of high birth rates in many regions of the world. One way of considering the characteristic difference between the birth patterns of industrialized and non-industrialized economies is the realization that, whilst we have been considering the relationship between population and food availability in aggregate terms, the actual decision about whether or not to produce children (i.e. whether or not effectively to increase the birth rate) is made at the family or household level. Following T. P. Schultz (1971), we might suppose, on the assumption that the reproduction decision is the subject of planning, that families will assess the decision with respect to the costs and benefits, and the following aspects will be significant. Although children represent a 'consumption' benefit to their parents, i.e. parents 'enjoy' their children, other factors are present. In infancy, for example, a child also represents a cost, since it must be cared for, although the actual period of parental responsibility varies from society to society. On the other hand, there might exist the possibility of material gains to the household if the child undertakes some form of production and contributes to the running of that household. Third, an important cost to be considered is the opportunity cost of resources forgone as a result of child-rearing; important here will be the cost of the parents' (or more usually the mothers') labour time. Fourth, parents will consider the possibility of children dying in infancy; if it is felt that only a proportion of the children will survive to maturity then, *ceteris paribus*, we should expect to find more being produced. Finally, parents may view their children as security provisions for old age, arguing that the production of children could serve as an investment for the long-term future.

If we now consider the rearing of children purely from the investment point of view, we can go on to suggest conditions that would lead families to select a larger rather than a smaller family size as the optimum. First, it should be the case that children should be able to make a productive contribution to the household at as early an age as possible. Second, the opportunities forgone in terms of the mother's labour time should be low. Third, infant mortality should be high and, fourth, long-run household security should depend upon the new generations. A region of the world where such conditions are clearly *not* met is Western Europe. Here, children are excluded from production until they reach some legally enforced school-leaving age (mid-teens) and they must therefore be subsidized by the household up to this time. As production in European countries is typically organized via the factory or office system, parents often find it difficult to maintain regular employment whilst simultaneously devoting themselves to child care, i.e. reproduction is likely to involve the cost of one parent's income. Finally, in such systems, infant mortality is very low owing to medical provisions and high nutritional standards, and the existence of private or state pension and insurance schemes means that children have little impact upon the parents' long-term security.

By contrast, our required conditions are most exactly met in many of the non-industrialized economies of the world, especially those characterized by household-based subsistence agricultural production. Here children may enter the labour force at an early age, owing to the technical simplicity of the tasks involved, and they serve as a complement to adult labour. Furthermore, the tasks of cultivation and child care do not represent the same problem of substitution as they do in factory production; both can, to some extent, be carried on simultaneously. In the absence of social security systems in such economies, parents depend far more on their children for support during illness and old age. All such arguments lead us to the conclusion that one reason for high birth rates in pre-industrial economies is the likelihood that the optimum family size, given the prevailing socio-economic conditions, is far larger than that for the industrialized economies. In short, it is 'rational' to have large families.

The study of Peru by Chaplin (1971b) provides some empirical support for the points made above. In the first place he notes:

> The depressing effect on fertility of female employment is a well-established pattern for developed nations, with the extremes found in communist countries whose inheritance and welfare programs appear to remove the last of the practical advantages of having children (pp. 225–6).

Contrasting this with findings for Turkey, Puerto Rico and Peru, where the incidence of female labour has a negligible fertility effect, he suggests:

> The essential reason for this finding is that most employed women are in occupations which permit, or at least do not conflict with, high fertility i.e. agriculture, service occupations and artisan handicrafts (*loc. cit.*).

Although there is a sizeable factory employment sector in Peru, Chaplin notes that there has been a tendency for firms to discriminate against women because of the specific and rigorous welfare legislation relating to their employment, which has proved expensive to employers. Coinciding with a decline in the female participation ratio, Chaplin observed an increase in fertility, which presumably results from the diminished opportunity cost of child-rearing. An additional finding of relevance is the result obtained by Stys (1957), which relates to peasant production in nineteenth-century Poland. It was discovered that family size tended to vary with the size of land-holding and this is suggestive of (i) larger holdings being able to sustain more people and (ii) more people being necessary to work larger holdings.

In addition to this purely private calculus, the reproductive decision will also be a product of the overall ideological and cultural structure of the society in which the family lives. A number of the world's major religions extol procreation and the natural increase of mankind as divinely inspired virtues in their own right and, in some cases, teach that children are an essential ingredient of a marriage. In certain countries the existence of a large number of children secures social status for the parents, being taken as a sign of potency in the man and femininity in the woman. We should bear in mind that the costs and benefits of a large family are unlikely to be interpreted equally by both father and mother. In his study of the Zulu household, Scotch (1963) discovered that desirable social status was an increasing function of family size although the incidence of hypertension amongst mothers caring for children also increased with family size. This factor became particularly pronounced when more than five offspring were involved. If we were to suppose that Zulu fathers do not suffer from such psychological hardships, we might suggest that the mother's notion of optimum family size might well be at odds with that of the father and the family size actually chosen would depend in part upon the relative authority of each individual in the family decision structure. Finally, we should note the frequent equation of population with military power; nations have, in the past, held it as desirable to increase population in view of the strategic threat posed by neighbours with greater levels of manpower.

6.2.2   POPULATION POLICIES

When it is suggested that a contemporary society 'needs' to adopt a population policy this invariably implies that it should contemplate steps towards reducing fertility. This has not always been the case. In the 1920s and 1930s, for example, the birth- and death-rate trends in Britain gave rise to the belief that the population in that country might actually be declining. This led economists like Reddaway (1939) to speculate upon the undesirable consequences of such a decline to the extent of outlining measures for fertility increases. Suggestions in this respect included the heavier taxation of unmarried individuals and the limitation of female employment opportunities. Even more recently, the French people were exhorted by General de Gaulle to produce more children for the good of France. Such views are no longer fashionable, nor, for that matter, is the other brutally effective method of population limitation, namely an increase in the death rate.

In order to be successful, a fertility-reduction programme must satisfy four requirements. First, it must be ethically acceptable, or viewed as legitimate, by the population concerned. Second, it must be technically viable. Third, it should be designed so that the individual household decision makers find that fertility reduction is economically and socially optimal from their own private point of view. Fourth, the programme must obey the general economic criterion of cost-effectiveness.

As we have suggested, covert population limitation has probably been employed by households since time immemorial, using such 'natural' methods as sexual abstinence, coitus interruptus and infanticide. However, as an explicit goal in national policy terms, the idea is relatively recent in origin and did not really get under way until the 1960s. As Berelson (1971) observes, by 1960 only India, Pakistan and Hong Kong had developed population policy proposals although, by 1970, 25 countries in Africa, Asia and Latin America (comprising two-thirds of the existing population of these regions) had established programmes. In spite of the rapid growth in concern, it is important to recognize that the success of such policies has been variable. Two oft-cited instances of success are Korea and Taiwan where large-scale government contraception and sterilization programmes certainly assisted in bringing about significant fertility declines during the 1960s. Rather than confirming these successes, however, let us contemplate some of the problems with which population policies have to contend.

First, and under the rubric of ethical acceptability, we may cite the ideological and cultural norms mentioned earlier as being possibly inimical to the legitimacy of population control. Certain religions, especially Roman Catholicism, are overtly hostile to many forms of contraceptive practice on moral grounds, either because such practices are held to interfere with the natural consequences of matrimony or because they are thought to encourage sexual promiscuity. We should bear in mind that the fact that certain contraceptive techniques are outlawed does not, of itself, constitute grounds for expecting fertility limitation to be impossible – Catholic countries such as France, Spain and Ireland have all secured substantial reductions in the birth rate over the past century. However, it does seem reasonable to suppose that fertility reduction is more likely to take place in countries where contraception is advocated rather than castigated. Even in cases where religious doctrine is not involved, government population policies might be interpreted as an illegitimate infringement of personal liberty – i.e. it could be held that families have a 'natural right' to produce children as a response to their own private decisions. In the past in fact, Marxists have come close to viewing population control as a neo-imperialist conspiracy. For the Marxist, the weakness of a pre-revolutionary economic system is the imperfect organization of production. The policy of population control (to influence consumption) therefore tackles the problem from the wrong direction; indeed, it focuses attention away from the problem's root cause.

Second, technology has yet to provide us with the 'perfect' contraceptive. The most effective technique – sterilization – carries with it the considerable private cost of probable irreversibility, and thus the restriction of choice. A method that is both cheap and fairly effective – insertion of the intra-uterine device – has proved unsatisfactory in a number of cases, owing to patient rejection and the occurrence of discomfort. The other major methods – condoms, diaphragms, spermicides and oral contraceptives – are all relatively expensive. They therefore represent a considerable long-term cost to the family using them, or the government supplying them, depending upon who is to pay. Furthermore, if the latter forms of contraception are to be at all effective in reducing fertility, they require substantial back-up and distribution facilities – local medical clinics, instruction classes and inspection services. Even with these facilities, fertile couples must still have the motivation to practise contraception. Clearly, the provision of contraceptive services in a country like India, with 800 million people spread over 3 million square kilometres, is an expensive proposition, especially when we consider the opportunity costs of resources in such a materially poor economy.

Finally, we must note that, if a government wishes to inhibit the production of children, it must make such a limitation seem worthwhile from the family's point of view. One possible strategy is to provide financial inducements to those who elect to use the contraceptive techniques, especially those who volunteer to undergo sterilization. The problem here lies in the identification of the appropriate level of remuneration. Presumably a government would find it worthwhile to compensate, say, a man for a vasectomy equivalent to the non-private costs saved from each child that he would have sired. What is likely, however, especially in the agricultural economies, is that the potential father would value the benefits of his children at a higher level than society would value their social costs. Whilst one extra person represents an infinitesimal cost rise to a national economy, it might represent considerable input to a family smallholding. The level of government compensation necessary to prevent the father producing children could therefore be uneconomic. An alternative approach might be to make the production of children more costly to the household by, say, imposing extra taxes on larger families. This strategy has unfortunate consequences in that, first, it immediately imposes additional burdens upon those who are, in all probability, the least able to sustain them and, second, it is likely to prove somewhat unpopular from an electoral point of view in democracies where large families are the norm. In reality, it is only when there is a significant shift in the nature of production that the smaller family becomes optimal from the family's point of view although, in many cases, it is the existence of high rates of population growth that is acting as a brake upon this transition in the nature of production.

Since the 1940s, the dramatic reduction in death rates in pre-industrial societies brought about by the control of disease and limited production improvements led many observers to assume that birth rates would be controllable in a similar manner. The experience of the past two decades has suggested that this is not necessarily the case. Although certain economies have indeed undergone demographic transitions with respect to births as well as deaths, the problems of fertility control in other cases have proved quite intractable. Indeed, Dasgupta (1977) concludes the following in the case of India:

Unless the people are motivated towards family planning and the material conditions in their life are so changed as to make family planning worthwhile, even the most extravagant and spectacular family planning campaigns backed by material incentives and coercive measures for sterilisation are unlikely to succeed. In the immediate future, there is no easy and cheap solution to India's population problem. Even compulsory sterilisation which, apart from raising uncomfortable ethical issues, would be difficult to administer. Hence, any plan for domestic food production will need to take account of the on-going population growth rate (pp. 6–7).

Although we have so far restricted our observations, by and large, to the problems facing those nations with population pressure on the supply of food, this is not to say that the growth of population in the nutritionally rich countries of Europe and North America is necessarily acceptable. Despite the fact that the average citizen of such nations has more than enough to eat, there might nevertheless exist certain causes for concern. In the first place, whilst the household consumption of materially poor nations is heavily weighted in favour of foodstuffs, a significant determinant of consumption standards in the richer nations is energy. This is either consumed directly (as heating or lighting) or indirectly (as an input to production of consumer goods). Energy is, of course, a scarce resource and is, some would argue, becoming distinctly more finite as time goes by. We could therefore use an exactly analogous argument in favour of population control in 'energy-consuming' nations as opposed to 'food-consuming' nations as explored earlier.

Second, the industrialized countries of the world are, with rare exceptions, highly urbanized. Whilst an industrial, urban existence has, to some extent, been the result of perceived advantages of such a lifestyle, it must also be recognized that it can give rise to certain costs. Put simply, to any one individual, other people may constitute pollution. The negative externalities of traffic congestion and atmospheric contamination, for example, may be charged directly against the increasing number of automobiles. Given that motorcars generally do not drive themselves, the prime culprits must be the people inside. Recreational facilities, such as public parks, bathing beaches and the countryside, often yield a lower level of utility to the individual when it is discovered that, come the public holiday, he is obliged to share them with tens of thousands of other town-dwellers. Further, and given that industrial societies generally make a substantial public allocation to the young in terms of health and educational services, an increasing birth rate would presumably necessitate further spending in such areas at an opportunity cost to other sources of welfare. In overall terms, therefore, a society might well discover that its welfare optimum in terms of the 'quality of life' is quite distinct from the optimum defined in terms of the 'quantity of life'.

Finally, and although we have so far been concerned exclusively with the consumption aspects of population, we must bear in mind that population as labour is a key ingredient of production. Population growth in industrialized countries could thus be legitimated in terms of its contribution to output. This production role forms the subject of the next chapter, although we should note here that the technological developments of the past few decades appear to have drastically reduced labour's technical input requirement and the trend shows every sign of continuation. Labour supply no longer appears as a constraint upon growth of output, its place having been taken by general resource availability and the possibilities of demand expansion. Unless industrial societies are willing to reverse the trend of technological innovation, they will be obliged to come to terms with increasing and permanent unemployment of labour. If such unemployment is to be considered an economic problem, then a long-term solution could be found in further reductions in the rate of population growth.

The issues raised above are relevant not only to the industrialized world. We might make similar points in the context of the agricultural economies, and further factors can be added to our general list. In the absence of constitutional change, population growth within an economy might mean that the 'representative democracy' becomes less 'representative'. Since 1830, the population of the United Kingdom has increased by more than 100 per cent, although the number of elected Members of Parliament is presently slightly smaller than it was in 1830. In recent years, concern has grown over mankind's destruction of the natural environment in the search for living space. Whilst such concern is nothing if not well-meaning, the advocates of population control are faced with two unpleasant possibilities. First, even if population limitation is taken to represent a global optimum, it might prove difficult to persuade all individual decision makers, either at the level of the nation state or, particularly, at the level of the household, that it also represents a private optimum. The reasons for this were discussed earlier. Second, given the dynamics of population change, it is clear that, if we wished to effect substantial alterations to the population patterns of the present time, then we should have started two or three decades ago. Ruling out natural (or unnatural) calamities, the labour forces and the number of mature consumers for the year 2000 have already been determined. This is not to say, of course, that demographic momentum is omnipotent. Nevertheless, it is equally clear that the effects of a population control policy will be seen not in a year but, rather, in a generation. A generation is a long time in the life of any individual and, indeed, of any government. In establishing the United States Commission on Population Growth and the American Future, President Nixon wrote: 'When future generations evaluate the record of our time, one of the most important factors in their judgement will be the way in which we responded to population growth' (in Singer, 1971, p. 332). The evidence to date suggests that their judgement is likely to be somewhat unfavourable.

Summary

The individual's consumption decision is influenced by the availability of commodities, his tastes and preferences, his income, time preference and the existence of external effects. Empirical studies of household behaviour suggest that the income elasticity of demand for food is positive but less than unity. Household consumption is also influenced by social class and the age and occupation of the head of the household. Farming households appear to have a high marginal propensity to save, because of uncertainty, reinvestment needs and tenancy arrangements. In his book, *The Joyless Economy*, Scitovsky has warned against equating increased consumption with increased welfare. He argues that the assessment of personal welfare involves comparisons with the welfare of others and that consumers continually redefine their consumption norms at higher levels. Novelty is an important ingredient in welfare. Increases in production disutility necessary to generate consumption utility must also be considered.

Evidence suggests that nutritional standards vary from country to country. Certain economies find themselves in a position where the growth of population is exceeding the growth of food supply. Amongst the factors that have contributed to population growth are rises in living standards and advances in medical technology. In certain economies, the structure of productive organization means that it is optimal for the household to produce many children. In general, larger families are more likely where children enter employment at an early age, where the opportunity cost of the time spent in child care is low, where infant mortality is high, where children are a source of security for parents in old age.

Policies for population control have been advocated for those economies where population growth rates remain high. To be successful, a population control policy must be ethically acceptable, technically viable, cost-effective, and optimal from the individual's point of view. Although such policies have been successful in some countries, their impact in others has been marginal to date. Despite the fact that population growth rates in industrial economies are low, and widespread poverty is not in evidence, there is no reason to suppose that continued population increase even in these countries is desirable.

Further reading

The behaviour of consumers is a central theme of neoclassical microeconomics; representative texts in the field include Green (1976) and Deaton and Muellbauer (1980). Hansen (1972) and Powell (1974) approach consumer analysis from the empirical or applied point of view. Burk (1968) offers a more multidisciplinary approach, whilst Ferber (1973) surveys the literature.

Data for UK household expenditure are derived from Department of Employment (1980) and Central Statistical Office (1980). Data for the FAO nutritional levels are from UN (1980b), pp. 246–62.

Petersen (1975) is an excellent basic text on the subject of population in general. Ridker (1976) is specifically concerned with population issues in poorer economies. In this context, both National Academy of Sciences (1971) and Easterlin (1980) incorporate papers of relevance. India's population problems and policies are examined by Cassen (1978). For a stimulating reappraisal of 'popular population fallacies' see Parsons (1977). Hartley (1972) deals with population growth from the 'quantity versus quality' point of view. In 1974, a World Conference on population growth took place; its findings are reported in UN (1975b). Boserup (1981) discusses the relationship between population and technological change. For an optimistic view of the population issue, see Simon (1981). Overbeek (1974) is a comprehensive survey of population theories.

Chapter Seven

People as Producers

Only a very small minority of the items regularly consumed by individuals occur naturally and can therefore be consumed directly; air is perhaps the most obvious example. The remainder, the great majority, require the transformation of natural resources into welfare-generating items by means of the application of productive inputs, primarily labour power and capital equipment. In this chapter we shall consider aspects of man the consumer's *alter ego*, namely the individual as a labour unit of production. Economists typically describe the transformation process by means of production functions, which we may think of as recipes of input combinations for the output of particular goods and services, and the relevant question to be answered relates to the choosing of the 'best' production function for the purpose. The identification of the optimal function involves us, however, in the discussion of a number of issues related to the nature of production.

In the first place, what determines the feasible set of production alternatives that a society faces? One important class of determinants are really constraints representing the technical laws of the real world. We should not expect, for example, iron to melt at less than around 1200°C, other things remaining equal, irrespective of whether or not we employed more or less labour or, for that matter, whether such labour was organized under a 'socialist' or a 'capitalist' system. Similarly, it seems most improbable that the basic chemical reactions that produce sulphuric acid would be noticeably influenced by the ideology of the chemist. However, even given these technical constraints upon production, most goods will admit the possibility of being produced by a number of possible techniques. Take the case of road construction, for example. Observation of the world tells us that roads may be constructed in at least three ways. First, we could employ a labour-intensive technology, with thousands of men shifting earth by hand. At the opposite extreme, a capital-intensive technology is feasible, involving a handful of men operating giant earth-moving equipment. The intermediate posi-   143 tion could be represented by a factor combination, e.g. a road gang, each member of which is armed with a shovel. If our society attaches welfare to consumption that, in turn, is derived from production, the optimal technique amongst the three must clearly be the one that generates the maximum output per unit of input used. The identification of such an optimum entails the estimation of the opportunity costs and productive contribution of the factors involved.

Second, it is the case in most societies that to consider labour solely as a productive input implies the missing of an important feature of employment. We have seen earlier that many ideologies accept the view that the individual's share of aggregate output should be related in some way to his contribution to the creation of such output. Societies may accordingly aim at the maximization of employment for two reasons: first, more labour inputs should generate more output, other things remaining equal, and, second, employment entitles the individual to a share in national output. Thus, not only can they survive physically, but they do not require subsidization from the contributions of others, assuming that such social security exists in the society in question. However, because of the existence of necessary non-labour factors in the production function, there is no guarantee whatsoever that the production technique that represents the optimum in the sense of maximizing output is identical to the one that maximizes employment. Indeed, a feature of the industrial revolution in Europe was the replacement of labour by capital in certain branches of activity, on the grounds of cost-effectiveness.

Finally, to consider the production function in terms of aggregate labour and capital units is misleading, for labour (and for that matter capital) is not homogeneous. Rather, it has a qualitative as well as a quantitative dimension. If we consider two roads being built by road gangs of ten men each, it seems reasonable to suppose that a gang of ten robust individuals, skilled in the art of shovel-wielding, would perform the task more rapidly than would, say, ten arthritic economics teachers whose abilities do not lie in that direction. The quality of labour with respect to a particular task is not only likely to vary but can be made to vary, and this variation is itself the result of a production process. In this particular case, we might suppose that a great number of individuals (including economics teachers) could become useful road gang members if they were provided with medical and training resources to raise their health and educational statuses to the appropriate level. Clearly, we now have a more subtle production function and it becomes relevant to examine the extent to which we might improve the quality of labour in respect of its increased abilities in producing the particular output concerned. The significance of such labour quality forms the subject of our next section.

7.1 Human capital

Certain commodities typically consumed by individuals have effects additional to the direct satisfaction of immediate needs. Thus, for example, whilst the attainment of good health and a high educational standard may generate utility in their own right, a consequence of consuming health care and education is the likelihood of the individual concerned becoming more productive in the future by virtue of his ability to handle more demanding or more complex tasks. In other words, by purchasing health care and education the individual is not merely consuming in the present period but he is also investing in himself by adding to his productive potential. Economists refer to this as the creation of 'human capital', an analogy to the capitalization process, which increases the productivity of inanimate factor inputs. Let us consider the possible benefits of the increase in human capital, first of all from the point of view of the whole society. We shall use as our example investment in education.

Although the realization that increases in educational levels have a positive impact on the growth of material output has been with us since the time of Adam Smith, attempts to quantify this influence are of only recent vintage. Perhaps the best-known attempt is that of Denison (1967). Denison estimated an aggregate production relationship for the output of a number of Western economies in terms of changes in factor inputs (essentially capital and labour). In particular, he demonstrated that output growth in the 1950s could not be explained solely in terms of input increases; indeed, less than 50 per cent of total growth could in general be put down to changes in input levels. Denison suggested that this 'residual' growth determinant must include factors such as increasing economies of scale, trade expansion and, most importantly, the rising educational standards of the labour force. More recent work by Psacharopoulos (1973) has suggested that the specific contribution of education to economic growth is around 11 per cent for the industrialized economies studied by Denison. More significantly, the recent work also suggests that education's contribution rises as material living standards fall – i.e. up to 16 per cent of economic growth can be ascribed to education for economies with very low levels of aggregate output. In itself of course, education is a heterogeneous commodity, for it embraces different age groups and different subjects of study. The data reported by Psacharopoulos suggest that, of the total contribution of education to economic growth, primary education accounts for perhaps one-half, whilst the contribution of secondary education is higher than that of tertiary, or higher, education.

An alternative way of looking at the same phenomenon is to estimate the social rate of return to education. The procedure involved is the same as the one we might employ to estimate the rate of return for any project involving social costs and benefits over time. In the case of an individual undertaking educational investment, the time profile will typically be as follows. In the short term, society will incur costs, as the individual consumes education. These costs will have two components. First, society will lose the production that the individual would have generated had he not elected to undergo full-time education. Second, it is likely that society as a whole will be obliged to make some direct resource contribution to the individual to permit his education to proceed. The extent of these latter costs will depend upon the extent to which the society in question believes that the individual should be responsible for the finance of his own education. In some cases, he might be obliged to purchase education at market prices; in others, he might be subsidized by the provision of 'free' tuition, maintenance grants and so forth. In the longer term, however, benefits begin to accrue to society as the now-educated or trained individual begins to contribute to aggregate production as an employee. If the education has had the presumed effect, the value of the production created by the educated worker should now exceed what he would have produced had he remained uneducated. Given this profile of costs and benefits, the rate of return can now be estimated. In principle, the calculation takes the following form.

Suppose an individual undergoes 10 years of full-time education and thereafter works for 40 years. For each year (t) of study, society provides him with C_t units of educational resources. Further suppose that, without education, his annual production capability is P_0. As a result of education, this may be raised to P_1. Throughout the individual's training, therefore, society incurs costs equivalent to the educational resources supplied plus the production forgone as a result of the individual not working. Once training is completed, society will gain, to the value of the net production increase that results from education. The social rate of return is the rate of interest that makes society's discounted costs just equal to the stream of anticipated benefits, i.e. it is the rate of interest (i) that solves the equation

$$\sum_{t=0}^{t=9} \frac{(C_t + P_0)}{(1 + i)^t} = \sum_{t=10}^{t=49} \frac{(P_1 - P_0)}{(1 + i)^t}.$$

In effect, society's provision of educational facilities is a gamble, a trade-off between short-run costs against expected increased production in the future. The success of this gamble is measured in terms of the magnitude of the rate of return. Empirical findings, such as those reported by Psacharopoulos (1973), attest to a wide degree of variability of such rates. For a sample of 32 country studies, Psacharopoulos found that social rates of return appeared to lie, on average, in the 10–20 per cent per annum range. Rates seemed to be generally higher in poorer economies although, in all cases, rates declined as the level of education increased. Measured in these terms, primary education appears to be 'worth more' to society than, say, university education. Across countries, there appeared to be a considerable difference in rates of return from male, as opposed to female, education. This finding presumably reflects the differing extents of female participation in the labour force, since P_0 and P_1 will be estimated from the prevailing labour market conditions. If female employment is uncommon in certain sectors, or if wage discrimination against females is prevalent, returns to female education will naturally appear to be low. Finally, the overall type of education was also significant in determining rates of return. From a technical point of view, some subjects are more conducive to material output growth than others.

Although empirical results do differ from one country to the next, reflecting as they do the specific demand and supply conditions within each, the evidence does suggest that educational investment has a strongly beneficial impact upon a nation's pursuit of economic progress. The same can also be said in the case of the individual's pursuit of material prosperity. Most societies reward increased production on the part of the individual with increased income, although the equivalence is not always one-for-one. In their analyses of the United States, for example, both Becker (1964) and Denison (1964) estimated that the proportion of personal income gain attributable to a college education was approximately two-thirds. A more recent study of the United Kingdom (Psacharopoulos and Layard, 1979) suggested that some 50 per cent of the individual's earning power could be explained by the level of his educational attainment. Such evidence leads us to suppose that it is likely to prove optimal for the individual, purely from his own private point of view, to invest in education to enhance his earning prospects.

The individual's investment decision can be modelled in a fashion analogous to the social rate of return calculation described above. Suppose that a society requires that an individual finance his own training, at least in part. He might therefore be required to pay, say, annual educational fees (F_t). The other major cost incurred by the individual whilst undergoing education is the income forgone (Y_0) net of taxation (T_0) that he might otherwise have been earning. Having received his education, the individual will subsequently earn more income (Y_1) although, assuming that the society's tax system is progressive, he will be required to pay a higher amount in taxation (T_1). For the individual, therefore, the private rate of return is the rate of interest (i) that solves the equation

$$\sum_{t=0}^{t=9} \frac{F_t + (Y_0 - T_0)}{(1 + i)^t} = \sum_{t=10}^{t=49} \frac{(Y_1 - T_1) - (Y_0 - T_0)}{(1 + i)^t}.$$

The prospect of a positive rate of return will clearly be an important factor in influencing the individual's demand for education, although other such factors might well exist. Individuals might also, for example, enjoy education as a consumption good – i.e. they might associate positive utility with the process of being educated *per se*. Further, education may permit them to attain desirable social status. The empirical evidence, again as summarized by Psacharopoulos (1973), suggests that the broad patterns of private rates of return are similar to those of the social rates of return, with the exception that the former are usually a few percentage points higher than the latter. Considered in these terms, it seems that education is 'worth more' to the individual than to the society. One reason for the difference in rates arises from the fact that, in many countries, the individual's education is subsidized, and the present value of his future additional tax contributions, resulting from his higher earning power, is insufficient to cover this subsidy element.

Accepting the pivotal role of human capital formation in the creation of material progress, two policy issues raise themselves. First, how much investment in human capital will be required? Social rate of return analysis provides a broad guide because a positive rate indicates that net benefits are accruing to society. More precisely, economic theory suggests that society will find it desirable to invest in projects, of which the formation of human capital may be considered as one amongst many, until the rates of return are equal for all. Indeed, such a criterion might be employed within the education sector itself. If a society estimates that the social rate of return from higher education exceeds that of university education, it might devote its resources to the expansion of the former at the expense of the latter.

In reality, investment decisions are likely to be more subtle for a number of reasons. First, an economy is a complex interactive system and returns from investment in one area of human capital formation might well be contingent upon investment in another. Thus, for example, it might only prove worthwhile to train additional airline pilots if society also trains more engineers to build the extra aeroplanes for these pilots to fly. Similarly, society might be unable to find employment for all its trained garment makers if it has an insufficient number of people able to weave the cloth. Second, the realization of returns from education may be complicated by time lags. A society that suddenly finds itself in need of more doctors might well have to wait ten years before these doctors became available – five years for the medical schools to be built and five years for the first graduates to enter practice. Third, the level of capital formation that a society deems necessary will be determined by its view of the minimum standards of capital provision with which all citizens ought to be provided. Certain countries, for example, stipulate that all children must attend school for at least a minimum number of years; other countries do not. Fourth, the realized returns from invest-ment may be contingent upon changes in technology. The automation of a productive process, for example, can easily render redundant labour skills that, at the time, proved costly to acquire.

Such complexities take us onto the second policy issue, namely the organization for the provision of human capital formation. For most real-world economies, the complications mentioned above are sufficient to support a case for a certain amount of centralized direction of resources. Indeed, the case is strengthened by the acknowledgement of the existence of externalities, whereby one person's investment in human capital has implications for the welfare of others. An individual who does not voluntarily invest in health care, for example, may be more likely to transmit communicable diseases to others and would also probably make a lower contribution to overall production than would a 'healthy' individual. Amongst the educational externalities identified by Blaug (1972) are income gains to future generations resulting from a better-educated present generation, assistance in occupational mobility, the transmission of cultural values, and benefits to others as a result of the individual's increased productivity. Left to his own devices, therefore, the individual might undertake 'too little' investment from society's point of view, either because of his own personal preferences or because he has insufficient resources to purchase the investment. Society might accordingly intervene, by means of legal compulsion or subsidy, to ensure that the external benefits are realized.

The individual, we have argued, will be interested in investing in himself in the expectation of securing a higher income. He will therefore demand education in conditions where the expected rate of return is sufficiently high. To some extent, society is likely to share his enthusiasm because of the educated (or healthy) individual's increased productive contribution. However, this does not mean that society will necessarily be interested in supporting *all* forms of educational or health care investment. Considered as a selfish entity, it will allocate its resources, in the form of government expenditure, to the areas that appear most productive from its own point of view. It is widely accepted, for example, that the social returns to primary education, which imparts literacy and other social skills, are so high as to warrant major disbursements from public funds. At a later stage in the individual's career, a particularly attractive form of education from society's point of view is 'on the job' training, because it lowers society's net costs during the training period (as opposed to the higher costs of full-time education). Eason (1963) noted that major improvements in the quality of the Soviet labour force were made at low cost using this method. Expected returns will play a part in determining the precise nature of government provision, in the sense of determining what types of education will be subsidized. A growth-oriented government, for example, might be more willing to subsidize engineering students than artists. Finally, we might consider the assertion of Youngson (1967) that 'education is the most powerful of all solvents of existing institutions and ways of life' (p. 161). Government interest in supporting education might therefore be influenced by the extent to which it regards the dissolving of existing institutions as desirable.

A general idea of the importance attached by contemporary societies to human capital formation can be obtained by examining expenditure allocations. Global public expenditure on education in 1979 was around 6 per cent of world GDP. Of the regions, Latin America was the smallest spender, with an allocation of some 4 per cent of regional GDP. The United Kingdom, the United States and the Soviet Union, in contrast, were amongst the highest spenders (6–7 per cent of the total outputs). The average public expenditure on health care for the OECD group of countries in the mid-1970s was also around 6 per cent of GDP. Such public expenditure data provide only a minimum value for total spending on education and health care because (i) in market economies, health care and education are also purchased from the private sector, and (ii) an 'informal' sector also exists in most economies, for example, 'on the job' training in the education area.

We have suggested that, by a process of investment, the individual can be made more productive. However, the entire argument thus far rests upon a crucial assumption – that the individual will actually be able to use his new-found skills or improved health to generate output. Clearly, if society is unable to find any use for the individual's abilities, then the investment expenditure (as investment but not necessarily as consumption expenditure) represents a waste of scarce resources. The efficient use of labour is accordingly a question of relating manpower supply, both qualitative and quantitative, to manpower requirements. Let us now examine the position of labour supply in one specific set of circumstances.

7.2   Industrialization and the dual economy

In Chapter 6 we examined the consumption aspects of population. Specifically, we were concerned with cases where the growth of societies' outputs was being matched or even surpassed by the growth of populations hoping to consume such outputs. In general, the economies that are experiencing population pressure of this nature are predominantly agricultural; the bulk of economic activity is devoted to the production of the basic means of subsistence. Of course, at an earlier stage in human history, *all* economies were agricultural but, since then, a number have become highly industrialized. In the economies of Western Europe and North America, output has expanded and diversified to a considerable extent. It is instructive to enquire into this industrialization process if only because of the possibility of the experience of the industrialized world serving as a guide to economic policy in those agricultural economies that have not yet made, but wish to make, such a transition in production. In this analysis of industrialization, we shall now view population in a different light; the emphasis will be less on man as a consumer and more on man as a producer – i.e. population considered as a supply of labour input.

The following analysis rests on the formative contributions of, amongst others, Lewis (1954), Jorgenson (1961) and Fei and Ranis (1964). We shall begin by constructing a highly simplified model and then explore the implications of some of our assumptions at a later stage. Consider an agricultural economy characterized by a large number of household producers. Each household is engaged in production for family subsistence. We shall assume that each member of the household participates in production, i.e. population is equivalent to labour supply. As families reproduce, we might expect the household labour input to rise accordingly. However, with a fixed technology, the law of diminishing returns suggests that a point will be reached beyond which further increases in the labour force have no positive impact upon output. Indeed, a point could even be reached where increases in labour input cause output to fall, owing to diseconomies of scale. Thus we can construct a total agricultural product function for our model economy; this is TP_A in *Figure 7.1*, with production reaching a maximum at Q_A. The output for any production period will be devoted to two uses, immediate consumption and investment for production in the next period. We shall take total consumption (TC) to be a simple linear function of population, and the slope of this line (a) indicates the average subsistence level.

Suppose our economy is presently in an equilibrium position with

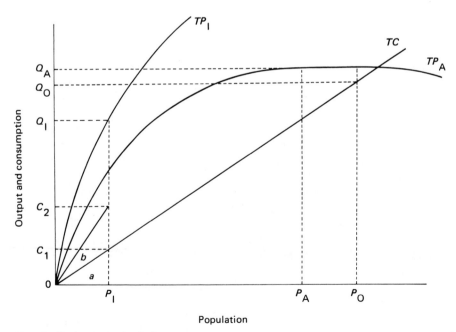

Figure 7.1 Production in the dual economy

population P_0. It is producing an output Q_A, of which Q_0 is consumed. The residual $(Q_A - Q_0)$ we shall take to be just sufficient to ensure the reproduction of the same output in future time periods. For convenience at this stage, we shall assume that population remains constant at this level, P_0. Let us now introduce a second form of activity into our model, creating a two-sector or dual economy. This activity we might label 'industry' and we shall endow it with an initial capital stock. The essential feature of this industry is that, at all points, the marginal product of labour is higher than that for agriculture. We can therefore construct a total industrial product function, TP_I. At present, of course, this function is purely notional because all our available labour force is engaged in agricultural production. Consider what happens, however, when we begin to move labour out of agriculture and into industry. If we remove an amount of labour $(P_0 - P_A)$ from agriculture, total agricultural output remains unchanged (Q_A). However, we have now liberated labour for employment in industry, equivalent to the amount $P_I = (P_0 - P_A)$. By redeploying this labour, the total output of our economy will rise, from Q_A to $(Q_A + Q_I)$. From a collective point of view, this movement must be seen as beneficial because we are now producing more output from the same labour input. However, can we necessarily convince the individual agricultural worker that he ought to move into industry in order to generate the increased production?

A simple expedient might be to coerce the agricultural labour surplus $(P_0 - P_A)$. Assuming that it possessed the power, the government of our economy might simply round up the spare labour and set them to work in the factories under threat of dire penalties. The more faint-hearted might prefer a milder alternative. Suppose our society were to offer potential industrial workers a reward for leaving agriculture, in the form of increased consumption benefits. This reward is represented by the slope, b, in *Figure 7.1*. Such discrimination in consumption benefits between industrial and agricultural workers has a consequence of twofold importance. First, the prospect of a higher consumption level resulting from industrial employment should induce voluntary labour migration from agriculture, compensating the individual for the costs of relocation and such like. Second, it is likely that, in industry, the extra consumption benefits paid out to workers $(C_2 - C_1)$ will be less than the gross industrial output produced (Q_I). Industry will thus generate an output surplus that represents an investment fund. Such resources can now be employed, in either the industrial or the agricultural sector, to raise labour productivity, and therefore aggregate output, still further. Once this has taken place, a further productive surplus will again be generated. Such industrialization accordingly brings about economic expansion and also produces the resources necessary to fuel continued expansion.

To summarize, the model sees population pressure as a labour surplus in an activity where the marginal product of labour is low. Indeed, between P_A and P_0, marginal product is zero. The strategy of relocating labour to a new economic sector where its marginal product is higher will give rise to a net output increase, in addition to an investible surplus to facilitate further expansion. The questions we must ask of our model are therefore (i) how realistic a description is it of the industrialization process that actually took place in those countries where output expansion and diversification occurred, and (ii) what insights does it provide for economic policy in pre-industrial economies where a labour surplus might conceivably exist?

The hypothesis that labour transfer during the industrialization process, from low to high marginal product sectors, is an integral factor in economic growth can, in general, be sustained. Growth studies of the industrialized economies, such as those of Denison (1967), confirm that this is a major factor in explaining growth differentials. The point is perhaps made most forcibly by Kaldor (1966) in his explanation of the low rate of growth of material output in the United Kingdom since 1945, relative to the growth rates of other Western countries. Kaldor argues that aggregate output increases result primarily from the growth in manufacturing production, owing to a relatively high labour productivity realized by scale economies. The economies of Western Europe (excluding the United Kingdom) have experienced rapid growth of manufacturing since 1945, largely due to the fact that they had available substantial reserves of low-productivity agricultural labour. Denison (1968) records, for example, that, whilst the British agricultural population in 1950 was some 5 per cent of the total labour force, the corresponding proportion for economies such as France, West Germany and Denmark was 25–30 per cent (p. 254). Since 1950, the agricultural population has declined considerably in such countries, being accompanied by high overall growth rates as displaced labour enters more productive areas. By contrast, the agricultural population of the United Kingdom had fallen to the 25 per cent figure by the beginning of the nineteenth century. This source of potential growth was therefore exhausted by the beginning of the twentieth century.

However, whilst we can safely assert that labour relocation of the form described is certainly a *potential* engine of economic growth, we should be careful not to make any stronger generalizations. There is no evidence that labour shake-out *must* lead to higher growth rates. Deane and Cole (1967) have estimated that the British growth rate was a little less than 3 per cent per annum at the beginning of the nineteenth century, and that it fell, during the middle decades, to 2.0–2.5 per cent. The highest growth rates – slightly in excess of 3 per cent per annum – occurred at the end of the century. However, the average British growth rate for the period 1950–64 was 2.8 per cent per annum. It seems clear, therefore, that the growth rate in Britain during the nineteenth century relocation period was not noticeably different from the rate in the 1950s and 1960s, when the source had been exhausted.

We should further add that the existence of an agricultural labour surplus cannot be considered as a prerequisite for growth because of the effects of other factors of production. Refinements in production technology, and the substitution of labour by other inputs, can easily give rise to material growth without necessarily requiring any alteration in the balance of employment. Given the histories of the Western economies, which involve invention and innovation, international trade and imperialism, developments in commerce and in transport, it becomes clear that the relocation of labour forms only one factor in a complex pattern of causation of output expansion.

Let us now turn to our second point, the relevance of the approach to contemporary economies characterized by subsistence agricultural production and a labour surplus. The first implication to notice is the contrast between the 'dual economy', composed of the agricultural and the industrial sectors, and the 'Malthusian economy' that we met in Chapter 2. This latter type of economy was locked into a low-level equilibrium from which it could escape only by the injection of a sizeable 'critical minimum effort'. Policy in this case would involve the application of a once-and-for-all resource injection. By contrast, the dual economy model permits policy at the margin. Although we have described it in terms of transferring 'blocks' of labour, the processs will clearly still operate on an incremental basis, albeit with smaller and slower increases in production levels per time period. Labour can, in other words, be gradually removed from agriculture with no loss of production and can be relocated, equally gradually, into industry to begin to yield the productive surplus to sustain growth. In theory, therefore, policy is not an 'all-or-nothing' choice as in the low-level equilibrium case, but a question of setting a rate of labour transfer appropriate to the costs of relocation, the availability of industrial capital (the amount of which need only be small for the model to operate) and the expected benefits from industrial production. Governments with small budgets at their disposal and that do not happily contemplate the social tensions precipitated by dramatic economic change may well be encouraged by the prospects for gradual transition that the dual economy approach suggests. Unfortunately, the reality is not so rosy as the picture we have been painting, for, in developing our model, we have made several implicit assumptions that may legitimately be called into question.

In the first place, our model suggests that there exists a proportion of the agricultural labour force whose marginal contribution to production is negligible. Although such workers might appear to make a contribution to output, they are, in effect 'unemployed', for their removal would have no effect upon the level of output. This phenomenon is referred to as 'disguised unemployment'. However, does it exist in reality? There are good reasons for suggesting that, in certain cases, it might not. Sen (1968) makes the important distinction between the number of labourers employed and the amount of labour-time involved and argues that what we see as 'disguised unemployment' is simply a relatively large number of people working relatively few hours each. To say that such a pattern represents labour redundancy necessitates establishing some sort of criterion of the amount of daily labour-time that the individual 'ought' to work, and such a criterion can hardly be established objectively. Those empirical studies that have been undertaken, such as those of Schultz (1964), Mathur (1964) and Desai and Mazumdar (1970), do not indicate that labour can be easily relocated without output declines. Furthermore, the fact that agriculture is very much a seasonal activity means that whilst, on occasions, a proportion of the agricultural labour force might be observed to be idle under any criterion, at other times farms might experience labour shortages, e.g. during planting and harvesting. Indeed, the practice of hiring additional labour during peak periods in many agricultural economies attests to labour's positive marginal product in such cases. The possibility of agricultural labour having a positive marginal product poses a problem for our dual economy model, for it means that labour can only be transplanted into industry at the expense of some level of agricultural production. Whilst, in aggregate, the agricultural loss could be more than compensated for by industrial output gains, it will pose a specific problem for economies at a very basic subsistence level. For such economies, it will entail, at the limit, starvation, which could only be alleviated by expenditure on food imports. Such a revenue cost might well outweigh the anticipated industrial output benefits.

Second, our model assumed that population was equivalent to labour supply. This is unrealistic because, whilst household subsistence production is indeed characterized by the participation of most members of the family, we should expect at least some members (such as the extremely old and the extremely young) to make no productive contribution whatsoever. These individuals would be pure consumers. Such an objection can be accommodated within our model, however, if we consider the 'household', rather than the individual, to be the unit both of consumption and of production. As long as we can assume some fixed ratio of individual producers to dependent consumers within each household, the analysis can be made to apply. Rather, it is our assumption about the fixed level of population that creates the problems. If we permit the population to grow in our model, beyond P_0, then the investible surplus and agricultural output will decline. Changes in population growth will lead to a changing ratio between producers and dependants. Further, if we subscribe to the Malthusian argument, it is conceivable that any gradual change in material living standards will evoke a direct response from population growth.

The existence of population growth will, of course, have a potentially beneficial impact by making available still more input for industrial production. Here, however, we encounter a third problem; we have no guarantee that industry will actually require all the labour available. Indeed, there are at least three reasons for supposing that our new industrial sector will not take up as much labour as we might like. First, much of the capital equipment employed in the industrializing world is obtained from the industrialized economies. Such equipment tends to have been developed to permit factor substitution away from labour. Second, if industrializing economies are to manufacture commodities for the world market they will be obliged to produce items that are attractive to buyers in the industrialized world. Such commodities often have to be produced using capital-intensive technologies, by virtue of the nature of the commodities. Third, capital will not employ labour in the dual economy case if the displaced agricultural labour does not possess the necessary skills. Overall, therefore, a policy of induced labour migration might well result in the creation of high levels of unemployment, in view of a relatively low demand for industrial labour. In his study of Egypt, Mabro (1967) noted that the industrialization process was being accompanied by population growth and an emphasis on capital-intensive technology. As a result, the industrial labour surplus was being maintained. A similar experience has been recorded in the case of Taiwan (Ho, 1972), although some changes have been recorded more recently with the influx of capital from Japan.

Fourth, we come to the problem of the wage differential between the agricultural and the industrial sectors. The setting of this differential requires careful consideration for two reasons. First, we might expect that the knowledge that industrial workers were receiving higher consumption benefits would induce some reaction on the part of those still producing in agriculture. In an effort to redress the balance, the latter might be tempted to adjust agricultural prices or outputs to secure outcomes favourable to themselves. To prevent the industrial labour force being 'held to ransom', some form of government control over agricultural production will presumably be required. Such control was practised in the Soviet Union during the 1930s. In this particular case, the government actively discriminated against the agricultural sector in an effort to provide capital and labour resources for the nascent industrial sector. Second, the setting of a wage differential at too high a level will encourage a degree of migration that might not only bring about a decline in agricultural output but that might also yield a quantity of labour in excess of industrial requirements. Many industrializing economies are currently experiencing an industrial labour surplus, indicating that the wage differential might well be excessive.

To this list of principal objections to the approach we may easily add others. Our model presumes, for example, that in some sense the industrial sector is more productive than the agricultural. Although, in reality, this tends to be the case, there is no universal rule that says it must be so. If the reverse were indeed true, we should presumably wish to encourage migration from industry into agriculture. Again, we have assumed that 'industry' and 'agriculture' are discrete and independent sectors, although it is quite possible for the production functions of the two to be interrelated in some fashion. Finally, we have yet to identify the origin of the initial capital endowment of our industrial sector. The indigenous industrialization of the European economies was facilitated, to a large extent, by the mobilization of an agricultural surplus through established capital markets. In the Soviet Union, such a surplus was mobilized by centralized government direction. In the poor economies of the present day, the agricultural surplus is, on average, extremely low. Therefore, some exogenous source of capital, such as international economic aid, may be crucial in determining the extent to which industrialization might be brought about.

The problems entailed by the dual economy approach to industrialization have not been examined with the intention of demonstrating that the gradualist approach to economic policy, especially in poor economies, is invalid. Rather, we have been concerned to show that prospective solutions may well give rise to inadvertent outcomes. One of these outcomes is the creation of overt labour unemployment, and the problem of unemployment is not confined to the industrializing nations. Indeed, the 1970s witnessed the gradual expansion of labour unemployment in many industrial economies, and we shall now consider this aspect of 'people as producers' (or, more accurately, people as non-producers) in more detail.

7.3   The unemployment problem

Unemployment is an extraordinarily difficult concept to measure on a comparative basis, due, in part, to the heterogeneity of economic systems. We have already seen, for example, that, for economies where subsistence agriculture is the predominant form of production, it is quite likely to be the case that a substantial proportion of the labour force may appear to be unemployed for parts of the year, whilst being in great demand at other times. In contrast, such seasonal unemployment will be far less significant in the highly industrialized, wage-labour economies. Second, the precise definition of the labour force might be ambiguous. The position of female labour is a case in point. Because of the particular historical evolution of pre-industrial societies, female labour is commonly considered as integral to overall labour effort. Industrial societies have evolved the role of 'housewife', whose productive contributions are not sold in the market. If all the 'housewives' of affluent countries who are not currently registered with their local employment offices as being available for wage-labour suddenly did register, then the unemployment rates in these countries would increase by several hundred per cent overnight! A third possible source of confusion is between labour (on a head-count basis) and labour input. This will be a function of the particular occupational practices of the economy concerned. Suppose an economy of 200 adults had 125 of them putting in eight hours of labour per day, whilst the remaining 75 pairs of hands were idle although actively seeking work. Unemployment in this economy is 37.5 per cent. However, suppose the economy were to be restructured so that everyone worked a five-hour day. Note that we have magically eliminated unemployment on a per capita basis although the actual amount of real resource input – labour-time – remains the same. The essential point is that unemployment rates are only comparable if we can assume identical working practices.

Given these problems, it is hard to make robust statements regarding the unemployment position in various parts of the world. We are on the safest ground with the Western industrial economies, which possess established social accounting procedures as well as a certain homogeneity of industrial and employment structures. Even so, comparisons between countries are difficult to make because, for example, unemployment data based on sample surveys of the labour force often present a different picture from data compiled from registrations with unemployment offices. Individuals might well be unemployed but not registered as such. Nevertheless, the data presented in *Table 7.1* do support the view that unemployment in Western economies generally rose throughout the 1970s, although some countries clearly fared better than others in this respect.

TABLE 7.1 Unemployment rates in Western industrialized economies (per cent)

Country[a]	1970	1979
Australia	1.6	6.2
Austria	2.4	2.0
Belgium	2.9	10.9
Ireland	7.2	9.3
Italy	5.4	7.7
Japan	1.1	2.1
Netherlands	1.1	5.1
Spain	1.1	7.9
Sweden	1.5	2.1
UK	2.6	5.7
USA	4.9	5.8
West Germany	0.7	3.8

[a] Data for Australia, Italy, Japan, Sweden and the United States are compiled from sample surveys; remaining data compiled from administrative records.

Source: International Labour Office (1980), *Yearbook of Labour Statistics*. Geneva, ILO, pp. 282–4

Our knowledge of unemployment in other parts of the world remains more limited. With respect to the Soviet Union, Nove (1977) remarks that 'unemployment naturally exists in the Soviet Union, though we do not know its extent' (p. 219). Ellman (1979) asserts with more confidence that the USSR 'has experienced continuous urban full employment since 1930' and he goes on to suggest that this has also been the case for the remaining European socialist economies (p. 160). Ellman argues that the goal of full employment has been emphasized over the past 50 years, and that a number of factors have been instrumental in attaining it. There have always, for example, been legal restrictions on labour migration from agriculture, the effects of which have been reinforced by a deliberate policy to restrict wages in the industrial sector. Such a policy also permitted the accumulation of sizeable investment surpluses, which gave rise, in turn, to expanding employment opportunities. More recently, the Soviet Union has favoured the expansion of educational opportunities and the reduction of the retirement age, resulting in the effective contraction of average labour-time per worker. Thus the demand for labour on a per capita basis has increased.

For the pre-industrial and industrializing economies of Africa, Asia and Latin America, such data as are available suggest there exists a considerable degree of variation in rates of industrial unemployment. Labour market surveys for Egypt and the Philippines, for example, record unemployment rates of 3.6 and 4.4 per cent respectively for 1978. Similar surveys of urban areas of Colombia and Chile suggest 1978 rates of 8.9 and 13.7 per cent respectively. In the case of India, employment office statistics recorded that some 10 million individuals were registered as being available for work in 1977. Given a total non-agricultural employment figure of around 20 millions, this suggests an unemployment rate for India of a far higher order of magnitude.

It is widely accepted that employment opportunities in economies such as those cited above have been contracting over the past two decades. Gregory (1980), however, challenges this view. The analysis of employment data for some 40 low-income economies leads him to the following conclusions. First, most poor economies have experienced the expansion of employment in secondary and, especially, tertiary sectors in recent years. In the majority of cases, the fastest-growing occupation group has been that composed of managerial, clerical and professional workers; the second most rapid growth has been sustained by craftsmen and industrial labourers. As a proportion of the total labour force, agricultural workers have declined in virtually all the countries that Gregory examined. Second, there has been an 'unambiguous decline' in the contribution of the self-employed farmer and the 'unpaid family worker' to agriculture. Third, trends in unemployment rates are difficult to identify, although no single economy appears to have experienced a distinct increase in 'open' unemployment. As Gregory appreciates, these conclusions are very much conditioned by the nature and the availability of the data; we noted earlier that the extent of unemployment within the subsistence agriculture sector is difficult to define. Further, irrespective of the past unemployment record, high levels of unemployment still exist in many of these economies. The future absorption of such unemployment cannot but be hampered by population growth rates of 2–3 per cent per annum.

Although our estimates lack precision, we must clearly conclude that the unemployment of labour resources is widespread. However, should unemployment necessarily be considered a problem? There are several reasons why it should. First, we have argued that material plenty is an objective espoused by most societies and, in general, the more inputs we can push into production, then the more output we can obtain. By not using a productive input, such as labour, we are denying ourselves the welfare benefits of the output that it might have produced. Second, at the level of the individual rather than the society, lack of participation in production usually entails ineligibility to participate in consumption. As, in most economies, consumption rewards are related to productive input, the unemployed person will find himself presented with severely restricted consumption opportunities. Now, most industrialized economies operate social security systems under which the unemployed without incomes receive consumption benefits via the government. Such benefits, however, are merely transfer payments. The necessary resources are taxed away from those actually in employment. Higher levels of unemployment therefore require a higher subsidy from the employed to the unemployed. Whilst this might prove perfectly acceptable to the inhabitants of societies with collective consciences, economies composed of persons with more individualistic dispositions might well find it unpalatable. Finally, we should note that unemployment can give rise to some undesirable sociological outcomes – boredom, frustration, anomie and hostility. If all these assertions are correct, therefore, unemployment certainly seems to constitute a problem demanding a fairly immediate solution. Although the problem is a universal one, however, it is likely that it will be manifested differently in different economic circumstances. Let us therefore consider just one example, the nature of unemployment in East Africa.

7.3.1 UNEMPLOYMENT IN EAST AFRICA

The countries of East Africa, notably Kenya, Tanzania and Zambia, are in many respects 'classic' examples of dual economies, for they possess industrial, wage-labour sectors emerging alongside the predominant subsistence agriculture sector. Since independence in the 1960s, these economies have all experienced labour migration from agriculture, partly as a result of the industry/agriculture wage differential. As industrial demand for labour has not kept pace with migration and population growth, all now possess high levels of urban unemployment – Fry (1979a) has estimated that the rate of unemployment in the urban areas of Zambia may be as high as 22 per cent, and at least 9 per cent even allowing for 'informal' employment such as domestic service (pp. 57–62).

Morawetz (1974) has identified three approaches to policy formulation with respect to reducing industrial unemployment. The first, the 'laissez-faire' solution, is to permit market forces to lower the industrial wage rate to an equilibrium level that ensures full employment. Second, we might argue that the market solution is not predictable in this context and what is required is some form of government regulation such as migration control or incomes policies. Finally, we might argue that such 'tinkering' with the system will do nothing to resolve its inherent defects and the only solution is a radical restructuring of ownership rights and industrial organization.

A rigorous testing of the market solution hypothesis in the case of Kenya has been undertaken by Rempel and House (1978). Taking data for the period 1964–72, they discovered that the rate of growth of wages in industry exceeded that for agriculture and the public sector, and also exceeded the rate of growth of industrial employment. The average urban/rural wage differential over the period was around 2.5:1 although a certain degree of regional variation appears to have existed. The co-existence of relatively high and stable wages with labour surpluses in most areas of the 'modern' industrial sector of the Kenyan economy, and indeed the perpetuation of wage growth in spite of increases in labour availability, led Rempel and House to conclude that the determination of wages was effectively divorced from the normal demand/supply mechanism. They accordingly began to search for other factors to explain the specific pattern observed.

Economic theory suggests that wage levels might well be a function of the strength of unionization in an industry or firm, i.e. the extent of the collective coercive power that labour can direct against management. However, it was discovered in the Kenyan case that unionization could not satisfactorily explain wage levels in different areas of the industrial sector, although it was thought to be a contributor to the urban/rural differential. Also, there appeared little evidence that the government was acting as a 'wage-leader' by paying high salaries to public sector employees that served as a standard for industrial wages. Rather, it appeared to be the case that the main determinants of wages were, first, the historical structure of payments that had evolved at the time of independence and that had become established as a norm and, second, the 'ability to pay' of particular firms. Indeed, this ability to pay was selected by Rempel and House as 'the most consistent determinant of inter-industry wage differences' (p. 179) and the ability to pay was especially strong in cases of product monopoly, capital-intensive production and where firms were foreign-owned. Indeed, 'within the manufacturing sector, the level of wages paid was found to be correlated positively with both plant size and the presence of foreign-owned firms in the industry' (p. 41). Actually, the existence of large monopolies in the industrial sector has wider implications. Rempel and House point out that, not only do such firms act as a magnet for rural labour by paying high wages, but they also discourage small-scale enterprise (by virtue of its inability to compete) whilst generating little economic spin-off (as most of their operations are contained within the firm).

The conclusion to be drawn from this analysis would seem to be that, for the Kenyan economy at least, the 'laissez-faire' solution – the obtaining of a labour market equilibrium via competition to lower wage rates – is unlikely to be successful. Some form of government intervention therefore appears to be a prerequisite and, if the objective is to reduce labour mobility brought about by wage differentials, an obvious candidate for implementation is an incomes policy. In fact, Kenya, Tanzania and Zambia have all had experiences of incomes policies since the mid-1960s although, as Fry (1979a) has shown, their roles have been disparate.

The most fruitful comparative analysis is that between Zambia and Tanzania, for both countries invited the International Labour Office to send missions in the late 1960s to design incomes policies appropriate to the country concerned. Fry makes the important point that the potential success of an incomes policy is crucially dependent upon a government's resolution actually to redistribute incomes, and he notes three broad contrasts between the Zambian and Tanzanian proposals. First, whilst the Zambian proposals had little to say about minimum wage determination in absolute terms, the Tanzanian solution was to establish rural living standards as a norm for industrial wages. Second, whilst the Zambian plan was to improve the lot of the agricultural population by expanding the marketing potential, the Tanzanian proposal involved the development of positive incentives for increased production, especially by means of tax reform. Finally, the Tanzanian plan was more explicit in its advocation of profit-sharing and the taxation of high profit levels in cases where firms were protected from the rigours of competition.

In terms of the outcomes of the two policy proposals, Fry concludes that the Tanzanian experience has proved the more positive to date. In the case of Zambia, he notes that many of the institutions set up to implement the incomes policy were rapidly dissolved. A 'pay restraint' policy initially established appears to survive only in a 'voluntary' form. In contrast, Fry accords a certain degree of success to the Tanzanian policy. Between 1967 and 1972, real wages in industry were roughly constant whilst industrial employment rose by 20 per cent. The enlarged gap between total output and total wage bill permitted a doubling of the gross investment level over the same period (p. 161). Fry cites the one failure of the Tanzanian policy as the government's inability to peg industrial wages to living standards in agriculture.

The possibilities for government intervention to solve the unemployment problem are not, of course, limited to incomes policies. Depending upon the nature of the economic system, a reorganization of land ownership might have the effect of increasing average incomes in agriculture and thus of staunching the flow of labour to the urban centres. Land reform in Kenya, for example, began in the pre-independence period with the consolidation of small-scale holdings. Coupled with land regis-tration, this provided a far higher level of security of tenure than that obtaining under the former system of 'customary tenancies' and the process has continued. A major thrust of reform in the post-independence period has been the settlement of farmers on land formerly farmed extensively by Europeans, notably in the 'White Highlands' north of Nairobi. Maina and MacArthur (1970) note that this particular policy had a four-fold objective: to reduce European influence, to improve the popular 'status' of agriculture, to introduce farmers to new agricultural methods and to relieve population pressure on urban areas. Kenya is also attempting to reclaim relatively poor farming land by means of government-sponsored irrigation schemes and, although the capital costs are high, this clearly represents a potential for employment. Indeed, Clayton (1970) has suggested that the land consolidation schemes have proved to be the most cost-effective by far in terms of employment genera-tion. Since the late 1960s, Tanzania too has made a most determined effort to restructure land ownership patterns, mainly by the creation of agricultural communities of a size closer to a socio-economic optimum (in terms of resource use) than was the case in 'traditional' agricultural practice. However, in this particular area, Zambia is hastening more slowly.

A third possible avenue for government policy, although not one being followed to any great extent in East Africa at present, is the direct control of migration. It seems to have been the case that the absence of large-scale migration from agriculture during the initial industrialization of the USSR and China can be attributed partially to legal prohibitions against such movements. Whilst liberal societies might see such a policy as an illegitimate interference with human rights, it did, in these instances, have the additional effects of lessening the decline of agricultural output that might have resulted from migration, of preventing the build-up of urban unemployment, and of facilitating the rational evolution of industry via planning. Finally, a government policy that should prove acceptable to most ideologies is the provision of facilities for human capital development, to increase the skill level of those in towns to facilitate their employment, and to initiate and sustain productive ventures in non-urban areas.

We noted earlier that a distinction might be made between the 'inter-ventionist' and the 'revolutionary' approach. From the policy point of view, however, this might be very much a distinction in degree rather than in kind. A liberal government might be just as willing to implement land reforms, incomes policies and educational development as a revolu-tionary socialist one if these policies appeared to be necessary in order to attain the specific objectives required. Revolutionists would probably argue, however, that it is not in the interests of non-revolutionary governments to pursue policies to the extremes demanded by the magnitude of the unemployment problem. As we have seen, some East African governments appear to be more revolutionary than others in this respect.

Summary

The production that a society might undertake is a function of technology and the availability of factor inputs, both qualitative and quantitative. By spending on education and health care, the individual can be rendered more productive. This process is termed investment in human capital. Evidence suggests that human capital formation has been a significant factor in economic growth. Although society will be interested in such capital because of the productivity consequence, the individual is more likely to invest because of resulting gains in earning power. A model of the investment decision can be derived using economic analysis. The returns from such investment depend on several factors, e.g. educational level, nature of training. Rates of return provide a guide to resource allocation. The complexity of the economy, time lags, changes in technology and ideological criteria are likely to make some centralized direction and manpower planning desirable in most economies.

The dual economy model is a way of analysing industrialization in an agricultural economy. The process involves the removal of labour to a sector where its marginal product is higher. Such a labour transfer did indeed occur during the industrialization of the European economies, although this is not sufficient to explain economic growth in such cases. In applying the basic model to contemporary agricultural economies, we must question some of its assumptions. It remains debatable whether labour's marginal product in agriculture is low. Labour released from agriculture might not be taken up by industry, owing to the use of capital-intensive production methods. Labour absorption problems will be compounded by population growth and inflexible industrial wages. The source of industrial capital is uncertain. The model points to the likelihood of rising unemployment in poor economies.

In fact, throughout the 1970s, unemployment rates rose in most of the world's economies. Unemployment constitutes an economic problem because it implies unused resources and personal deprivation. In the case of the East African economies, government intervention appears to be necessary to resolve the urban unemployment problem. Policy options include wage limitation, land reform, and direct control of migration away from agriculture.

Further reading

Investment in education is appraised specifically by Becker (1964) and Psacharopoulos (1973). Grossman (1972) examines investment in the context of health care. The human capital approach is invariably discussed in texts in such areas – Blaug (1972) for education, Cullis and West (1979) for health care, Culyer (1980) for social services in general. Blaug (1976) is a survey of human capital theory. Correa (1963) is an important early attempt to demonstrate how 'human variables' might be integrated into an overall economic framework. Mincer (1970) and Sahota (1978) survey the evidence for relationships between human capital creation, employment and earnings. Labour training programmes, their design and implications, are analysed by Loken (1969) and Hamermesh (1971). Bartholomew (1976) is a useful introduction to the subject of manpower planning. The data for public expenditure allocations are taken from UN (1981) and OECD (1977).

As indicated in the chapter, the basic dual economy industrialization model derives from Lewis (1954) and incorporates the modifications made by later writers. The present stock of literature relating to the problems of 'labour surplus' economies is large. More recent contributions include Dixit (1968, 1971), Marglin (1976), Ho (1972) and Newberry (1974). Griffin (1969) assesses the relevance of the model for Latin America. Kelley et al. (1972) examine it with reference to Japan, whilst Myrdal (1968) appraises it in the Asian context.

Data for British growth rates are taken from Deane and Cole (1967), p. 283 and Peaker (1974), p. 11. Unemployment data for pre-industrial economies are derived from ILO (1980), Tables 5 and 10. Bardhan (1978) raises some questions about the measurement of unemployment in poorer economies.

Mention was made of the problems posed for the rural economy by industrialization and migration away from agriculture. A model used to examine this process is that of Todaro (1969, 1976). Such problems are considered by Dasgupta et al. (1977) and by Connell and Lipton (1977). The fortunes of the urban unemployed in pre-industrial economies are explored by Bromley and Gerry (1979). Stewart (1975) and Hunter, Bunting and Bottral (1976) deal with aspects of employment creation, the latter being especially concerned with employment in rural areas. Jolly et al. (1973) and Mouly and Costa (1974) are general approaches to employment policy in poorer economies.

Many of the issues covered in this chapter are the 'standard fare' of labour economics – a representative text is Bellante and Jackson. (1979).

Chapter Eight

Using Non-Labour Resources

The question posed at the beginning of the previous chapter about the nature of the feasible set of production alternatives has, as yet, received only a partial answer; our discussions have been limited to the labour contribution to production. To obtain the complete picture, a parallel analysis of non-labour inputs is required and this forms the subject of the present chapter. Broadly speaking, we may consider two types of non-labour input into the process of production and eventual welfare creation. First, there is a class of 'natural resources', resources that are not the outcome of some human productive process. Examples include animal and plant life both on the earth and under the sea, and also subterranean mineral deposits, such as coal, iron ore and oil. The extent to which such items represent resources available for human use depends both upon mankind's technical ability to transform them into welfare-creating products and upon any ethical code that might have become established to govern usage. Thus, for example, uranium deposits were not regarded as productive inputs of any consequence until the evolution of a process that was able to unlock the usable nuclear energy contained in such deposits. Again, the past few decades have witnessed the growth of a body of opinion that argues that it is morally wrong to hunt animal species to extinction or, in Western countries, to use animals as the subject of medical experimentation.

Animals, plants and minerals come into being and, evidence suggests, could quite happily exist without any form of human intervention. This distinguishes them from the second type of non-labour resource, namely capital, which is itself the consequence of a productive process – i.e. capital is created by man and does not exist independently of him. One of the earliest forms of capital must have been the stone axe, made by the application of labour power to a natural resource (flint or obsidian in this case). Once created, this capital input can now be combined with other factors to generate consumption goods or still more capital – we might chop down trees to construct boats or fishing rods. Capital may beget capital and thus we could, in principle, trace the pedigree of any contemporary piece of capital equipment back through the previous generations of capital implicit in its production.

Natural resources exist logically prior to capital for, presumably, mankind must create capital out of something. If such resources therefore serve as the basis of both consumption and production, via capital creation, the way in which such resources are used is likely to be a highly significant determinant of the level of welfare of the society that owns them. Let us examine the characteristics of natural resources in a little more detail.

8.1   Natural resources

Natural resources are those produced by, and reproduced within, the non-human environment. Because of the differential forms of reproduction and human consumption, economists typically subdivide natural resources into two categories, those considered 'renewable' and those considered 'non-renewable'. Mineral deposits are an example from the latter category. Coal, for instance, results from the long-term geophysical reactions upon decayed vegetation and is therefore constantly being produced under the earth's surface. However, as the coal deposits currently being mined began to form some 300 million years ago, and as the present availability of coal under very modest assumptions about consumption suggests that existing supplies could be exhausted in, say, 1000 years, it is realistic to assume that such stocks are finite and fixed at a specific level. Mankind cannot, in other words, renew the stock of coal once it has been used up and the same is true for most other mineral deposits such as oil and metal-bearing ores.

Animal and plant populations represent examples of 'renewable' resources and we can demonstrate the nature of this renewal by a simple model. Suppose we have available to us an empty lake into which we release a pair of fish. Nature being what it is, we might expect this pair to reproduce, as will subsequent pairings that result from the mating. Over a number of time-periods, the fish population of the lake will gradually increase although the net additions to the fish stock should become larger during each period as more and more fish begin to breed. Such a process cannot continue indefinitely, however, for our lake will only be capable of sustaining a specific fish population, in terms of the availability of food and space. After some point, therefore, net additions to the fish stock will start to decline until this upper limit is reached, at which time the fish population will stabilize. We can represent this relationship between growth in stock at any time (g), the stock at any time (n) and the maximum sustainable stock (N) by the equation

$$g = kn(N - n)$$

where k is an arbitrary constant, and this equation demonstrates that additions to the stock per period increase at first and then diminish as the technical limit is reached. The relationship is illustrated in *Figure 8.1*.

If we are going to use these fish as a source of consumption, the question now arises how many fish should we eat? Clearly, a trade-off is involved because increasing present consumption (producing increased welfare) lowers the potential for future consumption owing to the depletion of the breeding stock. At the extreme, for example, we might consume all the fish now and starve in all future periods! However, a more sensible alternative would seem to be the following. If we consume fish at the same rate as the fish reproduction rate then the stock of fish

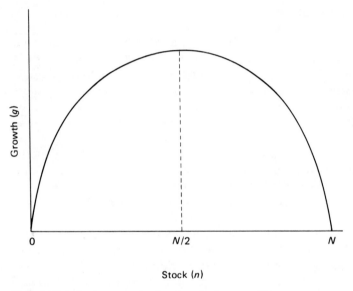

Figure 8.1 Relation between growth and stock of a renewable resource

will remain constant by self-renewal and will generate a stable and perpetual stream of consumption benefits. The maximum sustainable consumption level will be, in this case, equivalent to the maximum value of the above equation, which occurs at $n = N/2$. Assuming that we possess the necessary information about piscine reproduction and the life-sustaining properties of our lake, we can accordingly estimate the amount of fish that can be removed each time-period without destroying the source of our subsistence. The limitation of consumption thus permits the resource regularly to renew itself without our intervention (except, of course, in the case of our harvesting). Although we have used the example of fish, the model would apply to most reproducing populations with suitable modification; in the case of species with extended reproductive cycles (such as trees), the appropriate time-period might be decades rather than months.

Whilst we shall be primarily concerned with resources of the above two types, mention should be made of a special case of the renewable resource category. This is where we receive a constant flow of resources from a more-or-less infinite stock. The classic instances here are energy from solar radiation and power from tidal movements. Although it is, of course, true that the nuclear reactions within the sun will one day come to a halt, it is equally true that, when this finally happens, earthly debates about optimal resource exploitation will have ceased to be relevant.

Given these characteristics of resources, a primary issue of interest is the determination of the rate at which they ought to be exploited to yield the welfare benefits that form the end of human activity. We shall consider some of the factors involved in the identification of this rate. Perhaps the most obvious is the question of cost. Natural resources are seldom free goods in the sense that they can be used in consumption or production directly; rather, fish have to be won from the sea and minerals have to be mined and refined. We might suppose, for example, that mankind would be even keener to take uranium out of the ground if the costs of extraction, the costs of building nuclear power stations and the costs entailed by the risk and uncertainty associated with this energy source were all lower. In turn, a determinant of the costs will be the level of technological sophistication that a society possesses, to obtain and process the resources into usable form.

A second contributory factor is society's rate of time preference, that is, its view of the relative merits of present versus future consumption. Suppose a society were to say that benefits at all times were to be valued equally; a fish today yields the same level of utility as a fish in ten years' time yields today. In the case of our renewable resource, and ignoring the cost aspect, the society should clearly harvest at the maximum sustainable rate as estimated above. In the case of the non-renewable resource such as coal, the calculation becomes a little more complex. If we make the heroic assumptions that available coal stocks will replenish themselves in a further 300 million years by geological processes and that technology will not change, the above criterion suggests that we should consume, presumably, at a rate that spreads the existing stock over the 300 million year period! This would imply, incidentally, an annual future consumption of 10–20,000 tons, approximately one-millionth of current world annual demand.

A more realistic view of human nature, however, is one that suggests not only that people make decisions over far shorter time-periods, but that they actively distinguish between present and future values. In particular, it is widely assumed that an individual values the welfare generated by a given resource now at a higher level than the welfare generated by the same resource at some point in the future. There are two reasons for this. First, the possession of a resource now means that it can be put to some productive use to give rise to still more benefits by the time the future arrives. Second, the existence of uncertainty in the world, and the tendency of individuals to be risk-averse, would induce societies to prefer the certainty of present benefits to the prospect of future ones if the actual amount of both benefits was to be the same. Birds in the hand, the proverb tells us, are worth two in the bush. It accordingly follows that societies that place a higher value upon present as opposed to future consumption will favour a higher rate of resource depletion than societies for which present and future values are equivalent. In the case of renewable resources, this might well represent a rate in excess of the maximum sustainable yield leading to the eventual destruction of the available stock – we have already met the limiting case where all future benefits were valued at zero. Paradoxically, a high rate of exploitation could also be favoured by societies operating with the reverse set of time preferences, valuing the future more than the present. Suppose a society were to contemplate the industrialization of its economy by means of an austerity programme. All efforts were to be directed, in other words, to create a prosperous world for future generations at the expense of the present one, by means of lowered present consumption levels and high rates of investment. The essential point is that such a process of intense capitalization is equally (if not more) likely to raise the demand for exploitation of natural resources that are necessary for the creation of the capital.

We observed above that natural resources were not free in the sense that costs had to be incurred in order to render them productive. They are also not free in another sense in that they generally constitute the property of an individual or a nation. It is accordingly likely that the nature and distribution of property rights in the resource will influence the chosen rate of exploitation. Consider oil. The oil supplies of the world are owned by a relatively large number of countries and, in many cases, oil production and exportation are a major determinant of national economic welfare. The behaviour of the oil industry is, in many respects, similar to the behaviour of firms within any single industry. The existence of competition in the Middle East led to increased production (i.e. a higher rate of exploitation) and subsequently the formation of a cartel (OPEC) to protect the interests of producers. Cartels are, of course, unstable at the best of times for, although OPEC might agree that it is collectively optimal to lower exploitation rates to maintain prices, it still remains privately optimal for individual members to act competitively under the cartel's price umbrella, entailing increased exploitation of their own resources. The decision facing non-OPEC oil-producers such as Britain and Mexico is also problematic. The present policy appears to be to follow the lead given by (OPEC-influenced) world prices and thus to accept the world exploitation rate. An alternative might, however, be to lower the present rate of exploitation to conserve resources until such a time as competitors' are exhausted and then to re-enter the market as a monopolist. Such a decision will naturally depend upon the particular rate of time preference deemed appropriate, and upon an assessment of the likely speed of technological change.

The specific market model adopted will depend upon the particular allocation of rights for the particular resource. Copper, for instance, should be viewed as an oligopolistic market shared by Zambia, Chile and the USA. However, another type of problem arises when rights in the resource are not well defined, that is, when a number of individuals or nations possess 'common access'. Again, the case of fishing is a useful example. When we made our earlier decision about the amount of fish that we ought to take from our lake whilst still maintaining a stock, we were making the assumption that it was 'our lake' containing 'our fish'. If we consider the oceans of the world, however, the model breaks down. Ownership rights in the sea are, to say the least, ill defined. Even though there are cases where specific territoriality has been established we should bear in mind that fish are no respecters of political boundaries. If we now become just one amongst several societies all fishing in a particular area of ocean, our strategy is likely to be affected. In our lake example we conserved stocks of fish in order that we might consume in the future; now, we may argue, we shall be conserving our stocks simply such that the fleets of other nations can have them. This being the case, it makes no sense to any particular society to exploit at anything less than as high a rate as possible on the assumption that all competitors will also do this. Therefore, given this shared logic, we should anticipate very high exploitation rates for resources with common access.

A final factor that a society might wish to consider when deciding upon depletion rates relates to the dual nature of many of the resources currently in use. A particular piece of land, for example, might represent not only, say, a source of stone for building purposes, but also an attractive stretch of countryside that is, in itself, a source of pleasure. When deciding upon how to exploit that particular resource, society will be faced, in the case of quarrying, with both the direct extraction costs and the opportunity cost of loss of visual pleasure. Again, it appears that nations currently view the oceans of the world in two distinct ways: first, as a source of food and, second, as a repository for nuclear waste, surplus oil and general human effluent. The essential point is that, whilst either activity might be considered legitimate in its own right according to society's values, the use of the resource in the second manner is bound to have implications for its use in the first. At some point, we should presume, the magical regenerative properties of nature are bound to break down. It is clear that the existence of common access to the seas is an additional contributory factor to the problem of dual usage.

We therefore see that the selection of the optimal exploitation rate for any one country involves consideration of a wide range of factors. There is every reason to believe that nations will display variations in their assessment. One society with a highly effective extraction technology and a strong preference for short-term benefits might opt for a high exploitation rate; others may be more cautious. Given the existence of finite resources, and the likely depletion of non-renewable resources, it seems legitimate to ask the question at a wider level and enquire into the conditions for globally optimal resource exploitation. We shall, in fact, return to this issue towards the end of our enquiry; now we shall examine the second non-labour resource, capital.

8.2   Sources of capital

We have already specified one defining characteristic of a capital resource, namely that it is a productive input of human creation. The second important notion is that the process of capital creation and accumulation is essentially 'the production of production'. The capital resources we create are not demanded or consumed directly, for they do not provide immediate welfare gains; rather, they are contributory inputs to further processes that eventually generate goods and services for our enjoyment. Thus, for example, machine-tools are of no significance in their own right (excluding any psychic benefit we might derive from an aesthetically pleasing design); the significance lies in their contribution to the production of consumable items such as automobiles and refrigerators. As for the rationale of capitalization, we met this in an earlier chapter. Societies, we argued, would be willing to forgo the present consumption of resources in anticipation of the future and higher benefits generated by such resources when invested in the appropriate productive process. As yet, however, the origins of these resources are unclear. Restricting ourselves in this chapter to the discussion of a closed economy, we may consider two potential sources: first, individual economic agents such as households and firms and, second, the society as a whole as represented by its government.

8.2.1   SAVINGS

Societies typically make available to the individual agents of which they are composed stocks and flows of resources, the allocation of which is left to the discretion of the individual resource-owners. Broadly speaking, such agents may either consume or not consume their resources and it is clearly the second option, savings, that is of interest in the present context. An agent's decision whether to save or consume will be dictated by two factors, the overall level of resources at his disposal and the relative attractiveness of the savings option vis-à-vis the consumption alternative. Given that different societies possess different time preferences, different resource distributions and different institutional structures for the purpose of resource mobilization, we should anticipate that savings habits and patterns will also be diverse; indeed, this is the case.

At this juncture, a few generalizations derived from economic theory are relevant. First, we might deduce that the lower an agent's level of resource stock or flow then the less is he likely to save, since a proportionately greater amount must be consumed for the simple purpose of physical survival. Second, and at the opposite extreme, extremely rich agents or individuals should be better disposed towards saving as the opportunity cost of benefits forgone should be correspondingly lower if basic consumption needs can be easily satisfied. However, a moot point is whether a rich individual, who might save more resources, will also use such resources for the purpose of capital accumulation. Our savings model is based upon the assumption of diminishing marginal utility of expenditure, that is, additional welfare gains become progressively less valuable as consumption rises. Is it reasonable to assume that a rich individual, who places such a low value on marginal consumption as to leave some of his resources unconsumed, will then use these resources in production and thus deliberately create even more consumption goods? Third, and irrespective of whether or not the individual is wealthy, the extent of the amount of savings must always be dependent upon the degree to which the consumption/savings trade-off can be made to look an attractive proposition from the individual's point of view.

Until recently, it has been widely held that the very low level of aggregate savings in the pre-industrial economies of Africa and Asia arises from the extreme poverty of their populations. Griffin (1979), however, cites a number of studies that suggest that this is not necessarily the case. In such economies, the unit of consumption and production coincide in the household and recent evidence suggests that a high savings potential exists under specific conditions. Families have been observed to exhibit high savings ratios (as much as 30 per cent of income) in order to undertake specific, household-initiated investments, such as the purchase of improved seed-corn, fertilizer or 'low-technology' capital equipment. During periods when such investment is not deemed necessary, savings tend to fall to a low level as the bulk of household output is consumed. Such evidence is corroborated by that of Lluch, Powell and Williams (1977), as discussed in Chapter 6, and the conclusion seems to be that a high savings potential exists even in relatively poor economies as long as some form of incentive to save is also in evidence. We might deduce, therefore, that the reason that the average savings propensity appears low in many economies is not lack of potential but lack of opportunity; agents are not being encouraged to forgo consumption. A likely source of such encouragement could, of course, be government economic policy.

Turning to the case of the Western industrial economies, the analysis of Baran and Sweezy (1966) suggests that the use of savings in the creation of capital might be hindered in other ways. Simplifying the picture considerably, their model runs as follows. Baran and Sweezy believe that Marx's image of nineteenth-century capitalism is not an appropriate description for the twentieth century. In countries such as the United States, capitalism has given way to 'monopoly capitalism'. The independent factory-owners of the earlier period have been replaced by a new breed of capitalist, the operators of the giant corporations that have come to dominate production. In common with their predecessors, these new capitalists are keen to increase their profits by undertaking cost-reducing innovation. They are far less willing than their ancestors, however, to compete in terms of price. Rather, they actively collude with one another in a variety of ways, e.g. price leadership and secret agreements, to control the level of market prices for mutual benefit. Given price fixing and continued innovation of cost-reducing technology, monopoly capitalism will therefore generate an economic surplus, defined as the difference between the value of output and costs of production. Moreover, suggest Baran and Sweezy, this surplus displays a tendency to rise over time, owing to the strength of the capitalists' bargaining power and the nature of technological change.

If economic stagnation is to be avoided, this surplus must be 'ploughed back' into the system in some manner. One possible method is simply to reinvest the surplus; clearly, some reinvestment will be required to develop new production methods and products and to supply a growing population. Beyond a certain point, however, reinvestment will become counter-productive. If capital formation leads to increases in capacity in one period, then all that will happen will be the generation of a greater economic surplus in future periods. The problem for reabsorption will therefore be compounded. It is Baran and Sweezy's contention that both reinvestment and the consumption of capitalists are together insufficient to account for all of the surplus. For the system to support itself, they argue, the remainder must go to 'waste'. In this category of waste they include such items as expenditure on the sales effort (which represents 'permissible' non-price competition between the corporations) and the maintenance of the military establishment.

Baran and Sweezy's approach is difficult to test empirically owing to its data requirements and definitional problems. For example, how exactly should the surplus be measured and how influential is the collusion between the corporations in fixing prices? Further, there is no reason to accept that a given society should necessarily regard, say, expenditure on armaments as inherently 'wasteful'. However, the model is of considerable theoretical interest because of the manner in which it combines elements of the Marxist model with the views of Keynes. In his *General Theory*, Keynes himself pointed out the possibility of private wealth-holders being faced with insufficient investment opportunities. Under such conditions, he argued, the capitalist economy would indeed stagnate. Keynes wryly noted that the ancient Egyptians were perhaps fortunate in having property-owners with a passion for pyramid-building. This occupation kept the labour force in employment and created no additional productive capacity.

The discussions above are not intended to demonstrate that individual economic agents will not generate savings for use in capital formation. Rather, they serve to demonstrate a general possibility that the optimal level of savings from the point of view of the individual might differ from an optimum defined in social terms. It might be argued, for example, that the Asian farmers mentioned above were saving 'too little' to generate long-term output growth. The Keynesian view of the mixed economy also allows for the 'paradox of thrift' whereby households save 'too much' and thus lower the level of aggregate economic activity in both present and future terms. In fact, the realization of disparity between the two optimality criteria is widespread, as is evidenced by the general employment of government direction of savings in most economies of the world.

8.2.2 GOVERNMENT DIRECTION

When Keynes published his *General Theory* in 1936, his views on the necessity of some form of governmental intervention or resource mobilization were regarded as little short of revolutionary (as far as the non-socialist world was concerned), for they seemed to herald the imminent destruction of the prevailing individualistic ideological orthodoxy. Keynes defended his views in the following terms:

Whilst, therefore, the enlargement of the functions of government, involved in the task of adjusting to one another the propensity to consume and the inducement to invest, would seem to a nineteenth-century publicist or to a contemporary American financier to be a terrific encroachment on individualism, I defend it, on the contrary, both as the only practicable means of avoiding the destruction of existing economic forms in their entirety and as the condition of the successful functioning of individual initiative (Keynes, 1964, p. 380).

Even though the 1970s witnessed the growth of a degree of scepticism about the possibility of using a 'purely' Keynesian system of economic management in Western economies, Keynes' fundamental point about the necessity to synchronize the optima remains valid. In principle, closed economies may use two types of policy techniques to obtain this synchronization – monetary policy and fiscal policy. Let us make a few observations regarding each.

In the classic market economy model a central role in channelling the saved resources into capitalization is played by the financial market. In general, this market offers savers an incentive by payments on loans whilst borrowers wishing to invest are charged a price for the privilege of using such savings. Both this incentive and the price are represented, of course, by a rate of interest. Whilst a central theme of the Keynesian critique of this classical approach was that the availability of investible resources, even at a very low price, could not guarantee actual investment under conditions of poor expected returns, it must nevertheless be the case that the existence of a market *per se*, either privately or government operated, offers a more positive inducement to private savers than would exist in the absence of such a market. Furthermore, the existence of an organized fund of investible resources should be more attractive to entrepreneurs than would an absence, *ceteris paribus*.

The existence of a defined market in saveable resources should thus increase the savings potential of an economy, although, to date, it is only the Western mixed economies that have utilized the capital generated from such voluntary savings to any great extent. In most such cases, analysts have concluded that the existence of such markets was significant in the attainment of material progress. In her study of the UK, for example, Deane (1965) suggests that a well-developed money system was one of the advantages possessed by the UK during its industrialization period and she concludes that this system made 'an important direct contribution to the finance of British trade and industry' (p. 185). Gerschenkron (1952) made an equivalent claim for the role of financial institutions in central Europe during the nineteenth century. In comparison, the significance of markets in loanable funds in the rest of the world has been far smaller. In many African and Asian economies, the evolution of a formal financial sector began only in the late colonial/ early independence period and has yet to reach a degree of involvement within the economy such that an impact might be made. In his study of economic policy in Bangladesh, for example, Islam (1977) clearly sees the absence of formal money markets as a factor hindering economic growth and he concludes that, throughout the 1970s, the 'need for continuous improvement and expansion of financial institutions and instruments for the mobilization of private savings remained paramount' (p. 243). Private savings also play a very limited role in the socialist economies; Nove (1977) notes that their main role in the USSR is in the area of housing finance (p. 243).

Whilst the existence of a positive rate of interest in a money market might well induce people to save, the imposition of a tax obliges them to do so. Such 'forced saving' has a key role in fiscal policy. In effect, the power to tax means that governments are permitted to confiscate and transfer resources from any one economic agent to another according to whatever criteria are laid down by the social choice process. We might now think that the creation of the optimal resources saving rate is but a simple matter, for all the government has to do is to enforce the appropriate tax and channel the resulting resources into whichever area it decides will generate the most benefits. The central problem, however, revolves around the fact that governments typically have multiple objectives, over and above the rate of accumulation, and these might be regarded as being of higher priority. In post-war mixed economies, fiscal policy (the variation in the levels, composition and incidence of government revenue and expenditure) has also been an important management technique for the control of price stability and the level of employment. Because of their economic structure, this role is defined differently in socialist economies; the tax level is an important instrument in equating consumer demand with planned producer supply. In virtually all economies, governments act as entrepreneurs by providing goods and services, which range from major items such as national defence to relatively inexpensive services such as the maintenance of public parks. If, as is true in many cases, individuals are not required to pay directly for consumption, the provision of such goods must be financed from taxation. Finally, taxation is perhaps the most effective short-term measure to redistribute income or wealth in a society, in cases where the government feels the prevailing distribution is sub-optimal.

Taxation is therefore a weapon directed against many enemies. The essential point is that the optimal level of tax necessary to achieve one particular objective might well be detrimental to the attainment of another; a classic case of goal conflict and its consequences is provided by the analysis of the UK economy by Bacon and Eltis (1978). In brief, they argue as follows. The UK is a mixed economy in which manufacturing output is largely the concern of privately owned industry. However, over the past two decades, the non-market or government sector has expanded its interests, prompted by the desire of successive governments to redistribute income and to engage in public service provision. A principal facilitator of this expansion has been the tax revenues gleaned from private industry, which, argue Bacon and Eltis, lowers its profitability and potential for reinvestment. In turn, declines in profitability act as a positive disincentive to external investors and such private savings as exist will be drawn, more and more, towards investment in the government sector. Accepting that it is manufacturing industry that is the essential engine of material growth, a principal factor in the explanation of low UK output growth is thereby identified. We should, in fairness, add, however, that there seems to be nothing inherently illegitimate in a society wishing to trade off increases in output against increased government provision and redistribution as this model suggests has occurred in the UK case.

A further consideration to be taken into account when applying a tax for the purposes of resource mobilization is the design of the tax itself. A given sum of taxation revenue for investment may be raised in a variety of ways, for example by levying a proportional tax on personal incomes (direct taxation) or by a tax on expenditure or property (indirect taxation). Key factors to be considered in making the choice will include the economic effects of the form of taxation and the actual economic efficiency of the tax itself. Progressive income taxes, whereby richer individuals or firms pay larger proportions of their income to the treasury, would appear to be sensible measures if the objective is to achieve a more egalitarian income distribution and to gain control of large volumes of resources. On the other hand, it might be argued that such taxes act as a disincentive to effort, and productive input could accordingly be reduced. Evidence on this point is so far inconclusive. Furthermore, the collection of an income tax requires a sophisticated recording, monitoring and policing system to support it. Where such a system has not been developed, as in many pre-industrial economies, the costs of operation might prove prohibitive. Ilersic (IEA, 1979) has established that, even in the UK where a relatively elaborate system does exist, some £7000 million in 'rightful' taxation is not collected each year (p. 35). For this reason, more easily administered indirect taxation, such as customs duties and sales taxes, form the mainstay of the tax yield in the pre-industrial nations. Ghatak (1978) shows that materially poor economies (those with incomes below $500 per capita) collect two-thirds of government revenue as indirect taxes, whilst richer economies, such as those of Western Europe, collect this proportion in the form of direct taxation. One particular form of tax that has grown in significance in these Western economies in recent years is the value-added tax (VAT), whereby tax revenue is gathered at each stage of the productive process. Although a virtue of VAT is the possibility of putting the whole indirect tax structure onto a consistent and unified basis, it has proved, in many cases, to be a remarkably expensive tax to operate. Davies (IEA, 1979) has estimated, for instance, that whilst small firms in the UK contribute at present some £170 million in VAT revenue, the costs of collection from them are around £220 million (pp. 72–3). Such figures clearly make a fairly positive statement about the way in which such a tax should be administered.

In summary, therefore, the ways of ensuring that resources are saved for use in capital creation are many and varied and depend, to a great extent, upon the institutional structure of the economy concerned. In cases where money markets are well established and the government has considerable power to tax, there will exist the potential for a high savings rate, if not the desire. Where individuals have little personal incentive, or few obligations, to save, we should expect that the rate would be low. However, assuming that there exist at least some possibilities for capital creation, we are now in a position to ask the question – how should we combine all our productive inputs in order to generate output?

8.3   The optimal factor combination

At the beginning of the previous chapter we noted that the mix of inputs chosen by a society would depend upon the prevailing feasible technology, the quantity and quality of resources available and the specific objective function that the society set itself. Since then, we have been concerned with an examination of the characteristics of various resource inputs and the time has come to integrate these into the whole. Let us begin by constructing a simple abstract model that demonstrates possible consequences of assuming the existence of different objective functions.

As a starting point, we shall hold a number of our potential variables constant. We shall assume that our economy has already mobilized an initial and fixed amount of non-labour resources and also that there exists some determined technology that specifies the relationship between the input combination and output. The essential variable in our initial model is thus the amount of labour that may be employed in production. With fixed non-labour inputs we should expect output to exhibit diminishing returns as represented by the total product (TP) curve in *Figure 8.2*. Let us define a consumption level per individual at the subsistence minimum as a. Therefore the line TC represents total consumption at different employment levels. (For convenience, we shall assume population is equivalent to labour supply.) Suppose the government can set employment at any level it wishes. Now, if the objective function were to be the maximization of aggregate output we should select the level N_0 giving output Q_0. On the other hand, we might be more interested in maximizing the productive surplus – the difference between output and consumption; in such a case, we should set employment at N_S giving output Q_S. A final option would be the objective of ensuring a high level of labour employment; let us therefore choose the output level corresponding to the point where most people have a job. Depending upon the structure of our economy, this point might lie anywhere along the employment axis but, for the sake of illustration, let us suppose that we are the government of a 'labour surplus' economy. We might therefore arbitrarily choose employment level N_E, giving output Q_E.

Note that, for our particular model, a production surplus is generated whichever of the three possible objectives we follow. Indeed, this is true for all employment levels less than those beyond the point S. However, this productive surplus is highest for the employment level N_S and lowest for the level N_E. After the production round has taken place, suppose we collect up this surplus and add it to our initial stock of non-labour resources. The surplus, in other words, now becomes capital. With a net capital injection, output should be increased for all levels of employment, but the extent of this increase will depend upon the amount of capital accumulated. Thus our potential production relationship will show a small increase in the case where we selected high employment as our objective (for this gave a small surplus) but a large rise in the case of the surplus-maximization objective. The output-maximization objective would yield a function in an intermediate position. These three potential production relationships are represented as TP_E, TP_S and TP_0 respectively in *Figure 8.2*.

The implications of each of the three possible objectives are clear from an examination of *Figure 8.2*. With the particular production functions

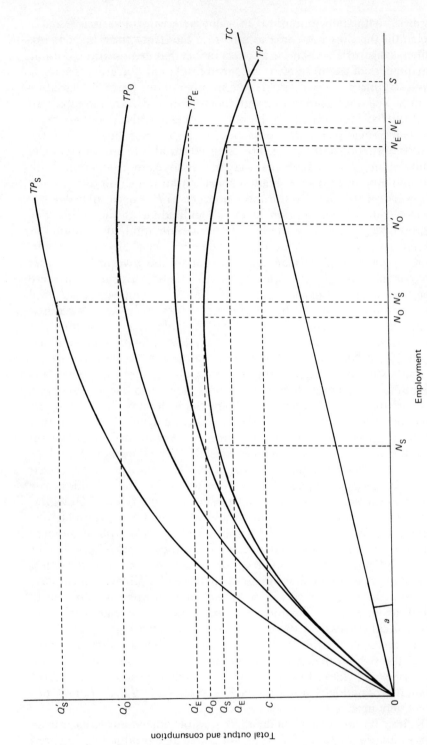

Figure 8.2 Choice of optimal strategy

specified, the surplus-maximization objective has led to a higher output level in the second production period, increased the employment opportunities for labour substantially (from N_S to N'_S) and given rise to an even bigger investible surplus for use in a possible third production period. By contrast, the option that favoured high employment levels has increased output and the investible surplus by only a small amount, the output-maximization policy again occupying an intermediate position. It follows by analogy with the first and second production periods that the surplus-maximization policy will rapidly outperform its rivals in subsequent production periods, in terms of the level of output attained and the employment opportunities generated.

Now, all this is very well if we are really in a position magically to produce or eliminate the members of our labour force as we assumed. Suppose our economy actually contained N'_E individuals. Thus, in choosing the surplus-maximizing strategy we have conveniently forgotten that $(N'_E - N_S)$ individuals still remain and, presumably, have to be fed. Our economy will have, in other words, a constant minimum consumption requirement (C) and this fact limits our alternatives. Given this constraint, the output-maximizing strategy now appears quite attractive in providing both output and the highest investible surplus $(Q_0 - C)$. Unfortunately, we still have rather a large number of people out of work in the first period $(N'_E - N_0)$ with the prospects of continued, although diminished, unemployment in the second production round $(N'_E - N'_0)$. Does this matter? The answer is 'most probably' for three reasons. In the first place, unemployment would not matter to the individual if society divided up output amongst all members without respect to their productive contributions. Typically, however, societies feel that consumption benefits should be allocated in some relation to the individual's productive effort with the result that, unless we govern our economy along purely altruistic lines (a manner not particularly characteristic of most modern economies), the lot of the unemployed section of our population will be relatively hard. Second, and quite simply, unemployment is a problem because it represents a waste of resources that could be used in production. Finally, notice that we have not specified the length of the time-period involved in moving from one production round to the next. If such periods were ten minutes long then we would not be particularly concerned by the unemployment created by the surplus-maximization or the output-maximization objectives, for either would probably soak up the surplus within an hour! If, however, each period was to be measured in years, then we might be rather more worried. Unemployment could then be, for all practical purposes, permanent in view of the constant supplementation of the labour force by population growth.

Our dilemma over which of the possible objectives we should choose as the specific goal of our economic policy could, of course, be easily resolved by the sudden appearance of vast stocks of capital, although our assumption about minimum subsistence levels implies that the economy must have been mobilizing as much as possible. Excluding the possibility of obtaining such stocks from external sources (a possibility to be discussed in the next chapter), perhaps a resolution is obtainable by relaxing some of our earlier assumptions. First, production within an economy is, in reality, not homogeneous in the way our model suggests. It is likely that different production activities will use different resource inputs in different ways, depending upon technology. Thus each activity will have a different implication for employment creation and the generation of output and the investible surplus. Second, it is likely that, even for one particular form of productive activity, be it automobile manufacture or education, there will exist a variety of technically feasible input mixes to generate output. The solution to our problem of selecting the 'right' objective for economic policy might therefore lie in identifying the different social costs and contributions of specific productive sectors and in exploring the possibilities of factor substitution, whereby inputs that are in short supply can be replaced by those more readily available.

The consequences of the relaxation of these assumptions can again be explored by recourse to a simple model. Consider an economy composed of just two productive sectors, A and B, both of which use two factor inputs, labour (L) and capital (K). Assume the factor supplies to be fixed at $\bar{L}$ and $\bar{K}$ respectively. From the point of view of sector A, it might be technically possible to produce any given level of output from a variety of input combinations; at the extreme, production might be possible using a large capital input coupled with a small labour contribution, although output could be maintained by progressively substituting labour for capital in the input mix. In *Figure 8.3* the isoquant Q_0 represents such a fixed output level for all such factor combinations, a high capital/labour ratio at one extreme and a low one at the other. The essential point is that the selection of any one particular capital/labour ratio on this isoquant automatically defines the availability of inputs to sector B, for total supply is fixed. Suppose we initially select the combination K_3,L_3. Whilst this certainly permits the production of Q_0 from A, sector B is now constrained to employ $(\bar{K} - K_3)$, $(\bar{L} - L_3)$ and, in *Figure 8.3*, the highest feasible output level in B using this combination is Q_3. Aggregate production of the economy is therefore $(Q_0 + Q_3)$. All other permutations of factors yield equivalent results; thus the use of combination K_1,L_1 in A will constrain the output of B to Q_1, although a movement in this direction would seem desirable for Q_1 is greater than Q_3. The combination K_2,L_2 is of the greatest interest for, whilst continuing to produce Q_0 in sector A, the economy can now produce Q_2 in sector B and the aggregate output $(Q_0 + Q_2)$ is the highest of the three possibilities discussed. If, as would seem reasonable to suppose, we should prefer more output to less from given resources, then the combination K_2,L_2 is clearly the one we want to employ in sector A. In contrast, the selection of any other technology represents a positive

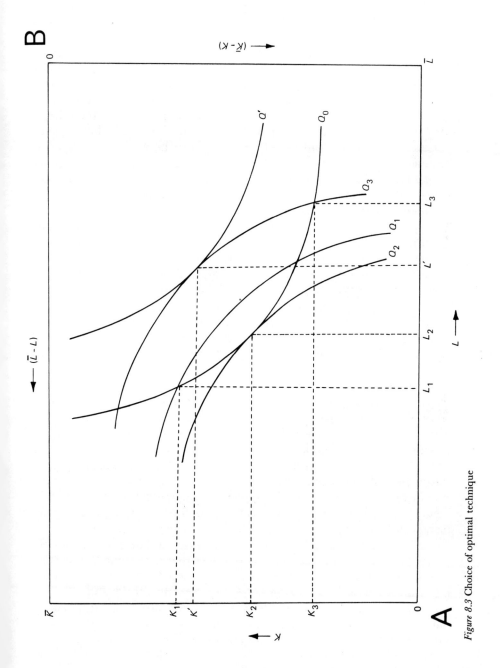

Figure 8.3 Choice of optimal technique

opportunity cost, the combination K_1, L_1 representing, for example, a cost of $(Q_2 - Q_1)$.

By holding the output of sector A constant, therefore, it seems we can reach a decision about the optimum mix of inputs, assuming the objective to be output maximization. In so doing, however, we have only dealt with one half of the problem. Suppose that we decide to increase the output of sector A by increasing the input of both factors of production; in the previous case, output was held constant at Q_0 by the substitution of one factor for another. Such an input increase might take us to the isoquant Q' and the resources available to sector B now give rise to a best possible output level from B of Q_3 under the criteria used above. The identification of the optimum is now a little less clear, for society is being confronted with a choice between $(Q_0 + Q_2)$ as opposed to $(Q' + Q_3)$, although both positions represent an optimum in the technical sense in that these are the maximum feasible outputs for given input combinations. This particular dilemma can only be resolved by recourse to society's assessment of the subjective valuation of output gains and losses, for it is being required to trade off the increases in output in one sector against the decreases in output in another. Thus if it were felt that output increases from sector A more than compensated for the welfare losses resulting from an output decline in sector B, society might opt for output combination $(Q' + Q_3)$ in preference to combination $(Q_0 + Q_2)$. Were sector A to represent capital goods and sector B consumption goods, this might be the decision taken by an economy whose objective was long-term growth maximization. Alternatively, if A were agriculture and B were manufacturing industry, the position might represent that chosen by a pre-industrial economy particularly concerned with the immediate problem of subsistence.

One final theoretical consideration is that of cost, and we can demonstrate the relationship between this and the choice of technique by an extension of the analysis in *Figure 8.3*. Let us assume that the factors of production, capital and labour, are all owned by someone or something and thus recompense is required for factor usage. Again, considering sector A to begin with, let us give the entrepreneur in charge of production a fixed sum of money to purchase his inputs; this budget can be expended on labour, on capital or on some combination of the two. A defining characteristic of the input purchase will be the price charged by the owners of the factors for the use of their services. Let us contemplate two (arbitrarily chosen) sets of possible factor price relatives that determine the possible combination of input purchases from a fixed budget; these are represented by the lines $X_1 Y_1$ and $X_2 Y_2$ in *Figure 8.4*. For ease of illustration, suppose that the highest output level available from the inputs purchased is the same, namely, Q_a; the isoquant is thus tangential to both budget lines. Now suppose that factor prices happen to be fixed according to the constraint $X_1 Y_1$. Our entrepreneur would therefore purchase an amount K_1, L_1 to produce Q_a and this leaves $(\overline{K} - K_1)$, $(\overline{L} - L_1)$ available for the pro-

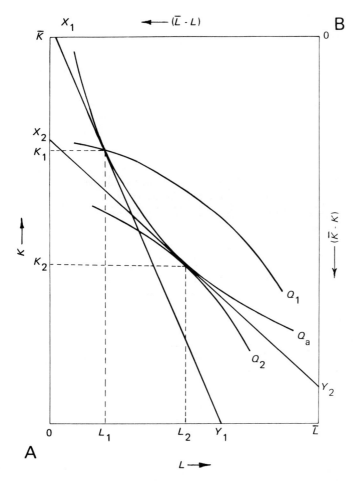

Figure 8.4 Cost and the choice of technique

duction of Q_1 in sector B. However, under a factor price regime specified by $X_2 Y_2$, Q_a is still the optimum in sector A where K_2 and L_2 are the amount of inputs purchased, although this now leaves sufficient inputs for sector B to attain a higher output level, Q_2. In aggregate terms, a change in the ratio of factor prices has clearly given rise to a higher output level.

Up to this point we have limited ourselves to a purely theoretical discussion of the issues involved in selecting the optimum output mix in terms of the maximization of an objective function given fixed inputs. Our models have been quite unsophisticated but, even if we developed them in n-dimensional space to cater for a variety of productive inputs (e.g. different types of capital and labour with different skill levels) and a multiplicity of productive sectors, we still need to apply a little more flesh to the bones in order to use them as an analytical base for real-world economies. Following on from the example above, it would appear that the alteration of factor prices can have a positive effect in channelling resources into the socially optimal areas of activity. There are two problems here: first, that factor prices determine not only resource usage but also the returns to factor-owners and, second, the possibility that what is socially optimal from the aggregate point of view may not be individually optimal from the factor-owners' point of view. In securing the output increase above, we effectively lowered the price of labour relative to that of capital and this will have the effect of an income redistribution. This, in itself, could be considered as undesirable and unjustifiable even in the face of prospective output increases. Many societies, indeed, apply minimum wage legislation that establishes a level below which the price of labour cannot fall. If this level is above that implied by the factor price ratio X_2Y_2 in *Figure 8.4* (and assuming that we do not permit unemployment), then the optimum cannot be reached without the violation of the legislation and society will have to decide which of its two objectives is the more important. From a private point of view, labour is likely to regard the lowering of its wage rate with a certain amount of displeasure and could take steps to ensure that this does not occur. In the face of the threat of wage cuts we should anticipate the establishment of labour unions whose purpose is to create a restrictive practice, i.e. to offer the employer an all-or-nothing deal at a fixed price. Note that, although we have only considered a fall in the labour price, there is no reason to suppose that the owners of other factors might not take equivalent strategic steps should they feel their interests threatened.

This likely 'stickiness' of factor prices does not constitute the sole imperfection in factor markets; other issues determine the extent to which factors can be successfully combined. Throughout our theorizing, we have blithely assumed that factors are perfectly adaptable and can be dropped into productive processes at will. Experience suggests that this is unlikely to be the case in reality. The productive potential of both labour and capital is likely to be specific and not general; just as we should not expect lawnmowers to be capable of baking bread so we should not expect untrained farm labourers to be able to programme computers. Our theoretical isoquants might not be attainable, therefore, because we do not possess the 'right kind' of productive inputs. Changing the factor mix is thus likely to necessitate, from the labour point of view, a sizeable investment in the creation of human capital. Intuitively, pre-industrial economies would appear to be in a particularly poor position, for much of their capital equipment will come from the industrialized world. From a purely technical point of view, such equipment is likely to be labour-saving and this would seem effectively to limit the potential for factor substitution whilst denying to such economies the use of their most plentiful input.

Finally, another discrepancy between theory and practice should be noted. In our models, we have assumed that sectors will combine factors in ways that are technically efficient; that is, such that all productive inputs are permitted to perform to the best of their abilities. To believe that this must be the case, however, requires the presumption of a high degree of managerial skill on the part of the entrepreneur plus 100 per cent commitment on the part of the employees. It seems unlikely that both of these conditions can always be guaranteed. Within any one industry, therefore, it might be possible to detect firms using the 'wrong' input mix owing to managerial incompetence and also firms using the same mix and input volumes as others but producing different levels of output owing to differential efficiencies.

Accepting such problems might exist, what scope is there for factor substitution in the selection of the optimum input mix? Tyler (1974) opens his study of Brazil, a country with unemployment rates of the order of 10 per cent, with the observation that it is widely held that labour absorption during the industrialization process of poorer economies is precluded by virtue of the absence of a viable labour-using technology in many industries and the tendency of firms in such countries to imitate the labour-saving technologies of the industrialized nations. His empirical findings suggest, however, that these arguments could be invalid; even in the most capital-intensive sectors, clear scope for substitution was detected. Tyler focuses his analysis on imperfections in the labour market and concludes that an obstacle to substitution is the inflexibility of real wages. Having estimated the elasticities of substitution between inputs, he concludes that the elimination of such distortions could increase total employment in Brazilian manufacturing industry by some 10 per cent overall. He is at pains to point out, however, that remedial policies must not be deduced from this observation in isolation from an analysis of other market imperfections, such as those likely to exist in capital markets, and the overall objectives of economic policy.

Although he approaches the topic from a broader perspective, Pack (1974) comes to similar conclusions about substitution possibilities. He compares a number of productive activities common to several countries in terms of both factor combinations and technical efficiency. As a basis for the analysis, Pack constructs isoquants for activities in terms of input usage per unit of output and this permits him to identify plants at the limits of the 'efficiency frontier'. From this, he is able to derive estimates of the elasticity of substitution, which shows a fair degree of variation depending upon the type of activity concerned – the figure was lowest in the case of bicycle manufacture and highest in the case of grain milling. Plants at the extreme of the isoquants often displayed a very large variation in the capital/labour ratio; the ratio for capital-intensive Japanese woollen textile plants was nearly 20 times the ratio for the labour-intensive Indian plants and the difference was even greater in the case of grain milling. Such calculations led Pack to conclude that 'considerable substitution possibilities exist in a number of manufacturing industries' (p. 403). Pack also examined the effects of differential efficiency in the specific context of India, asking what consequences would result if all firms in an industry were as efficient as the most efficient firm in that industry. Not surprisingly, his model suggested that both employment and output benefits would accrue; paint production was the most extreme case, in which he suggested that efficient production could increase both output and employment by around 300 per cent in total. Pack suggests that the obstacles to the realization of such increases may be maintained wage and profit rates that favour relatively less efficient, capital-intensive production methods. All these conclusions are significant in view of their implications for our earlier analysis; it seems that the possible conflict between the objectives of output and employment maximization could be resolvable by the appropriate choice of technique.

Summary

In addition to labour, natural resources and capital are essential inputs to production. Natural resources are those resources not resulting from some human productive process. They may be renewable or non-renewable. Non-renewable resources, e.g. mineral deposits, exist as a fixed stock. Renewable resources, e.g. animal populations, will reproduce themselves if left to their own devices. Given a knowledge of how renewable resources reproduce themselves, we can calculate the quantity that may be consumed without reducing the size of the stock. In deciding upon the rate of exploitation of a natural resource, society will consider the costs of exploitation, its rate of time preference, and the nature of technological change. The choice of exploitation rate is also influenced by the allocation of property rights in the resource and the market structure.

The two sources of capital in a closed economy are voluntary savings and resources raised by government. A savings potential appears to exist in the majority of economies, although incentives to save may be lacking. Similarly, certain types of economic structure could serve to stifle the incentive to invest. Governments use both monetary and fiscal policy to mobilize savings for investment. Although taxation is used to generate investment funds, taxation is also applied by governments to achieve other goals, e.g. macroeconomic stabilization. Conflicts between goals may therefore occur. One determinant of the effectiveness of a tax is its administrative design.

The optimal combination of factors of production depends crucially upon society's objective function. Different policies may be pursued, depending upon whether the society wishes to maximize employment, output or economic growth. In all cases, factor costs are instrumental in determining the optimum. Amongst the obstacles that might prevent the optimum from being achieved are the 'stickiness' of factor prices, the existence of inputs that are qualitatively inappropriate, and managerial incompetence. Empirical evidence suggests that considerable scope exists for factor substitution in many economies.

Further reading

Texts relating to the economics of natural resources include Leacomber (1979), Banks (1976), Herfindahl and Kneese (1974) and Kneese (1977). The data source for the depletion of coal stock calculation is Meadows *et al.* (1972). The behaviour of cartels is analysed by Whynes and Bowles (1981).

Capital is so widely recognized as a determinant of output growth that it finds its way into virtually all treatises on material progress; Cairncross (1962) is a basic statement. Capital's contribution to UK economic growth is assessed by Deane and Cole (1967). For India, see Rosenstein-Rodan (1964). Readers with an interest in capital theory might care to contemplate Harcourt (1972) and the readings in Harcourt and Laing (1971). Thirlwall (1978) has excellent sections on resource mobilization. Atkinson and Stiglitz (1980) and Brown and Jackson (1978) are basic texts on public finance and taxation principles. Fiscal policy in Africa is discussed by Taylor (1970), whilst practices in the Soviet Union are described by Wilczynski (1970) and Nove (1977). Two lively contributions to the debate over the operations of the tax systems of mixed economies are IEA (1977) and IEA (1979).

The standard work on optimal factor combinations is Sen (1968). Sen (1975) relates the choice of techniques to employment policy, as does Standing (1978). White (1978) surveys the empirical evidence about factor combination and substitution in poorer economies.

Chapter Nine

International
Economic Relations

All the dimensions of progress discussed up to this point have had one thing in common. Whenever we discussed the various possibilities for the social choice process, the design of legal and property systems, the choice between present and future consumption and the identification of the optimal technology, our implicit context has always been the single national economy. We have seen this entity as some geo-political combination of consumers and productive inputs, to be used for the creation of welfare; the existence of a multitude of national economies, each using its own resources to further its own specific objectives, has not been relevant for our enquiries. In this final chapter of the second part of the book, however, the assumption of insularity will be abandoned. The real world is indeed composed of diverse economies, just as any one society is composed of diverse individuals. Just as we, as individuals, appreciate that our fellow members of society may help or hinder us in the pursuit of our private objectives, so do we, as a society, accept the existence of a similar potential for aid or hindrance within the other economies of the world. What makes the external dimension different from the others, however, is the possibility, nay almost certainty, of the conflict of sovereignties. Our earlier discussions of policy have all assumed that the nation state, in designing its strategy for progress, could in principle do very much as it wished in terms of designing political procedures, using factors of production and so forth. In exploring relationships between, as opposed to within, nations, the feasibility of *our* particular strategy will be contingent upon the extent to which it also represents an attractive option to fellow nations.

Economists model the interactive behaviour of two or more sovereign bodies by means of the theory of games. Considering for simplicity a two-economy world, we may derive three possible outcomes for any form of, as yet, unspecified relationship that might exist between our sovereign economies. First, the game relationship might be negative-sum; as a result of interaction, both economies find themselves in an inferior position in terms of welfare or whatever. Under the standard economic assumptions, we should not expect economies voluntarily to indulge in this type of relationship. Second, the outcome of the game could be positive-sum; both economies find the relationship produces welfare gains and, accordingly, this would seem to be the sort of relationship that both might encourage and into which both would wish to enter. Finally, the outcome might be zero-sum, that is, one economy gains at the direct and equivalent expense of the other. Presumably we should discern something of an imbalance of interest in the forming of such a relationship and it seems likely that the potential loser (assuming that it could foresee the outcome) would only enter such a game, not from choice, but as a result of coercion. In this chapter we shall mostly be concerned with positive-sum games – particular strategies pursued by one nation that would be approved of by others. Games of the other types we shall meet again in our concluding chapters.

What, then, are these national strategies that give rise to mutual benefits? Perhaps the most obvious are the gains resulting from the international transfer of resources. If we accept the current political division of the world and that nations 'own' the resources on which they stand, it is clear that Nature has endowed nations with a particularly inequitable distribution. Cultivable land, mineral deposits, labour populations and so forth are not spread evenly amongst the various economies and, in any case, the actual resource balance of one particular economy might be totally inappropriate for producing the type of consumption items that it favours. An industrial nation with vast stocks of iron ore but no coal might therefore profitably strike a bargain with another country in which the balance of resources is reversed and, from this bargain, both might expect to gain by virtue of now possessing the necessary ingredients for steel production. Clearly, the precise terms of the exchange agreement will depend upon each economy's valuation of its own resource vis-à-vis the value of the welfare created by the resource to be gained. In a sense, this logic also applies to commodities; if the French enjoy 'English cheese' and the English enjoy 'French wine', a basis for exchange producing mutual benefits obviously exists.

Gains from commodity exchange can also exist in the case of homogeneous commodities. Suppose that, by virtue of factor endowments, organization and technical skill, our economy was a particularly cheap and efficient producer of just one commodity. On the other hand, other economies, we shall assume, are rather good at producing other items, the production of which for us is far more expensive. A beneficial outcome would be for us all to agree to concentrate our productive efforts in that area in which each is the most efficient and each country can then trade its efficiently produced commodity for others, equally efficiently produced by those economies with the particular advantage. This argument to the effect that national specialization and exchange increase aggregate welfare is, of course, directly analogous to the argument about the desirability of the division of labour within a given economy. The proposition can be demonstrated simply. Suppose the opportunity cost of the production of a good was 10 per unit in country A but 20 per unit in country B. If a trading regime was established, the total production of the good could be maintained at a fixed level and, for every unit extra that A produced (at a cost of 10), B need produce a unit less (at a saving of 20). The effective price of the traded commodity could be set such that B could compensate A for its costs but still remain in profit itself.

This bilateral exchange of resources or commodities is perhaps the simplest example of the positive-sum game, although more subtle ones can be devised. Suppose, for example, that an enterprise discovers that the return on capital is likely to be higher in a country other than the one in which it is currently based, owing to, say, lower labour costs or higher market potential. Investors from economy A might therefore be willing to offer to establish production in economy B in order to reap these benefits. In turn, B might also find this solution optimal if such investment, not available internally, were to offer employment opportunities and other multiplier effects. Again, aggregate welfare might be increased by what in the first instance appears to be a unilateral resource flow. Country A may actually donate resources to country B (to B's fairly obvious advantage), A's return being either 'psychic', i.e. the welfare produced by the act of charity, or more long term – A donates resources to B in the expectation of, say, trading advantages to be gained via B after B has put the donation to productive use.

9.1   Patterns of trade

Between 1963 and 1980, the total volume of world output doubled, whilst the total volume of world trade – the direct exchange of resources and goods between economies – rose three-fold (GATT, 1980, p. 193). In 1979, the total value of traded goods reached $1625 billion, a figure considerably greater than the combined output values of all the economies of Asia, Africa and Latin America. Clearly international trade therefore constitutes an important issue, but the first question to ask is – just which countries are engaged in trade and what is it that is being traded? The question can be answered by considering data at three levels of aggregation.

At the most general level, *Table 9.1* displays the share of total world trade flowing between and within the four main trading groups of economies, which are (i) the Western industrialized economies, a group that includes Western Europe, North America, Japan, Australia and South Africa, (ii) those partially industrialized economies whose main form of industrial and trading activity involves oil production, e.g. Nigeria, Venezuela and the Middle East, (iii) the Eastern trading bloc, essentially China, the USSR and Eastern Europe, and (iv) the remaining

TABLE 9.1 Share of world trade, 1979[a]

Exports from: / Imports into:	Industrialized economies	Oil-exporting pre-industrial economies	Other pre-industrial economies	Eastern bloc	Share of world exports
Industrialized economies	47.6 (−5.4)	4.8 (+2.2)	9.7 (−1.2)	3.3 (+0.6)	65.8 (−4.5)
Oil-exporting pre-industrial economies	9.7 (+5.0)	0.2 (+0.2)	2.7 (+1.7)	0.2 (+0.1)	12.8 (+7.0)
Other pre-industrial economies	8.3 (−0.6)	0.7 (+0.4)	2.5 (0.0)	0.7 (−0.2)	12.2 (−0.3)
Eastern bloc	2.8 (+0.2)	0.4 (+0.4)	1.0 (−0.3)	4.7 (−2.3)	9.2 (−2.1)
Share of world imports	68.4 (−1.2)	6.1 (+3.0)	15.9 (+0.2)	8.9 (−1.8)	

[a] Data indicate percentage share of total value of world trade. Data in brackets indicate absolute change in share since 1968. Totals may not add owing to rounding errors and omissions of unspecified flows.
Source: Calculated from GATT (1980), *International Trade 1979/80*. Geneva, GATT, Table A22.

pre-industrial economies of Asia, Africa and Latin America. The first point to note is that the Western industrial economies occupy the dominant position in the world trade picture. Not only does this group account for some two-thirds of the world total, but around 70 per cent (nearly 50 per cent of the world total) of their trade takes place between the group members themselves. In contrast, the non-oil-producing pre-industrial economies, which contain perhaps 50 per cent of the world's population, are only responsible for 12–15 per cent of its trade. It is clear that a significant shift in trade shares occurred during the 1970s due almost exclusively to one factor – the increasing importance of the oil-producers. At the expense of the other groups, their import and export shares more than doubled. Note also that, not only is the extent of trade between the non-oil-producing pre-industrial economies insignificant in the world total, but that the share did not change during the period considered.

The next level of analysis involves consideration of the trading groups in terms of the composition of imports and exports. *Table 9.2* displays the proportion of each group's trade in four commodity categories: (i) foodstuffs and raw materials, (ii) minerals, fuels and non-ferrous metals, (iii) capital equipment, machinery, motor vehicles, and (iv) other manufactured goods, including iron and steel, chemicals and textiles. Again, some clear patterns emerge. First, there is a clear difference between the export compositions of the industrialized and pre-industrialized economies. The former's share of primary production – categories (i) and (ii) – in its export total is 22.3 per cent. The latter's is 57.9 per cent (97.8 per cent for the oil-producers). Second, the import balance appears broadly similar for all groups, with the notable exception of the oil-producers. This group, we would presume, is unlikely

TABLE 9.2 Commodity composition of trade, 1978[a]

Trading group	Food and raw materials	Fuels and minerals	Capital equipment	Other manufacturers
Industrialized economies:				
Exports	14.5	7.8	43.7	34.0
Imports	16.9	24.5	29.8	28.8
Oil-exporting pre-industrial economies:				
Exports	0.0	97.8	0.0	2.2
Imports	12.4	2.4	52.8	32.4
Other pre-industrial economies:				
Exports	35.3	22.6	12.9	29.2
Imports	15.9	20.3	33.9	29.9
Eastern bloc:				
Exports	12.8	23.2	35.7	28.3
Imports	17.4	15.4	41.0	26.2

[a] Data indicate percentage share in value of exports and imports of four commodity categories.
Source: Calculated from GATT (1980), *International Trade 1979/80*. Geneva, GATT, Table 21.

to require oil imports, which are the main item in category (ii). Given the balance of trade from *Table 9.1*, it appears that the pre-industrial economies are net exporters of food and raw materials to the three remaining groups. Third, the main differences between the Eastern and Western economies' trading position occur in the net export share of fuels and minerals, and in the relatively high import share of capital equipment in the case of the former group. These facts may be accounted for by the rich resource endowments of the Eastern bloc and the differential development of indigenous technology within the member states.

Finally, *Table 9.3* provides specific data on the commodity composition of trade for selected countries from all four groups. The first three mentioned in the table, two Western and one Eastern industrial economies, display a certain similarity. Metal-based manufacturing products constitute over one-half of total export value and other industrial sectors are well represented. Naturally, dissimilarities are also in evidence. Japan, for example, appears obliged to import far more fuel and food supplies in relative terms than do the United States or Czechoslovakia, although its reliance upon external sources for machinery, vehicles and consumer goods is correspondingly smaller. These differences can be explained in part by Japan's poor natural endowments of land and raw materials, and its efficient production of manufactures. The second set of three countries in *Table 9.3* are examples of relatively low-income economies in which agricultural production is the main form of economic activity. As may be seen, agricultural output, either in its 'raw' or 'processed' state, accounts for 60–80 per cent of export value

TABLE 9.3 Commodity composition of trade for selected countries[a]

	USA 1977	Japan 1977	Czechoslovakia 1976	Argentina 1976	Brazil 1977	Tanzania 1976	Saudi Arabia 1976	Zambia 1975	India 1976
Imports:									
Food	9.5	13.9	7.9	4.7	6.6	13.4	10.4	7.1	27.1
Industrial supplies	25.5	31.5	34.5	49.7	31.2	30.4	29.7	36.5	26.7
Fuels	29.1	44.0	14.0	17.4	33.4	18.2	0.7	13.4	25.7
Machinery	8.9	5.0	32.3	20.6	22.2	19.0	23.8	21.2	16.0
Transport	14.8	1.4	5.6	5.6	4.6	13.1	18.8	15.7	3.3
Consumer goods	12.2	4.2	5.7	2.0	2.0	5.9	16.6	6.0	1.2
Exports:									
Agricultural goods	15.7	0.4	1.8	41.7	34.2	80.0	0.0	1.4	23.2
Mining/quarrying	4.0	0.1	4.1	0.2	9.6	4.5	95.1	0.2	11.3
Processed agricultural goods	6.2	0.9	2.7	30.9	28.4	6.5	0.0	0.1	12.4
Textiles	2.6	5.6	10.0	7.5	6.9	2.9	0.0	0.0	26.7
Chemicals	12.1	8.0	7.5	4.3	2.6	5.5	4.7	0.3	3.3
Basic metal industry	2.4	14.2	10.0	2.4	2.4	0.1	0.0	96.0	10.9
Metal manufacturing	50.1	65.7	56.1	11.7	12.5	0.2	0.2	1.7	9.0
Other manufacturing	6.9	5.1	7.8	1.3	3.4	0.3	0.0	0.3	3.2

[a] Data indicate percentage share in country's total value.
Source: United Nations (1978), *Yearbook of International Trade Statistics*. New York, UN, Vol. I (Country Tables); calculated from Table 2 in each case.

in each case and therefore, when compared with the industrialized nations, the various other forms of manufacturing seem far less significant. Capital imports, especially machinery, are far more prominent than in the Western industrialized cases. Next, Saudi Arabia and Zambia are two graphic examples of economies whose trading activity is dictated by the extraction of a specific natural resource, oil and copper respectively. In both cases, at least 95 per cent of export value is directly attributable to the countries' possession of the particular resource; again, their capital requirements make up a sizeable proportion of the import total. Finally, data for India are included. Although very poor materially, India's export balance is quite different from that of many other countries at similar levels of prosperity such as Tanzania. Whilst agricultural production remains important in the export mix, other industrial sectors, notably textiles, figure more prominently. This may be accounted for by the relatively longer length of India's basic industrialization period. Note, however, the importance of food imports in India's import total; this would seem to be a reflection upon the country's concern and ability to feed itself.

So much for the basic state of world trade. Let us now continue with our overall line of enquiry and ask a second question – what form of trade policies ought a country to pursue in the context of a strategy for progress? The general arguments made earlier would seem to suggest that some involvement in trade is desirable. We have examined evidence of economies gaining, via trade, resources and commodities that they either did not possess in the first instance or that they found could be more profitably purchased from abroad rather than produced internally. Other arguments may also be brought into play to support the gains from trade idea. A vigorous policy of export promotion on the part of a government, for instance, should have positive multiplier effects on the economy as a whole and should act as a spur to the capital accumulation process. Other things remaining equal, the more one is able to offer to other economies in exchange then the greater should be one's ability to import items not otherwise available. Thus social welfare may be increased (we are assuming, of course, that other economies will not be persuaded to part with their output without receiving something in return). All in all, the arguments seem to imply that the global optimum is specialization within national economies and exchange between such economies. Consider, however, the following problems.

First, we should presume that a movement towards national specialization would involve substantial costs of relocation. In the case of the United Kingdom, for example, the opportunity cost argument would probably suggest that the productive inputs currently employed in the manufacture of UK textiles and UK automobiles should be allocated elsewhere. Such goods are importable relatively cheaply. Were it possible suddenly to uproot in excess of 1 million workers from such occupations and instantaneously set them to work in another in which the UK had a comparative advantage, then there is little doubt that this would yield a higher aggregate welfare level, *ceteris paribus*. Similarly, we should have to assume that looms and lathes are equally adaptable to other forms of production. In reality, however, such relocation would involve the UK in major short-run costs of retraining and re-equipment that, depending upon the time preference rate chosen, could well be regarded as prohibitive.

Second, and although we have suggested that all trading partners can gain from exchange, we have not yet specified how the gain might be distributed. The trading bargain finally struck might result in country *A* gaining a great deal whilst country *B* only gains a very small amount. Although gains from trade are positive in absolute terms, the existence of a gain gap, one that would widen over time, might engender a certain amount of concern in the country, *B*, that was getting better off less quickly. Third, a high degree of specialization that involves the concentration of economic activity into a small number of areas greatly increases the level of risk that a society faces. A country that specializes in, say, the production of coffee will presumably do quite well as long as the rest of the world is happy drinking coffee; the sales of its exports will pay for the importation of all those items not produced domestically as a result of specialization. However, should the world suddenly develop a passion for tea, or if some unkind soul were to invent a cheap, acceptable coffee-substitute, the fortunes of our specialized economy would decline, for it would possess abundant supplies of a commodity that people no longer wanted. If such circumstances were envisaged as possible, the appropriate strategy might be industrial diversification rather than specialization. In fact, this problem is especially acute for those real-world economies whose welfare depends, to a large extent, upon the exploitation of a non-renewable natural resource. In such cases, specialization will only be feasible for a finite period until the resource is exhausted, although the length of this period presumably remains at the society's discretion. Such economies must, one assumes, use the export revenues gained by trading in their particular resource to enable them to import the requirements of a production structure suitable for a continued economic existence once the resource is exhausted. Paradoxically, eventual diversification may only therefore be obtainable by means of specialization.

Finally, we should note that the particular form of industrial structure entailed by specialization might not appear attractive to an economy in wider social terms. In spite of a particular trading advantage in manufacturing, economies might not wish to turn their green and pleasant lands over completely to the dark satanic mills of industry. Even though their advantage lies in continued agricultural production, agricultural economies may see the industrialization process as a desirable means for transforming what they consider to be out-moded social structures. For any or all of these reasons we might therefore find that, not only are economies not interested in the trading option, but actual positive steps are taken to ensure that trade does not occur. Suppose an economy is faced with the prospect of imports from another at a low enough price to divert consumer demand from the products of its own industry. These cheaper commodities are now to be bought at the price of the decline of the home industry; should the government feel that this is too high a price to pay, it might take steps to restrict the import flow by imposing a quota (a volume limit) or a tariff (a tax on imports that effectively raises their price). Either should have the effect of maintaining consumer loyalty to the products of the home industry. Whilst in the theoretical world of instantaneous factor adjustments this represents a sub-optimal outcome with respect to efficiency, this clearly need not be the case with respect to distribution.

Perhaps the most important contribution to the argument against a multilateral free trade system involving both industrial and pre-industrial economies was that made by Prebisch (1964). It employed the general characteristics that we observed in *Table 9.2*, namely that industrial economies tend to export manufactures that agricultural economies then import, whilst the latter concentrate on primary production that is sold to the industrial world. Prebisch concluded that the nature of the exchange deal between these two trading groups, in terms of the relative prices of the particular commodities involved, had altered over time, to the detriment of the pre-industrial group. In the Prebisch model there are two causal factors, the first involving the differential effect of technical change. Owing to labour pressure, productivity gains and buoyant demand conditions, the price level of manufactures in industrial countries has generally increased over time. In contrast, world demand for primary production (excepting oil and certain rare minerals) has been less pronounced and, owing to rapid population growth in agricultural economies, the wage level (and thus the price level) has not risen significantly. The prices of manufactured goods (i.e. the cost of agricultural economies' imports) have accordingly outstripped the prices of agricultural products (i.e. the revenue gained from agricultural economies' exports). Put another way, each unit of export value for an agricultural economy gradually buys less and less imports. The second factor involves elasticity of demand. It might appear that the first problem facing the primary producer might be overcome by a reduction in price. Demand should be stimulated and export revenues should rise. Prebisch contends, however, that the industrial economies' demand for primary production is so unresponsive in this respect that such a strategy would simply lead to a net decline in export earnings.

The Prebisch thesis presents three problems when we come to empirical testing. First, it is difficult to generalize about primary product prices that are subject to such high degrees of short-run fluctuation. Second, different pre-industrial economies tend to produce different primary commodities. Each of these will be subject to different long-run trends owing to specific demand and supply trends, technological developments, and so forth. Third, any conclusions about changes in variables through time depend crucially on the selection of the base year against which comparisons are to be made. Prebisch, in fact, used the early 1950s as a reference point, a time when primary commodity prices were high owing to the Korean war boom. Arguably, the choice of a different base period – when primary prices were low – would lead to the conclusion that the terms of trade had improved rather than deteriorated. However, if we accept the Prebisch doctrine – that the gains from trade are heavily weighted in favour of the industrialized world – at face value, what are the strategies open to the pre-industrial economies?

Leaving aside multinational solutions for the moment, the main contender would appear to be a process of industrial diversification. The problem, nevertheless, is quite specific to those economies that we care to consider. It is not, for instance, true to say that *all* primary product prices have remained at a low level and are characterized by low income elasticities of demand. Demand and supply conditions for each vary. The price of Zambian copper, for example, doubled when one of its co-producers, Chile, was embroiled in political and economic turmoil in the early 1970s. Even so, the principle behind industrial diversification appears to have proved attractive to many economies in the recent past. This involves the establishment of a manufactured export goods sector on the one hand, producing items with a higher income elasticity of demand than that prevailing for most primary products, and the evolution of import-substituting industry on the other, which is required to diminish reliance on high-priced manufactures from the industrialized world. Such diversification is not without its problems. The creation of any new industry requires additional resource inputs that might well be unavailable. Again, the establishment of export-oriented industry gives no guarantee that production will necessarily prove profitable or even saleable on world markets. Further, all such industrialization takes place within the context of the existing primary production being the most valuable source of export revenue. The unfortunate consequence is that, the more an economy attempts to mobilize and marshal its resources to industrialize away from its reliance upon primary production, then the more is it driven to rely upon primary production as the source of revenue, at least in the short run.

Little has been said so far about the nature of trade between the Eastern bloc and the other three economic groupings. Detailed analysis of the area is precluded owing to the non-availability of data, although the evidence that does exist suggests that international trade is becoming more important to the Eastern bloc. This represents a certain shift in thinking, as compared with the earlier periods of socialist development. The Stalinist model of Soviet socialism – 'socialism in one country' – was widely copied at the time by the other socialist states. Heavily oriented towards autarky, the policy was influenced by ideological considerations, and also the overt hostility of the rest of the trading world. Whilst the sheer size and particular resource endowment of the Soviet Union mean that an autarkic strategy is probably more feasible there than elsewhere, the need for trade has nevertheless been felt. Such a need has possibly been more acute in the other Eastern European states, which have been less fortunate in their resource endowments. At present, the areas of Eastern interest appear to number two: the first is the importation of Western manufactures (implicitly, Western technology) and the second is the importation of basic foodstuffs. In this latter respect, the Soviet Union and Eastern Europe benefit considerably from their ability to purchase the food surpluses that result from the agricultural support systems practised by the United States and the European Economic Community. However, it probably remains fair to say that East–West trade is, at present, still governed more by political and strategic considerations than by any appeals to the economic rationality of static comparative advantage.

9.2   International resource flows

We noted earlier that trade was only one of a number of possible international economic interrelationships into which countries might enter.

Although, in quantitative terms, international trade is certainly the most important of such relationships within the world economy, let us now consider some of the other possibilities. First, instead of exchanging resources with country B, country A might be prepared to lend them to B for the latter's use. The more that B is willing to recompense A for the services of its resources, in the form of higher interest payments, then the more attractive is such a proposition likely to become from A's point of view, other things remaining equal. In practice, such loans could be financial or physical, e.g. the loan of capital equipment. Second, in the case where A and B are potential trading partners, A might wish to advance credit to B to enable the latter to purchase A's exports. The extension of such credit should yield a double benefit to A: country A will receive interest on the loan and will also reap the benefits of a trade expansion, e.g. the stimulation of its export sector. Such an expansion would not have occurred in the absence of purchasing power being extended to the buyer. Third, country A might wish to invest its resources directly in country B, assuming that such a practice was acceptable to both parties. It might therefore establish, for example, a productive enterprise to serve B's internal market or to make use of a resource with which B was well endowed. The higher the expected yield on such investment, then the more likely is it to occur, *ceteris paribus*.

A fourth form of relationship – official development assistance (ODA) – involves the international transfer of resources under concessionary terms. ODA may be subdivided into two broad categories. First, country A may simply present resources to B in the form of an outright gift or grant. In such a case, no reciprocal repayment is anticipated. Second, country A might invest, lend or extend credit under terms that are particularly favourable to country B. The interest rate on the negotiated loan, for example, might be low relative to the prevailing market rate. Alternatively, B might be permitted an unusually long 'grace period' before the repayment of the loan commences. In principle, we can think of such a concessionary loan as being made up of a 'normal' commercial transaction, plus a grant element. To qualify for inclusion in the ODA statistics compiled by the international agencies, concessionary loans must have at least a 25 per cent grant element. They must, in a sense, be '25 per cent more favourable' to the borrower than a 'normal' loan.

Although we have so far only considered these international resource flows as theoretical possibilities, all of them are readily observable in the real world. As might be expected, the evidence suggests that the principal sources of loans, credit provision, investment funds and ODA are the richer economies of the world. In the case of direct investment, the principal hosts of such funds are also rich economies. Whilst it is difficult to put a precise figure on the value of the internationally owned capital stock, owing to different accounting conventions and ownership arrangements, it has been estimated that some 75 per cent of the late 1970s' international capital stock resulted from the investment by rich economies in other rich industrial economies (ICIDI, 1980, p. 187). The major United States' automobile firms, for example, all have subsidiaries in Europe. In the present section, however, we shall focus our attention on the flow of resources from the richer economies to the poorer ones. For the purposes of analysis, we can divide the former into three groups: (i) the members of the Development Advisory Committee (DAC) of the OECD, the 17 richest Western economies including the United States and the United Kingdom, (ii) the Organization of Petroleum Exporting Countries (OPEC), which represents the major oil-producers, notably the states of the Middle East, and (iii) the Eastern bloc, comprising China, the USSR and Eastern Europe.

The international flow of resources has, in the past, proved subject to fluctuation from year to year. This is perhaps not surprising. It seems reasonable to suppose, for instance, that the potential profitability of foreign investment could vary with the economic climate of the host country, and this will have an effect on the investment level. Similarly, political developments within the recipient country might condition the extent to which a donor feels disposed towards the granting of ODA. However, bearing such points in mind, we may nevertheless make a number of observations about the flow of resources from rich to poor economies during the 1970s.

In the first place, the annual net flow of resources to poor economies clearly increased during the 1970s. Net inflow for 1970 was $19 billion; by 1979, the value had risen to $81 billion. Second, the proportion of non-concessionary flows (credit, loans and direct investment) in the total was always higher than the proportion of ODA. During the 1970s, the share of ODA fluctuated between 30 and 45 per cent, the 1979 figure being 35 per cent. Third, bank lending was the most important form of non-concessionary resource flow throughout the 1970s, and its significance increased as the decade advanced. In 1979, the contribution of bank lending to the total net resource flow was 21 per cent. In the same year, the share of direct investment was 17 per cent and export credits made up 13 per cent. Fourth, of the three groups of rich economies mentioned above, the DAC group was by far the most significant source of all forms of funds throughout the 1970s. Although the share of the other two groups appeared to rise throughout the decade, OPEC's share only reached 18 per cent in 1979, and the Eastern bloc's share rose to 7 per cent. Fifth, the DAC group's contribution to non-concessionary resource flows was even more important: in 1979, 98 per cent of such resources came from DAC sources.

Irrespective of whether loans or credit are arranged on concessionary or non-concessionary terms, an increasing volume of loans, such as occurred during the 1970s, is likely to imply an increasing amount of debt on the part of the borrowers. IMF (1981) has estimated that the outstanding medium- and long-term debt of the poorer economies increased four-fold between 1972 and 1979, reaching a value of $360 billion in 1979. Such a debt naturally requires servicing, in the form of interest repayment. Between 1972 and 1979, the annual service payments made by these debtor countries rose five-fold, from $12 billion to $63 billion.

Having gained some idea of the magnitude of the resource flows involved, let us now examine in more detail two specific forms. The first of these is direct foreign investment.

9.2.1 FOREIGN INVESTMENT

The empirical study conducted by Reuber *et al.* (1973) sought to discover why firms originating in the rich industrialized economies might choose to invest in countries at earlier stages of industrialization. Reuber's findings led him to classify such investment into three categories. First, the investment of some firms is 'export oriented'. In such a case, the firms are concerned to seek out new sources of inputs, either for use directly in their own production plans, or for more immediate resale. The main purpose of such investment is to generate an output that is exported from the host country, and this characteristic distinguishes it from the second type, 'market development'. In this case, resources are being invested in a productive process, the output of which is to be sold *within* the host country itself. The investment decision will therefore be made with reference to the economic conditions prevailing within the host economy rather than with reference to world market conditions. Finally, certain investments might be 'government initiated', implying that, although market or cost conditions make the investment appear unattractive in the first instance, incentives provided by the government make the project viable on balance from the investors' point of view. Such incentives may include tax concessions or the provision of support services.

In many respects, Reuber's three categories equate well with particular types of commodity production. Export-oriented investment is likely to take place in the area of primary production. Firms specializing in, say, metal-based manufacture would be concerned to secure supplies of the raw material concerned. On the other hand, market-development investment is more likely to occur in manufacturing industry, especially if production costs in the host country are less than those in the investor's country, after due allowance has been made for transport costs. Bulky items, such as automobiles, should certainly generate economies for firms if they could be manufactured in close proximity to the eventual market. For reasons discussed earlier, government-initiated projects are likely to be found in the area of import substitution, or in industries where employment multipliers are high.

In developing these categories, Reuber undertook sample surveys to determine investment behaviour. He discovered that investment plans were typically made to cover a relatively long time-period; the horizon was 9–12 years in the case of North American investors. Such a response would imply that short-run profitability is not always a relevant consideration, and, similarly, short-run fluctuations in capacity would not influence investment to any great extent. As might be expected, the surveys revealed that liquidity (i.e. realizable returns and mobility of profit) exerted a strong influence upon the investment decision. Reuber concluded that two of the most successful inducements that the government of a potential host country could offer to investors were the prospect of long-term political and economic stability and guarantees of the protection of the market from competition, both domestic and international.

Looking at the investment flow from the opposite direction, what benefits can local investment by foreigners provide for the host nation? We may consider four classes of benefit. First, the inflow of foreign capital represents a net increase in the input endowment of the host economy. Resources not previously available to it have now appeared. Depending upon the precise nature of the investment, we should anticipate that this would give rise to an increase in the level of economic activity, with production and employment multiplier effects. For a project concerned, say, with mineral extraction, these benefits could be quite small; operations would, most probably, be export oriented. In the case of market-development investment, where linkages might become established between the foreign firm and local activity, greater benefits could be anticipated. Second, international investment can represent a transfer of technology and knowledge from the investing economy to the host. If the investing firm is contemplating a labour recruitment and manpower training programme, then such investment could represent, for the host, a cheap source of human capital accumulation. Third, the government of the host country might find an influx of foreign firms attractive because their profits could represent a source of tax revenue. Once appropriated, such resources could be channelled into other deserving areas of economic activity. Finally, it might be argued that the arrival of foreign firms will stimulate the evolution of a market structure in hosts where such a structure does not yet exist. Where markets already occur, the foreign firm can provide a competitive edge and thus encourage the more efficient allocation of resources.

These, it should be emphasized, are all *potential* benefits. Under particular circumstances, and with certain types of investment, a host might well find that the investment project being contemplated will not in fact contribute to welfare at all. The game could be such that the investors receive all the gains and exclude the host from any benefit. When an investment project is on offer, hosts will clearly be assisted if they have available some set of criteria that distinguish 'good' projects from 'bad' ones. One such set, based upon the approach developed by Little and Mirrlees (1974), has been advocated by Lal (1975).

Lal argues that hosts must, first of all, consider the prospective investment project in the light of alternative strategies. In the case of an international firm offering to establish production facilities for a particular
good, the host has a number of options available. It might, quite simply,
decide to do without the good entirely. It might be found that the good
could actually be imported more cheaply from elsewhere, or perhaps
the domestic industry could produce it at less cost. Alternatively, the
contract might be awarded to a rival foreign firm in a position to offer
the host a more favourable deal. For each of these possibilities, it will
be necessary to calculate the benefits relative to the costs incurred. What
factors should enter the calculation? Perhaps the most important general
consideration is the need to evaluate costs in their true economic sense.
The prices of the goods and factors employed in the estimates must,
in other words, be 'shadow prices', determined by the opportunity cost
of the good or factor concerned. These prices might be quite different
from the observable market prices, which may have arisen from the existence of market distortions and imperfections. Such distortions might be
the result of taxation, subsidy or concentration of market power. In a
labour-surplus economy, the prevailing market price for labour is likely
to be much higher than its real economic cost. Little and Mirrlees (1974)
have recommended the use of world prices, rather than internal prices,
as a more accurate proxy for opportunity cost.

Having established a cost criterion, the alternative strategies may now
be appraised in terms of their benefits. Significant amongst these will
be the effects of employment multipliers, the potential impact of
technical change and the influence of each strategy on the distribution
of income. Consideration must also be given to the precise terms of the
investment agreement between the foreign firm and the host government.
Important issues here will include the extent to which profits may be
repatriated and commitments to further investment in the future.
Further, a host government's valuation of benefits might well depend
upon its own specific objectives. A growth-oriented host, for instance,
might consider that X units of reinvestible taxation revenue are more
valuable than X units of immediate consumption gain; a more hedonistic
economy might have a contrary valuation.

In his study, Lal (1975) supplements his guidelines with some
empirical appraisal of foreign investment in specific sectors of the Kenyan
and Indian economies, e.g. tourism and food processing. He concludes
that 'it is platitudinous that POI [private overseas investment] can be
an important aid to development' (p. 261). Such a conclusion does not,
of course, mean that *all* such investment must necessarily benefit the
host. Indeed, the role of investment appraisal criteria is the identification
of the alternative that yields to the host the highest prospective gain.
Naturally, criteria other than the Little and Mirrlees method employed
by Lal also exist. An example is the method developed by the United
Nations Industrial Development Organization (UNIDO, 1972). In

common with the method described above, the UNIDO approach requires the estimation of shadow prices for inputs. However, whilst the basic Little and Mirrlees method considers the benefits and costs largely from the point of view of contributions to government income, the UNIDO method favours the assessment of the project's impact upon present consumption levels. It is quite possible, therefore, for the same set of projects to be ranked differently, depending upon which set of criteria is chosen. The implication is clearly that a society should choose its criteria for investment projects with reference to its own specific objectives.

9.2.2   OFFICIAL DEVELOPMENT ASSISTANCE

Given that the material prosperity of their citizens is a principal objective of most economies, it seems somewhat surprising in the first instance to find that a number of them appear freely to donate their resources to others. We must conclude that either such donors are being perverse or, and this seems more likely, the nature of the game being played is more subtle than in previous instances. Let us begin with an examination of some of the evidence.

We have already identified the donors of ODA as the richer economies of the world, and we have seen that ODA consists of both grants and loans. A further distinction to be made is that between 'bilateral' and 'multilateral' assistance. In the former case, country A will simply transfer resources to country B in a direct fashion. In the latter case, a number of donors will pool their ODA resources, which are then allocated to recipients via an established agency. In fact, virtually all donors presently employ both methods. The major multilateral agencies are the United Nations, the World Bank Group (including the International Bank for Reconstruction and Development), the EEC multilateral fund, the OPEC fund, and the regional Development Banks (African, Asian and Inter-American). *Table 9.4* displays the nature of assistance provided by the Development Advisory Committee (DAC) of the OECD, OPEC and multilateral donors, at the beginning and towards the end of the 1970s. One clear change during the period is the increasing significance of OPEC's involvement. This tendency parallels the one we noted earlier, regarding the oil-producers' increasing involvement in international trade. Although the United States remained the largest single donor by the end of the 1970s, its importance clearly diminished. In 1971, the United States' contribution was double that of France and West Germany combined; by 1977, it was only equal to the combined contribution. Throughout the period considered, grants accounted for a slightly higher proportion of assistance than loans, 58 per cent in 1977. Also, as a proportion of the total, the share of multilateral assistance (as opposed to bilateral) rose from 16 to 26 per cent.

TABLE 9.4 Assistance allocations from DAC/OECD and OPEC
(US$ million)

	1971		1977	
	Loans	Grants	Loans	Grants
Bilateral:				
EEC	1249	1528	1573	3749
USA	1585	1548	1564	1738
Japan	375	125	824	237
OPEC	—	—	787	2977
Others	191	431	293	1479
Multilateral:				
EEC	14	218	151	441
UN	—	561	—	1404
OPEC	—	—	1475	14
World Bank Group	289	—	1197	—
Development Banks/IMF	254	—	690	8
Totals	3957	4411	8554	12047

Source: OCED (1978), *Geographical Distribution of Financial Flows to Developing Countries.*
Paris, OECD, pp. 266–7

Having identified the main origins of ODA, we now turn to its destinations. Considering solely the DAC disbursements, resources flow to all corners of the globe. The continents of Africa, Asia and Latin America each received 25–30 per cent of the 1977 total. When we come to examine the levels of assistance provided to specific countries, however, we find a curiously unbalanced picture. The DAC countries allocate assistance to more than 150 recipients, yet just six of these account for 25 per cent of the total. In 1977, these countries were Brazil (by far the largest single recipient), Indonesia, India, Algeria, Mexico and Korea. Furthermore, it appears that some assistance allocations fluctuate considerably over time. For example, in 1975, the Philippines received $401 million in assistance, an allocation that more than doubled to $1072 million in 1976. By contrast, Nigeria discovered that its 1975 allocation of $685 million fell to $75 million in 1976. At the same time, we observe stability in the annual shares of other recipients, about a constant or moving trend. Burma's annual assistance hovered between $50 million and $80 million between 1971 and 1976, whilst Kenya's gradually rose from $108 million to $354 million.

We noted earlier that the resource transfer from the Eastern bloc to the poorer economies was insignificant when compared to the flow from the DAC countries. Between 1954 and 1973, the Eastern bloc committed capital to the value of $18 billion for use by the poorer economies. Approximately 50 per cent originated from the Soviet Union and 20 per cent came from China. The principal recipients of this capital were Egypt, India, Iran, Iraq, Algeria and Indonesia. Together, these six economies absorbed 54 per cent of the total capital supplied. By the end of the 1970s, the annual ODA allocation of the Soviet Union and Eastern Europe was approaching $2 billion (approximately 6 per cent of world ODA). Nayyar (1977) notes that, in the past, ODA from socialist economies has been concentrated within the public sectors of the recipients. Typical projects have included the exploitation of natural resources, infrastructural development and the establishment of heavy industry. By contrast, the portfolio of ODA disbursements from DAC sources has been far more diverse.

Although assistance is a bilateral or multilateral resource transfer, it results essentially from a unilateral decision. We should presume that donors cannot be forced to provide assistance if they do not wish to. In order to understand why assistance allocation has evolved along the lines that it has we need to consider the motivations of these donors. In general, there are three possible reasons for donation to be an appropriate strategy from the donor's point of view: first, that donation actually confers an economic benefit upon the donor; second, that donation leads to the gaining of wider political or strategic advantages; third, that the donor gains the psychic benefits associated with a charitable act.

In their study of the United Kingdom assistance programme, Hopkin et al. (1970) demonstrated quite clearly that the donation of X units of resources need not represent the loss of X units to the donor economy. In calculating the real cost of assistance, there are three effects to be taken into account. The first of these is 'induction'. In providing resources to a recipient, the donor is giving purchasing power to enable that recipient to buy the donor's exports. The donor economy is thereby stimulated. Indeed, this will be especially true if assistance is 'tied' as is frequently the case in reality – i.e. the recipient is given purchasing power but, under the terms of the assistance, is constrained to purchase items specified by the donor. Second, there exists the 'reflection' effect, which involves the trading relationships of third parties. Economy A may give resources to economy B, which then purchases goods from economy C. Given the nexus of international trade, this might cause economy C to increase its purchases from economy A, again providing benefits to the initial donor. Opposed to these two positive effects we must consider the third, 'switching'. This term describes the possibility that, as the recipient would have bought the donor's exports in any case, the provision of assistance means that funds formerly earmarked for such purchase can now be employed elsewhere. Aggregating these effects, Hopkin et al. discovered that, whilst assistance donation did not actually yield a profit to the UK, the real economic cost was probably only one-third of that suggested by the financial figure. Although the study was concerned essentially with UK bilateral assistance, Hopkin did note that the UK was in a favourable position as regards multilateral aid as its share of world trade with recipients was higher than its share of contributions to the multilateral assistance budgets. The induction effect should accordingly generate positive returns.

If rich countries were to allocate assistance with the express purpose of improving the welfare of fellow nations we might expect them to adopt one of two criteria. In the first place, they might send resources where need is the most immediate, e.g. to countries experiencing acute food shortages. Second, they might decide to allocate investible resources to economies that display the most potential for using these resources in long-term output generation. Evidence suggests that they do neither. In his empirical study of assistance donation, Davenport (1970) discovered that neither of these two factors appeared relevant in explaining the pattern of assistance allocation; in fact, there was stronger evidence to support the hypothesis of positive discrimination against particularly needy countries. This is not to say, of course, that charity is totally absent from the international scene. Given the enormity of the problem of world poverty, the relatively small sums of money available when we consider the number of people that the assistance budgets have to reach (the average assistance receipt in 1976 was a little under $10 per head per annum) and the extreme difficulty of ordering priorities (deciding where resources may be 'best' employed), perhaps a clear relationship should not be expected. In certain respects, we are appraising the wrong sort of data. International charity, in the Western world at least, tends to be more a question of private conscience than collective policy. Governments may therefore be content to leave this aspect of assistance to the informal sector, represented in the British case by organizations such as Oxfam and Christian Aid.

There is little doubt that political, strategic and historical considerations are major factors inducing donors to offer assistance to particular economies. As a general rule and in order to attract a large assistance donation, Thirlwall (1978) concludes with tongue in cheek that 'it would seem advantageous to be a small island of ex-colonial status in a politically sensitive area of the world' (pp. 320–1). This being the case, the impact of assistance on the recipient becomes less clear-cut, for we might, in the first instance, have assumed that assistance as a free gift would always prove acceptable. However, if we now see the offer of assistance essentially as a bribe in order to purchase a recipient's acquiescence to some activity of the donor, assistance becomes a legitimate subject for appraisal. In theory, we could undertake the calculation in the same way as before, evaluating the costs and benefits, although it might be expected that the shadow price of items such as 'diminution of political sovereignty' could prove a little difficult to quantify.

Because of the existence of such intangibles, the estimation of assistance benefits to the recipient is extraordinarily difficult and it is quite possible that, at the end of the day, the recipient might find that there is no such thing as a free lunch. Whether or not the lunch consumed represents value for money is another matter. In a study of UK assistance to Southern Africa, for example, Jones (1977) suggests that certain mutual benefits have resulted. He argues that, as a result of the resource inflow into Botswana, Lesotho and Swaziland, levels of investment have been raised to support the long-run viability of these small economies; at the same time, 'productive' consumption opportunities in the field of education and health care have also become available. Jones believes that, in this particular case, the political and economic aspirations of the donor and the recipients are completely coterminous. Whilst these small economies are anxious to minimize their economic dependence upon South Africa, the UK, with a foot in both camps, sees these states as an important buffer zone between 'black' and 'white' Africa, each of which offers the UK excellent trading possibilities and neither of which the UK wishes to antagonize.

9.3   Economic cooperation

In the previous sections of this chapter we have examined instances where economies have found it optimal to exchange commodities or resources or transfer them from one to another. Although we have considered this as taking place very much on an *ad hoc* basis, the possibility also exists that economies might find it advantageous to enter into a more formalized arrangement of cooperation via the formation of an economic community. Such a community would be in the form of a club wherein member states would agree to abide by a set of rules governing conduct, adherence to which is designed to ensure a superior welfare outcome for all parties. There are two main reasons why the formation of such a club could be considered desirable *ex ante*.

First, it is argued, single economies left to their own devices have a tendency to restrict trade, usually by means of the imposition of tariffs and quotas on imported goods. There are several reasons why they do this, such as the desire to protect domestic industries from foreign competition and the desire on the part of the government of the importing country to raise revenue. However, if one economy imposes a tariff it is likely that trading partners will be obliged to retaliate – otherwise, they would find themselves in a position of being unable to sell their exports whilst being subjected to competition in home markets by the exports of the tariff-imposing economy. Over the longer term, we should anticipate successive rounds of tariff increases as each trading partner attempts to gain a trade advantage over its rivals. This is clearly a negative-sum game, for the volume of international trade will diminish as prices rise; at the limit, it could imply a zero level of trade in a world of perfectly protected markets. As it is unlikely to prove optimal for any one country to remove its trade restrictions without an equivalent response from its partners, the impasse can only be resolved by some formal and binding agreement by all the economies concerned to dismantle their trade barriers simultaneously. Using the standard trade theory of Ricardo, developed in this context by Viner (1950) and Lipsey (1957), we can demonstrate that the increase in trade brought about by collective tariff reduction will be likely to increase the welfare levels of all partners involved in the agreement.

Second, formal cooperation can lead to a more rational use of scarce resources via the coordination of economic policies. Under certain circumstances, for instance, international competition can be inherently wasteful as the desire to maintain home output of certain goods can lead to expensive subsidization and overproduction. Again, to resolve this sort of problem economies might agree to delegate responsibility for the production of such goods to the most efficient producers, who would then act as the (relatively cheap) providers to the entire community. Further, there might well exist investment projects with such high initial costs that they are beyond the reach even of the government of a modern industrial economy. Such projects could become viable, however, were a number of governments to agree to cooperate by pooling resources.

These two factors – trade liberalization and coordination for the more efficient use of resources – were fundamental to the establishment of perhaps the best-known modern example of an international club, the European Economic Community (EEC). In this particular case, however, we can identify two more significant motivating causes for cooperation. First, on two occasions during the twentieth century, the European economies found themselves involved in bitter conflict and it was felt that the transcendence of the boundaries of nationalism via closer formal ties would be more likely to prevent a repetition of infra-European hostilities. Second, the European economies at the time undoubtedly felt that, individually, they were in some sense 'too small' to compete in a world dominated by the economic and political might of the USA and the Soviet bloc. The EEC thus represented the establishment of a countervailing power in the world economy.

The formal birth of the EEC is generally taken to be the Treaty of Rome, which came into force in 1958. The Treaty was principally concerned to establish (i) free trade between member countries, (ii) free mobility of factors of production, (iii) harmonized economic policies, involving necessary changes in national legal systems, (iv) the development of a coordinated policy towards the transport industry and agriculture. Since that time, these general aims have become more specific; for example, the principle of the harmonization of taxation systems was accepted in 1970. In terms of these objectives, it is clear that the trade liberalization aim was the first to achieve any success, and the decline in internal tariffs accounts, in part, for the EEC's growing share of world trade; since 1968, intra-EEC trade has risen from 16 per cent to 20 per cent of the world total. In contrast, many of the remaining aims have given rise to a certain degree of discontent on the part of club members.

There exists, for instance, the likelihood that, in certain cases, community-optimality and member-optimality will differ, although this is less true in the case of trade liberalization and probably accounts for the speed at which liberalization has proceeded. Two examples will suffice. First, all EEC members agree that, if left to the whims of market forces, agricultural prices would fall such that European farmers would only receive very low incomes. Members therefore make a contribution to a common fund to support farm incomes, although there is disagreement at present over the method by which support policies should be implemented. The existing EEC policy is to support farm prices at a sufficiently high level to guarantee 'reasonable' levels of farm income, even for the most inefficient producers. However, as we might expect from the most elementary economic theory, this policy results in general agricultural overproduction, plus the requirement that consumers be obliged to subsidize the inefficient producers. Not surprisingly, the major contributors to the agricultural budget are unhappy about this state of affairs. Second, by the late-1970s, there had arisen a substantial disagreement between Britain and the other EEC members bordering the North Sea regarding fishing rights. By entering the EEC in the early 1970s, the UK surrendered many of its 'private' fishing rights to the common EEC pool and it subsequently found that the club's proposed allocation of fishing territories between members put it in a far less preferred position than had obtained previously. In both of these instances, the games being played may seem, to the disadvantaged members, to be zero- rather than positive-sum.

A second problem, common to all collusive agreements, is that the individual club member may well find it optimal to 'cheat'. A provision of the Treaty of Rome was that economic competition between EEC members should be 'fair', so that markets would be won by the most efficient producers. However, on the assumption that all other members will abide by this rule, it becomes optimal for a single economy to provide a disguised subsidy to its industry in order 'unfairly' to gain a greater market share. Since what is optimal for one is also optimal for all (individually but not collectively), we are likely to be able to discern a trend towards increasing subsidization and overproduction; this seems to be the case with certain EEC industries at present. In fact, both this and the previous problem are related to one general failing of most international collusive agreements, namely the likely existence of a conflict between national sovereignty and the supranational authority, represented in this case by the Council of Ministers and the European Parliament. The source of the authority of such bodies is hard to discern for, whilst national governments can at the limit enforce their domestic decisions by force of arms, the authority of the supranational body, short of the declaration of war, is probably the ability to expel a member from the club. Given that members are supposedly participating in a positive-sum game, even this option would result in a net welfare loss to the remaining club members and it is therefore not a sanction that we should expect to see imposed.

A full appraisal of the EEC is difficult to make for a number of reasons.

First, the community remains, in terms of meeting the objectives specified in the Treaty of Rome, very much in its infancy; accordingly, such problems as discussed above could simply be regarded as those of short-run transition from discrete nationalism to the formation of an integrated European economy. Second, the character of the EEC has changed quite dramatically in recent years with the addition of new members and prospective members, each with its own special class of economic problems; examples are the addition of the UK, Ireland and Denmark in the early 1970s and Greece in 1981. Third, and possibly as a result of the extension of membership, the long-run aims of the EEC are now less precise. Whilst the immediate post-war hopes were, almost, in terms of a 'United States of Europe', with a common currency, a common system of economic management and an embracing political structure, this unilinear trend no longer seems to be such an accepted goal, especially in the light of the substantial European recession of recent years, which has induced member countries to resort, more and more, to essentially domestic economic policies. In particular, there seems to have been a growing interest in protectionism, which, if vigorously applied, would reverse the earlier trade liberalization trend.

Summary

Game theory suggests that trade is likely to be mutually beneficial to trading partners. In recent years, world trade has grown faster than world output. One-half of world trade takes place between the Western industrialized economies. The share in trade of the poorer economies has stagnated, whilst the oil-producing nations came to prominence in the 1970s. Eastern bloc trade remains insignificant in the world total. The nature of trade varies from country to country; resource endowments and technology are determinants. Poor economies tend to export food and raw materials whilst importing manufactures and capital goods; the reverse is true for the industrialized economies. For any one economy, specialization and exchange may give rise to relocation costs, unequal distribution of gains, increased uncertainty and undesirable social consequences. Protectionism may be a privately optimal strategy. Prebisch argued that the trading prospects of poor economies were hampered by the nature of demand and technical change. The Eastern bloc has shown a small but increasing interest in Western technology and food supplies.

Trade is only one of a number of international economic relationships. Amongst the others are loans, export credits, direct investment, concessionary loans and grants. Together, the last two are termed official development assistance (ODA). Direct investment may be classified as export oriented, market development or government initiated. Investors are influenced by long-term profitability and politico-economic stability.

Amongst possible benefits of investment to hosts are net capital inflow, transfer of technology, sources of tax revenue and the evolution of market structure. Hosts will need to employ investment criteria, which account for opportunity costs, when deciding which investment project to select.

ODA originates mainly from the Western economies. It is allocated unevenly between recipients. Political, historical and strategic factors seem to be the major determinants in allocation. Donor benefits may be economic, political and psychic. Because of the induction, reflection and switching effects, the real cost of ODA differs from the nominal cost.

Economic cooperation is a way of expanding trade and of using resources more efficiently by the coordination of economic policies. In addition to these reasons, the desire to avoid political tensions and to increase European competitiveness in the world economy were factors in the formation of the EEC. Collusions are unstable owing to the possibility of cheating and divergences between the interests of individual members and the interest of the community as a whole. The EEC has experienced conflicts of interest in the areas of agricultural policy and fishing.

Further reading

Issues discussed in this chapter all fall within the sub-discipline of 'international economics', which is well served by comprehensive texts; Meier (1980) and Lindert and Kindleberger (1981) are examples. It should be borne in mind that data inaccuracy in this area is particularly problematic; the Eastern bloc, for instance, is most secretive about many of its international relationships. The state of East/West trade is examined by Masnata (1974).

The role of international investment flows is discussed in UN (1975a), Dunning (1972), Ady (1971), ILO (1976) and Bos, Sanders and Secchi (1974). The economic implications of the multinational corporation for the host country are discussed in Kindleberger (1970). Sigmund (1980) considers some of the political implications. Contributions to the debate about the benefits of official development assistance are contained in Bhagwati and Eckaus (1970). Papanek (1973) also examines the contribution of such assistance. Arnold (1979) considers assistance to Africa; Datar (1972) examines Soviet assistance to India. Nayyar (1977) contains a number of papers surveying socialist economic relations with poorer economies. Investment planning in poorer economies is the subject of Newlyn (1977) and Fitzgerald (1978). The specific problems of international indebtedness and loan repayments are discussed by Feder (1980) and in a special issue of *World Development* (1979), Vol. 7, No. 2. Data on international flows are derived from OECD (1980a), pp. 85–7 and UN (1979), Table 204.

The principal sources for the cooperation section are Bracewell-Milnes (1976), Swann (1975) and Robson (1972, 1980). The European Economic Community is dealt with specifically by Denton (1974), Paxton (1976) and Ionescu (1979). Tsoukalis (1981) appraises the problems of EEC enlargement. K. Twitchett (1980) contains analyses of European economic cooperation in general. Krause and Mathis (1970) and Cáceres (1979) explore cooperation and integration in Latin America and Arnold (1979) does the same for Africa.

Strategies for Progress

Part III: Introduction

In the past, economists have devoted a considerable amount of time and effort to the classification of different national economies into typologies of economic systems. At the same time, other economists have been equally industrious in attempting to show that such classifications are unhelpful, if not downright wrong. Now, casual empiricism does tell us that there do exist certain features in a number of economies that permit us to discuss them at a level of generalization, for the purpose of convenient discussion if not detailed analysis. Throughout this book, for example, we have used the term 'pre-industrial' to describe those economies in which agriculture remains the primary form of domestic economic activity and, at the level of generality at which the term has been employed, such usage does not appear illegitimate. However, perhaps a more rigorous classification system is feasible. If so, what defining characteristics might we use in devising a typology?

Virtually every classification of economic systems yet devised owes a certain intellectual debt to Karl Marx who, in suggesting that the history of all societies was the history of class struggle, brought the question of the ownership of productive property to the forefront of economic analysis. Modern texts on the classification of economies into a typology of systems, such as that by Holesovsky (1977), maintain that the ownership criterion is a key factor in any such classification. We may see, for instance, the existence of private property in the USA, socially owned property in the USSR and small-scale communal ownership in countries like Yugoslavia and Spain. Certain pre-industrial societies hold property on a feudal basis. Given this fairly clear set of ownership characteristics, we seem to have at least one solid base for classification. In addition, other writers such as Neuberger and Duffy (1976) consider that the nature of the decision-making and motivational processes is also significant in categorizing national economic behaviour. In particular, these authors focus on three issues. First, different societies operate different systems of enterprise control; in Western Europe, the owners 217 of the firm (i.e. the owners of the firm's capital) in principle control its operations whilst, in the USSR, firms' activities are government directed. Under conditions of industrial democracy, we might expect the labour force to have at least partial control over enterprise operations. Second, different economies have different forms of communications between economic agents. Again, the communication between the firm and the consumer in the West is typically via the price mechanism whilst, in the East, the central government is the intermediary. Finally, different economies use different methods to motivate the producers; in some cases there is the lure of private profits, in some the worker is rewarded at the team rather than at the individual level, whilst in yet other cases the motivational reward might simply be the knowledge that society has benefited through the individual's efforts.

In reality, of course, the decision-making and motivational structure is largely an adjunct of the property relationship. It is the structure of ownership rights that distinguishes the nature of control (i.e. who may do what with what) and that dictates the rewards gained from participation in production. It accordingly seems likely that the nature of ownership in its widest sense may be the central characteristic of our typology of economic systems. However, by looking at the problem in this specific way, we are concerning ourselves not with what economies do but rather with the way in which they do it. We therefore seem to be concerning ourselves with means rather than with ends. An alternative schema would be to classify our systems in terms of the sort of objectives that they set themselves, i.e. in terms of ends rather than means, although, in this case, the former will embrace the latter. What might be the typological categories in this case?

Consider first the manner in which we might classify the UK, Japan and the USSR under the former typology using the ownership and organization criteria. Naturally all three economies have specific peculiarities but we might also note that, whilst the public ownership of property and the centralized direction of resources are features of the Soviet economy, the UK and Japan can be characterized by a fair degree of private ownership with autonomy of enterprise activity. In our classification, Japan would presumably be positioned 'nearer' to the UK than to the USSR. However, what has been the nature of the tasks that these economies have set themselves over the past few decades? In the case of Japan and the USSR, both economies have implemented policies involving substantial resource savings from present-period consumption whilst encouraging, via a variety of techniques, a high degree of resource utilization; the end result has been sustained economic growth over a long period. By contrast, the economic growth performance of the UK has been relatively modest over a similar period. A conclusion that we might draw is not that the UK economy is incapable of growth (for the UK government possesses ample powers of resource mobilization) but that the desire for a high growth rate has not occupied such a position of prominence in the UK objective function as it has in the Soviet or Japanese case. We might find, for example, that the UK has been more concerned with high present consumption levels, with trade policy or with some other objective. Whatever the precise nature of the UK range of goals, we now have grounds for suggesting that, in terms of overt policy and performance, the Japanese economy has more in common with that of the USSR and less with that of the UK, and this is quite contrary to our classification based on ownership patterns.

Other examples of apparently perverse groupings can easily be devised. The industrial structures of France and West Germany, for instance, are clearly comparable in terms of the nature of commodities produced, the patterns of ownership and the extent of government control, and all these characteristics are quite dissimilar to those prevailing in many pre-industrial African economies, such as the Ivory Coast. Evidence suggests, however (Appendix to Part I, Table A1), that the German distribution of income has a far higher correspondence with that of the Ivory Coast than with that of France. We might conclude that, as the French taxation systems would be quite capable of engineering a radical shift in income distribution, perhaps France does not weight the objective of income equality particularly heavily. In objective terms there is no reason why it should, but we again could suggest that, from the point of view of recorded performance, West Germany and the Ivory Coast now belong to the same category of 'egalitarians' whilst France would enter the class of 'inegalitarians'. The data suggest that countries like Peru could also enter this latter class, whilst India could join West Germany in the former.

The purpose of these remarks upon the observed behaviour, and imputed motivations, of certain economies is, most emphatically, not to support the introduction of yet another typology of economic systems, purely for the sake of classification. Rather, it is simply being suggested that what economies are apparently trying to do may be at least as important as the manner in which they are apparently trying to do it. Economic structures and institutions only make sense in the light of the objectives that societies set for themselves, the realization of which provides the rationale for the creation of such structures and institutions. Organization and objective cannot therefore be divorced but must be considered as a totality.

From the expositional point of view, such logic presents problems. We know, for example, that classification by 'means' will generate an extensive set of classes and sub-classes of differing forms of ownership and control. If we now plan to cross this 'vertical' division of the world with some form of 'horizontal' one involving all the possible permutations of objective function that societies might have (even assuming that they could be identified with precision), we shall end up with a number of classes equalling the number of economies in the world (in theory, probably quite a few more). Our proposal for Part III of the book is somewhat more modest. We shall appraise four broad strategies for progress, i.e. organizations of means for the attainment of particular ends. As such, the strategies discussed represent neither exclusive nor exhaustive classifications; rather, they represent convenient ways of handling empirical observations about economic policy, which are necessary to complement the largely theoretical range of alternatives discussed in Part II.

The first strategy to be discussed will be termed the 'growth strategy' and, in this context, we shall examine the historical experiences of two economies that appear to have attached a great deal of weight to the attainment of long-term increases in material output. Correspondingly, they have both placed far less emphasis upon other possible goals of economic policy. Second, and in contrast to this strategy, which is based upon an essentially unbalanced objective function, we shall consider an example of a 'balanced strategy'. In such a case, societies appear to set themselves a range of equally weighted goals, the object being to realize them all simultaneously if at all possible. Third, we shall consider instances of a strategy termed, rather grimly, the 'survival strategy', which is relevant to those economies that, in material terms, are exceptionally poor and that therefore exist on the threshold of economic viability. Finally, and whilst our first three strategies operate at the national level in keeping with much of our earlier analysis, we must also examine a class of strategies that makes explicit recognition of international political and economic relationships.

Chapter Ten

The Growth Strategy

Almost without exception, each economy in the world currently produces more material output than it did a century ago. However, within this overall upward shift in global production, we can observe considerable variation in national performances. Over the past 100 years, for example, some economies have grown at a much faster rate than others; in some cases, growth has been the subject of occasional and erratic spurts; in others, the growth trend has been smooth over an extended period of time. When we come to consider just those economies that have been able to maintain high long-run rates of sustained output growth, our attention naturally focusses upon two prime examples, the first being the USSR. Over the period 1930 to 1960, Soviet material output rose approximately ten-fold, implying a crude average annual production increase of at least 8 per cent over the 30 years. Since 1960 there has been a slight decline in growth performance, to around 7 per cent per annum for the period 1960 to the present day. Our second example is Japan, whose high-growth phase dates from the end of the Second World War. From this time up to 1970, the average growth of Japanese national product exceeded 10 per cent per annum; during the 1970s, average rates declined to around 5 per cent. To a certain extent, a fall in the long-run growth rate after an extended period is to be expected; as output grows, the same absolute output increase becomes smaller relative to the increasing total. However, the point remains that few other economies have performed in such a way; given that these experiences therefore represent quite impressive growth performances, the USSR and Japan seem prime candidates for consideration under the rubric of the growth strategy.

10.1   Soviet economic growth

At the time of the Russian Revolution in 1917, the basic economic structure of what became the USSR was quasi-feudal and predominantly agricultural. The decade after the revolution is of great interest to the student of strategies for progress, for, during this period, almost every conceivable option in terms of objective and organization was rehearsed if not actually implemented. The immediate post-revolution period, usually labelled the period of 'War Communism', had, as the name suggests, two distinguishing features. First, economic organization was geared largely to the consolidation of the new regime's power base, which was vulnerable to the overt hostility of the Western capitalist powers and also to dissenting forces within Russia itself. Second, the new government was clearly establishing communistic organization at one fell swoop, for it proceeded to attempt to nationalize all industry, to ban private exchange and to eliminate money. In the light of this, the so-called New Economic Policy (NEP) of the early 1920s appears to have represented something of a volte-face; private enterprise, which had been maintained in the peasant-based agricultural sector, was slowly re-established in many industrial areas with the exception of large-scale industry (the 'commanding heights of the economy' in Lenin's words). A role for prices and money accordingly re-emerged. The death of Lenin in 1924 heralded a prolonged debate on two related issues, namely who was to succeed Lenin as leader of the new nation and exactly which possible strategy of progress was to be followed in the future. In fact, many of the economic strategies that economists in both East and West discuss today made their first appearance at this time. Some Soviet thinkers argued, for instance, that agriculture represented the USSR's potential strength and therefore the concentration of efforts to establish a secure and efficient agricultural base should be the first priority. At the opposite extreme there were those favouring industrialization at the expense of agriculture. There were also representatives of the 'middle way' who favoured the balanced and simultaneous development of agriculture and industry. The appropriate role for private markets was examined as were the possibilities for foreign trade; at the opposite extreme again, cases were made out for the abolition of such markets and economic progress on a completely autarkic basis.

In the study of economic policy, one does not always come across a precise specification of the strategy being contemplated by the social decision maker. However, for the Soviet case, the following statement made in 1927 by the Central Executive Committee encapsulates not only the specific objective function that was finally selected but also the particular method that was to be employed to realize this objective:

> The five-year economic plan which is being worked out at present must be con-
> structed in conformity with the fundamental objective of strengthening the socialist
> nucleus of our economy, based on the industrialization of the country and on a
> rate of economic development which will allow us in the shortest possible time to
> catch up and overtake the capitalist countries. Industrialization is the hub of all
> our economic policy (in Carr and Davies, 1974, p. 921).

Such a statement appears to represent not only a commitment to a radical shift in production structure away from agriculture but also a commitment to industrial growth that is both high-speed and engineered by a process of economic planning. How did the proposal operate in practice?

Let us first of all consider the basic system of resource allocation that came to be adopted in the USSR. The 'plan' referred to in the above quotation was the First Soviet Five-Year Plan, which ran from 1929 to 1933. Although the planning machinery became more refined as time elapsed, the essential nature of the allocation system was founded at this time, and this was the system that guided the Soviet economy through the high-growth phase up to the 1960s. Nove (1972) has sketched the principles of this planning mechanism in the following terms. Reversing the trend towards decentralization that had begun in the 1920s, all enterprises, with the exception of those of purely local concern, were placed under the ultimate control of a department of the central government. As the system evolved, the extent of this control became virtually limitless. Departments made decisions regarding all aspects of the enterprises' operations, from the appropriate level of output to the composition and origin of inputs, pricing policy, wage levels and so on. Whilst the operations of all enterprises were supervised by the department responsible for the particular category in question (e.g. chemicals or textiles), a newly created agency, Gosplan, was charged with the task of co-ordination of the various individual sectors in line with the overall objectives of national economic policy as determined by the central government. The principal technique by which Gosplan accomplished this task was the method of 'material balances'. For any one enterprise, a material balance represented a record of the available physical output and necessary physical inputs for that enterprise; in effect, it was a micro-production equation. As inputs and outputs of enterprises were inevitably interdependent (i.e. the output of enterprise A would form the input of enterprise B), Gosplan's task was in reality the solution of a nationwide set of simultaneous equations, in order to integrate the activities of all single enterprises. As a result of its reconciliation of individual balances, and taking into account the specified social objective function set by government, Gosplan was then in a position to calculate specific requirements to be passed down to individual enterprises as operational targets for the immediate production period. It should be noted that, in such an allocation system, there is no role for the formal price mechanism as resource allocater.

The First Plan established a range of targets to be attained by all the various sectors of the economy. In aggregate terms, the value of national production was planned to double by 1933; in fact, it rose by 86 per cent. The target for gross industrial production was growth of 135 per cent, a figure that was reached almost exactly. In particular, the growth of capital goods production far exceeded its target with a five-year expansion of 285 per cent. The poorest performances, relative to the hoped-for targets, were those of the consumer goods industries (with an actual 64 per cent expansion). In order to explain these differential performances we must examine the economic policies actually applied.

The theoretical foundations of the Soviet industrialization drive were laid in the early 1920s by, amongst others, Preobrazhensky. His analysis of the early stages of capitalist development, which he derived from Marx and the British classical school, suggested that investment was the key to growth and, in the European case, such investment had been obtained by imperialist exploitation, the absorption of the agricultural surplus and land enclosure. Given the absence of a Russian empire, Preobrazhensky argued that this model of 'primitive capitalist accumulation' was not directly applicable and he accordingly suggested that the Soviet variant (primitive socialist accumulation) would have to give the role of surplus mobilizer exclusively to the agricultural sector. When Preobrazhensky was advancing such ideas (during the NEP), agriculture remained in private, peasant hands. Whilst it was conceded that it was possible that the necessary agricultural surplus might be realized on a voluntary basis, Preobrazhensky doubted that such an 'optional' system would generate sufficient investible resources to permit the rapid expansion of the socialized industrial nucleus of the economy. Compulsory taxation would therefore be necessary but, more importantly, a system of unequal exchange would have to be initiated. This was to involve a shift in the terms of trade between industrial and agricultural goods, the government using its power to inflate the prices of the former. Investible resources would thus be effectively drawn out of agriculture.

The specific policy applied to Soviet agriculture in the 1930s was derived from the above model, although it certainly went further than most of the theoreticians had envisaged. Reforms of the late Tsarist period, and the policies of NEP, had created an agricultural structure in the Soviet Union characterized by owner-occupier peasants. From the time of the revolution, a gradual consolidation of land-holding had occurred, as the richer peasants managed to acquire the land of their poorer neighbours. Stalin, however, planned for consolidation on a grand scale. Land was to be held collectively at the village level and farmed as a cooperative enterprise – the average collective farm of today covers an area of 6000 hectares and employs some 500 persons (Nove, 1977, p. 27). There were three major justifications used to support this policy. First, it was felt that large-scale farming would be more efficient than agriculture under the peasant structure. To rationalize the use of capital, Machine Tractor Stations were established that supplied equipment to the collectives. Second, Stalin was conscious of Lenin's warning that the survival of a peasant-based agriculture could, in the long run, bring about the return of the capitalist system. This, of course, had to be avoided at all costs. Third, it was felt that a collectivized agriculture would make it easier for the government to implement the terms of trade policy and would assist in the withdrawal of the surplus from agriculture. Collectives, for example, paid for the equipment hired from the Machine Tractor Stations with agricultural produce.

Irrespective of the rationale of collectivization, it remains unclear to this day why the change in ownership and production practices amongst tens of millions of agricultural workers had to be made so rapidly and dramatically. Ulam (1974) suggests that Stalin made the decision 'on impulse, even if it was cunningly pursued later on' (p. 355). It was largely the experience of collectivization that accounted for the poor performance of agricultural production during the period of the first few five-year plans. Indeed, the legacy of collectivization remains with Soviet agriculture to the present day. The peasantry reacted to the confiscation of their surpluses, and the attempts to force them onto the collectives, by slaughtering their livestock and by withdrawing their labour efforts. The reorganizers, on the other hand, were not even able to argue that the collectives were more efficient, for they were often poorly administered and starved of capital. In retrospect, the collectivization policy is impossible to understand in purely material terms. It imposed fearful costs in terms of lost production and lost lives – many millions of peasants were eliminated directly during the collectivization drive, especially the richer ones who were considered 'class enemies', and an even greater number of people perished as a result of the famines that ensued as a consequence of the production cutbacks. With the benefit of hindsight, we now know that pre-collectivized Soviet agriculture was no more 'backward' than the agricultural sectors of many other economies at the time. The fact that overall Soviet economic growth was so high during the Stalinist era becomes even more intriguing when we consider that it received precious little direct assistance from agriculture.

Despite a degree of disarray, resources nevertheless became available for investment. Indeed, one positive contribution that collectivization was able to make to industry was the liberation of a large number of peasants from the land. Discontented with their lot, these individuals made themselves available for industrial employment. As a migration of such a magnitude had not been foreseen by the planners, the effect was to make the industrial targets far more feasible, as a higher input of labour became available. On the debit side, however, urban amenities such as transport found themselves under severe pressure. The spending power of this unexpected labour force also contributed to urban price inflation.

Irrespective of the specific form of policy for reorganization, the early plans had always envisaged agriculture as being the prime source of investible resources. In the beginning, mobilization was brought about by the imposition of a 'turnover tax', first brought in in 1930. The government purchased agricultural production at a low price, charged the consumers a high price, and retained the difference for its own use. Nove (1972) notes that two-thirds of the investment plan was financed by this method in 1935 (p. 211).

Having briefly examined the origins of the Soviet growth strategy, let us now turn to the situation in and around 1960 and discover what subsequently emerged. The most obvious change was the sheer scale increase in the economy, with a shift in structure particularly towards the capital goods industries. To a considerable extent, this move resulted from the explicit decision on the part of the government to aim for as high a rate of accumulation as was possible, i.e. to trade off short-run consumption for long-run consumption, and the proportion of annual product reinvested between 1930 and 1960 was of the order of 20–30 per cent. As we have just seen, the turnover tax was the major source of resource mobilization in the earlier period, although, as industrialization proceeded, the government began to extract more resources from the surpluses of industrial enterprises. By 1960, enterprises were contributing 50 per cent of the central government's budget. The general turnover tax accounted for most of the remainder, given that the Western preference for direct personal taxation was not shared by the Soviets. In turn, a little less than 50 per cent of state receipts were put back as investment for material production, the rest being allocated to the equivalent of the capitalist 'public sector', i.e. the collective provision of education, health care, defence and so forth.

From our earlier examination of the nature of technology, it is clear that an annual growth of capital of 10 per cent, such as the USSR sustained over the 1930–60 period, cannot in itself generate material growth. Complementary factors of production will always be required. As far as natural resources were concerned, the Soviet Union found itself well endowed. The exploitation of primary minerals such as coal, oil and iron ore was given a prominent position in all of the five-year plans. The supply of 'raw' labour likewise presented few problems before the 1960s owing to natural population growth and the general shift of labour out of agriculture, partially as a result of agricultural reorganization. The question of labour quality was, however, a more difficult one to resolve and it was approached in three ways. First, the expansion of the formal education sector became a priority target, resources being allocated to school construction and teacher training, particularly in relation to those areas directly oriented towards material production. Second, relatively cost-effective informal education was introduced, e.g. apprenticeship schemes and 'on the job' training. Finally, an incentive payments structure was implemented at an early stage that not only served to increase the basic labour supply but also encouraged those with the skills to enter the most socially productive occupations. Significantly, and especially in the Stalinist period up to the mid-1950s, international trade was given only the most minimal role to play in the mobilization of resources.

Detecting shifts in economic strategy is always a problematic exercise, for it is hard to detect where one ends and another begins. In the Soviet case, however, the 1960s can with some justification be regarded as such a period of shift. Niwa (in Wiles, 1971) has shown that, in spite of the massive output increases experienced by the Soviet economy over the 1930–60 period, the level of real wages was not significantly different at the end of the period from its level at the beginning. Indeed, there is evidence of a decline in the 1930s, and a corresponding upward trend emerged only in the early 1950s. Clearly, this represents a stark measure of the extent of short-term sacrifice involved in the Soviet case. It is surely significant that the Party Programme adopted in 1961 established as a principal goal the doubling of the real wage level by 1970; all previous plans had been centred upon output targets. In practical terms, this was not taken to mean that the accumulation strategy was wrong *per se*; rather that the particular emphasis might be misplaced. A diversification away from the heavy industrial base was seen as justifiable.

In parallel with this concern that the composition of the output and investment mix might be in need of some adjustment, there was the growing belief that the resource allocation system being employed might be giving rise to production inefficiencies. Although administrative change, methodological advance and improvements in data accuracy and availability had taken place between 1930 and the 1960s, the basic material balance framework remained the central pillar around which each Soviet plan was built. However, there are a number of reasons why a material balance planning framework might give rise to a sub-optimal allocation of resources.

First, the material balance approach may well lead to a waste of resources. When an enterprise negotiates with Gosplan regarding its output targets and input requirements for the planning period, it is clearly in its interests to incorporate as much 'slack' as possible. Without suitable incentive, no enterprise manager would choose to operate at 100 per cent efficiency, preferring instead some level of 'breathing space', which would be provided by a lower output target, or a higher availability of inputs, than was strictly necessary. Wastage might also come about if the plan fails to incorporate the precise specification of consumer demand. If nobody wishes to consume the output, the product yields no welfare irrespective of the degree of technical efficiency by which it is produced. Second, if the planners allocate investment goods and raw materials to enterprises without any consideration of opportunity cost, not only will the inefficient hoarding of inputs be encouraged but society will be unable to adopt any rational criterion for the allocation of scarce resources. Third, the practice that existed in the USSR up to the 1960s of operating simultaneously a system of centralized direction of resources and a system of quasi-market allocation via prices (generally politically determined) naturally gave rise to conflicts and anomalies. Fourth, whilst the material balance approach might be very effective in regulating the flow of resources between enterprises where production functions are well established, the volatility of consumer demand implies that, without almost perfect knowledge, a plan will be virtually guaranteed to produce either surpluses or shortages of particular consumption items. Fifth, and questioning the assumption made above, the use of established input–output coefficients in formulating enterprise targets (i.e. the principle that, in order for enterprise A to produce X units, enterprise B must always supply it with Y units of input) means that the possibility of technical progress – the more efficient use of inputs – could well be overlooked. Sixth, an excessively autarkic attitude (which characterized the USSR at the time) could deny an economy access to foreign products and technology. Finally, as the material balance system is administered bureaucratically, the possibility arises that the particular objective function of the bureaucrat could differ from that of society, leading to a socially sub-optimal resource allocation (Ellman, 1979).

This is a rather impressive list of objections. Not surprisingly, when such matters were openly discussed in the Eastern bloc in the 1960s, changes were suggested. However, in this respect the course pursued by the USSR was somewhat different from that pursued by its East European neighbours who, ever since the Second World War, had followed the Soviet model quite closely. Let us therefore consider the 'East Europe' alternative first of all. If the individual enterprise, it was argued, is to perform efficiently, it must be given some incentive to do so (or, alternatively, some disincentive not to do so). Further, centralized resource direction can be rationalized if enterprises are obliged to bear costs for the resources that they employ; this will discourage resource hoarding and the use of inefficient production techniques. Finally, production incentives ought to be related to the extent to which output satisfies consumer demand, i.e. social efficiency should be maintained. Taken together, these conditions imply a very positive role for markets in a socialist economy; specifically, they imply a role for the price mechanism and the 'profit' motive. Enterprises, it is argued, should be required to purchase inputs and market the output, the difference in the values of costs and revenues acting as an indicator for the incentive payment to be made to the employees of the enterprise. We should then expect the enterprise to attempt to minimize its input costs or, alternatively, to maximize its output value, which will be accomplished by satisfying the prevailing demand conditions.

This economic structure looks deceptively like a capitalist model. Its supporters, however, argue that there are significant differences. In this Eastern European solution, often termed 'market socialism', the central government still plays a key role in fixing the price levels of producer goods. Indeed, this does make all the difference. By manipulation of these prices, the government is able to effect alterations in the balance of production, for the producer price level, by changing the enterprises' input costs, influences profitability. To discourage production in sector A, therefore, it might raise the price of A's inputs, which should have a disincentive influence. Also, the whole concept of profit is quite different in the market socialist case. Socialist profits are simply methods of ensuring efficiency; they are not the object of production as in the capitalist case. Because of the degree of price control, an enterprise cannot manipulate its market to increase its profit, whereas capitalist firms, especially monopolies, of course can. In the socialist case, profit is not privately owned as it is under capitalism; rather, it serves as a guide to where enterprise should be rewarded and such rewards are to be shared amongst all factor-owners, not simply the owners of capital. Finally, profitability is a criterion for investment in capitalist societies. No private investor will place his resources in an unprofitable venture. In the socialist case, the government retains the freedom to invest wherever it wishes, irrespective of the profitability criterion, i.e. there ought to be no 'failure' in the investment market.

Amongst the Eastern bloc, and with the exception of Yugoslavia, which left the Soviet fold in 1950, it is Hungary that has gone the furthest in the market socialist direction. As a result of the 1968 reforms, enterprises found themselves free of many of the earlier restrictions on employment and wage payment. In turn, however, enterprises were given far more responsibility in resource mobilization, as enterprise taxation replaced the turnover tax as the prime source of state revenue. This liberalization procedure was also applied to agricultural enterprises, which, although not de-collectivized, were now free to make their own production decisions. The government maintained its general control over the economy nonetheless, via involvement in trading relations, investment and by means of its pricing policy. The prices of basic capital goods and essential consumption items were strictly managed, whilst goods regarded as being of less importance had price controls eased or withdrawn completely.

The difference between the market socialist alternative and the strategy employed by the USSR at present is not in terms of the 'prices and profits' policies. A restructuring of the incentive system and the rationalization of allocation by pricing was a basis of a 1965 Soviet reform. However, rather than decentralizing decisions to the level of the enterprise, the USSR appears to be better disposed towards the integration of existing enterprises, essentially for the purpose of gaining economies of scale. The present Soviet attitude to planning also seems to differ from, say, the Hungarian conception. The market socialist view appears to be that any economy is such a complex system that, not only is it difficult to understand, it is impossible to control from a central standpoint. Accordingly, it is necessary for large areas of economic activity to be governed automatically, a market being the classic example of automatic regulation. The current Soviet view, on the other hand, seems to be that, granted an economy is complex, every step must be taken fully to understand and direct it. The 1970s have therefore witnessed attempts to develop cybernetic technology in the form of sophisticated methods of data processing, economic modelling and automatic management structures. Ellman (1979), incidentally, is dubious about the possibilities of success of this approach, believing that no computer technology can be *that* effective, especially in view of the existence, as in all economies, of uncertainty. In this, he echoes the sentiments of the early critics of central planning who had doubts about its technical feasibility (Hayek, 1935).

Owing to its reluctance to publish data, and its particular technique of national accounting, the USSR presents problems for observers wishing to appraise its current circumstances. The annual growth rate for the mid-1970s appears to have been a little over 5 per cent. Gross capital formation, as a proportion of output, declined slightly during the 1970s, reaching 26 per cent in 1978. High industrial growth rates stand out in stark contrast to the performance of agriculture. For the period 1970–76, annual average growth rates by sector were: manufacturing industry, 7.6 per cent; construction, 5.6 per cent; transport, 7.0 per cent; agriculture, −0.3 per cent. Such data add weight to the assertion of Ulam (1974) that agriculture remains the 'Achilles' heel of the entire national economy' (p. 356). Soviet population growth has been relatively modest and the annual growth of per capita output averaged 4.8 per cent between 1970 and 1976. In spite of an emerging interest in foreign trade, especially with other socialist states, the Soviet economy remains insular – net exports contributed 1 per cent to total output in 1978.

10.2   Economic growth in Japan

Whilst the Soviet growth strategy grew out of political and economic revolution, the Japanese experience was prefaced by military defeat. Neither, however, began in a vacuum. In the Soviet case, certain of the basic foundations had been laid in the Tsarist era. There had been attempts, for example, to develop heavy industry and transport, and agricultural reforms had been implemented. The corresponding initiative in the Japanese case was taken by governments after the

restoration of the emperor in 1868 (the Meiji restoration). Meiji governments were especially concerned to liberalize trade, to restructure the
ownership patterns of agriculture and to build up the basis of a financial
economy. As a result, a certain amount of economic growth took place
in Japan during the late nineteenth and early twentieth centuries; even
so, the Japanese 'growth miracle' remains very much a post-1945
phenomenon.

In their detailed study of Japanese economic growth, Ohkawa and
Rosovsky (1973) argue that Japan in 1945 exhibited a number of features
of the 'dual economy' type of model that we met in Chapter 7. One
of the most important was the nature of technology. The legacy of the
Meiji and subsequent periods was, they argue, the prevalence of
'traditional' technology, production being based on capital-saving and
land- and labour-using techniques. The technology of the post-war
world, however, was 'modern', essentially capital-intensive. Significantly, modern technology is characterized by fixed proportions production functions whilst the traditional technology admits greater scope
·for factor substitution.

In what way was the dualistic development of Japan realized? An
important consequence of pre-war industrialization was the institutional-
ization of some very specific labour practices, characterized by the
phrases 'seniority wage scale' and 'lifetime commitment' (p. 135). In
purely economic terms, this implied the production of distortions in the
Japanese labour market. In the first place, it became the practice to
relate wage payments not to marginal product (as neoclassical economic
theory would suggest would be the optimum strategy) but to more
individualistic aspects such as the worker's degree of education, his length
of service, his status and the overall cost of living. Second, in a number
of industries, both firm and worker came to accept the belief in permanent employment, each acknowledging a long-term responsibility for
the welfare of the other. Coupled with this, however, it appears that
the labour force was extremely 'flexible', i.e. it required only a small
change in the going wage rate to induce a large amount of labour to
migrate from the traditional sector and complement the capital in the
modern sector.

After 1945, and because of the nature of modern technology and the
particular labour market structure, there existed a strong tendency for
wages to lag behind labour productivity in the modern sector. Enterprise profitability was accordingly high and the anticipation of high
profits caused firms to save and reinvest at a substantial rate. In this
investment drive, firms received positive assistance from the Japanese
consumer, for not only did wage growth lag behind output growth but
private consumption did not keep up with rises in incomes. An increasing
amount of private savings, in other words, became available to firms
via financial intermediaries. Exactly why the Japanese consumer had
such a high marginal propensity to save during the 1950s and 1960s

still remains unclear although a number of reasons have been advanced. First, Japanese tastes appear to have been conservative, with individuals disinclined to alter their purchasing habits in spite of income and wealth increases. Second, the public provision of welfare programmes was rudimentary with the result that the Japanese family was obliged to cater for its own 'social security' insurance and to finance children's education; in contrast, such items were the responsibility of government in most other industrial economies. Third, the peculiarities of the Japanese banking system made personal credit difficult to obtain so savings became vital to future individual consumption. Whatever the precise cause, we know that the total savings ratio of the Japanese economy (savings as a proportion of national output) reached 35 per cent in the early 1960s, half of which was accounted for by savings of individuals and companies. Private savings made up one-third of this amount.

This high investment potential is not sufficient to explain Japanese economic growth, just as it was insufficient in the Soviet case. Whilst the USSR was blessed with enormous endowments of natural resources and an extensive internal market, the opposite was more true for Japan. The external dimension therefore becomes of crucial importance in explaining the Japanese achievement, and two factors were significant in this respect. First, the fact that Japan was a relative late-comer in the adoption of modern technology permitted it to 'tool up' with the most recent innovations initially imported from other industrial economies. Second, high productivity and low labour costs gave Japanese exports a substantial competitive advantage over those of many other countries. As a result of the increasing world interest in Japanese manufactures, Japan was able to, first, restructure its output in favour of import-substitution industry and, second, begin to import those essential primary products (such as minerals, food and fuels) with which it was poorly endowed and that formed inputs to its productive processes.

Two further constituents of Japanese economic growth must also be noted. The first consists of a simple proposition. Japan has been unique amongst the countries of the world in including in its constitution a formal renunciation of the legitimacy of the use of war as a means of resolving international disputes (Article 9). This implies that the acquisition of the means of warfare has not ranked high in the Japanese objective function. Throughout the 1970s, Japan devoted less than 1 per cent of its gross annual output to military expenditure; this is a stark contrast to the much higher GDP commitments of other industrial nations with no such antipathy towards violence – USA, 6 per cent; UK, 5 per cent; USSR, 11 per cent. By not consuming the 'defence' commodity, Japan has accordingly been free to consume others. Put another way, the opportunity cost of the USA's consumption of defence, over and above that consumed by the Japanese, is of the order of 20–30 per cent of its possible rate of non-defence capital creation, other things remaining equal.

The role of the second constituent is somewhat more complex. Our description of Japanese growth thus far records it as mechanistically following an almost perfect textbook account of growth via 'laissez-faire' and private enterprise. However, what part has the Japanese government played in the growth experience? In his study of the modern Japanese economy, Halliday (1975) argues that the relationship between government and private industry has in fact been most intimate. By virtue of the government's acceptance that the overall Japanese objective function was coterminous with the objectives of private enterprise, the government has responded both positively (by giving assistance to firms) and negatively (by not hindering the activities of private firms) in the management of the economy. Two areas, for example, where many other Western economies have felt a need for intervention are in wage policy and monopoly policy. In the former case it is frequently held that the superior bargaining position of capital as opposed to labour may cause a disproportionate share of the production surplus to be distributed to the owners of capital. It is the task of the government to step in and establish a 'fair' wage minimum. In the latter case it is held that, if a firm attains a position of monopoly in an industry, it will be able to influence the market by the restriction of output and will thus appropriate consumer surplus. Accordingly, the government might intervene to enforce a competitive industrial structure, ensuring that the surplus goes to the consumer and not to the producer. In both of these areas, however, intervention on the part of the Japanese government has been conspicuous by its absence, and the effect over time has been the considerable strengthening of the power and the wealth of the industrial corporations.

Indeed, Japan at present is very much a 'corporate economy', an oligopoly of a small number of industrial/financial conglomerates known as *zaibatsu*. This basic structure actually dates from the early twentieth century and has become more and more refined since then, despite post-war American attempts at 'trust-busting'. A 1970 survey showed that the 13 largest conglomerates accounted for 92 per cent of capital in heavy industry and were responsible for 75 per cent of the total sales of the top 170 Japanese manufacturing firms (Halliday, 1975, pp. 275–6). In a more positive sense, the government appears to have facilitated the formation of such an industrial structure by engaging in forms of economic planning (e.g. by establishing agencies to coordinate enterprise activities and to provide management services) and by easing the potential for the mobilization of industrial credit. In addition, the rate of taxation levied by central government has been low and therefore the reinvestment possibilities for firms have been high. Even though taxation levels have slowly risen in Japan over the past two decades, Japanese government revenue in 1978 was only 24 per cent of gross domestic product; corresponding figures for other Western economies were: United Kingdom, 39 per cent; West Germany, 43 per cent;

Sweden, 60 per cent. We must also note that Japanese trade policies have favoured output expansion, with government assistance being given to exports and degrees of protection of the home market against the incursions of foreign competition.

In appraising the present circumstances of the Japanese economy, it is perhaps instructive to consider the impact of growth upon two interested parties who, to a large extent, were responsible for it. These are, first, the Japanese worker/consumer and, second, Japan's trading partners. We have already suggested that labour made sacrifices during the high growth period of the 1950s and 1960s by virtue of the fact that productivity growth rose faster than wage growth. Sacrifices were also made in the sense that, over the period, the Japanese did not consume many of the sorts of products that inhabitants of other industrial economies appear to enjoy. Although its per capita income by 1970 was equivalent to that of many Western economies, Ohkawa and Rosovsky (1973) argue that Japan was particularly deficient in social overhead capital:

Measured in terms of number of rooms per person, diffusion of water supply and sewage, ratio of paved roads, or area of city parks, Japan lags sadly behind countries with which it likes to compare itself.... The ratio of social stock to national income fell steeply from the early 1950s until the early 1960s and since then it has not risen significantly (pp. 242–3).

Indeed, a comparison between Japan and other Western industrialized economies yields interesting conclusions as regards the nature of consumption goods purchased. Of the 25 OECD countries (essentially Western Europe, North America, Australia and Japan) in 1978, Japan occupied thirteenth position in a ranking of output per head and per capita private consumption. In terms of the number of telephones owned in proportion to the population, Japan was in fifth position. By contrast, for the indices of doctors per head, and television sets and car ownership per 1000, Japan ranked twenty-first, seventeenth and twentieth respectively. We should note that over 30 per cent of Japanese exports to the USA, and over 20 per cent of exports to Western Europe, was made up of motor vehicles and television equipment.

There is naturally no reason whatsoever why the Japanese consumer should necessarily feel that a different basket of goods 'ought' to be consumed. The point remains, however, that were tastes to change in order to generate the consumption bundle more characteristic of, say, Western European economies, this would have implications both for the private individual's marginal propensity to save and also, in the case of social overhead capital, for the level of taxation necessary to finance such provision. In fact, there seems to be no particular indication that such a change is occurring. During the late 1970s, productivity rises were greater than increases in unit labour costs, especially in manufacturing industry. The Japanese labour movement has shown little desire to appropriate the gains from its increasing contribution as has been the case in the majority of Western economies. An important factor explaining this must be the peculiarly Japanese structure of employment mentioned earlier.

The second party interested in Japan's economic growth – Japan's trading partners – appeared to react quite positively during the 1970s. In a sense, the strategy for growth that Japan has employed has much in common with the one that developed in the UK in the nineteenth century, i.e. the import of raw materials and the export of manufactures. The important difference, however, is that when Britain was the 'workshop of the world' not only were there few other nations engaged in the same business but the supply of world resources appeared to be limitless. Japan presently finds itself trying to export to other countries that, although they want the welfare gains derived from the consumption of Japanese goods, have become worried about the effects that the availability of such goods is having on their domestic industries. Further, the increasing scale of global production means that the stock of world resources in relation to demand has become unpleasantly finite and Japan is now obliged to compete for this stock with many other industrial powers. Japan experienced problems in its trading growth during the 1970s, from both the export and the import side. Based upon the high growth rates in the 1960s, the Japanese Economic Research Centre in 1970 forecast a 10 per cent share in world trade by 1975 (Ohkawa and Rosovsky, 1973, p. 241). In fact, the Japanese share in 1975 amounted to a little over 6 per cent and this proportion remained constant for the remainder of the decade.

Several factors contribute to the explanation of this stability. First, North America, and especially the USA, has always been a 'target market' for Japan; 27 per cent of total Japanese exports went there in 1979. In terms of global growth, however, North America is a contracting market; its share of world imports fell to 14 per cent in 1979, from 20 per cent in 1968. Second, evidence suggests that the demand for Japanese exports is fairly price-elastic with the result that the appreciation of the yen disturbed the smoother upward trend that characterized the 1960s. Third, there is growing evidence of the emergence of protectionist proclivities on the part of the Western industrial importers who fear the effects of Japanese exports on their own industries. In February 1981, the US Ford Motor Company announced the biggest trading loss in American business history and partially ascribed it to consumers' preference for imported Japanese automobiles. The late-1970s saw the start of 'gentlemen's agreements' between Japan and the United Kingdom, whereby Japan 'voluntarily' limited its exports to the UK in order to prevent the creation of serious economic difficulties in the latter's car and engineering industries.

Because of its poor natural resource endowment, Japan depends heavily on primary imports to sustain production. The increase in oil prices in 1973–4 of some 200–250 per cent plunged the economy into depression. Between 1974 and 1975, output actually fell by 2 per cent whilst the price level rose by 15–20 per cent. The competitiveness of Japanese exports was accordingly reduced and export growth was restrained. Significantly, as the trend in wage levels at this time did not follow the output path, real wages in fact rose at the expense of short-term profits and long-term investment. These problems were reinforced by a further oil price rise in 1978–9 although, in this second instance, the Japanese government appeared more willing to intervene with monetary and fiscal management policies, which had not been widely employed during the earlier periods.

10.3   Some observations

Both the Soviet and the Japanese examples illustrate the simple point that we have affirmed and reaffirmed throughout our enquiry, namely that high rates of long-term material growth necessitate high rates of short-term material sacrifice. In the Soviet case, this sacrifice resulted from a unilateral decision on the part of the central government to transfer resources into the accumulation process as rapidly as possible in the first instance. This was engineered by taxation and a radical restructuring of the country's economic base. In the Japanese case, however, the government's role was less overtly coercive because the prevailing economic structure and conditions appear to have made the savings option attractive from both the firm's and the consumer's point of view. It remains a moot point whether the sacrifices for the attainment of growth and the resultant benefits from growth have been equally distributed. In the earlier periods of Soviet industrialization, agriculture was heavily penalized although Wiles (1974) suggests that the post-Stalin income distribution has moved fairly rapidly towards egalitarianism. Surveying the most recent evidence, Ellman (1979) argues that the USSR in the 1970s was a society 'in which the great mass of the population was quite equal ...', although the actual standard of living was low as compared to many Western states (p. 190). Japan, on the other hand, is placed in the 'high income/low inequality' category by Chenery et al. (1974) and it appears that post-war Japanese growth has always been characterized by a comparatively egalitarian income distribution.

Further insights into the growth strategy may perhaps be gained by some tentative prognoses of the Soviet and Japanese economies. The USSR has three great advantages. First, its sheer physical size and geographical location mean that, from the natural resources point of view, it is possibly the best-endowed economy in the world. It has abundant supplies of both primary raw materials, such as iron and copper ores, and energy sources, such as oil, coal and natural gas, even though Nature has not seen fit to locate them in convenient positions. The enormous distances involved, and the inaccessibility of resource fields such as those of Siberia, will continue to impose extraction and transportation problems. Second, because the allocation of investment remains the responsibility of government, there should arise none of the Keynesian type of depressionary problems that supposedly characterize capitalist economies, namely market failure and deficient aggregate demand. The government's power to tax and spend is probably higher in the USSR than in any other country. Third, the Soviet Union is, to a large extent, insulated from the economic fluctuations of the outside world, owing to its extremely limited involvement with that world.

On the 'debit' side, we should recall the comments of observers who suggested that the Soviet resource allocation mechanism might come under pressure from the growing complexity of the economy. Sustained growth may therefore only remain feasible if the planning system can be made more sophisticated. Second, the Soviet Union continues to be a net importer of agricultural products, reflecting its decades-old inability to secure agricultural production increases that match its industrial performance. The raising of agricultural productivity has been a perennial concern of the Soviet leadership, one that gives rise to recurrent proposals to extend private ownership in this sphere. Third, the USSR carries one of the highest defence burdens (the ratio of defence spending to national output) in the world, a burden that generates severe opportunity costs in terms of 'civil' consumption. However, it might be considered that such costs are overstated if it can be shown that military spending yields net multiplier benefits, when compared to alternative activities, or that the behaviour of rival nations jeopardizes Soviet security.

We noted that, in 1927, the Soviet Union set itself the task of catching up with, and overtaking, the capitalist nations. In aggregate terms, this objective has undoubtedly been realized. The USSR presently out-performs the capitalist economies in many fields of industry, and its military strength must clearly be considered to be at least equal. In particular areas, however, the gap has closed over the past half-century but nevertheless clearly still exists – examples include agriculture, technology and labour productivity. Even so, we must conclude that, given the confusion in which the contemporary capitalist world appears to find itself, and the remarkable ability of the Soviet Union to maintain a high rate of economic growth in spite of all the charges that theoretical economics might level against it, a further narrowing of those differentials that remain must appear feasible.

As for the future of Japanese growth, one very positive factor must be that economy's exceptional capacity to generate savings. The national savings ratio in 1978 was 33 per cent of GNP, the second-highest in the OECD group after Luxemburg. Another is the continued saleability of Japanese products in world markets, despite decreases in price-competitiveness owing to cost rises and exchange rate appreciation. On the other hand, the very narrow Japanese resource base implies that the country's economic fortunes are heavily dependent upon the willingness and ability of other economies to keep it supplied with the basic resource inputs. In addition, Japan's trading prospects depend upon the degree of international protection that might be practised by its trading partners. Over the past decade, the Japanese have been evolving two policies to come to terms with such problems. First, as 90 per cent of all energy inputs are imported, Japan has attempted to promote both energy-conservation measures and the development of new energy sources. Second, in an attempt to maintain its competitiveness, Japan has found it profitable to move capital to cheap-labour economies such as Korea, Taiwan and other states in South-East Asia. Direct investment in Western industrial economies has also taken place, stimulated by the reduction in Japanese/Western wage differentials and the fear of restrictions being placed upon imports.

Given this high degree of interdependence with the rest of the world, the Japanese economic future is difficult to forecast. Almost certainly the 'growth miracle' phase, with annual rates in excess of 10 per cent, is over. Ohkawa and Rosovsky (1973) forecast an annual average growth rate of 6.5 per cent for the period 1970–90. As the average for 1970–78 was only around 5 per cent, this forecast now appears wildly optimistic, especially in view of the escalation of the world's energy problems over the past ten years. On the other hand, the potential for demand-induced growth on the part of the Japanese consumer must remain extremely high. Hedging our bets, therefore, we shall forecast a continuation of the present trend in economic growth, whilst emphasizing that particular circumstances, such as a further doubling of oil prices or the rise of market protection in the West, could influence it to a considerable extent. Although the Japanese growth performance in the past, therefore, has not quite matched the Soviet record, Japan's future growth rate should remain one of the highest amongst capitalist nations.

We cannot conclude this chapter without reviewing the costs of growth – the opportunities forgone as a result of the adoption of the growth strategy. In the Soviet case, growth was undoubtedly purchased at a high price in terms of the sacrifice of immediate consumption. With the benefit of hindsight, we might even say that the price was too high. Soviet growth resulted not so much from productivity or technological improvements but rather from the increased input of basic factors of production on a massive scale. Had the Soviet record of productivity increases over the past 50 years matched, say, that of the Western economies, it seems clear that the same rate of growth could have been achieved with a lower level of consumption sacrifice. Looked at another way, higher productivity in the Soviet Union, coupled with the same level of investment, could have given rise to an even higher growth rate than the one actually obtained, other things remaining equal. Western observers often add that the Soviet people incurred a substantial cost in terms of the limitation of political freedom. However, as we saw in an earlier chapter, Soviet ideology is unlikely to admit the validity of this argument.

In the Japanese case too, we noted that high consumption sacrifices were made, especially in the area of the government provision of goods and services. In addition, during the earlier part of the post-1945 industrialization drive, the Japanese urban inhabitant had to endure particularly high levels of environmental pollution. One factor that initially contributed towards Japanese competitiveness was low costs, made possible by minimal expenditure on pollution control. However, whether the Japanese, and the Soviet, governments were right to impose such costs on their citizens at the time is essentially a metaphysical, and not an empirical, question.

Summary

Compared to most other economies, rates of economic growth have been very high in the Soviet Union, since 1930, and in Japan, since 1945.

For a decade after the 1917 revolution, a variety of economic strategies was discussed and/or applied in the USSR. These included agricultural development, a return to private ownership and decentralization. By 1930, the policy of high-speed industrialization had become accepted, with emphasis being placed on the expansion of capital goods industries. Resources were allocated by a process of economic planning. Enterprises came under central control and their targets and requirements were coordinated via material balances. The theory of socialist accumulation suggested that resources must be liberated from agriculture. Policies to accomplish this included the collectivization programme, price control and turnover taxation.

The 1960s witnessed a certain change in emphasis in the USSR. Industrial diversification appeared necessary. Critics argued that the existing planning system was wasteful, inefficient and inconsistent. It was thought to be incapable of dealing with changes in consumer demand and technology. The reaction of some Eastern European economies was to decentralize and to introduce incentives, individual discretion and a form of market structure. Although the USSR made some reforms of this nature it also appeared interested in developing a more sophisticated centralized system.

Japanese economic growth can be interpreted as dualistic. Important factors in growth included institutionalized labour practices and wages lagging behind productivity. Savings propensities have been high owing to conservative consumer tastes, lack of public welfare provision and the nature of the banking system. Trade expansion was a vital determinant of growth. Japan had the advantages of modern technology, high productivity, low defence spending and an oligopolistic market structure. In recent years, Japanese growth has slowed down, owing to the decline of target markets, exchange rate appreciation, international protectionism and input price rises.

The experiences of both economies demonstrate that high growth rates entail short-term sacrifice. Soviet growth has been assisted by a rich resource endowment, centralized control and isolation from international economic fluctuations. Future problems may include agriculture, inefficient planning and the burden of defence spending. Japan has had the advantage of high rates of accumulation but is especially vulnerable because of its dependence upon energy and raw material imports, and on trade generally.

Further reading

The principal sources for the section on Soviet growth are Ellman (1973, 1979), Nove (1972, 1977), Carr and Davies (1974), Wilczynski (1970, 1973), Bowles and Whynes (1979), Turner and Collis (1977) and Preobrazhensky (1964). Data for the performance of the First Plan are derived from Nove (1972), p. 191. Adam (1980) examines the present Soviet incentive system. A detailed analysis of the state of Soviet technology is provided by Amann, Cooper and Davies (1977). The circumstances of the Soviet labour force are debated in Schapiro and Godson (1981). A useful source of Eastern bloc data in general is the annual *Statistical Yearbook of the Member States of the Council for Mutual Economic Assistance* (CMEA Secretariat, Moscow). An English edition is published by IPC Industrial Press, London.

The account of Japan rests on Ohkawa and Rosovsky (1973), Halliday (1975) and OECD (1980b). Kelley and Williamson (1974) assess the extent to which Japan might serve as a model for economic development. Data on defence spending derive from IISS (1978), pp. 82–3. The ranking of Japan relative to other OECD countries is estimated from summary tables in OECD (1980b), pp. 87–90. Data on the recent performances of the USSR and Japan are taken from UN (1980a), Vol. I, pp. 1398–9 and Vol. II, pp. 266–7 and pp. 314–15. Japan's trade share is calculated from GATT (1980), Table A22.

Chapter Eleven

Balanced Strategies

In Chapter 10, we examined a strategy that could be described as 'unbalanced', in the sense that it was concerned with the attainment of a limited range of objectives at the expense of others. The Soviet Union in the 1930s, for example, expressed a desire for high-speed industrialization that implied consumption sacrifices. Faced with a similar set of circumstances, there is no reason to suppose that another society would have made the same decision. Indeed, a more 'balanced' strategy might have been preferred, i.e. maintaining a 'reasonable' level of consumption with a 'reasonable' rate of economic growth. We can think of balanced strategies in general as those that aim at the simultaneous achievement of goals drawn from a broad range. As there exists a multiplicity of goals for economic activity, there must accordingly exist a multiplicity of possible balanced strategies. Rather than consider all the permutations, we shall confine ourselves here to just one example, an example of considerable interest and importance in the analysis of comparative economic behaviour. This is the balanced strategy associated with the notion of the 'welfare state'.

In the century leading up to the Second World War, it slowly dawned upon the capitalist economies that the system of private property and free markets under which they operated was, by and large, rather better at accomplishing some tasks than others. Amongst its more obvious deficiencies were the following. First, the experience of the 1930s demonstrated that decentralized decision making gave rise to the possibility of instability at the macro-level, generating high levels of factor unemployment. What appeared to be optimal from the point of view of the individual firm in the short run proved to be distinctly sub-optimal for society in the long run. Second, the existence of private ownership and commodity exchange gave rise to inequalities in income and wealth. Highly prized resources or skills could earn monopoly rents for their fortunate owners. As Keynes pointed out, the distribution of wealth is not only an ethical issue; in a capitalist economy, it is a vital   241

determinant of the level of economic activity. Third, decision making
at the individual level entailed the under-provision of goods with 'public'
characteristics, i.e. goods whose production is socially optimal but
privately sub-optimal. Fourth, such individualistic decision making did
not take account of externalities, either positive (e.g. social benefits from
education) or negative (e.g. pollution).

Market failure of the above types led most Western capitalist
economies to accept government intervention as a means for the realization of certain desirable goals. Taken together, these objectives form
the basis of the welfare state ideology. Considering the post-1945 Western
European economies as a whole, we can detect a degree of unanimity
about the range of goals to be attained. At one time or another, the
governments of such countries have made policy commitments along
the following lines. First, welfare state ideology holds that governments
should try to maintain the full employment of factors of production,
especially labour. Second, the distribution of income should tend towards
the egalitarian, this belief justifying a system of progressive income
taxation and transfer payments from rich to poor. Third, welfare states
hold that, irrespective of the individual's productive contribution, he
must be guaranteed a minimum level of consumption opportunities for
a basic set of commodities, e.g. food, housing, education, health care.
Individuals are permitted to consume such items by virtue of centralized
provision at zero price or income supplements where necessary. Fourth,
welfare state governments typically hold the general long-term increase
in material living standards to be a desirable goal. However, this is not
a goal to be pursued exclusively and at the expense of the attainment
of other objectives. Finally, the welfare state is intended to be both
stable and secure. As far as the citizen is concerned, this means that
the effects of any personal calamity not elsewhere provided for will be
cushioned by a government response, e.g. insurance benefits in the event
of sickness or unemployment. From the collective point of view, stability
can be interpreted as the maintenance of aggregate employment, price
stability and an external trading equilibrium.

Thus seen as a portfolio of parallel objectives, the concept of the
welfare state is one of the twentieth century's most intriguing inventions.
How did the ideology emerge? Two models appear feasible and each
probably contains an element of truth. Culyer (1980) argues that the
social policy aspects of the welfare state in Western Europe – the guaranteed provision of certain minimum welfare standards to all citizens –
came about because, quite simply, people care about one another. In
neoclassical terms, this means that your utility appears as a positive
argument in my utility function and vice versa. Further, he suggests,
the 'very *existence* of the Welfare State is evidence *for* the proposition
that specific caring exists, for if individuals did not care for one another
then no externality would exist and there would be little reason for
collectivist action' (p. 65). If we follow Culyer's logic, however, the

rapid increase in the scale of welfare provision on the part of Western European governments would seem to imply that concern for others has been the twentieth century's main growth area. Quite frankly, this seems unlikely. Whilst it is certainly true that Western political leaders have become more concerned about the imbalance of welfare in their societies over the past century – witness, for instance, Disraeli's description of nineteenth-century industrial society as 'two nations', the rich and the poor – an additional factor of significance must be the evolution of the facility by which care and concern for others might be manifested. Surely the increasing democratization of social choice in the capitalist economies of the late nineteenth century, which effectively meant the enfranchisement of the poor, implied that the specific concerns of this latter group came to the forefront of politics. This is precisely how B. Gilbert (1966) appraises the evolution of the national insurance system in the United Kingdom at that time:

> The poor refused any longer to suffer in silence. The aim of the eighteen-thirties had been to induce people receiving relief to work. By 1890, the old problem of pauperism had become a problem of poverty and the essentially economic dilemma was political and social: what, it was asked, can the governors of the nation do to prevent the poor from using their franchise to overturn a society based on capitalist wealth? As it turned out, the defence against socialism was social legislation (p. 19).

In sum, therefore, it could be that it was not the concern that was lacking at the earlier stages of European history but rather the effective mouthpiece for voicing that concern. Given the franchise changes, the social policies of the welfare state became avenues for the electoral competition of political parties in the representative democracies of the capitalist world.

Critics of capitalist society suspect that there was a more insidious causal mechanism. This view is put rather elegantly by Fry (1979b) in his analysis of the Swedish welfare state:

> The comprehensive and generous delivery of an unprecedented barrage of social services is the most visible activity of the state, and thus it appears its primary business is ensuring the well being of its citizens. Indeed this is one objective and it would be inaccurate and unfair to deny its value and primacy in the minds of many socially conscious reformers. However, just as it would be ludicrous to conclude from the fact that a farmer heats his henhouse well, pipes in relaxing music, feeds the chickens a nourishing diet and makes sure the veterinarian visits at the first sign of illness among the hens, that his primary interest is in the intrinsic happiness and fulfilment of his chickens and not in their productivity, so it is naive to view social services in Sweden and elsewhere as being delivered for the sole purpose of benefiting the less fortunate (pp. 2–3).

The argument here is that the provision of welfare services by the government is not necessarily motivated by any 'concern' that the government might claim to exhibit; rather, provision occurs because such investment yields a strongly positive social rate of return. That this is indeed the case we have already concluded from our discussion of human capital in Chapter 7; we should perhaps add that one does not have to be a 'capitalist' to appreciate the virtues of social investment, as is evidenced by the widespread provision of social services in socialist economies.

Irrespective of the reasons for the evolution of the welfare state ideal, it is instructive to consider how the many Western economies that like to use this label to describe themselves actually operate. We shall, first of all, turn to a case-study of Sweden, regarded by many analysts as the 'model' welfare state. Possibly Schnitzer (1970) comes the nearest to eulogy when he asserts that 'Sweden has combined perhaps the highest standard of living in the world with a highly developed welfare system to create what is perhaps the closest thing to a utopian society in existence' (p. 10).

11.1   The Swedish welfare state

Myrdal (1965) has commented that, in reality, welfare states do not actually exist; rather, they are perpetually in a process of coming into being (p. 45). No such society ever accepts that it has arrived at the ultimate and definitive position but argues that it is continually striving to reach it. Just as we cannot observe ends, so we cannot detect origins; it is difficult to pinpoint the exact date when a country starts to become a welfare state. For our discussion of Sweden we shall accordingly impose some rather arbitrary criteria and deal with the period between 1935 and 1975, which we shall take to represent the foundations and erection of the welfare state structure. First, however, a few words about the background of the modern Swedish economy.

Swedish industrialization dates from the second half of the nineteenth century, making the country a relatively late arrival on the European industrial scene. Prior to this time, land reform had generated a substantial increase in agricultural productivity and Sweden discovered that its primary products (mainly grain, timber and iron ore) were in great demand in neighbouring countries. On the import side, Sweden became a major importer of capital, much of which was directed by the government towards the improvement of the infrastructure. In contrast to the public initiative here, many other industrial advances were made on the basis of purely private initiative, especially in the field of banking and, thanks to Swedish invention and innovation, in engineering. This rapid spurt of industrialization, coupled with a high level of migration of surplus labour (mainly to the USA), gave the Swedish economy a high annual per capita output growth rate up to the beginning of the First World War. Indeed, amongst the Western nations its growth record at the time was matched only by that of Japan. However, as trade made a sizeable contribution to the overall level of economic activity, Sweden was finally obliged to contend with the same economic difficulties that confronted other Western economies in the 1920s and 1930s. Even though the Swedish currency was to an extent undervalued, and world demand for primary products was not so sharply depressed as the demand for manufactures, Sweden still experienced unemployment of the order of 10–20 per cent during its depression years. Such a problem clearly required a policy.

In 1932 the Swedish Social Democratic (or Labour) Party gained a victory in the national elections and, excepting a brief interregnum period in 1936 and during the Second World War when a coalition was in office, this party was in power until 1976. Without doubt, the particular ideological stamp of the party had much to do with subsequent developments in the Swedish economy. In the pre-war period, the new government gave early indications of a commitment to the expansion of the level of social welfare services by, for example, passing extensive pensions legislation in 1937. From the management point of view, it was, furthermore, arguably 'Keynesian before Keynes'. At the same time as Keynes in his *General Theory* was patiently lecturing to the American and British governments that a policy of balancing the budget in periods of economic disequilibrium was, to say the least, misguided, the economists of the Stockholm School (such as Myrdal, Ohlin and Lindahl) had managed to convince their government of the advisability of counter-cyclical deficit financing. Whilst it is quite wrong to say that Sweden weakened the effects of depression by massive governmental intervention (for intervention on a large scale simply did not take place), this early acceptance of what we now term Keynesian management techniques of fiscal disequilibrium was instrumental in facilitating post-war economic change.

We can see the period 1945–1975 not only as one in which the Swedish objective function was gradually broadened to accommodate more and more policy goals but as one in which established goals became more and more refined. The major policy debates of the 1940s and 1950s revolved around the familiar management problems of the maintenance of full employment and price stability and the creation of economic growth, the immediate solution being sought in the imposition of direct government controls. This had the effect of causing 'hidden' inflation, for both world and domestic markets were potentially buoyant. When the controls were relaxed in the early 1950s Sweden experienced a rapid rate of open inflation, exacerbated by the additional boom precipitated by the Korean War. This, in turn, caused a fourth policy objective to appear as a priority, namely the maintenance of an external payments equilibrium. Immediately after the Second World War, pensions remained the main area of government involvement in social policy; in 1946 a universal flat-rate pension scheme was introduced, replacing the former system, which had been based both upon insurance contributions and upon means-tested benefits. The value of the pension was enhanced after 1950 when a form of index-linking was introduced to counter inflationary effects; further reform in 1960 linked pension levels to pre-retirement incomes.

The policy goals added to this basic range belong almost exclusively to the category of 'social' goods and services. In 1955 a system of national health insurance was introduced, designed to provide financial support to every citizen in times of illness and to provide recompense for necessary expenditures on medical care. The responsibility for the provision of such care was placed upon local, rather than national, government, and the establishment of the system necessitated substantial expenditure at this level. During the 1960s, spending on public health care increased at twice the rate of aggregate national output. Although the Swedish government had always maintained an interest in education, the 1960s witnessed wide-ranging reforms of the system. By 1971, every child was guaranteed nine years of basic schooling to be followed by a choice of further education opportunities. A range of grants and loans was introduced to encourage the continuation of education by those otherwise unable to afford it. Such a provision of financial resources can also be seen as a manifestation of a more general desire to redistribute income in favour of the poor, a further example of which was the 1969 legislation providing rent allowances to support the less well off families.

Having therefore painted in the basis of its conception of the welfare state with broad brush-strokes, Sweden, in the late 1960s and early 1970s, began to concern itself with finer points of detail. The earlier blanket commitment to the maintenance of full employment via government management, for example, was slowly disaggregated into a number of component objectives. By the 1970s, therefore, we see specific attention being paid to the employment problems of married women and handicapped persons. Important in the former respect was the 1974 legislation that guaranteed support for the family when one parent was obliged to leave employment in order to care for the children. Measures were also introduced to ease the particular economic problems of single-parent families. Lindbeck (1975) has detected some recent and subtle changes in policy emphasis. He suggests that the desire for the balanced regional growth of economic activity has become more noticeable, whilst the balance of payments target is no longer that of equilibrium but one of surplus to finance assistance to less affluent economies. In addition, there appears to have been a growing concern about the effects of industrialization on the environment, both natural and social (e.g. working and living conditions), and the degree of worker participation in management.

Clearly, during the period under consideration, the Swedish juggler threw more and more balls into the air – how did he manage to keep them all aloft? To answer this question, let us examine the structure of the Swedish economy in the mid-1970s, by which time the basis of the welfare state would seem to have been established.

In certain respects, Swedish economic policy has always conformed to the textbook 'mixed economy' strategy by virtue of its economic structure. The great bulk of industrial production has been generated by private enterprise, the governments of the past having confined their activities to, for example, resource exploitation in the far north of the country where the adverse climatic conditions and prohibitive transport costs make the region unattractive from the point of view of a private firm. The mid-1970s public contribution to manufacturing output was of the order of 5 per cent of total value. Rather than engaging in industrial production, the Swedish government has concentrated on the twin activities of the provision of social infrastructure and public goods and services on the one hand, and of the redistribution of income via transfer payments on the other. Where Sweden departs from the standard mixed economy model, however, is in its possession of a cooperative sector. The cooperative movement first emerged during the earlier stages of industrialization in the mid-nineteenth century and, in certain areas, it developed in parallel with the more formal private sector. By the mid-1970s, consumer cooperatives were playing an important role in retailing and housing whilst, on the production side, they had always been extremely significant in agriculture.

Although there is no single simple answer to the question of how the Swedish welfare state came into existence, we can hardly ignore the increasing role played by the government in the management and direction of economic activity. In 1950, the public sector (measured in terms of the taxation resources and social security contributions mobilized by the central and local government) accounted for 21 per cent of GNP. By 1976, this proportion had risen to more than 50 per cent; the increase in public expenditure was, of course, of equivalent proportions. In terms of the rapid growth of public intervention in the economy, post-war developments in Sweden have been somewhat different from those experienced by the other industrial nations. For the period 1950–70, the annual rate of growth of Swedish public expenditure was some 25 per cent *higher* than its annual growth of aggregate output, whilst, for the OECD group as a whole, the average public expenditure growth was 25 per cent *lower* than GNP growth. By 1975, Swedish expenditure on social services – health care, poverty relief, education, family benefits and pensions – accounted for one-half of government spending, i.e. over 25 per cent of GNP. Subdividing further, we find that health care and pensions were the major areas of government involvement in this respect, each taking around a 40 per cent share of annual government social expenditures.

This massive degree of resource mobilization on the part of the government not only enabled it to indulge in the provision of facilities that it felt were socially desirable, but the magnitude of this involvement gave it the leverage necessary for aggregate economic management. At least until the 1970s, Swedish fiscal policy was essentially Keynesian, stabilizing the levels of aggregate demand (especially the level of private investment) with the appropriate counter-cyclical action. Particularly during the 1960s, this was buttressed with an active policy towards improving the labour market, by means of the establishment of retraining agencies and the provision of subsidies to encourage spatial mobility. Interestingly enough, it would appear that Sweden has rarely been tempted to use this leverage in order to attempt the type of 'growth planning' popular in other European economies, especially France and the UK, during the 1960s. The idea in this latter case was to try to lead the private sector onto a high-growth path by means of specific *ex ante* commitments of public resources coupled with comprehensive economic forecasts. Sweden, however, appears to have been content to delegate the growth decisions to the enterprises concerned, policies being designed not so much actively to encourage growth but more to avoid discouraging it. The level of company taxation and the use of an investment reserve (i.e. the extent to which corporate reinvested profits may escape taxation) have been important policy instruments in this respect. The post-war Swedish growth up to the mid-1970s was, in fact, not particularly dissimilar from the average rate of Western industrial nations.

Observing the Swedish economy as it moved into the 1970s, Schnitzer (1970) applauded its balanced progress towards the realization of four general objectives. First, he argued that Sweden had been able to maintain consistently low levels of unemployment of both capital and labour (of the order of 2 per cent). Second, strides had been made towards an egalitarian distribution of resources, not only in terms of income (by means of heavily progressive taxation) but via the comprehensive system of welfare services. Third, a gradual rise in average material living standards had been maintained. Fourth, there had been an 'emphasis on the quality as well as the quantity of life' (p. 241). We do not have to agree with Schnitzer's view of Sweden representing a 'model society' to accept that movements in these directions have indeed taken place since the 1930s. However, we must also bear in mind that many of the developments that we have discussed in the Swedish context have also taken place in other Western industrial economies, as we shall now see.

11.2   International comparisions

Sweden is simply one of a number of industrialized capitalist economies that share an approximately common organizational structure and a range of objectives that we have loosely defined as the creation of a welfare state. This does not mean, however, that the operations of all such economies are identical; just as there exist similarities, so there exist differences, both in terms of economic circumstances (e.g. resource endowments and degree of openness) and in terms of the specific method by which a country chooses to realize its objective. Thus, for instance, whilst all economies might agree that full employment of inputs is a desirable objective, some might place more emphasis on the role of Keynesian management techniques than others. Some of these similarities and differences will become clear when we examine the structures and performances of six Western economies at various levels of detail.

TABLE 11.1 Breakdown of GNP by expenditure and by economic activity for selected industrial economies, 1978 (percentages of total GNP)

	France[a]	*West Germany*	*Netherlands*[b]	*Sweden*	*UK*	*USA*
Economic activity:						
Agriculture	5	3	5	4	2	3
Industry	30	42	30	27	31	29
Construction	7	7	6	7	5	5
Internal trade	13	10	12	9	9	18
Transport	5	6	7	4	7	7
Services	31	32	32	38	33	37
Unspecified	9	—	8	11	13	1
Expenditure:						
Private consumption	61	55	59	53	59	64
Government consumption	15	20	18	29	20	18
Capital formation	23	23	23	17	19	20
Exports	21	25	47	29	30	8
Less Imports	20	23	47	28	28	10

[a] 1977.
[b] 1976.
Source: UN (1980) *Yearbook of National Accounts Statistics 1979.* New York, UN, Vol. II, Tables 2A and 3. Adjustments have been made to conform to data in Vol. I (Country Tables)

For the purpose of analysis at the most distant perspective, *Table 11.1* provides a disaggregation of total national output, by expenditure and by economic activity, for five European economies and the USA. Viewing such data, the essential similarities that seem to emerge are the following. First, and in all cases, agriculture's contribution to GDP is minimal; the UK's agricultural sector is especially small relative to the total. Second, the contribution of industrial output to aggregate production is correspondingly substantial, of the order of 40–50 per cent if we include construction and transportation in the category. Third, the service sector accounts for around one-third of economic activity in all six cases, this category being composed of (i) financial operations such as insurance services and property transactions and (ii) the private or government provision of such commodities as health care, education and community services. Fourth, for all these economies the balance of

trade is in an approximate equilibrium, the level of exports corresponding to the level of imports. Turning to the more obvious dissimilarities,
we observe, first, the importance of internal retail and wholesale trade
appears to differ from country to country, being of least importance in
the Swedish and the UK cases and of most importance for the USA.
Second, the balance of consumption between governments and private
households is also a variable; whilst the Swedish government is responsible
for 35 per cent of total consumption, the French government's share is
around 20 per cent. Third, the balance between current consumption
and current investment differs from case to case. Fourth, some economies
are clearly more dependent upon foreign trade than others; for the
sample, the Netherlands emerges as a highly open economy, whilst trade
is of the least relative importance in the US case.

Having examined the overall profiles of our six economies, let us

TABLE 11.2 Growth, savings, government revenue and expenditure data for selected industrial
economies, 1978

	France	West Germany	Netherlands	Sweden	UK	USA
Annual average growth of GDP (%)[a]	4.8	3.5	3.9	2.1	2.2	2.9
Share of government revenue in GDP (%)	42	43	54	60	39	33
Composition of government revenue (% of total):						
Direct taxes	19	30	30	40	37	46
Indirect taxes	33	29	23	24	36	26
Social security payments	39	32	33	24	16	24
Other taxes	9	9	14	12	11	4
Composition of government outlays (% of total):						
Current transfers	51[b]	40[c]	54	40	33	35
Capital formation	8	7	6	5	7	5
Final consumption	34	44	34	47	51	59
Subsidies and capital transfers	7	9	6	8	9	1
Annual average growth of real government consumption (%)[a]	3.5	4.1	3.2	3.6	2.1	1.1
Proportion of disposable income saved (%)	14	14	14	6	8	7
Proportion of gross accumulation financed by savings (%)	52	53	58	31	38	32
Composition of savings by source (% of total):						
Enterprises	9	20	20	−79	19	26
Government	1	16	10	65	−23	9
Households	90	64	70	114	104	65

[a]Growth rates are for period 1968–78.
[b]1976.
[c]1977.
Source: Derived and/or estimated from OECD (1980), *National Accounts of OECD Countries, 1950–1978*. Paris, OECD, Vol. I; UN
(1980), *Yearbook of National Accounts Statistics, 1979*, New York, UN, Tables 11 and 12; OECD (1980), *National Accounts of
OECD Countries, 1961–1978*. Paris, OECD, Vol. II.

focus attention upon a couple of specific areas, namely government involvement in economic operations and the nature of savings. *Table 11.2* provides some relevant data. What do such comparative data tell us? The first observation is that some countries have experienced higher growth rates than others over the past decade; France, for example, has grown twice as fast as the UK and the USA. Second, the degree of government involvement in the economy clearly differs; whilst government revenue is only one-third of GDP in the USA, its share approaches two-thirds in Sweden. In other words, the extent of the 'public sector' varies considerably. Incidentally, it must be pointed out that the share of government revenue is only one possible definition of the public sector, an alternative one being government expenditure relative to GDP. A difference between the two definitions will emerge in cases where governments finance expenditures via borrowing rather than by taxation. The most sizeable divergence between these two approaches probably occurs in the UK where government borrowing is indeed significant; in terms of the expenditure definition, the UK public sector probably exceeds that of France and Germany.

Given that all these governments appear to wish to appropriate substantial tax revenues, it is interesting to notice that they go about it in different ways. The three major forms of taxation are (i) direct taxation (e.g. taxes on household income and company profits), (ii) indirect taxation, levied on expenditure on goods and services (e.g. VAT), (iii) social security contributions, which are paid by both employer and employee. At a superficial level, we might think that a government would be indifferent as to the manner in which cash was raised, the important feature being the fact that it is actually raised. This is not so, however, partly because of the implications that different taxes have for the distribution of income. Taxes may be thought of as 'progressive' or 'regressive', defined in terms of the extent to which they advance or retard the attainment of an egalitarian income distribution. Indirect taxes on expenditure are thus regressive in that both rich and poor consumers pay the same rate of tax on their expenditures. By contrast, most direct taxes are progressive, for marginal tax rates are generally adjusted such that rich individuals pay more tax relative to their income than do poor individuals. The extremes of the direct/indirect tax balance are represented by France and the USA. Social security contributions have an additional distributional aspect by virtue of the fact that both employer and employee are involved in the taxation. Wilson (1979) notes that, in the case of France, employers contribute two and a half times more than do employees, whilst in the Netherlands the employee's share is larger than that of the employer (p. 136).The distributional effects also depend on the particular system of payment adopted. Many economies gear social security payments to income (i.e. they become a form of direct taxation) although, in the United States and Britain, there exists a maximum contribution that anyone is obliged to make.

Above this level, the marginal contribution rate is therefore zero, i.e.
the tax is initially progressive but subsequently becomes regressive. One
component of the 'other taxes' category is taxes on property, although
it should be noted that only in the case of the UK and the USA do
property taxes make any sizeable contribution to government; their
significance appears to be the least in the case of Sweden.

An appropriate distribution of income is not, of course, the only
criterion used by governments when choosing which tax to employ.
They will be concerned, for instance, with the economics of administration in terms of collection costs. 'Tax psychology' is of undeniable
importance and we may cite two examples. First, the principle of the
establishment of social security payments in most Western economies
was usually that the government would operate a national and actuarially
sound insurance scheme; by making contributions, individuals would
therefore see themselves paying for the benefits that they would actually
receive when the need arose. In reality this is not the case for, in many
economies, contributions do not actually cover the benefits provided
and the deficit is made up from the general tax fund. Arguably, however,
citizens are more happy to pay taxes if they believe that they are
obtaining specific benefits than if they are asked to contribute to a tax
fund with a non-specific purpose. Second, a view that appeared
especially prevalent in the UK and the USA in the early 1980s was the
idea of giving the consumer more freedom of choice, by lowering direct
taxation to increase disposable income. Unless the government contem-
plates a substantial reduction in its activities, such a policy will require
the raising of the level of indirect taxation to recoup the revenue lost
from lower direct taxation.

Having collected its revenue by whatever means is felt to be
appropriate, the government is now faced with the problem of spending
it. *Table 11.2* shows there are two major forms of government outlay –
consumption and transfer payments. Under the former heading, the
government uses its cash to provide goods and services for the economy,
usually in the fields of defence, health care, education and civic
amenities. Under the latter, it effectively gives resources away to those
deemed to be in need, generally the unemployed, the sick and the
elderly. As may be seen, some governments are more consumption-
oriented than others (those of the USA and the UK being the extreme
cases), whilst the Dutch government has the highest allocation of transfer
payments. Relating the trends in government consumption to GDP
growth, we may see that this aspect of government activity has grown
in importance in the German and Swedish cases.

Possibly the strongest contrasts between the six economies come in
the field of savings and accumulation. Not only do three economies
typically save a higher proportion of their disposable incomes but, as
might be expected, savings in these cases are more significant in the
finance of gross accumulation (the other main source is the consumption

of fixed capital). Sources of savings vary widely from country to country; note that, whilst savings from households are invariably the most important source, Swedish enterprise and the British government are both net dis-savers.

This brief examination of just six economies allows speculations rather than conclusions. *Tables 11.1* and *11.2* suggest a general relationship between economic growth and savings or capital formation as might be intuitively expected. Interestingly enough, the size of the relative tax yields does not appear particularly influential in determining growth. Such speculations, however, are not the point of presenting the data, which were designed to demonstrate nations' approaches to essentially similar economic problems. One specific problem that we shall focus upon now relates to the decision whether to provide a commodity via the public sector or the private market. Depending on the decision reached, provision will appear as either 'government' consumption or 'private' consumption in the breakdowns above, and there will be corresponding implications for taxation. Let us consider the case of the provision of health care.

11.2.1   THE PROVISION OF HEALTH CARE

In theory, the 'mixed economy' that characterizes the Western welfare states could arrange for the provision of health care in any one of a number of ways. Let us consider just two. In the first place, we might entrust the supply of care to private enterprise, which would sell the commodity to those individuals who wished to consume at a price determined by the free market. Such enterprises, we might suppose, would operate according to the normal profit-making criterion of other forms of enterprise in capitalist economies. Given that individuals are likely to experience substantial degrees of uncertainty with respect to their demands for treatment, we might anticipate the formation of an insurance scheme. On receipt of a regular premium, private insurance companies would make resources available to individuals in times of need such that they would be able to purchase the required treatment. An alternative system for health care provision would be for the citizens of the economy concerned to place the responsibility for the supply of medical care with some central agency, presumably the government, and to contribute to the finance of this body in the form of taxation. From this tax fund, the agency could subsequently supply the citizens on demand at zero price. A key distinction between these two methods is that, in terms of our system of national accounting, the former constitutes private, and the latter constitutes public, consumption. Whilst neither of these models accords with the real world in every respect, the former alternative nevertheless bears a certain resemblance to the practices of the USA whilst the latter is a reasonable description of the UK National Health Service.

The evolution of the American health care system demonstrates immediately the likely sub-optimality of a pure market approach to health care provision. Markets are likely to fail in the case of this particular commodity owing to the existence of externalities and the maldistribution of income. It is, for example, not generally optimal for one individual to invest in maintaining his health status if he risks infection from other individuals who are less concerned about their own health levels. Further, if the objective is to ensure minimum health standards for all, the poor and the chronically sick will be particularly disadvantaged by the existence of a free private market in health care, owing to inability to pay. To counter these problems, the US system has developed into its own form of 'mixed economy', a private sector in parallel with a public sector centred on Medicare (the provision of treatment facilities for the elderly) and Medicaid (the provision for the poor). At present, private care accounts for around 60 per cent of total medical expenditure in the USA. However, this proportion is quite unlike that of the UK where the vast majority of health care resources are allocated by the government.

If we intend to compare health care delivery systems, we require some notion of performance. Unfortunately performance is difficult to estimate in this context because of the multiplicity of factors influencing an individual's health status. The incidence of death and disease is related not solely to the level of medical treatment supplied but also to factors such as climate, health education, nutritional standards and pollution; in the case of accidental injuries, it is related to the number of motor vehicles on the roads. We are reduced to making the most general of comparisons. In the first place, we can establish that the significance of health care is agreed upon by all the economies in our earlier sample. Each of them regularly devotes 5–10 per cent of GDP to medical care, making this commodity far more important than agriculture in terms of proportion of national output. Further, the analysis by Newhouse (1977) suggests that, amongst the richer nations in general, income-elasticity of demand for medical care exceeds unity. *Table 11.3* provides data that illustrate other aspects of performance in the widest sense, namely the provision of medical facilities amongst the sample and also death rates and life expectancies. As may be seen, the differences between these economies is in most cases slight, especially if we compare the group as a whole with, say, Africa or South-East Asia. Population per physician figures for these regions are around 10 000 and 5000 respectively, whilst infant mortality rates often exceed 100 per 1000 births. Life expectancy differentials were apparent in *Table 6.1*. Assuming that the data of *Table 11.3* do not indicate an excessive dissimilarity between the performance of different health care delivery systems, let us pose a more specific question – do the particular forms of health care provision chosen by, say, the UK and the USA pose any distinct economic problems?

TABLE 11.3 Health statistics for selected industrial economies, late 1970s

	France[a]	West Germany[b]	Netherlands[b]	Sweden[b]	England and Wales[c]	USA[a]
Population per physician	613	490	583	563	659	595
Population per hospital bed	90	80	100	70	120	160
General mortality (per 1000)	10.2	11.8	8.2	10.8	11.9	8.8
Infant mortality (per 1000)	10.6	14.7	9.6	7.8	13.8	13.6
Life expectancy (years)	73.0	71.3	74.8	74.5	70.8	72.6

[a]1976.
[b]1978.
[c]1977.
Source: World Health Organization (1980), *World Health Statistics Annual 1980*, Geneva, WHO, Vol. I, Table 4; Vol. III, Table 1. Also Table 6.1.

The two major charges levelled at the American health care system are, first, that it is 'unjust' despite increasing government involvement since the 1960s and, second, that the private sector generates inflation. Indeed, the former complaint is also made against the UK system, so let us first consider the latter. Newhouse (1978) has shown that, for the period 1949–75, the average annual price increase for hospital services was three times that of goods and services as a whole, whilst the price for physicians' services grew at one and a half times the annual inflation rate. Such a relative rise in prices clearly implies the existence of a demand/supply imbalance. On the demand side, there are two causal factors. First, the existence of an insurance system greatly increases the effective demand of the individual consumer. As the costs of treatment are automatically covered by a scheme, the individual will have few worries about the direct market price of the service. The insurance company will meet the bills and will react by spreading its losses incurred by the expenditure amongst all policy-holders in the form of a marginal increase in average premium. This is a general problem characteristic of all insurance systems and is referred to as 'moral hazard'. It means that, once an individual has insured himself against a certain eventuality, it might well become optimal for him to ensure that the eventuality actually occurs, given that the cost of the event will be spread amongst all participants in the insurance scheme. Second, health care is a curious commodity in that the principal guidance about whether the good should be purchased comes from the supplier. Given their monopoly of expertise, physicians are in a strong position to persuade consumers that a health care purchase is necessary. Turning to the supply side, it is clear that the monopoly position of the medical profession as a whole has been instrumental in restricting the supply of medical care, in terms of the limited creation of medical schools, restrictions on training and the constrained availability of licences to practice. In sum, price inflation is exactly what one should expect in a monopoly market characterized by rapidly expanding consumer purchasing power in the form of insurance.

It would appear that the UK has also experienced an increase in effective demand for health care in recent years although, given that the British health service only imposes a limited and nominal range of charges on supply, excess demand in this case has not resulted in an increase in the direct price of treatment. The potential health care consumer has been faced not with price rises but with an increase in queuing time; since 1950, the length of waiting lists for most forms of surgical treatment has increased. The essential problem for the UK system therefore becomes one of devising criteria for the rationing of medical facilities, given that rationing by price is explicitly rejected on ideological grounds. The criterion usually adopted is that of 'normative need'; the medical profession devises, in principle, a priority ordering of diseases, illness, complaints, urgency, degrees of pain and so forth, and allocates resources accordingly. This implies that, if an individual wishes to undergo treatment for a complaint that has been accorded a low priority, he will, other things remaining equal, be faced with a longer waiting time. In a market system, we should presume he would be able to purchase the treatment immediately at the going rate, assuming that he could afford to pay this rate.

Most of the industrialized capitalist economies discussed throughout this chapter appear to exhibit some degree of interest in the principle of 'equity' in the provision of health care and, indeed, in all social services. Equity, however, can be interpreted in a number of ways. First, consider equity of access, the idea that any single individual ought to be able to consume the resources required, from a medical point of view. Most economies fall short of this norm. Evidence suggests that, whilst the incidence of disease or complaints requiring treatment in a purely medical sense varies inversely with income, the actual purchase or use of medical facilities tends to vary directly with income. Examining data for the USA, Cullis and West (1979) suggest that 'it seems reasonable to conclude that some Americans, especially the members of the poor minority groups, do not receive or have potential command over an "equitable" share of the nation's health care resources' (p. 264). This suggests that, if equity is indeed the target, the USA should become involved in more income redistribution or more public provision at subsidized rates. In the case of the UK, these authors conclude that 'not only do members of higher social classes make greater use of preventive services, but they also receive better care in some respects because of the unequal distribution of facilities and their ability to communicate with doctors more effectively' (p. 241).

A second equity criterion is the belief that access to health care should be equally available irrespective of the individual's geographic location. Again, in most economies, this goal has yet to be realized, as metropolitan regions tend to be better served than the more remote rural areas at the present time. Third, one might suppose that a legitimate equity criterion could be equal treatment of patients irrespective of the nature of complaint. However, we have already seen that, in the UK case, positive discrimination is necessary as a means of reconciling demand with available supply. A fourth concept of equity could be that the net costs of health provision should fall on the rich rather than the poor. Wilson (1979) suggests that this is indeed the case in Sweden, although Fry (1979a) makes the important point that the burden of financing Swedish social services 'falls exclusively upon the wage earning class', as opposed to the property-owning class (p. 6). Clearly, the specific concept of equity chosen by a specific government will be a prime determinant of the form of health care delivery system chosen.

11.3   Recent developments

In our earlier discussion of Sweden, we compared the welfare state idea to a kind of juggler attempting to maintain all the balls of policy objectives up in the air and in some form of balanced equilibrium. For many countries, the 1970s was the decade in which all these balls came crashing to the ground. In general terms, post-war economic evolution of the Western nations had taken place with governments first satisfying themselves of their ability to attain the primary targets of employment, growth and stability via management techniques; onto this base, the wider edifice of the welfare state – social services and the other necessities of the 'good life' – was gradually erected. Unfortunately, in recent years it is just this base that has undergone the most erosion.

We have already remarked in Chapter 7 upon the growth of unemployment in Western economies during the 1970s. *Table 11.4* presents unemployment data in a slightly different form by showing, in index terms, how the level of unemployment in our six sample economies changed during the 1970s. Only Sweden and the USA appear to have escaped substantial increases in unemployment rates, although we must

TABLE 11.4 Indices of unemployment rates, consumer prices and money wages in manufacturing industry, for selected industrial economies, 1979 compared to 1970 (1970 = 100)

	France	West Germany	Netherlands	Sweden	UK	USA
General level of unemployment	485[a]	543	464	140	219	118
Consumer prices	221	156	191	212	306	187
Average money wages in manufacturing	330	198	246	239[b]	375	200

[a]French unemployment is estimated from employment data.
[b]The base for Sweden's wage figure is 1971.
Source: Estimated from data in ILO (1980), *Yearbook of Labour Statistics*, Geneva, ILO.

bear in mind that, whilst the Swedish level has been maintained at around 2 per cent, the USA level has been stable at 5–6 per cent. *Table 11.4* also includes data on another aspect of the 'base', namely inflation. Over the 1970s decade, all our sample economies experienced regular increases in consumer prices, the UK representing the most extreme case with a three-fold rise in the price level. Taking the data for wage growth, we note that its trend runs parallel with that of prices although growth has been somewhat higher. This means that average real wages have in fact risen in all our sample economies, although the rise has been highest in the case of France (around 50 per cent) and lowest for the USA (around 10 per cent).

How are we to account for this manifest failure of most of these economies to maintain the basic foundations of a welfare state? Naturally we must expect there to be a plethora of theories in this respect, especially in view of the important differences in approach towards specific problems that we noted earlier. Let us consider just one model here, a model that has the distinct advantage of operating at a fair degree of generality. This is the analysis by Watt (1978), which offers the following hypothesis to explain the coexistence of inflation and unemployment in many Western economies. Watt suggests that the situation has arisen owing to the simultaneous operation of several forces. The rapid expansion of the labour force during the 1970s was fuelled by the increased birth rates of the 1950s. The number of individuals attempting to find employment during the 1970s was higher than at any previous time and, rather than appearing gradually as had happened in the past, this new supply arrived rapidly as the 'population bulge' grew to working age. Further, the 1970s were characterized by capital-intensive production methods that discouraged the employment of labour. This tendency developed from the nature of technological innovations made during the period, the level and growth of wages in industrial economies making substitution into capital-intensive production techniques more sensible from the point of view of the private entrepreneur's profitability. Taking these effects together, we therefore see more labour becoming available just at the time when, from the technical point of view, it was least needed. Watt sees the central cause of inflation as the growth in global demand for scarce resources, particularly primary inputs such as energy. Indeed, we have already commented on the impact of oil price inflation in the Japanese context (Chapter 10).

The manner in which our economies have reacted to such problems has further generated some curious outcomes. For instance, in an effort to maintain international competitiveness, many governments appear keen to subsidize their industries, especially with regard to energy inputs. The long-run implication of this strategy is that, the more one economy subsidizes in an effort to raise market share, the more other economies must subsidize in an effort to prevent their shares from being eroded. The resultant fall in the market price will lower the profitability of the industry in question and necessitate further subsidization on the part of the competing economies. Such a game is quite clearly negative-sum. Further, the typical policy response of Western governments in recent years has been the implementation of short-term monetary and fiscal policy at the cost of higher unemployment, although, if Watt (1978) is correct in his diagnosis, such policies are unlikely to exert a significant impact on inflation. We note in passing that one reason for governments' preference for short-term policy may be found in the models of political behaviour that we explored in Chapter 4. Governments anxious to secure their re-election in the short term are unlikely to pursue radical policies that yield benefits only in the long term.

Although they may be faced with similar forms of economic problem (essentially the specific problem of attaining the basic targets of full employment and price stability), it would be quite wrong to suggest that the policy responses of the Western economies have been identical in every respect. In its annual *Economic Surveys* of member countries for the late 1970s, the OECD noted that 'a reduction of energy dependence and progress in the restructuring of industry' to soak up the existing labour surplus would be important goals for policy in the immediate future. France and West Germany, it suggested, had made 'substantial progress on both these fronts' in recent years (OECD, 1980c, p. 69). OECD was more dubious of the efficacy of the policies being pursued by other members, such as the USA whose government was heavily oriented towards demand management and which was a major claimant on world resources. OECD suggested that a demand management policy would be successful only in the longer term and 'relying primarily on demand management runs the risk that continuing price shocks will undermine progress, or that society might find the costs of running the economy at below capacity unacceptable'. A 'tax-based incomes policy' (for income redistribution and control of wage inflation) was recommended for the United States (OECD, 1980d, p. 50).

Turning now from the general to the specific, what have been the recent trends in the sector that we singled out earlier, namely health care? In its recent survey, OECD (1977) notes that expenditures on health have been 'possibly the most rapidly rising component of public spending in the OECD area' (p. 83). Although methods of finance vary from country to country, as we have seen, there appears to have been a general movement away from private, and towards public, provision. Such an expenditure rise has, however, confronted the OECD economies with a particular problem:

A very real fear now appears to exist in the governments of Member states that the demand for health services is insatiable on the basis of any pricing system to consumers that is socially and ethically acceptable. And despite the increase in expenditures there is no very clear evidence of declining morbidity (p. 86).

The conclusion is therefore that, not only have diminishing returns to care become prevalent (entailing higher spending levels for progressively smaller improvements), but attempts to introduce direct charges for treatment, as in the UK for example, have neither limited demands nor provided an acceptable level of finance to the exchequer.

In many respects this problem confronting the health care sector is merely representative of the wider problem confronting balanced strategies in general and welfare states in particular. As an economy creates for itself a multiplicity of simultaneous targets, then the more difficult does it become to realize one without necessarily sacrificing the others. Economies are therefore obliged to make 'hard political choices'. However, these choices are not simply those between, say, more or less public provision of health care; rather they are choices in the entire area of public policy towards all the accepted goals of the welfare state. In this respect, one further speculation may be warranted.

If the objective function of industrialized economies is to continue to include the parallel objectives of full employment, price stability, a movement towards a more egalitarian income distribution and the provision of certain minimum welfare standards for every citizen, then it is hard to see how this might be accomplished without the influence of the government upon the economy. As Keynes appreciated, what this comes down to is the central government's powers of control, specifically its power to tax. Our evidence suggests that this is different in different economies; arguably the Swedish government is more powerful in this respect than is that of the UK or the USA. Although we might count the increased mobilization of resources on the part of the government as a positive factor in terms of the likely feasibility of policy implementation, we must naturally weigh this aspect against any negative effects induced by such a resource redistribution in the government's favour. In times of depression, the Keynesian would argue, such negative effects would be insignificant because individuals would not otherwise find it privately optimal to employ their resources in a collectively optimal manner, nor would they be induced to undertake a restructuring of the economy such as might be necessary during an epoch of rapid technological change. At the present time, there exists a view that Keynesian policies are incapable of bringing about the restoration of equilibrium given the specific historical conditions of the 1970s and 1980s. Again, however, the Keynesian might reply that the supposed failure of fiscal techniques over the past decade in certain cases is due to the fact that they have not really been applied in the strictly Keynesian sense. Keynes himself pointed out that the required extent of government involvement in the economy during periods of imbalance was extremely large, arguing with a distinct degree of sadness that it was only during periods of warfare that Western governments would be induced, or even permitted by the tax-payers, to mobilize resources on the scale necessary for adequate demand management. As we saw earlier, there are one or two exceptions to such a generalization, for public expenditure has indeed continued to grow rapidly in certain Western economies, West Germany and Sweden being cases in point. In other cases, however, it might be argued that the extensive increase in public sector involvement necessary to obtain these goals would lead to the creation of a society that places an excessive constraint upon individual freedom of action.

By way of conclusion let us simply make the point that, although we have talked in this chapter solely of the welfare state as an example of a balanced strategy amongst capitalist economies in the West, it is not true to say that concern over the attainment of multiple goals is confined to such economies. As we shall see in the next chapter, many of the materially poor economies of the world can be considered in such terms, although the specific economic problems that such economies encounter require us to consider them separately. Furthermore, and in spite of its clear growth orientation, the USSR too is concerned to provide its citizens with minimum welfare standards; indeed, McAuley (1979) observes that, in the USSR, 'there are far more doctors per head of population than in either Britain or the USA' (p. 234). However, he does suggest that overt Soviet interest in social welfare policy is very much a product of the recent past, dating from the end of the 'high growth' phase, perhaps the late 1960s. In its relatively new commitment to improve real living standards McAuley suggests the Soviet government is 'feeling its way', although he concludes that if the test of civilization is the degree to which a society provides for its poor (as Dr Johnson suggested) then 'the USSR bids fair to become more civilized than the rest of Europe' over the longer term (p. 317).

Summary

Western economies have come to appreciate the undesirable consequences of market failure. These include unemployment, inequality, negative and positive external effects and the under-provision of public goods. The ideology of the welfare state includes a commitment to full employment, the maintenance of minimum consumption standards for all, an egalitarian (as opposed to an inegalitarian) income distribution, security and stability. This ideology may have arisen for a number of reasons – growth of social concern, changes in political structure, efficiency.

In the case of Sweden, the range of policy goals has widened since the 1930s. The earliest objectives were full employment, growth and price stability. Over time, new goals were added, e.g. external equilibrium, adequate provision of pensions, health care, education, housing. Recent policy has been oriented towards the specific problems of sub-sets of the population. Since the 1930s, government involvement in the economy has risen dramatically. Government activity centres on the provision of the social infrastructure and redistribution. It has been argued that the Swedish economic structure has given rise to high employment levels, egalitarian distribution, increasing living standards and improved quality of life.

Western welfare states have several features in common, e.g. low agricultural contribution to aggregate output, large service sectors, trade equilibria. However, there exist important differences, e.g. investment rates, size of public sector, tax structure. Government involvement in the finance of accumulation varies from country to country. Tax psychology is an important ingredient in tax collection.

In principle, health care can be provided via either the public or the private sector. A private system might give rise to price inflation and an inegalitarian distribution of health care resources. However, depending upon the criterion of equity adopted, a public provision system might be considered unjust. Excess demand in the public case will be manifested as waiting time.

Amongst the problems currently facing welfare states is the undermining of the basic goals. Unemployment and inflation rose during the 1970s. A possible explanation is technological change and increased costs of energy. Welfare states have reacted to their problems with defensive policies, e.g. subsidization and protectionism. It is likely that solutions will be economy-specific. Although only capitalist economies have been considered, other nations might well share some 'welfare state' objectives.

Further reading

Approaches to the analysis of market failure and the welfare state include Culyer (1980) and Whynes and Bowles (1981).

The principal sources for Sweden are Wilson (1979), Fry (1979b), Lindbeck (1975) and Schnitzer (1970); also two statistical publications – *Statistical Abstract of Sweden* (National Central Bureau of Statistics) and *The Swedish Budget* (Ministry of Economic Affairs and Ministry of the Budget), both published annually in Stockholm. The taxation data are derived from Lindbeck (1975), pp. 177–8, Wilson (1979), pp. 129–37 and Normann and Södersten (1979).

Data on comparative taxation are derived from the same source as the data for Tables 11.1–11.3; also Brown and Jackson (1978), pp. 183–7. Sources for the health care section are Cullis and West (1979), Culyer (1976, 1980), Newhouse (1978), Maynard (1975) and OECD (1977). McLachlan (1980) and Maynard (1975) are comparative studies of health care provision, the latter being concerned with the EEC, the former examining countries such as West Germany, Sweden and the USSR. Sources for section 11.3 are the OECD's 1980 annual *Economic Surveys* of the countries concerned.

Chapter Twelve

Strategies for Survival

It goes without saying that, in designing their individual economic strategies, all economies are attempting to survive in some general sense, by arranging for the provision of at least the basic requirements for subsistence. History presents us with few examples of human, or indeed of non-human, societies that have embarked upon a deliberate collective suicide in the absence of external pressure. What is abundantly clear, nevertheless, is that some societies have found the target of survival far easier to reach than others. Observing the present 'state of the world', Seers (1971) remarks

> ... there are hundreds of millions of people who are illiterate and inadequately sheltered even from the rain, virtually without furniture and shoes, perpetually undernourished, provided by the twentieth century with little except the growing awareness of their misfortune. This has, however, always been the case. The striking fact about the world economy today is that tens of millions of people live very differently and that moreover those with high incomes, high enough (say) to spend a third of them on food, are not scattered evenly over the globe, but are heavily concentrated in a dozen countries bordering the North Atlantic (p. 13, new paragraph omitted).

In our discussions in Part I of this book we made the point that there is no reason to suppose that the social objective functions of different nations should be identical, given the possibility of a variety of views on the appropriate aims of human conduct. However, it is difficult to believe that any human society could be sufficiently transcendental as to opt deliberately for a policy of starvation and physical deprivation of the form described by Seers above. Clearly, the problems faced by such very poor economies are of a different order from those faced by, say, the industrialized welfare states examined in Chapter 11.

Just as the aims of society might be dissimilar, so too will be the relative importance attached to any particular aim in the overall social 263 objective function. What is interesting, however, is that if we rank economies according to any number of indices of material prosperity (such as nutritional levels, life expectancy, per capita output or income and so on) we find that all these indices are, in the main, highly correlated. Nations with the lowest incomes, in other words, tend also to be those with the lowest level of medical care provision, the lowest average calorie intake or the highest death rate. This implies that the ordering of nations by means of some generalized prosperity index, including all the elements mentioned above, would produce a ranking that was largely insensitive to the weights that we attached to any particular element. In whatever manner we defined material poverty, we should find, by and large, that the same group of countries always appeared at the bottom of our ranking. It is with the problems of this particular group that we are concerned in this chapter.

12.1   Changing attitudes towards India

In 1947 India gained its independence from the British Empire as one of the poorest states in the world. Myrdal (1968) has studied the condition of the Indian economy at that time and his conclusions paint a picture of exceptional material deprivation under all the headings considered earlier. On the nutritional front, he cites surveys suggesting that over 90 per cent of the population was probably undernourished from the point of view of individuals being unable to maintain their existing health status (p. 545). This was due not only to the non-availability of foodstuffs but also to the fact that those foodstuffs that were available (primarily cereals) were incapable of providing the necessary balanced diet. Another survey cited suggested that as much as 95 per cent of the urban housing stock could be considered as 'unsatisfactory for healthful habitation' (p. 554) whilst only a tiny proportion of the Indian population had access to protected water supplies, unpolluted by human waste and potential disease. The very low per capita income figure for India was complicated by a high degree of income inequality; even by the mid-1950s it was estimated that 50 per cent of the population was living on 10 US cents per day or less. Even so, Myrdal concludes, 'the very low average income does not begin to plumb the depths of misery in India' (p. 565).

That India was on the brink of economic collapse in 1947 does not therefore appear to be in doubt and, not surprisingly, the improvement of material living standards was the task to which post-independence India addressed itself. What makes India an interesting example from our point of view is the fact that India's economic policies, and the policies proposed by external observers who have used India as a case-study to test their models, have gone through a number of reasonably distinct phases. Within the Indian context, therefore, we can appraise the implications of a number of survival strategies.

The initial strategy, which dominated the years between 1950 and the mid-1960s, set industrialization as the target and economic planning as the means. The strategy owed much to the theories of Mahalanobis, who was the chief architect of the first few five-year plans. The question to which Mahalanobis addressed himself was how might it be possible to make India economically independent and self-sustaining in the shortest possible time? Observing the prevailing conditions in the Indian economy, he ruled out the possibility of the agricultural sector serving as the engine of economic growth. Given the composition of Indian exports, and the inelastic world demand for primary exports of the Indian type, an active external policy likewise appeared non-feasible. Growth would therefore have to come from indigenous industrialization, although Mahalanobis argued that it would have to be industrialization of a specific type. The expansion of both consumption goods and capital goods production depended, he suggested, on the increased production of capital goods in the first instance, for such goods are vital to all forms of subsequent production; concentration on capital goods production in the short run would enable both types of production to be realized in the medium run. By contrast, an industrial strategy favouring the initial expansion of consumption goods would be frustrated by in-adequate supplies of capital goods. Furthermore, the more one expanded capital goods production then the higher would be the resulting output of the economy, the higher would be the income generated and, most importantly, the higher would be the level of savings for reinvestment to maintain the growth process.

Such was the theory behind the First and, especially, the Second Indian Plan (1956–61). Those resources that could be mobilized by government (a substantial proportion of which came from foreign assistance) were directed, first and foremost, into large-scale heavy industry, such as iron and steel, machine tools and electrical equipment. In fact, this basic heavy-industry sector was planned to receive over one-third of the total investment allocation of the Second Plan. However, and although heavy industrialization represented the central thrust of the strategy, it was appreciated that industrialization could not proceed in isolation. Throughout these early plans, public sector services and the infrastructure also received attention, to lay the foundations upon which the evolving industrial structure was to rest. The production of consumption goods too was not totally neglected but, in Mahalanobis' view, primary responsibility in this area was to be given to small-scale or household enterprises, which would complement the centralized production of capital goods with more localized production for the consumer. Agriculture also received a share of the investment resources although its funding was subordinated to the interests of basic industries.

The Mahalanobis strategy of industrialization via planning did not pass without criticism, both from within India and from without. It was argued, for example, that the decision to concentrate on the production of domestic capital goods would deny India the possibility of gains from trade – i.e. India would be producing capital equipment at high cost owing to comparative disadvantage, when such equipment could be imported more cheaply from the industrialized world. Second, the emphasis on capital production implied the necessity of capital-intensive production techniques, owing to the realities of technology in this respect. The strategy therefore appeared to take little account of the problem of the absorption of the labour surplus. Third, and as Shenoy (1971) has suggested, a central problem with an industrialization programme is the increased reliance that becomes placed on imports. Not only does capital goods expansion necessitate certain capital goods imports, at least in the short run, but the relative neglect of agriculture could necessitate the increased importation of foodstuffs. Criticism was also made not so much with respect to the industrialization programme but with respect to the great emphasis that was being placed upon economic planning. A high degree of centralization, it was argued, not only permitted members of the planning administration to further their private interests via corrupt practices, but it discouraged individual enterprise and the formation of markets. Doubts were also expressed that India possessed the necessary data or 'know-how' to operate a planning system.

In his study of the Indian economy Mellor (1976) suggests that the industrialization-with-planning strategy was terminated (*de facto* if not *de jure*) by the severe drought of 1965–7. This drought depressed annual agricultural output by some 20 per cent and even the index of industrial production, which had tripled since 1949, showed a slight downturn. How had the Indian economy changed during the period? From the point of view of industry, Mellor suggests that three transitions had taken place. First, capital goods output in the mid-1960s accounted for a far greater share of total production than was the case in the 1950s. Second, the public sector had expanded at the expense of the private and, third, larger firms had expanded more rapidly than smaller ones. Compared to industry, agriculture had performed less well, with a 60 per cent production increase over the period 1949 to 1965.

In spite of the achievement of a high industrial growth rate, Mellor argues that the Indian economy did not realize its full potential because of the existence of three constraints. First, there was a constraint at the administrative level. The Indian economy is, of course, vast and complex, and Mellor argues that the planners simply did not possess sufficient information or the basic operational controls necessary to implement the optimal policy. Second, the industrialization strategy was dependent upon capital formation, which did not noticeably expand over the period. The profitability of most industries was low and the market for private savings was ill developed. Throughout the period, foreign assistance remained an important source of investment funds, and output growth was thus constrained by the extent of international generosity. Third, although agriculture appeared to play only a subordinate role in the industrialization approach, Mellor concludes that its relatively slow growth acted as a brake on the entire economy owing to the existence of important industry/agriculture linkages. The agricultural sector proved manifestly incapable of responding to demand changes by output adjustment, with the result that prices fluctuated dramatically. Such prices were a key determinant of the nature of aggregate activity. They determined, for example, the level of farm income, and farmers were of course a major demand factor as regards industrial output. Agricultural prices were also significant in determining the wage demands of urban industrial workers, and also their demand for food imports if the agricultural price level rose excessively.

It was in particular the observation of this last constraint that led analysts in the mid-1960s to believe that the rapid industrialization strategy might have been misguided. Agriculture, they suggested, appeared to be failing in three respects. First, the increases in foodgrain output appeared to be keeping pace only with population growth, implying zero improvement in the existing nutritional levels. Second, agricultural output was certainly growing at a slower rate than the increase in consumer purchasing power, implying excess demand for agricultural products, price inflation and higher import bills. Finally, agricultural growth was clearly insufficient to enable savings to be accumulated, i.e. the sector appeared incapable of generating a surplus for reinvestment either in agriculture itself or in industry. However, at the same time as the past performance of agriculture was being viewed with pessimistic gloom, developments in agricultural research were providing the basis for a more optimistic vision. It came to be believed that substantial expansion of the agricultural output of poor economies such as India was indeed possible by following through the logic of what has been termed the 'Green Revolution'.

The notion of the Green Revolution hypothesized that substantial increases in agricultural productivity, especially in the area of foodstuffs production, could result from advances on three fronts. The first of these would be the planting of high-yield varieties of cereals, particularly wheat and rice, which had been developed over the years since 1945. Not only did such varieties actually produce more output per unit of land area, but they were supposedly more resilient to disease and drought and they permitted multiple cropping by having shorter growing cycles. Second, changes in agricultural technology would be required involving, in particular, the increased usage of capital inputs, e.g. mechanization, irrigation schemes, the use of fertilizers. Finally, the Green Revolution had implications for institutional change. Land reform and reclamation, increased credit facilities and research and marketing assistance would, it was argued, all encourage the individual farmer to increase his output by making such an increase privately optimal. Singh (1974) has shown how the acceptance of the principles of the Green Revolution was explicitly included in the Fourth Indian Plan in 1965. Although agriculture had always received a slice of the central resource disbursements in the earlier plans, he notes that the 'new agricultural strategy' of the post-1965 period marked a change in emphasis. The Indian government came to favour investment in agricultural schemes that were quickly and directly productive, as opposed to those that involved a substantial time lag before benefits could be realized. Emphasis came to be placed on small-scale irrigation, soil conservation, forestry and animal husbandry, whilst a substantial effort was made to increase the use (and the production) of fertilizers. Between 1965 and 1970, both the annual production and the annual consumption of nitrogenous fertilizers approximately tripled.

The Green Revolution of the late-1960s was not a phenomenon peculiar to India; indeed, it was hoped at the time that it would provide a solution to one of the most fundamental problems encountered by all the poorer agricultural economies. Looking back over the past two decades we are in a position to ask how successful this revolution has in fact been. Perhaps the most surprising conclusion is that reached by Griffin (1979), who examines aggregate data over time for the major agricultural regions of the world. He concludes that there is no evidence of a significant shift in labour productivity after 1965 (when the Green Revolution was supposedly brought into operation) and, indeed, there are certain instances where agricultural growth rates have actually fallen after the introduction of Green Revolution techniques. For the Far Eastern group of economies (which includes India) Griffin notes an increase in annual food production rates in the post-1965 period of 0.11 per cent. Such data lead him to believe that, whilst the agricultural world is not heading for conditions of general famine, 'neither is it advancing rapidly to a state of abundance and adequate nourishment' (p. 6).

Evidence of this nature should not lead us to suggest that the Green Revolution has been proved to be a completely false hope; rather, we can see that, as a weapon to fight the agricultural production constraint, it has proved itself to be singularly double-edged. Specifically, the following are the sorts of problems that have emerged. First, it seems clear that, whilst the Green Revolution as a global phenomenon appears to have made little impact on aggregate growth trends, there have been some spectacular localized successes. Wheat production in Pakistan and northern India, for instance, has proved particularly responsive to Green Revolution techniques. On the other hand, there have been some equally spectacular localized disasters, for the high-yield varieties have so far proved to be far more temperamental than their predecessors. This might mean, for example, that, whilst the new variety is resilient to diseases A, B and C, it is especially vulnerable to disease D, an outbreak of which could annihilate the entire crop. The higher yields are thus bought at the price of periodic catastrophe. We should note too that, at present, higher yields are almost solely confined to varieties of wheat and rice; in economies where these crops are of only limited significance (such as those of Africa and Latin America) the Green Revolution has proved understandably less revolutionary. Second, it is clear that the impact of the new technology has been felt only by certain types of farmer. As the new varieties often require increased capital inputs to yield their full potential, innovation along these lines has largely been confined to the richer, larger-scale farmers. If only for this reason, therefore, the potential benefit of the Green Revolution is a function of the nature of land ownership, which, in turn, has distributional implications. Third, and following this argument through, the new input mix usually requires substantial government support, to introduce the new ideas and to make them financially feasible as far as the individual farmer is concerned. The gains from the revolution, in other words, must be obtained at some opportunity cost and there is no necessity for the returns from expenditures to be always increasing. Finally, the Green Revolution appears to exert a considerable influence on employment and social relationships. Griffin (1979) notes that, because the technically optimum size of farm increases with the introduction of Green Revolution technology, there is a tendency for the Asian peasantry to become transformed into a class of wage-earners employed by the larger farmers. Whilst in some cases the new technology has increased the demand for labour, in others the higher scale of operation has permitted farm-owners to economize on employment. In the face of a labour surplus, this can imply a fall in potential labour income and, Griffin argues, the penetration of the labour market into the rural areas may have the effect of polarizing the population into two antagonistic classes.

In view of criticisms such as these – to the effect that the Green Revolution has as yet been unsuccessful in either increasing agricultural output or relieving rural poverty – observers such as Mellor (1976) have suggested that a further shift in economic strategy might be necessary, to give agriculture possibly as much emphasis as the earlier strategy gave to industrialization. Mellor is especially concerned with the plight of the small farmer and the rural landless labourer in India, both of whom, as a result of the technological transition of the Green Revolution, find themselves in a severely disadvantaged position. In his view

Increased agricultural production must form the cornerstone of a strategy for the relief of poverty. Agriculture must provide the food to back higher incomes, and to improve health, and it must directly account for much of the rise in employment in the short and intermediate run ... [T]o be effective, the goals of agricultural policy must be supported by an employment-orientated, capital-conserving industrial policy (p. 106).

Some insights into the feasibility of such a strategy may be gained by considering the economic policies pursued in one of India's immediate neighbours, namely China.

12.1.1   COMPARISONS WITH CHINA

For perhaps the first ten years of their autonomous existences we can detect strong parallels between the strategies pursued by India and post-revolutionary China. In the first place, both the 1947 Indian and the 1949 Chinese administrations inherited primarily agricultural economies; even by 1970, by which time substantial industrialization had taken place in both economies, some 70 per cent of the populations in both cases were still directly engaged in agricultural production. Moreover, the industrial structure that did exist in China in 1949 was disrupted and fragmented by the prolonged civil and Sino–Japanese wars. Rampant inflation had further dislocation effects. Second, the strategies pursued by both governments during the first few years were essentially holding actions, attempts to come to terms with prevailing economic realities and to design long-term policies for the future. Third, the principal objective of both governments was similar, i.e. the creation of an independent and autonomous nation and the rapid increase in levels of material welfare. Fourth, the first long-term strategy adopted by both administrations (in the form of the First and Second Indian Plans during the 1950s and the First Chinese Plan of 1953–7) owed a great deal to the Soviet industrialization model. Both economies favoured a centrally planned, 'industry first' approach, emphasizing the need for a high rate of investment in capital-intensive heavy industry. Agricultural progress was therefore subordinated to industrial needs although, of the two, the Chinese strategy was the more explicitly 'Soviet', the ideology of socialism requiring the transformation of the institutional structure of agriculture by collectivization. After 1957, however, the policy lines of India and China began to diverge as the Chinese leadership rapidly rethought its strategy.

Although the First Chinese Plan was successful in generating substantial increases in industrial output (of the order of 15 per cent per annum) and in transforming the production base from consumer to capital goods, it became apparent that the plan was also giving rise to precisely the same problems as were being experienced by India. In particular, agricultural output was not growing at anything like the rate reached by industry. It was thus acting as a constraint to continued expansion, because of a diminution of available food supplies necessary to feed the growing urban population, added to the fact that industry was slowly being starved of its vital raw materials derived from agriculture, e.g. raw cotton, food for processing and so forth. Furthermore, a sluggish agricultural sector was clearly incapable of generating an investible surplus for capital creation. As a reaction to such problems, the Chinese leadership embarked upon a new strategy in 1958, a strategy popularly labelled the 'Great Leap'. This strategy emphasized, first and foremost, rapid and concurrent progress on both the agricultural and the industrial fronts. The means of realization was via the mobilization of China's most abundant factor of production, labour. Policies were accordingly devised not only to marshal the rural labour surplus but also to put it into productive use by encouraging the establishment of small-scale labour-intensive rural industries. Typical projects of the period were irrigation and land reclamation schemes, and the now-famous 'backyard' steel furnaces. In terms of overall economic policy, the Great Leap represents the first distinct manifestation of the theories of Chairman Mao, the earlier period having been heavily influenced by Soviet thinking. The immediate fortunes of the Great Leap were quite dismal for, within a couple of years, it was formally abandoned. A combination of poor harvests, the disruptions arising from collectivization and the simple technical inefficiency of small-scale production led to a serious depression in the rural economy by 1960, the effects of which soon filtered through to industry. Again, the need for a new approach was evident.

In 1961 China adopted a policy of 'agriculture first', representing a distinct volte-face from the early 1950s. This essentially involved the further reordering of priorities, with far less emphasis being placed on a high rate of investment to secure industrial growth. Rather than being the leading sector, industry was now required to play a more subservient role to agriculture, being encouraged to expand in those areas – such as the production of farm vehicles, electricity and fertilizer – that would yield the greatest benefit to agriculture. At the same time, incentive systems within agriculture underwent a certain transition. Whilst, under the earlier strategies, the incentives to produce in agriculture were largely in the form of moral exhortation supported by veiled coercion, material incentives in the form of pecuniary rewards for greater output now came to play a far larger part.

The economic progress of China between 1961 and the death of Chairman Mao in 1976 was really conditioned by the legacies of all three strategies. The 'agriculture first' approach had raised agriculture's status in the overall objective function, but the industrial structure laid down under the 1953–7 Plan was not, of course, neglected. As a result of the rapid switches in strategy, China in the 1960s and 1970s came to follow a path with agriculture and industry in some form of balance, the legacy of the Great Leap being perhaps more social and ideological than directly material. How well did the Chinese economy perform during the Maoist period? Considering simply material living standards, Eckstein (1977) estimates that the average per capita consumption levels of the 1970s exceeded the 1952 figure by some 70 per cent and he therefore suggests that 'the bulk of the Chinese population must have begun to reap substantial material benefits from the process of economic development' (pp. 305–7). The average annual GDP growth over the same period was around 6 per cent. Against this general background,

Aziz (1978) argues that China's strategies have yielded successful outcomes in four specific areas, and this serves to contrast the Chinese
experience with the experiences of other Asian economies such as India.
First, China has managed to increase food production to the extent that
malnutrition has become a relatively rare occurrence. In spite of having
a ratio of arable land to population 50 per cent lower than India,
China's per capita cereal consumption was in fact 50 per cent higher
in the early 1970s. Aziz suggests that this state of affairs arose from the
specific attention devoted to the agricultural sector over the previous
20 years, coupled with the egalitarian distribution of productive
resources and food supply that is a central principle of Chinese ideology.
Second, the pressure of unemployment has been less in China than in
other Asian economies owing to (i) explicit interest in employment-
creating rural projects in the Great Leap mould, (ii) direct policy that
positively discourages migration away from agriculture and (iii) an
active population control policy that has halved the population growth
rate over the past two decades. Third, by deliberate manipulation of
the prices that they control, Chinese planners have been able to maintain
the prices of many consumption necessities at a fixed level; Aziz notes
that the 1974 prices of rice and coal were actually lower than their
1950 levels (p. 65). Finally, and because the Chinese emphasis has been
upon holistic progress, the rural/urban imbalances that are typical of
many poorer economies are less prevalent in China. An element of the
post-1961 strategy was to bring to rural areas services such as education
and health care that, in other Asian economies, are usually concentrated
in the urban industrial centres.

The contrast between India and China is perhaps most marked in
terms of the large emphasis that the latter has placed upon rural development. Aziz (1978) notes five features that characterize the Chinese
strategy towards the problems of the rural sector. First, China ensured
a reasonably egalitarian distribution of resources by means of an extensive land reform programme. Second, the collectivization movement
had the beneficial economic effects of facilitating large-scale labour
mobilization for use on major agricultural projects, of allowing the
pooling of individual savings to purchase inputs, and of permitting a
higher degree of specialization. Third, the rural economy became
progressively diversified with the establishment of rural industry, either
related to, or even independent of, agriculture. Fourth, direct agricultural development was backed up with the provision of welfare services
to minimize any obvious rural/urban differentials. Fifth, the organization
of Chinese agriculture, based upon the commune, was made coterminous
with the political system. In other words, the individuals making the
economic decisions were also those making the political decisions; as
Aziz observes, 'no rural community can achieve sustained progress if it
is directly or indirectly exploited either by the tax system or the terms
of trade under which it operates' (p. 104). In most of these respects,

India and China are radically different. Land in India is predominantly privately owned and the distribution is inegalitarian: in 1970, 5 per cent of rural households held 35 per cent of available land, whilst 26 per cent of rural households held no land at all (p. 115). The absence of collective production makes the employment of such surplus labour particularly difficult. An insight into the problem is provided by the case of the Punjab region of India, which, in some respects, represents one of India's most successful experiments in rural development. Green Revolution techniques, in the form of the planting of high-yield varieties of crop, irrigation, the establishment of marketing and purchasing cooperatives, and a degree of land reform, all contributed to significant output increases in the region during the 1960s and early 1970s. However, as Rajaraman (1975) has shown, a side-effect of the expansion was the polarization of welfare gains; the consumption levels of many families in the region actually declined, there being no employment opportunities for the large class of landless labourers.

12.2   Lessons in survival

As a result of the experiences of economies such as India and China and, indeed, as a consequence of the varying fortunes of other economies such as Pakistan and a number of Latin American states that began the post-war period with industrialization drives, the fashionable terminology used in discussing strategies for progress in poorer economies has changed. Nowadays, we see far less emphasis being placed upon 'rapid industrialization' and 'capital mobilization'; rather, the key words appear to be, if not 'agriculturalization', then at least the 'balanced development' of agriculture and industry, with emphasis not so much on 'investment' but more on 'employment'. Perhaps the most obvious lesson that has been learned is that the poorer economies ignore agriculture, generally their dominant economic sector, at their peril. The beginnings of this new approach were observable in the mid to late 1960s; indeed, a chapter in the book by Maddison (1970) is entitled 'Has Industrialisation been too Costly?' Maddison argues particularly that the desire for indigenous industrialization, often behind protective tariff barriers, led the economies concerned to endure much higher costs than would have been experienced had they traded on world markets. He cites evidence that suggests that the relative inefficiency of industry in Pakistan, as compared with that of the Western economies, meant that its industrialization strategy may have cost it between 3 and 4 per cent of GDP per annum (p. 194). Whilst conceding that efficiency could conceivably rise in the long run, he points out that this is a high price to pay in the shorter term in view of the contemporary low material living standards.

   Representative of contributions to the 'new direction' of strategies in recent years are those by Mellor (1976) and Okwuosa (1976). Whilst the latter study proposes a strategy for Africa, the former uses India as a model for the development of a general argument. In spite of the fact that different areas are analysed in these studies, both authors make remarkably similar recommendations. Both see the fundamental problems facing the poorer economies as being (i) the inferior performance of the agricultural sector, which acts as a brake on industrial expansion, (ii) the inability of the production mix to come to terms with the existence of substantial unemployment of labour, and (iii) the continued existence of poverty, especially in the rural areas, despite apparent progress in terms of, for example, overall GDP increases. Mellor argues that, to deal with such problems, three areas of priority should be established. The first is the simple acceleration of the growth of the agricultural sector. He further suggests that, within agriculture, most poor economies would have similar concerns and he lists fertilizer production, investment in irrigation, rural electrification, research and manpower training as central issues requiring attention. For his part, Okwuosa emphasizes the government's role in encouraging farmers to adopt new techniques, as well as the need to provide assistance in marketing via the formation of cooperatives and by means of price regulation. Mellor's second priority is the need to expand small-scale industry; this would complement agriculture by soaking up the labour surplus and by creating effective demand for agricultural output as a result of employment. Third, Mellor argues that poorer economies should continue to make use of the comparative advantage principle by importing capital-intensive technology, to be paid for by means of an export expansion. The agricultural and small-scale industrial sector would have a key role to play in this respect.

To a certain extent, states such as India and China paid the price of being early starters in the post-war world. Colonial territories, such as those of Africa, that gained their independence in the 1960s and 1970s were in a position to learn from the others' mistakes (if we view such rapid industrialization as a mistake) and to move directly to the balanced expansion of agriculture and industry as the primary strategy. Even so, and in spite of the contemporary viewpoint, we must not be led to believe that the agricultural-based programmes proposed by the above writers represent the sole possibility for the poorer economies. Strategies depend crucially upon circumstances. A strong case might be made for those economies endowed with resources characterized by exceptionally buoyant world demand (e.g. Nigeria with its oil and Zambia with its copper) to consider rapid industrialization as a viable alternative, if such a path is desired. It could be argued that the opportunities for industrialization via the import of capital exist only in the short run (until the resource is depleted) and thus full use of the potential should be made in the short run.

Our second lesson concerns the nature of government in some of the materially poor economies. Throughout our discussions we have made the possibly naive assumption that the government is in some sense *concerned* with the problems of poverty such as low standards of living, unemployment and so forth. Suppose, however, we were to follow the argument of Wiles (1977):

> ... many people want political power only for the wealth it brings. In the comparatively honest politics of Northwest Europe, Canada and Australasia, where also private business provides a quicker and legally safer road to wealth, this is not so. But where standards of honesty are lower ... and especially if in addition private business is the football of government ..., the man greedy for wealth must seriously consider a political or even a civil service career. In countries where these conditions are extreme – much of Africa and Latin America – the whole tone of government is set by these people. These are the so-called *kleptocracies* (pp. 450–1).

For Wiles, a kleptocracy is a 'state which is really an estate', an economy run for the benefit not of its citizens but of its members of government, possibly at the expense of its citizens.

It is not necessary for us to accept Wiles's notion of the specific geographical distribution of political integrity. What is interesting from our point of view is the implicit proposition that a government might act, not as a facilitator of collective progress, but as a constraint upon it. The best we can hope for from a kleptocratic government is a second-best solution, for such a government will automatically rule out any policy that would prejudice its favourable position. What are the conditions that most favour the existence of a kleptocracy? Given Wiles's proposition, they would seem to be the following. First, kleptocracies would be more likely to flourish in a situation of minimal accountability requirements on the part of governments with respect to citizens. Restrictions on the franchise, infrequent elections and *de facto* military dictatorship would be advantageous here. Second, kleptocracies are more likely to arise when the political avenue offers the highest expected rate of return to the individual wealth-seeker. This implies not only that the political system should be manipulable for private ends, but that other economic sectors should offer poor material prospects.

It is likely that an examination of *any* national government would yield some evidence of kleptocratic tendencies as Wiles suggests. However, it is fair to say that such tendencies are particularly pronounced amongst certain poor economies. Attitudes towards property ownership are a specific example. In his study of Spanish-speaking America, Griffin (1969) notes that, in respect of agriculture,

> the latifundia system is both economically inefficient and socially unjust. The under-privileged groups in Spanish America appear to have little political power, are pushed to the margin of the economy as consumers and are strongly – and unfavourably for them – integrated into the economy as sellers of commodities

and their labour. This situation will persist as long as political power, land and capital are concentrated in the hands of a few families (p. 81).

Even a simple economic change, Griffin argues, is 'likely to be strongly resisted by the landowning class, precisely because it would undermine the props upon which their wealth and political power are built' (p. 82). By the same token, he suggests resource mobilization in the region is typically lower than might be anticipated owing to the governments' reluctance to levy high rates of taxation on the very rich. The taxation of the already poor is not a technique that secures the maximum reinvestment. Aziz (1978) employs similar criticisms in his appraisal of Indian rural development, arguing that the government in this case has not made the reforms necessary to realize the full potential of the Green Revolution. Indeed, this is suggested as part of a more general proposition to the effect that strategies for progress may not be directly transferable from country to country because of differences in ideologies. Put simply, property redistribution, irrespective of any economic benefits that it might confer in aggregate, may not be considered legitimate in an economy that believes in the sanctity of private property rights.

A third, and related, lesson concerns the manner in which strategies are implemented. Almost without exception, the beginnings of industrialization in the post-war poorer economies of Asia and Africa have been accompanied by a form of economic planning, ranging from limited government investment proposals to all-embracing blueprints at a national level. Surveying the experiences of 25 African plans during the 1960s, Okwuosa (1976) observes that the successes of these plans were subject to a high degree of variation. Whilst ten economies had plan achievement levels in excess of 75 per cent of target, three had achievement levels of less than 25 per cent, the remainder being somewhere in between (pp. 179–81). Such data raise questions about the efficacy of planning as a means of implementing an economic strategy. One reason for certain poor performances, as Okwuosa appreciates, was the fact that targets were often set at an unreasonably high level. A more substantial problem, however, is that planning in poorer economies is likely to be inherently difficult to implement. Even if we ignore the possibility of corrupt practices as alluded to above, the simple institution of planning, in the form of setting up government departments for administration and control, is an expensive proposition. There may also be doubts about whether or not a poor economy would possess sufficient skilled manpower or even the economic data necessary to formulate and implement a rational plan. Singh (1974) points to certain administrative inefficiencies in the case of India, for example the 'failure as a rule to fix responsibility and accountability on organisations', 'lack of adequate telephone and other communications facilities' and, more generally, the 'archaic and cumbersome methods of handling all public business' (pp. 447–8).

The type of planning implicitly referred to here uses as its model the sophisticated structures of the methods of, say, France or the USSR. However, it might be more appropriate in the case of a pre-industrial poor economy to consider the employment of a less formal type of planning structure. The analysis of Tanzania by Hyden (1979) is interesting in this context. Hyden argues that Tanzania, feeling itself to be amongst the poorest economies in the world, has adopted a strategy that may be termed 'we must run while others walk', implying that a tremendous sense of urgency is being attached to progress. Hyden suggests that this approach to policy making gives rise to several characteristics. First, he notes a desire to do everything at once, often without the advantage of an *ex ante* understanding of the likely policy outcomes. This entails a view of planning in direct contradiction to the generally accepted position whereby policies are fully appraised before resources are committed. In the Tanzanian case, Hyden suggests that 'the ultimate objective is considered so important that the cost of resources to attain it becomes a secondary matter' (p. 6). Second, there exists considerable reluctance to use the past as a guide for the future, this being justified on the grounds that experiences of the earlier colonial period have no relevance for the creation of a new nation. Third, Hyden believes that individuals responsible for administration are in positions such that the individuals' feasible attainment is always less than the public expectation of their performance. Clearly, all this runs very much counter to the conventional Western or Soviet wisdom regarding rational economic policy. However, its advantages are argued to be in terms of the spontaneity created within the economy; given that Tanzanian planning is quite decentralized, the dependence relationship of citizens on administrators built up by 'normal' planning is effectively counterbalanced. In many respects, the Tanzanian approach to policy formulation is an echo of the Chinese version, especially the belief that all problems are inherently soluble given human will and effort. However, just as we cannot objectively state that the Chinese approach to rural development represents the definitive model, so we should not declare the informal planning approach of Tanzania to be readily transferable. Once again, different circumstances require different strategies.

Perhaps the most sobering lesson that the supposedly rational social scientist may learn is, discounting a deterministic or fatalistic theory of history, the significance of chance in determining the legacies and thus the prospects of many of the world's poor economies. Only 50 years ago, most of Africa and South Asia was essentially a dominion of Western Europe; if we are willing to go back a few more centuries we can include North and South America and Australasia in this subject group. What happened during the colonial era has exerted a profound influence upon the present-day prospects of economies in such regions; a few examples will demonstrate the point. The present frontiers of African nations are largely the result of negotiations between the colonial powers of Europe

in the late nineteenth century and, at the time, precious little account
was taken of the interests of the indigenous populations, or of their
existing tribal boundaries. The Ewe tribe therefore found themselves
divided between Togo and Ghana, whilst the Yoruba group found
themselves split between Nigeria and Dahomey. Indeed, many newly
independent African states have found the conflict between 'tribalism'
and the more recent need for 'nationalism' a particular problem in
policy implementation. As most of the colonies were operated under
the umbrella of an empire, autonomous economic viability was not a
requirement at the time; it suddenly became so with independence,
however, giving rise to severe balance of payments problems in many
cases. Needless to say, many of the national boundaries remain the
subject of constant dispute at the present time (e.g. the dispute between
Ethiopia and Somalia).

To a considerable extent, the preconditions of post-independence
strategies were established by the colonial power's assessment of the
particular end that the territory was to serve. India's particular mis-
fortune was to come under the control of a ruling power interested in
India as a source of primary products and as a market for manufactures.
Free trade, the particularly subtle form of imperialism that characterized
the British Empire, effectively dismantled those steps towards domestic
industrialization that had already been taken, although Myrdal argues
that this policy was misguided, for a richer India would have increased
the marketability of UK goods (pp. 144–7). Many of the African
economies were used as providers of agricultural supply, efforts being
concentrated on specific cash crops in the regions best suited to their
cultivation; examples were groundnuts (Senegal, Niger, Nigeria), cocoa
(Nigeria, Ghana), coffee (Kenya, Uganda) and sisal (Tanzania). This
commodity specialization was naturally inherited on independence.
Incidentally, the 'luck' element in colonialism has also filtered through
into the post-independence period. Some economies, for instance, have
found that their arbitrarily enclosed boundaries contain natural
resources in great demand; again, some states have been more successful
than others in persuading their former rulers to part with development
assistance (Chapter 9).

Whether the imperial experience was irrevocably harmful to many
of the poor economies in the contemporary world, or, indeed, whether
a particular country might have done better had it been conquered by
European state *A* rather than European state *B*, is an interesting field
for speculation. However, from the point of view of a poor economy
devising a future strategy, contemporary realities are of far greater
significance. One possible line of thinking is the following. If the geo-
political engineering of the past was undertaken by the likes of maraud-
ing bands of Spanish *conquistadores*, treaty-making diplomats around the
table at the 1885 Congress of Vienna (where Africa was reallocated),
plus assorted plundering princes, generals and revolutionaries, then there

can be little about the existing geo-political structure that is sacred. Perhaps a feasible strategy for survival for poor economies is one involving the transcendence of existing national boundaries via economic cooperation.

The arguments in favour of some form of cooperation between poor economies are not so different from those used to support a community such as the EEC (Chapter 9). Briefly, they are the following. First, the creation of a free trade area between poor economies could encourage production by giving each of them access to a wider market. Second, cooperation in resource use would even out the imbalances in natural resource endowments; as we have seen, poor economies tend to concentrate most of their economic efforts in the production of subsistence goods plus one or two cash crops or minerals. Third, coordination and pooling of investment resources could make larger-scale projects feasible and, fourth, the formation of a wider community could increase bargaining power vis-à-vis other economies or communities.

In the face of these possibilities, however, we can find some fairly compelling reasons to explain why the formation of, say, a regional economic grouping of a number of poor nations is unlikely to be successful. In the first place, whilst we might assume that the reduction of trade barriers such as tariffs ought, other things remaining equal, to increase the volume of trade, the evidence suggests that the level of trade between poor economies is low in any case, for they are often all engaged in the production of the same type of commodity. Even if a trade increase were to be secured by tariff reductions, governments might well feel that this would require them to forgo an important source of investible revenue. Second, it is quite likely that differing economies within the grouping would have undergone differing degrees of industrialization. This being the case, we should anticipate that the liberalization of factor mobility, for example, would produce a gradual polarization within the community, the region with the existing comparative advantage in industry acting as a magnet for liberated resources. This was clearly the case for the East African economic community up to the mid-1960s, Kenya attracting the lion's share of resources at the expense of the less industrialized Uganda and Tanzania. Third, it is difficult to see how integration could ever take place amongst certain groups of nations distinguished by widely differing ideologies. Africa again is a good example, for we witness socialist states existing alongside capitalist and, in some cases, quasi-feudal regimes.

Although interest in economic cooperation continues at the present time, it is probably fair to say that less is expected of it now than was hoped for in the 1950s and 1960s, when there was a particular proliferation of economic integration attempts. In Africa, this spirit was fostered by the simultaneous independence of a number of colonies, many of which were under the leadership of prominent 'pan-Africans', for example Nkrumah of Ghana, Nyerere of Tanzania, Senghor of Senegal and Touré of Guinea. A specific concern of the Organization of African Unity, established in 1963, was the extension of economic links between African economies. Of all the economic communities amongst poorer nations at the time, that of Central America was held up as a model, for it had effectively abolished trade barriers and attempted to arrange for a fair distribution of industrial activity. However, by the 1970s, it was clear that this community was under stress; there were overt political antagonisms between members and clear imbalances in economic prosperity.

Whatever the particular failures or successes achieved by specific attempts at cooperation, it seems hard to deny that, in principle, some socially profitable opportunities must exist. Okwuosa (1976) points out the potential for agricultural cooperation in cases where geography or climate imply that economies are suited for producing complementary goods. He also notes that, as infectious diseases do not seem to respect national boundaries, their eradication will require supranational strategies (p. 105). Thus, the relative decline in emphasis on integration amongst poor economies is not necessarily due to any inherent weaknesses in the logic; rather, it seems to have arisen as a reaction to the changing structure of the world economy. World trade is presently dominated by a number of blocs – the USA, the EEC, the oil-producers, Japan and the Soviet group – and the strategy being followed by many poor economies entails access to one or more of these blocs. Rather than form their own coalitions, in other words, poor economies seem concerned to join with the existing coalitions. An instance was the 1975 Lomé Convention agreement (revised in 1979), which established economic linkages between the EEC and some 50 African, Caribbean and Pacific economies. Although designed specifically to achieve a rational allocation of economic assistance, coupled with policies to stabilize the export earnings of the poorer economies, the agreement, as Twitchett (1981) notes, has so far produced no concrete results.

Summary

Between independence and the mid-1960s, India adopted a policy of industrialization under economic planning. Emphasis was placed on public infrastructure and the capital goods sector. It has been argued that the strategy was misguided because it ignored trading opportunities, the existence of a labour surplus and agricultural development. Further, it placed excessive reliance upon imports, and the planning mechanism was inefficient. The strategy was constrained by administrative problems, lack of capital and poor performance of agriculture. In particular, agriculture acted as a brake by not yielding increased food supplies and savings, and by not responding to increased consumer purchasing power.

It was hoped that the Green Revolution would bring about increases in agricultural output. It involved the planting of new varieties, use of

new technology and institutional reforms. Amongst problems encountered were variability of yields, limited application possibilities,
cost, and the consequences for existing employment and social structures.

The Chinese strategy initially displayed similarities to that of India.
After experimenting with rapid industrialization, China adopted a policy
favouring small-scale enterprise, and subsequently a policy favouring
agriculture. As a consequence, China suffered less with respect to
inflation, unemployment and inadequate food supplies. The benefits of
the Chinese model of rural development are argued to derive from
egalitarian land distribution, labour mobilization, the establishment of
rural industry and rural welfare services, and the equivalence of political
and economic structures.

Attitudes to economic policy in poor economies have changed over
the past few decades. Large-scale industrialization is emphasized less;
small-scale, employment-creating industry and agricultural development are emphasized more. In certain cases, the government itself and
the prevailing structure of political power may act as a distinct obstacle
to the pursuit of progress. Many of the problems that poor economies
presently face are inherited and result from the previous histories. Formal
economic planning may not always be appropriate in such economies.
Economic cooperation may prove to be an answer to problems in the
long term, but little success has been achieved to date.

Further reading

Sources for India include Myrdal (1968), Streeten and Lipton (1968),
Hanson (1966), Shenoy (1971), Mellor (1976) and Singh (1974); also
the reference manual, *India*, compiled and published annually by the
Publications Division, Ministry of Information and Broadcasting,
Government of India. Bagchi (1976) examines the nineteenth-century
industrial experiences of the Indian economy. The sources for China
are Aziz (1978), Kuo (1976), Eckstein (1977) and Wilson (1977).

The 'Green Revolution' is appraised by Griffin (1979), Dasgupta
(1977), Nulty (1972) and Frankel (1971). A special issue of the journal
World Development is devoted to an examination of capitalist and socialist
agricultural systems in Asia (1979, Vol. 7, No. 4/5). Heyer, Roberts and
Williams (1981) examine rural development in the African context.
Income distribution in poor economies is the subject of Adelman and
Morris (1973), Chenery *et al.* (1974) and Fields (1980). Reynolds (1977)
is a development text emphasizing agriculture.

The Tanzanian strategy is discussed in Rweyemamu and Mwansasu
(1974), Uchumi Editorial Board (1972), Nellis (1972), von Freyhold
(1979) and the volume containing the paper by Hyden (1979). Shen
(1977) discusses the fortunes of African economic planning. Changing
attitudes to economic policy in poor economies are discussed by Healey
(1972).

Chapter Thirteen

Coercive Strategies

Consider a world consisting of just two hypothetical economies, Oleana and Pomona. Unless we draw a complete veil of ignorance over each, it is hard to see how the strategies for progress devised by one will be of no concern to the other, although the precise nature of this concern will depend upon the extent of the interrelationship between the two. At a minimum level we might anticipate interest on a comparative basis; depending on their ideology, citizens in Pomona might be happy or sad to see successful progress in Oleana. It is likely, in other words, that one nation will use the other as a benchmark in assessing its own welfare levels. In more concrete terms, and assuming that the two economies traded with one another, we might suspect that some innovation made by Pomona would be viewed with alarm by exporters in Oleana if it implied that the market for the latter's exports now declined. Again, the development of new forms of weaponry by one country could engender feelings of insecurity in the other, whilst different economic policies leading to, say, different tax or wage rates, could encourage factor migration to one economy's detriment. Finally, should Pomona suddenly discover a new supply of an unclaimed resource, its subsequent claiming of such a supply would deny the resource to Oleana.

The point of this anecdote is simply to suggest that, in the real world, it is probably inappropriate to consider the implications of a national strategy solely in terms of the interests of the economy employing it, for costs and benefits will inevitably spill over national frontiers. Put simply, the policies of Pomona will be of interest to the citizens of both Pomona and Oleana. This leads us to the conclusion that, to the extent that transnational issues are deemed relevant, any strategy devised by a single economy will be an interdependent strategy. The choice of 'best strategy' will thus be determined by both the economy's perception or forecast of strategies being pursued by others and the extent to which other economies will sanction the use of the 'best strategy'. Given this assumption of the necessary interdependence of national strategies, we can explore the sort of outcomes that might arise via a simple game theory model. Suppose that Oleana and Pomona have two possible strategies open to them, A and B. Consider the possible outcomes for Oleana. We shall assume that, if Oleana pursues strategy A it receives zero welfare benefits if Pomona also pursues A, but it gains 9 welfare units if Pomona pursues B. On the other hand, if Oleana pursues strategy B it gains 5 if Pomona also follows B, but it loses 3 if Pomona pursues A. For convenience, we shall assume that the welfare possibilities open to Pomona are exactly equivalent and we can therefore present the data as a symmetrical pay-off matrix, *Figure 13.1*, where the first term in each pair represents the pay-off to Oleana.

Oleana

	A	B
A	0, 0	-3, 9
B	9, -3	5, 5

Pomona

Figure 13.1 Two player pay-off matrix

Which strategies should our economies pursue? In the first place, let us suppose that each economy makes its decision in isolation from the other. Oleana's government has no knowledge of the strategies being contemplated by its Pomona counterpart and may reason thus: 'Pomona can follow either strategy A or B although we don't know which. However, if we pursue strategy A, there's a chance that we might gain 9 units whilst the worst we can do is stay where we are (zero gain). If we follow B our maximum yield is only 5, whilst there exists a distinct possibility that we could end up worse off by 3 units'. Given the uncertainty about Pomona's decision, we should expect Oleana to follow strategy A for, irrespective of Pomona's actions, this yields the superior outcome (0 beats − 3 and 9 beats 5). As the matrix is symmetrical the Pomonan government will reach an identical conclusion, i.e. both economies will pursue strategy A.

In this first case our two economies made their decisions in ignorance of the other's possible pay-offs; each has simply tried to do as well as possible irrespective of the other's strategy. As observers, however, we have the benefit of the global view and *Figure 13.1* tells us that both economies would have done better had they both pursued strategy B (5,5 beats 0,0). However, using the logic above, it is unreasonable to expect such an outcome to result from individualistic decision making, for it is only optimal for Oleana to pursue strategy B if it knows with certainty that Pomona will also pursue this strategy. The (5,5) solution can therefore only be reached via collusion, via a binding agreement between the two economies to cooperate to produce the collectively optimal outcome. Examples of this type of reasoning are quite common amongst real-world economies, an instance being the decision to form a free trade area. In this case, strategy A would be 'retain tariff restrictions' whilst strategy B would be 'abolish tariff restrictions', the latter bringing about an increase in the level of trade and therefore, we presume, an increase in the level of aggregate welfare. Note, however, that a single economy could not afford to relax its tariffs without the equivalent compliance on the part of its fellows for fear of finding its home market flooded with imports with no prospect of export expansion. Such is the rationale for free trade zones such as the EEC and, more generally, the General Agreement on Tariffs and Trade (GATT). Another such example is the decision of private manufacturing firms in capitalist economies to form cartels and thus increase market power against the consumer. Here strategy A becomes 'maintain competition' and B becomes 'collude to act as a monopoly'. Under B all firms would agree to a price rise to increase their profits, although this only remains optimal as long as all firms abide by the agreement.

From *Figure 13.1* it is not difficult to see that a third possible outcome exists. Whilst the collusive outcome represents a superior collective result to that derived from independent decision making, it is clear that there is an even better position from the point of view of one particular economy. As far as Oleana is concerned, this outcome results from persuading Pomona to adopt strategy B and then pursuing strategy A itself. Pomona will, of course, have identical plans for Oleana. The question that therefore confronts each economy is – how do I persuade my opposite number to adopt what from his point of view is a sub-optimal strategy? There are two possible solutions here, the first being to agree to form a collusion and then to 'cheat' by reverting to the opposite strategy. Following our cartel example above, all firms may agree to raise prices but one may then revert to competition, lowering its price again and thus stealing the market from its former partners. The success of the 'cheating' policy depends upon the extent to which cheating can be successfully concealed for, as soon as such cheating is detected, we should expect the disadvantaged players of the game to amend their own strategies accordingly. It is because of the private optimality of cheating that so many real-world collusions, in the absence of a supreme authority to enforce and maintain the collusion, are notoriously unstable. The second, and more dramatic, solution to the above question involves coercion. There might exist some way in which one economy can actually oblige another to accept a strategy that it would otherwise not voluntarily adopt. A resolution here will therefore depend upon the relative bargaining strengths of the players in the game and the coercive techniques at their disposal.

The protocol of international diplomacy has evolved a wide range of techniques designed to exert pressure upon a country's political or economic policies. A recent example was the abstention from the 1980 Olympic Games of several countries that refused to compete on the grounds that they felt that the host nation (the USSR) had violated the sovereign rights of another country (Afghanistan). In previous Games, a number of African nations had been non-attenders, protesting against other competitors' sporting links with South Africa of whose political regime they disapproved. As it seems implausible that such actions could directly bring either the USSR or South Africa to its knees, we must conclude that they represent coercion attempts of the mildest form. Stronger pressure of a purely political kind would include the 'stiffly-worded memorandum' to ambassadors and the threat to break off diplomatic relations. In such respects, however, all countries are very much equal. Any nation could refuse to compete in the Olympics or could withdraw its ambassador if it so wished. Let us now consider cases where international bargaining power is more unevenly distributed.

13.1   Bargaining power

The two coercive possibilities we shall consider here are bargaining on the basis of military power and bargaining by means of economic sanctions. The first technique concerns the reconciliation of disagreement by the ultimate mundane method of recourse to physical violence. A military solution to a dispute involves, at the limit, the conquest of one nation by another. By contrast, the employment of economic sanctions is more subtle and is relevant in circumstances where there exists economic interdependency between nations. In this context, country A is effectively saying to country B that, if B decides upon a strategy deemed offensive to A, A will retaliate with a counter-strategy designed specifically to hurt B in the economic sense. An analysis of the possibilities of economic sanctions thus requires an understanding of the interdependencies between nations.

13.1.1   INTERDEPENDENCE

We have already seen that much of the present political geography of the globe was determined by the imperialist proclivities of the Western economic powers over the past few centuries. By the early twentieth century, much of Africa and Asia was under direct European rule and the UK was the clear 'market leader' in this respect; in 1914, 20 per cent of the world's population acknowledged the sovereignty of the British monarch. The methods used in the creation of the empires had ranged from the outright use of force to skilful diplomacy, backed by the threat of coercion. The motives behind imperialism were most certainly economic, but there was an additional moral dimension. Coupled with their desire to gain access to new sources of raw materials, to expand markets and to discover new opportunities for capital investment (and, in so doing, to deny such potential to rivals), imperialist nations generally believed that the result of their interventions would confer the benefits of civilization upon 'backward' peoples. Whether this belief was correct is not the point at issue. What is certainly true is that one consequence of imperialism was the restructuring of both imperialist and conquered nation to form a dependency relationship. Indeed, this has probably been the case for all empires; just as the ancient Roman Empire depended on its Egyptian territories for grain supplies, so Britain looked towards its own territories for raw materials and marketing opportunities.

Observers such as Galtung (1971), Emmanuel (1972) and Amin (1973) argue that there were two specific structural characteristics of the system of imperialism that arose in the nineteenth and twentieth centuries. Each empire, they suggest, had a centre (the imperialist power) and a periphery (the conquered territories), which evolved in different ways. First, all external relationships entered into by each territory, such as trade and investment flows, were focused towards the imperial centre; by contrast, the centre in question had a wider range of external options open to it. Thus, for example, whilst India's activities in the early twentieth century revolved almost entirely around relations with the UK, the UK itself enjoyed linkages with its other territories, such as Kenya and Nigeria, and also with other imperial centres, such as France and Germany. Second, under the imperial system, territories were frequently encouraged or obliged to concentrate their economic activities into specific areas, such as the exploitation of particular minerals or the growing of particular crops to which they were environmentally suited. Again by contrast, the imperial centres sustained highly diverse economic activities. Although the formal empires were, by and large, dissolved by the 1960s, the implications of this model are obvious. If an economy has become economically dependent upon another, the issue of whether it is formally independent politically may be quite irrelevant. It is therefore argued that, because of the global structure of economic interdependence established during the era of overt imperialism, the nature of economic interrelationships between former powers and former dependencies is unlikely to be overthrown in the post-independence era and, indeed, continues to the present day.

Not all parts of the world, of course, became involved in the relatively recent European race to establish empires; Latin America is a case in point. Having successfully expelled the Spanish and Portuguese, much of Latin America became formally independent in the political sense in the early nineteenth century. Nevertheless, an interdependency relationship soon developed in this region, not so much because the territories were reconquered but more because they permitted the inflow of foreign capital. Much of the Latin American railway system, for example, was built by the British. In the case of Chile, we find that 85 per cent of the copper industry was foreign owned in 1901 whilst, by 1918, over 95 per cent of nitrate production was in non-Chilean hands (Behrman, 1976, p. 40). Clearly, therefore, from the point of view of the investors, profitability of such assets depended upon the economic policies of the host. The Second World War also had a significant impact on strengthening interdependence in other regions. Eastern Europe, for instance, suddenly found itself aligned with the Soviet Union. Further, the substantial volume of capital that flowed around the world to assist the war-ravaged economies after 1945 naturally increased the interests of donors and lenders in the affairs of recipients and borrowers. Such interests have been enhanced in the post-war era by the growth of the multinational corporation.

The world picture is therefore one of a complex network of inter-dependence based upon the legacy of history, the mobility of capital and the extension of trade. In the event of a conflict of international interests, who, then, is likely to succeed in a bargaining situation? The answer depends upon two factors. The first is the power that economies have over one another by virtue of abilities to implement economic sanctions. The second factor is the economies' 'emancipatory cap-abilities' (Deutsch, in Rosen and Kurth, 1974, p. 32), that is, their ability to resist the imposition of sanctions by the pursuit of an autono-mous strategy without the need for dependence on others. Let us briefly consider the dependency relationship between the United States and Chile in the 1960s and 1970s.

By 1960, Chile had become dependent upon the United States in at least three respects. First, the Chilean copper industry's output represented some 80 per cent of the economy's total export value and this industry was almost completely owned by US-based multinational firms. Second, the United States was Chile's single largest trading partner, providing over one-third of its imports and buying over one-third of its exports. Third, Chile was a recipient of official development assistance, both directly from the United States, and from the multi-national agencies in whose decisions the United States had an influential voice. In turn, US interest in Chile was a function partially of the receipt of Chilean exports and partially of the repatriation of profits from the copper industry. During the period 1945–72, the multinational firms made a profit of $7.2 billion on an investment outlay of around $1 billion (Rosen, in Rosen and Kurth, 1974, p. 125).

The governments of the Chilean presidents Frei (1964–70) and Allende (1970–73) took the view that the net outflow of profits from Chile was excessively high. Accordingly, post-1964 economic policies were oriented towards the attainment of some degree of economic emancipation, initially via the partial nationalization of the copper industry but subsequently via a more forceful 'Chileanization' policy. The nationalization procedure did not represent a particular threat to United States' interests because the negotiated compensation agreements were particularly favourable to the multinationals. By the early 1970s, however, it seemed that the position had changed. Allende's radical economic policies were aimed at the rapid restructuring of the Chilean economy along overtly socialist lines. As a result of these policies, the overall condition of the Chilean economy deteriorated. The United States therefore became more concerned about the prospects for profits from its investments and repayment on its loans. Rosen (Rosen and Kurth, 1974) notes that the US reaction to the changing circumstances of the early 1970s took three forms. First, the flow of US development assistance was abruptly curtailed. Second, Chile was assigned to the 'worst risk' category in the Export–Import Bank. Third, loan and credit proposals in favour of Chile within the multinational agencies were not supported, and indeed were obstructed, by the United States. Rosen concludes that the 'loss of international borrowing ability and U.S. trade credits led to an exchange crisis that stifled the flow of industrial imports', which eventually induced 'economic chaos' (pp. 127–8). Such a view does, however, seem extreme. Whilst the leverage applied by the United States, directly and via the multinational agencies, was certainly influential in bringing about the Chilean collapse, the economic policies pursued by the Allende government clearly engendered a profound destabilizing effect in their own right.

The above analysis suggests that the bargaining position of Chile vis-à-vis the United States was, at the time, particularly weak. If we are to believe Marxist writers such as Hayter (1971) and Frank (1966), we should conclude that the experience of Chile is simply characteristic of US dealings with Latin America in general. However, we have only considered one particular example. Can we go further and make embracing statements about the overall bargaining position between rich industrial nations and the poorer economies, typically reliant upon a limited range of primary products?

The study conducted by Stern and Tims (1975) attempts to go some way in this direction. Their argument runs as follows. Poor economies presently obtain some 80 per cent of their foreign exchange earnings from their primary production. However, primary products have a declining share in world market value owing to the development of substitute products and the effects of competition between primary producers. Prices are notoriously unstable and cannot be influenced by the individual exporter. Furthermore, revenue raised internally is not sufficient to meet capital requirements. As a result, there is an increasing need to import capital from abroad. The authors argue that one possible solution might be the formation of a producer cartel to raise world prices, but this would seem feasible for only a very limited range of items (notably oil) where cartels could be effectively policed and where there exists less possibility of substitution. Such conditions would preclude collusion amongst, say, producers of tea, coffee, rubber and sugar, who are widely scattered across the globe. Stern and Tims note also that, even in cases where a poor economy has the advantage of the monopoly of a specific mineral resource, it is usually the case that the exploitation of such a resource is already in foreign hands. They conclude that

> if the issue is drawn between primary commodity producers and other countries, the overwhelming strength lies with the latter, including control over major raw material supplies. The developing countries as a group remain heavily dependent on the industrialized countries for markets, for research and technology, for investment goods and, to an increasing extent, for such strategic requirements as food and fertilizer (p. 235).

Whilst such a conclusion is probably fair as a general statement, it is important to appreciate that historical circumstances vary and that the outcome of particular bargaining situations cannot always be easily predicted. For example, the bargaining position of the poor economies was certainly strengthened in the 1960s when many of them became politically independent. Anxious to establish spheres of influence, the richer groups of East and West found themselves in competition and the poor countries, in many cases, were quite successful in playing off one bloc against the other. Thus India and several states in Africa found both the West and the USSR almost falling over each other in an effort to offer project grants. Unfortunately for these poorer economies, however, such a game can usually be played only once, although occasionally a country gives evidence of wishing to 'recant' and is profitably welcomed back into the opposite fold. The outcome of any game depends, of course, on the number of players. To express its disapproval of the political regime in South Africa, the UK steadily reduced its sales of armaments to that country during the 1960s. In the early 1950s, South Africa imported 95 per cent of its weaponry from the UK and it might therefore have been thought that the UK was in a strong bargaining position. This subsequently proved not to be the case however, for France expressed itself quite willing to supply armaments; by the early 1970s, France was providing 75 per cent of South Africa's weapons imports, the UK share having fallen to 11 per cent (Whynes, 1976). More recently, Western governments have considered the withholding of Western grain surpluses from sale to the USSR as a sanction against Soviet policies. However, it seems unclear that this would be effective in view of the existence of other potential sources that the USSR might tap.

Possibly the most famous instance of successful resistance to sanctions imposed on nations with supposedly inferior bargaining strength was the case of Rhodesia (now Zimbabwe) after the unilateral declaration of independence from the UK made by the white-minority government in 1965. The reaction by the UK to this seizure of power was remarkably rapid; by early 1966 an almost total trade ban was in force. Other countries followed suit, the USA banning exports to Rhodesia and France restricting imports in the same year. By 1968, the United Nations had required the imposition of trade sanctions from all its members and, given that some 40 per cent of Rhodesian GNP was derived from international trade, the outlook from the Rhodesian point of view was particularly bleak. Circumstances, however, proved otherwise. In the first place, the Rhodesian government had anticipated the imposition of sanctions and had taken steps to protect the economy, for example by introducing anti-inflationary policies of credit restriction and rationing and by supporting employment. Rhodesia was also fortunate in having neighbours (South Africa and Portuguese-controlled Mozambique) that openly supported its policies and were in a position to act as 'staging posts' for its imports and exports. Vital oil supplies thus continued to get through, whilst many Rhodesian exports, especially minerals that were in great demand, easily found their way onto world markets. There was even some evidence that sanctions were having a beneficial effect on the Rhodesian economy in certain respects, for the government was obliged to adopt a rapid import-substitution industrialization policy. Whilst it would be clearly incorrect to suggest that the performance of the Rhodesian economy was totally unaffected by the imposition of sanctions, it is equally clear that the effect of these sanctions during the 1960s was nothing like as disastrous as was believed at the time.

Our conclusion, therefore, is that, whilst all economies are *in extremis* dependent upon others, some are far better able to sustain themselves in the event of economic pressure being applied and, likewise, are in a better position to apply such economic pressure upon others. Accordingly, the choice of strategy open to economies in a very weak position could well be very much a 'Hobson's choice' between following the strategy that appeals to nations stronger than themselves, possibly against their own interests, or, alternatively, following their own preferred strategy at the risk of being subjected to sanctions.

13.1.2   THE ECONOMICS OF WAR

The ultimate coercive strategy is coercion by recourse to actual or threatened violence, i.e. war. By making a declaration of war against another state a country is effectively saying that, unless the former conforms to the latter's wishes, conformity will be enforced physically. As even the most casual observer of history will appreciate, the war option has found frequent and regular employment amongst the nations of the world. As the power to coerce entails a command over the means of violence, economies will naturally devote resources to the production of such means; a parallel consideration is that, to a considerable extent, the power to coerce is equivalent to the power to resist coercion on the part of others. The war strategy, in other words, is about both attack and defence.

Social science at present lacks a theory of war in the sense of being able to generate predictions about its occurrence. On the other hand, we can get some way with some simple economic propositions, e.g. nations feeling threatened by successes of their rivals are more likely to resort to war, or nations requiring access to limited resources may be obliged to fight for them against rivals with similar aspirations. What makes war especially hard to analyse is its very explicit moral dimension. Mankind has a habit of making ideological judgements about the status of war and such judgements influence not only the use of war by nations but also the assessment made of such a use by observers. Amongst the possible moral stances that have been, or could be, adopted are (i) 'Nation A rejects the use of war as being inherently immoral', (ii) 'Nation A reserves the right to retaliate if attacked', (iii) 'Nation A will only fight using certain military techniques considered moral, e.g. harming civilians is not permitted', (iv) 'As all is fair in love and war, Nation A will use any means at its disposal to get its own way'. All these stances are, of course, ideological and none is objectively right or wrong. What is important, however, is that each position will have specific implications for the likelihood of war occurring, the nature of the war fought, and the quantity and quality of economic resources consumed during its perpetration. Some ideologies, in other words, are cheaper than others!

In our present context, we are concerned not so much with the morality of war as with the simple empirical proposition that it is a recurring phenomenon. The questions we shall therefore ask are: how successful is the threat of war, or its actual use, in coercing other nations into conformity, and what is the relationship between war *per se* and the pursuit of economic progress? We can gain some insights at a general level by considering the analysis by Barbera (1973).

Barbera suggests four possible hypotheses to explain how the act of war might be related to a nation's progress. In the first place, we could argue that involvement in wars is inherently progressive because crises demand instant solutions. Therefore, of necessity, in time of war people are prepared to work harder, managers devise better administration systems, rational planning for optimal resource use becomes vital, governments are empowered to mobilize resources on a massive scale, the wheels of commerce are oiled by the increased demand for war-related supply, and so forth. War thus creates a production-oriented economy that should be better equipped to deal with progress during times of peace, when such a time finally arrives. Nations fortunate enough to win wars might also gain advantages of acquisition of new resources. Second, and in direct contradistinction, we could argue that war is inherently regressive. Put crudely, it kills people and thus deprives society of their productive services. It also destroys property and causes industrial dislocation leading, more often than not, to serious depressions in post-war periods. The costs of war are therefore not confined to the war itself but spill over into the post-war reconstruction period; indeed, the expense of capital replenishment and care for the casualties and deprived could well exceed the cost of the weaponry involved in the first place. Both of these arguments ignore, of course, any of the additional moral criteria mentioned above. Barbera's third candidate is the hypothesis that war's influence on progress is unpredictable; depending upon specific circumstances it could be either progressive or regressive in the above senses. The final logical possibility is that war and progress might be unrelated; we could suggest that war is irrelevant in a nation's pursuit of progress.

Barbera sets himself the task of testing these hypotheses in the light of the economic experience of the twentieth century. For indices of progress he employs a variety of measures, ranging from aggregate output changes to the extent of the use of telephones (an index of communication not specific to socio-economic system). His conclusions can be stated quite simply; they are

that the two total wars of this century have neither helped nor hindered development or noticeably affected the inequalities between rich nations and poor. This broad finding lends substantial support to the irrelevant hypothesis about the relationship between war and development. These wars have proven to be unrelated to socioeconomic development and world inequality: nations continue their normal rate of material improvement whether or not wars occur (p. 121).

However, whilst we might be willing to accept Barbera's conclusions at the high level of aggregation at which he was working, the economics of war takes more devious twists when we operate at the micro-level.

First, consider the decision made by a particular economy regarding the amount of resources to be devoted to the means of instigating and resisting coercion, i.e. the appropriate level of military expenditure. As is the case for all economic decisions, this will involve an assessment of costs, benefits and probabilities. In this particular case, costs will include the opportunity costs of forgoing expenditure on non-military items, say, education, health care, investment in transport. Benefits will include the perceived increase in security from external coercion and the increased chances of being able to coerce others. The probability factor refers, of course, to the likelihood of it being necessary to employ the coercive strategy. However, the decision cannot be made without some acknowledgement of the likely military policies to be pursued by potential rivals. We can again use the hypothetical data of *Figure 13.1* to illustrate a point. Suppose that Oleana and Pomona presently possess equal potential coercive power over one another and that bundles of resources suddenly 'drop from heaven'. These bundles can be employed either in a military fashion to attempt to increase coercive power (strategy A) or in a civilian fashion to, say, expand educational facilities (strategy B). Clearly, if both economies choose to increase military strength, equality is maintained and no coercive advantage is obtained by either side (outcome 0,0). On the other hand, should Oleana choose to increase military strength whilst Pomona spends on education, the former will gain a substantial coercive advantage over the latter (outcome 9, − 3). If both choose to spend on education, there would be no change in the balance of power but each would probably secure net welfare benefits from its educational investment (outcome 5,5). However, for the reasons examined earlier, both economies, in the absence of collusion, will be obliged to follow strategy A for fear of incurring the high possible losses associated with strategy B. In the real world, this phenomenon is popularly referred to as 'arms racing', the model suggesting that military powers of equal strength will tend to increase their military allocations in parallel and thus continue to remain at equal strength. We should point out, incidentally, that we have assumed that the consumption of military output confers little direct utility *per se*; this might not be the case in reality. A society might indeed enjoy the panoply of military splendour although it is generally the case that more guns represent a less palatable addition to the diet than more butter.

That the global distribution of military coercive power is uneven is hardly debatable. If we take military expenditures as a proxy for coercive power, then the disparity between the USA and the USSR (which together account for around 50 per cent of global defence spending) and the rest of the world is staggering. Indeed, some 75 per cent of world military expenditure is accounted for simply by the two major alliances, NATO and the Warsaw Treaty Organization. In general, Whynes (1979) shows that there is an extremely high correlation between outlays on military activities and the level of material welfare (pp. 32–42). Combining this finding with that of the previous section, we are obliged to conclude that the bargaining position of the rich nations is far superior in both economic and military terms. As a caveat, however, we can detect instances where the equivalence between military expenditure and coercive strength appears to break down. Although the relationship might hold good during 'total wars', that is, at times when the entire resources of an economy are being devoted to the war effort, doubt could set in during conditions of 'limited war', which is a form of conflict more characteristic of the post-1945 period. A significant exception to this generalization was the protracted Vietnamese war (1955–73), which did have total commitment on one side. It is instructive to note that the USA lost (or at least did not win) this particular confrontation in spite of the fact that it had at its disposal some 25 per cent of the world's coercive resources. Much of its military technology (particularly the nuclear weaponry) was deemed inappropriate for the particular form of combat being undertaken and the coercive possibilities were constrained by fears of invoking disapproval on the part of NATO allies, the USSR and a fair proportion of the USA's own electorate. These facts do not mean, of course, that US military technology is necessarily inappropriate to future wars that the USA expects to fight.

A feature peculiar to modern warfare is its extraordinary capacity for destruction. This makes the calculus of warfare far more difficult to estimate. In the Middle Ages, for instance, international disputes could be settled by brief, if bloody, encounters involving a few tens of thousands of men, in total isolation from the bulk of the population and the material resources of the nations involved. However, SIPRI (1978) notes that the effect of high explosives on South Vietnam during the 1955–73 conflict was such that some 35 per cent of the rural land surface was adversely affected in terms of defoliation and overall ecological destruction. SIPRI estimates that an average size nuclear bomb could totally obliterate an area of 'several thousand hectares' whilst there would exist enormous long-term implications such as accelerated soil erosion and radiation-induced disease. Further, the possibilities of chemical and biological warfare give rise to unthinkable outcomes. SIPRI suggests that, in the case of the deliberate seeding of an area with anthrax, a 'single aircraft would easily be able to deliver a dose of spores initially lethal to three-quarters of the humans over an area of at least several thousand hectares' (p. 49). The essential point is therefore that, given the weaponry in current use, a short-term coercive attempt is likely to have extremely long-term implications. Furthermore, if the goal is the acquisition of territory, the aggressor might well be obliged to destroy the territory in order to 'win' it. It is, of course, this sheer scale of destructive power of modern warfare, and the inherent unpredictability of outcomes, that raise international war to the level of global concern; neutrality might not be possible where weaponry possesses such obvious and extensive external effects.

A model of the world characterized by economic interdependence and inequalities in bargaining power has several implications. In the first place, we should expect that nations with very low levels of bargaining strength would be somewhat unhappy about the state of affairs, having relatively little chance of getting their own way. They would presumably wish to argue in favour of a more equal power distribution even if they did not possess the power to enforce one. Power, however, is relative; the strengthening of the weaker implies the weakening of the stronger. Second, the obvious externalities of many strategies, such as the threat of nuclear holocaust (perhaps the ultimate externality), widespread pollution of air and seas, and the global competition for scarce resources, would lead us to suppose that nations in general will have an interest in the affairs of a nation in particular. Third, as we saw in the case of arms racing, it is quite possible for independent strategies to be self-defeating. Game theory tells us that all these implications lead to one thing, namely attempts at collusion. However, given the extent of the interdependence and the externalities, such collusion appears to be necessary at the global level.

13.2   The global strategy

The 'grand design' of proposals favouring a global strategy for progress is relatively recent in origin. On the other hand, it must be pointed out that there is nothing radically new about the idea of nations cooperating with one another in order to arrive at a mutually satisfactory outcome. One of the ironies about the entry of Greece into the European Economic Community was that Greece itself was responsible for one of the earliest experiments in national collusion. This was the Confederacy of Delos, an alliance of a dozen city-states formed to encourage trade and to facilitate common defence, established in 477 BC. William Penn (of Pennsylvania fame) advocated the establishment of a European parliament in the seventeenth century, as did Saint-Pierre in the eighteenth. What makes the contemporary proposals different is the fact that they are framed very much at a global, rather than at a regional level. This awareness of the existence of a global economy arose for a number of reasons. First, the European powers put many other areas of the world into a common orbit as a result of their imperialist exploits. Second, and particularly during the past century, the former supremacy of the tight-knit European group has been challenged by the emergence of new world powers – the USA, the USSR, Japan and, most recently, China. Third, the post-war period has witnessed the creation of a great many new nations as a result of the contraction of the former empires. Thus there now exist far more autonomous entities, each attempting to pursue its own path whilst coexisting on the same finite globe. Fourth, the international conflicts of the twentieth century proved to be far more expensive in lives and resources, and generated far more external effects, than any that had previously been experienced. Fifth, and as a direct result of these conflicts, attempts were made to establish international organizations whose function was to provide the means for the international solution of the problems of peace and progress.

Although it is impossible to pinpoint the birth of the 'world economy' at any specific time, it is convenient from the point of view of exposition to use the Second World War as a starting point. During the war, or immediately after it, a number of important international organizations were created: (i) the International Monetary Fund, whose role was to provide credit to ease particular economies' balance of payments problems, (ii) the World Bank Group, to provide long-term capital, (iii) the General Agreement on Tariffs and Trade, concerned with world trade liberalization, (iv) the United Nations, the closest that we have so far come to the creation of a truly world-wide forum for debate on issues of international concern. Naturally, all these organizations had small beginnings, membership being initially confined to the independent Western allies. After the war, however, more and more economies joined, with the result that, at the present time, organizations like the UN and the World Bank possess a membership of around 150 states and they thus represent, in some sense, the vast majority of the world's population. Let us therefore consider the sort of global proposals that have emerged from such organizations, and others, since 1945.

The most immediate problem facing the world economy in 1945 was, as far as the members of the international organizations were concerned, the restructuring of production along non-military lines; during the war, much of the output of the combatants had been funnelled into the war effort and much capital and labour had been destroyed. The priority was thus a return to 'normality'. In achieving this aim, the international financial organizations were meant to play a central role; indeed, this was one of the purposes for which they had been created. Given the distribution of need and resources, the flow of capital via the organizations was essentially from the USA to Europe. This unilateral flow represented a marked departure from earlier US policy; after the First World War, for example, President Coolidge had been adamant that the European war debt to America should be paid in full. By the Second World War, however, the USA had become a net exporter and appreciated that, unless the European economies were supported, its export markets would decline. In spite of the transfer of funds through the World Bank and the IMF, the cost of rebuilding Europe proved enormous. Thus the USA entered into direct bilateral transfer agreements with the European nations, agreements known collectively as the 'Marshall Plan'. This undoubtedly had a positive effect upon European recovery, the region reaching its pre-war output levels by the early 1950s.

Although, in many respects, the basic economic structure of the nations of the world was restored quite rapidly, steps towards a truly integrated framework were taken more tentatively. GATT, for instance, did not make significant headway during the 1950s. Many countries were reluctant to forgo the protective effects of high tariffs. Likewise, full currency convertibility (an explicit aim of the IMF) was slow to take off. Certain steps were taken to assist the poor economies of the world via the specialized agencies created after the war (e.g. the Food and Agriculture Organization and the World Health Organization), but the volume of resources allocated was quite insignificant when compared to the bilateral transfers made by individual countries. Towards the end of the 1950s, the United States in particular showed signs of dissatisfaction with having to shoulder the heaviest burden of official development assistance. Finally, a major nail in the coffin of the formulation of a global strategy in the immediate post-war era was the rapid political polarization of independent nations. The Marshall Plan (which ultimately evolved into the Organization for Economic Cooperation and Development) was exclusively Western-oriented. The Soviet bloc established a rival scheme – the Council for Mutual Economic Assistance – in 1949, and this led to the USSR's insulation from many aspects of the world economic scene. These economic alliances were overlaid by military pacts, the West's NATO in 1949 and, again as a reaction, the East's Warsaw Treaty Organization in 1955.

Attitudes to the world economy changed considerably in the 1960s with the arrival of many newly independent nations, which strengthened the voice of the poor economies in the international arena. At the time of the formation of the World Bank and the IMF, only Latin America and India amongst this group had been party to discussions. Quite naturally, the new nations saw the problems of the world economy in a radically different light. Their concern was not so much with the rebuilding of Europe and the emerging East/West hostility but rather with their own future relationships with the richer economies. Their views were strongly manifested at the first UN Conference on Trade and Development (UNCTAD) in 1964, where a number of poorer economies presented their case jointly. They argued in particular that the existing structure of world trading relationships and bilateral assistance was constraining their potential for independent economic progress; furthermore, they felt that the organizational structure of the international agencies gave disproportionate weight to the views of the richer nations. As a result of such criticism, the World Bank suggested an independent appraisal of relations between rich and poor economies, and the Commission on International Development was therefore established, under the chairmanship of the former Canadian prime minister, Lester Pearson.

In its report (CID, 1969) the Commission appraised the experience of post-war development assistance and made recommendations for the future. Amongst other things, the following were considered important. First, the Commission agreed that the protectionist strategies employed by the richer economies were indeed restricting the poor economies' scope for trade. It was accordingly suggested that rich economies should adopt preferential tariff schemes to permit trade creation with such poor nations. Second, the instability of export earnings that poor primary producers generally experienced as a result of fluctuations in demand and production was to be ameliorated by the establishment of buffer stock and price guarantee systems. Third, it was suggested that poor economies should make up their apparent shortfall in indigenous capital by encouraging international investment. However, the Commission noted the problems posed for domestic control in an economy with a large proportion of foreign-owned assets and it therefore advocated partial nationalization. Fourth, and this was perhaps the major preoccupation of the Commission, it was found that the existing system of allocating official development assistance was inadequate for any purpose. The bulk of resources appeared to be tied to specific projects, usually designed to benefit the donor at the expense of the recipient, and political leverage was frequently applied. Those loans that were made were generally unfavourable in that they involved the recipient in having to find substantial amounts of extra revenue for debt servicing. The Commission recommended that, not only should the rich countries provide far more assistance (a target being set at 1 per cent of GNP by 1975), but more of it should be provided on a multilateral basis to overcome the problems associated with the vested interests of the donors. A maximum interest rate of 2 per cent was suggested for loans. Finally, the Commission argued that the formulation and implementation of population policies and education policies and the encouragement of overall research were priority targets for development assistance.

Even though the Pearson Commission's findings served to deliver a sharp rap across the knuckles of the richer economies, which appeared to be becoming complacent in their generosity, its specific emphasis on methods of improving the flow of assistance from rich to poor was out of step with prevailing philosophy even at the time of the report's publication. The new approach that emerged towards the end of the 1960s involved the devising of an all-embracing cooperative strategy of which development assistance simply formed a part. A significant shift in international monetary policy took place in 1969 when the IMF announced the facility of Special Drawing Rights (SDR), a proposal first put forward by Keynes in 1944 although his opinion was not accepted at the time. The effect of SDRs was to increase the international liquidity of any member country, members being allowed to draw on newly created assets in proportion to their subscription to the IMF. Naturally, this distribution was heavily inegalitarian although it did serve, in theory at least, to provide the poorer nations with more purchasing power. However, in spite of the change in approach, the initial impact of SDRs was minimal owing to the small amount of resources made available. Thirlwall (1978) estimates that, for the period 1970–73, even if the poor economies had made full use of their entitlements, which, in practice, they did not, the net increase in resources available would have been less than 0.03 per cent of their GNPs (pp. 367–8).

The demands for widespread economic reform made by the poorer economies at the 1964 UNCTAD were reiterated at every one of UNCTAD's subsequent quadrennial meetings. In 1973 the non-aligned nations met and adopted a programme calling for the creation of a 'new international economic order' and some of their proposals were accepted by the UN in 1974 and 1975. However, just as the political views of the international organizations were slowly changing, so too was the basic structure of the world economy. A significant factor was the oil price rise of 1973, significant not only because virtually every economy in the world was adversely affected (excepting the oil-producers) because of their dependency upon oil, but also because, for perhaps the first time, non-industrial nations were seen to be displaying considerable bargaining strength. The shock that this price rise imposed upon the world economy, and the subsequent global recession that was caused in part by it, emphasized world interdependency more strongly than at any time since 1945. In 1977, the president of the World Bank suggested that a commission be set up to consider the problems of the world economy, and this suggestion resulted in the establishment of the Independent Commission on International Development Issues, under the chairmanship of the former Chancellor of West Germany, Willy Brandt.

The tenor of the Commission's report (ICIDI, 1980) is perhaps best summed up by the heading of one of its subsections – 'Unity to Avert Catastrophe' (p. 46). The central thesis is that the fundamental interests of each and every economy are not in conflict but are, in reality, mutual; the failure to appreciate this, and the failure to take the necessary steps towards cooperation, will lead to disaster in the longer term. An impressive list of economic failures is cited, the report noting that we currently witness a world picture characterized by poverty, economic stagnation, mounting international debt, competition for scarce resources such as food and raw materials, rapid population growth and unemployment, environmental destruction and 'overshadowing every-thing the menacing arms race' (p. 47). Given the extent of the disease diagnosed, it is not surprising that radical therapy is advocated. First, an implication of the poverty of nations is not only the inherent injustice of a world system that permits such poverty to exist, but that poverty in some nations prevents richer economies from becoming richer. Rich economies cannot sell if no one else has the money to buy. Accordingly, it is argued, it is in the long-term interests of both rich and poor nations alike for wealth to be transferred from the former to the latter. To make any impact, this resource transfer would have to be 'massive', i.e. at least double the present flow. Second, the international competition for energy and natural resources that presently prevails simply leads to the over-exploitation of non-renewable resources as each nation attempts to expropriate them before its rivals can. The gain to any one nation can therefore only be short term, even if it is in the strongest bargaining position. The long-run optimum is agreement to restrict the consumption of scarce resources and to pool information regarding conservation and substitution measures. Third, collusion is clearly optimal in cases of global externality, e.g. pollution of the oceans and the atmosphere. Fourth, the present international monetary system is seen as anomalous in that it allocates liquidity in inverse proportion to need, i.e. richer countries seem to have access to more credit than do poorer countries. The IMF should accordingly agree to reverse this criterion, to facilitate the indigenous industrialization of the poor economies and thus permit them to contribute to the world economy. For a similar reason, more flexibility should be employed in dealing with the balance of payments difficulties of individual economies; the inability to import on the part of one economy implies the inability to export on the part of another. Fifth, world trade must be liberalized by multilateral agreements to reduce protectionism. Finally, and to facilitate all these policies, a political structure to permit international collusion must come into existence; the UN 'needs to be strengthened and made more efficient' (p. 292). This would have the additional effect of assisting the resolution of international tensions and could therefore help in the reduction in the levels of military expenditure.

The above listing can give only the most general flavour of the sort of arguments presented in the ICIDI report, for it is an extensive and tightly packed document. Indeed, it may be taken to represent very much the present 'state of the art' of global strategies. It is unfortunate, therefore, that it does not go into the rather important question of feasibility. In his introduction to the report, Willy Brandt stresses the inherent logic of international cooperation, in terms that echo Myrdal (Chapter 4): 'Global questions require global answers; since there is now a risk of mankind destroying itself, this risk must be met by new methods' (p. 27). Further, he emphasizes the importance of transmitting such values on a global basis. At the same time, however, he notes that the United States 'has substantially reduced its international development efforts' whilst the economies of the Soviet bloc 'have shown little readiness to share responsibilities in favour of poor countries' (p. 27). Brandt expresses the hope that a change of heart will be forthcoming in this respect, but it seems relevant to pose two questions. First, unless the gains from collaboration are so immediate and so staggeringly obvious, why should nations such as the USA and the USSR, possessing immense bargaining strength, necessarily opt for a collaborative outcome with other economies when they might, equally well, achieve a beneficial coercive outcome? This is not to say that Brandt's hopes cannot be realized; simply, it is possible that economies that might consider themselves as potential 'winners' under the existing international economic structure would require a very great deal of convincing indeed before agreeing to change this structure. Second, our analyses have shown us that the collusive optimum will be individually optimal only if 'cheating' can be prevented. The USA, for example, can be expected to forgo its massive defence capabilities only if it is quite certain that the USSR will do the same. Collusions therefore have to be policed, which implies, in global terms, the existence of a supranational government with coercive power over individual nations. Nothing remotely approaching a world government presently exists although, again, the arguments of the Brandt Commission and other observers might well serve to encourage such international unity under a single government. In this respect, the Confederacy of Delos, mentioned at the opening of this section, was far in advance of us today. All member-states subscribed to a navy that, under the direction of the Confederacy government, was empowered to coerce any one member of the Confederacy that was found to be 'cheating'. It may be instructive to note that, as a result of Athens obtaining the monopoly of warship production, the Confederacy of Delos was transformed into the Athenian Empire in 454 BC.

Summary

International relations can be modelled using the game theory approach. This demonstrates that, under specific conditions, coercion may prove to be a more attractive strategy than cooperation. The model predicts the likely instability of collusions owing to cheating.

Major forms of international coercion include economic sanctions and war. Sanctions (e.g. trade or assistance embargoes) are most effectively applied where there exists a high degree of interdependence between economies. Existing interdependencies are the result of imperialism and trade growth. In general, bargaining strength lies with the rich industrial economies. In certain cases, economies may have sufficient emancipatory capabilities to resist sanctions successfully.

The use of war for coercive purposes will be determined, in part, by ideology and cost considerations. Given the uncertainty aspects and destructive potential of modern war, such cost estimates are difficult to make. War could be related to progress in a variety of ways, e.g. it might contribute or detract. Game theory predicts the likelihood of arms racing. There is a high correlation between economic strength and military strength.

Interest in global collusion has arisen because of the awareness of the external effects of warfare, the realization that competitive strategies may prove self-defeating, and the observation of global inequalities. The formation of the international agencies marked a step towards an integrated global economy, although the creation of economic and military alliances after 1945 was an obstacle to collusion. The emergence of the newly independent economies in the 1960s changed the focus of interest. The Pearson Commission recommended assistance to the poorer nations, trade liberalization, international investment and extension of credit. Demands for a 'new international economic order' were heard in the 1970s. The report of the Brandt Commission emphasized the gains to all economies that would result from a global collusion. It recommended trade expansion, energy conservation, international wealth redistribution and international monetary reform. The major obstacles to global collusion include the individual optimality of the coercive strategy and the difficulty of enforcement to preclude cheating.

Further reading

The game theory approach to international relations is discussed by

Spanier (1972), Bose (1977) and Whynes and Bowles (1981). Sources
for section 13.1.1 include Jenkins (1970), Barratt Brown (1974) and
Birnber and Resnick (1975). Sources for Chile are Behrman (1976),
Rosen and Kurth (1974), Skidmore (1974), Carlos Méndez (1980) and
Frank (1967).

Economic sanctions are discussed by Doxey (1971), which is also the
source of the Rhodesian example. Corbet (1975) is relevant to the
considerations of bargaining strengths. Graham (1978) and Hallwood
and Sinclair (1981) are relevant for the 'oil weapon'. Eldridge (1969)
appraises the 'assistance weapon' in the Indian context. Faaland (1981)
examines assistance to Bangladesh. The politics of Japanese aid is the
subject of Rix (1980). The economics of war is discussed by Kennedy
(1974) and Whynes (1979). The nature and usage of military power is
examined by Lider (1977, 1981). Gallie (1978) and Walzer (1977) are
excellent introductions to the philosophy and morality of war respectively. Winter (1975) contains articles on the general theme of the
relationship between war and economic development.

The historical background to global strategies derives from Davies
(1930). Richards (1970) is a history of the international institutions.
Views on the importance of trade liberalization are contained in Bergsten
(1975). Global inequalities are examined by Cole (1981).

Chapter Fourteen

Prospective

At the end of Part I we asked where do we stand? Then, the question referred to our choice between the conceptions of historical progress that had been advanced, and it prefaced the extended analysis of dimensions and strategies wherein we examined the range of issues confronting policy makers and the possible consequences of alternative policies. In some sense, therefore, this analysis provided an answer to the question although, now that this ground has been covered, we can impute an additional meaning of a temporal, rather than a spatial, nature. Where, in other words, do we stand at present in relation to the possibilities for the future? Although futurology does not presently enjoy the same respectability as it did at the time of Nostradamus, it should, nevertheless, not be avoided. The attainment of some preferred state in the future, or the avoidance of a non-preferred one, is contingent upon the strategies implemented in the present. Our future expectations and aspirations thus influence our present policies. We shall therefore conclude our analysis with a little speculation. In terms of target dates, the year AD 2000 has much to commend it. In the first place, children born today will, in most countries, be considered as adults by the year 2000 and many will be producing children of their own. Thus 2000 marks the emergence of the 'next generation' of *homo sapiens*. Second, this 'next generation' epithet applies equally well to economic policy, for a project implemented today could well take two decades fully to unfold, e.g. irrigation schemes, population control policies. From the point of view of economic policy and demography, AD 2000 is very much 'tomorrow'. Third, and this is probably the most significant reason for the choice of the year 2000 by futurologists, the date has non-scientific but aesthetic qualities in being 'round' and by representing the end of the millennium.

There are no facts about the future. All we can do is to make forecasts of events, although the degrees of certainty that we can attach to these events actually occurring vary widely. Two future 'facts' that most analysts would seem to be willing to accept are the following. First, the 303 basic resources of the world are limited and fixed; extra-terrestrial inputs will not be available for a long time (if at all) and certainly not by the year AD 2000. Second, world population will grow to a total not far short of 6 billion individuals, possibly higher; indeed, this figure was forecast by the UN as long ago as 1958 (Petersen, 1975, p. 358). Owing to the time-lag effect, this growth path is already in motion and population policies applied at this instant (excluding drastic measures such as nuclear holocaust and global plague) would produce only the most marginal impact upon the year 2000 figure. Based upon these future 'facts', we can immediately enquire into the simple Malthusian proposition relating population and resources. Can a world of fixed resources accommodate a 50 per cent increase in population? Following the stereotype of economists as 'dismal scientists', let us begin with a dismal forecast, *The Limits to Growth* (Meadows *et al.*, 1972). This analysis consists of the extrapolation of contemporary trends in some basic economic variables – population, raw material supplies, food and industrial production – into the twenty-first century. The central conclusion of the study is that population growth, demand for limited inputs and increasing pollution will impose a definite ceiling on material output, to be reached by around AD 2050 at the latest, followed by a rather abrupt fall in both population and production. Accepting this approach, we might suppose that the beginnings of this crisis would be manifest by AD 2000, even if they are not apparent at present.

From a purely mathematical point of view there is little doubt that the extrapolation of present growth rates must lead to an economic catastrophe somewhere in the middle of the twenty-first century; such is the impersonal logic of the law of compound interest. However, and accepting that the *Limits to Growth* scenario represents perhaps the worst possible outcome for mankind, let us be uncharacteristic and consider the diametric alternative. Let us examine what economists term the 'Golden Age' solution and try to establish what preconditions must exist for this Golden Age to be technically feasible. Then, by assessing the extent to which the formation of these preconditions is likely, we can finally decide whether we should be optimists or pessimists.

First, our Golden Age scenario would almost certainly require a fall in the growth of population, which represents the effective pressure on world resources. Now, from the medical point of view, this should present few problems, for post-war medical technology has devised a number of effective and fairly cheap control methods. In theory, therefore, and for a reasonably modest outlay, world population growth could be constrained to very low annual increases; quite possibly, it could be stopped in its tracks.

A second Golden Age requirement must be the availability of foodstuffs and, on this issue, Rostow (1978) makes two relevant observations. First, he notes that the consensus of informed opinion appears to be that 'at least twice as much land is physically available for crop production as is presently used' (p. 585). Second, the Green Revolution techniques of mechanization, irrigation and so forth have, as we have seen, been applied so far only on a very restricted basis. A more widespread application could therefore increase the total yield of foodstuffs from the land presently available. Assuming that the new land is opened up, and the new agricultural techniques are applied, simple mathematics tells us that a 50 per cent population increase could be accommodated rather easily.

A principal concern of economies over the past two decades has been the availability of energy. Our Golden Age scenario must therefore also be concerned with the availability of adequate energy stock. It seems quite clear that what we might consider to be in short supply at the present time is energy in particular and not energy in general. Many of the world's economies are almost completely structured on the consumption of oil and natural gas. Given present trends, both of these resources will probably be disappearing not long after AD 2000. On the other hand, even assuming very high consumption rates, there appears to be quite enough coal to last well into the twenty-second century, whilst nuclear energy is still a very 'young' source. Curiously enough, the sources of practically infinite energy – wind, waves and solar power – have yet to be tapped.

A fourth Golden Age requirement might be the attainment of an un-polluted environment. Meadows (1972) suggested that increased production must involve the creation of unacceptable levels of pollution, but here we can use an argument equivalent to the one used in the case of population, namely that pollution can be controlled from a technical point of view if only at some cost. For evidence of this we need only look at the records of industrial societies. The urban centres of the United Kingdom in the 1980s, for example, are in general far less polluted than they were in the 1880s, even though UK output has expanded enormously since that time.

Finally, we must admit that our production possibilities are constrained by our technology. Nevertheless, we note that the history of the past few centuries includes the rapid development of more efficient techniques, of invention and innovation, of the creation of substitutes for scarce inputs and so forth. Superficially at least, there seems no reason why this trend should not continue. Our future Golden Age could therefore be characterized by still more refinements to productive technology, and the problem of ultimately finite resources accordingly becomes less acute.

The Golden Age scenario therefore stands in direct opposition to the pessimistic point of view. *In extremis*, it might say that population growth can be curtailed, more food produced, new energy sources exploited, pollution levels regulated and inputs combined more efficiently. Even non-renewable resources might be made to last longer given reclamation and input substitution. Indeed, perhaps there exist vast stocks of such resources awaiting discovery. If we could accept that all the steps were going to be taken in the immediate future to bring about the Golden Age solution then we might also be willing to go along with Kahn who believes that even if 'the century does not end in glory, it will likely end well enough' (Kahn, 1979, p. 429). By implication, the problems of the economic catastrophe could be left to the economists of a dim and distant future. However, what is the likelihood of these 'necessary steps' being taken? Before commenting on the world economy overall, let us examine some tendencies within specific regions.

In his forecast for Latin America, Sunkel (in Bhagwati, 1972) notes three developments within the region since 1945. First, the annual growth in value of material output, after adjustment for price and terms of trade variations, appears to be generally declining. Sunkel argues that this has occurred because of the typical nature of Latin American industrialization. Import substitution yielded high initial gains but is beginning to precipitate stagnation, owing to deficient demand (both domestic and international) and regional inequalities. Second, the growth of employment opportunities in such industry appears incapable of matching the increase in population; the population of all Latin American economies (excepting Argentina) will at least double by AD 2000. Sunkel notes that, even during the post-war high-growth period, only around 25 per cent of the extra population was successful in finding industrial employment. Third, there appears to have been little change for decades in the distribution of incomes. For most Latin American economies, this distribution has always been unequal. Sunkel's conclusion is quite frank: '... the development strategies pursued hitherto in Latin America have come to a dead end. It is obvious that the present trends cannot continue very long, and certainly not for 30 years' (p. 218).

Turning to Asia, we should note that, at present, around 50 per cent of the world's population lives in India, China and in these countries' immediate neighbours, such as Pakistan and Bangladesh. The present annual population growth rates in such countries are of the order of 2 per cent, at least twice the typical rates for economies in the Western or Soviet blocs, which together account for around 25 per cent of the world's population. In the future, these Asian economies must expect to face the same sorts of problems of labour absorption as Latin America, although the absolute scale of such problems is, if anything, far larger. As we noted earlier, population control policy in these Asian economies has not been received with any great enthusiasm. Indeed, even China, which has experienced a radical shift in social consciousness since 1949 and which has promoted a fairly active control policy since the 1960s, acknowledges the existence of tremendous inertia in terms of policy take-up, especially in the rural regions (Eckstein, 1977, pp. 48–9). We argued earlier that the development of agriculture represented a major step in enhancing the prospects for progress in China. Even the best-laid plans, however, have to come to terms with the weather, and Asian agriculture generally (including that of the USSR) is highly vulnerable to climatic fluctuations. Actually, the overall future of China is a vital ingredient of any world scenario and also a source of considerable uncertainty. Whilst the Maoist strategy for progress was sophisticated and complex, its essential direction was at least amenable to forecasting with a reasonable probability of success. However, the years following Chairman Mao's death, and the deaths or demotions of many of his former close political allies, have yet to reveal a discernible post-Mao strategy. Presumably such a strategy will emerge in the near future and its implications could be enormous. First, China has long been a closed economy; should it suddenly decide to open its borders the size of the potential world trading market would be considerably enlarged. Clearly, this would exert a strong impact on potential trading partners. Second, of all the economies or regional groupings in the world it seems likely that it is only China that could be capable, over the next few decades, of disequilibrating the Western/Soviet balance of power; this might happen irrespective of whether or not China formally aligns with one or the other. Third, the continued expansion of the Chinese economy would clearly exert an influence upon neighbouring states, such as India, which, at one extreme, view such growth as a threat or, at the other, might be encouraged to form cooperative linkages with China.

Any prognosis for Africa must include all the observations made above regarding the other low-income economies. It seems fairly certain that Africa too will experience very rapid population growth into the twenty-first century and will accordingly run into the industrial unemployment problem. Many areas of the continent are already 'overpopulated' in terms of their agricultural potentials but, given the poverty of these regions, it is difficult to discern a ready source of investment to raise productivity. As we have seen, many of the African economies might be considered to be 'too small' to be economically viable, although, in the future as in the past, the existence of nationalism, tribalism and the diversity of ideology in the region is not likely to be conducive to integration. A factor that complicates the African scenario in particular is the antagonism between the 'white' south and the remainder. The minority white population of South Africa enjoys a standard of living comparable with, and in many cases superior to, the populations of the rich Western economies; the majority of 'black' African states argue that this standard of living is maintained at the expense of the non-white population. South Africa occupies a special place in the contemporary world economy for it, together with the Soviet Union, is a major source of commodities central to the Western economic structure, namely gold, platinum and diamonds. South Africa is therefore in the middle of a strange nexus. Both Eastern and Western blocs are politically hostile to the regime but have a strong vested interest in the nature of its output, the Eastern bloc because it forms the other half of a duopoly, the Western bloc because of the importance of gold in its currency system. Black Africa too is hostile but, by virtue of its history, maintains a strong dependency relationship with both East and West. If a dramatic change in government were to occur in South Africa towards, say, a democratic structure, the global implications would be equally dramatic although, at this stage, uncertain. Given the military strength of South Africa's regime, and the interests of East and West, such a transition appears unlikely in the immediate future. We should remember, however, that revolution and war are difficult to predict; had this book been written in the 1960s it seems improbable that it would have predicted the independence of the former Portuguese colonies to the north of South Africa (Angola and Mozambique).

Leaving aside these specific regional aspects, let us turn to some wider issues; first, the environment. It is somewhat fatuous to comment that mankind has had a substantial direct impact upon the physical environment over the past few centuries, for this impact is well known and immediately visible – quarrying, deforestation, urbanization, industrialization and so forth. In recent years, for instance, ecologists have been concerned to persuade the world that oceans do not in fact represent a bottomless garbage-can. The seas contain part of a highly complex food chain at the end of which stands man himself, and it is feared that the destruction of this chain, via pollution, could have an adverse effect upon the production of food over the longer term. Gribbin (1981) provides an even more graphic example of global environmental externalities. The actual consumption of fossil fuel (coal, oil and gas) in the industrialized countries entails the production and release of carbon dioxide. A proportion of this is immediately absorbed by ecological 'sinks' (oceans and vegetation) but a larger amount is simply added to the atmosphere. As carbon dioxide has the property of absorbing and re-radiating heat, the consequence of having an atmosphere that is becoming increasingly rich in carbon dioxide is that the earth's capacity to lose heat is reduced; this is the so-called 'greenhouse effect'. On the assumption that the rate of burning of fossil fuels is at least maintained into the twenty-first century, the mean temperature of the earth will be raised by perhaps $2°C$ within 50 years, although the effect is likely to be more extreme at higher latitudes. In turn, this might be expected to generate two results. First, the productive agricultural regions of the USA, Europe and the USSR would suffer drastic declines in yield as a result of the hotter conditions and the adverse climatic changes that they would produce; Gribbin notes that such a temperature rise 'suggests a return of the dust bowls to North America and elsewhere' (p. 83). By contrast, the economies of the tropical regions, experiencing a smaller climatic effect, might well find that their agricultural prospects are in fact enhanced. Accordingly, such a temperature rise would dramatically reverse the bargaining positions of the food-rich 'northern' economies and the poorer 'south', although, in the short run at least, the elimination of the North American grain surpluses would cause hardship to food aid recipients. Second, as Leacomber (1979) notes, the changing fortunes of agriculture may be a purely academic point, for a mean temperature rise of a few degrees would be sufficient to begin the melting of the polar ice-caps. Were this process (which appears to be irreversible once begun) to commence, the general sea level could be raised by as much as 100 metres, implying rather startling changes to the world's political geography.

The distribution of world income at present is exceptionally unequal. An important consideration in assessing future progress, both in the regions and for the world as a whole, must therefore be whether or not it seems probable that any significant shift in this distribution towards more equality is likely to occur. Such a shift would, of course, be a vital ingredient of progress in poor economies that lack the resources to develop their agricultural or industrial structures. The continued growth of the multinational corporation seems assured, if only because of its profitability and the extent of desperation that many host nations feel with respect to their lack of capital. Again, we have seen that many benefits may accrue to all parties as a result of this, although hosts must not ignore potential costs in the form of political leverage, inflation induced by the international demonstration effect and so forth. In terms of the prospects for a straightforward wealth reallocation – that is, the free donation of resources to the poor – it will be remembered that the Pearson Commission (CID, 1969) believed that the appropriate target for official development assistance from the rich nations would be 1 per cent of the GDPs by 1975. Were the Commission writing today, we should expect it to propose a higher figure in view of, say, the increased burden of oil prices on poor economies and the increased magnitude of their employment problems. It is sobering to note that the 1975 assistance level actually attained by the rich Western economies (the OECD group) amounted to 0.36 per cent of GDP on average, Sweden recording the highest individual figure with 0.82 per cent. The impact and influence of the Pearson recommendations can be judged by appreciating that the 1975 assistance allocation represented a net *decline* since 1965 when the level stood at 0.49 per cent. The World Bank has forecast that the assistance flow from OECD will still be 0.36 per cent of GDP in 1985, with only Norway (and possibly Sweden and the Netherlands) reaching the Pearson target by that date. Economies expected to display the greatest shortfall are Italy and the USA. We must, of course, acknowledge assistance from Soviet sources, although the range of recipients is strictly limited to those, such as Cuba, with sympathetic ideologies. OPEC assistance has expanded considerably in recent years, although it is doubtful whether its benefits have outweighed the harmful effects of the oil price rises throughout the 1970s.

To re-emphasize the point, rich economies would have at least to treble their present assistance allocations even in order to meet the Pearson recommendations, which, nowadays, appear quite modest. Does such a shift in policy appear feasible when rich economies are so much less confident of their own survival than they were, say, 20 years ago? The calculation of the necessary magnitude of the resource transfer from rich to poor in order to create growth in the latter to expand the markets of the former is a complicated issue, although one would suspect that, as in the case of Keynesian demand management, the shifts would have to be major rather than marginal. Some indication of this can be drawn from the fact that, at the time of the Marshall Plan for the reconstruction of Europe, US assistance of one form or another amounted to almost 3 per cent of its GNP (some ten times its present allocation). The population of Europe is only some 20 per cent of the population of the poorer economies at the present time.

Given the interdependencies between economies throughout the world, the framework of world trade and international activity (especially the international monetary system) must be a determinant of any one economy's future prospects. Since its foundation at the time of the Second World War, the international banking system has slowly lurched towards the structure that its more radical proponents hoped it would initially attain, i.e. genuine banking in the sense of being able to create substantial amounts of credit. In fairness, most of the reforms that have taken place since its birth have been responses to particular emergencies. The weakening of sterling in the 1960s left the US dollar, to all intents and purposes, as the only reserve currency and the USA began to find that its liabilities to foreigners exceeded its gold reserves. This obliged the world monetary authorities to move away from the traditional gold-exchange standard. Even so, such reforms still have a long way to go to reach the ideals set by Keynes in 1944. We have already seen, for example, that the allocation criterion for SDRs is such that poor economies are able to gain very little from them. The future role of gold is uncertain. On the one hand it is clear that some acceptable commodity of internationally agreed value is necessary for trade to take place. On the other hand, it is not immediately apparent why this commodity should be gold in particular, which, although being particularly useful in the fabrication of artificial teeth, does have the distinct disadvantage both of being scarce (i.e. its supply cannot be instantly increased to facilitate an increase in world trade) and, in its raw form, of being unevenly distributed across the globe. There seems, in general, little doubt in the minds of most economists that the movement towards 'real banking' (i.e. centralized creation and control of international money) on the part of the international monetary system must be in the long-run interests of most participating economies. However, economists such as Robert Triffin are dubious about the likelihood of progressive reform. The record of the international system he suggests,

inspires considerable pessimism ... as to the likelihood of an orderly evolution, effectively orientated by our so-called monetary and political 'leaders'. They have been led by events far more often than they have shown themselves willing and able to lead them. The major changes in the international monetary system have, nearly invariably, been misunderstood and resisted by bureaucrats and officials. They have come, in most cases, as the by-products of the failures of official policies and of the resulting crises of the system, rather than as the planned outcome of official intentions and pronouncements (in Bhagwati, 1972, p. 197).

Developments in environmental control, resource transfer between economies and the reform of international finance pale into insignificance when compared to a further global issue, namely the threat of nuclear warfare. Should a full-scale nuclear conflict break out in the future, many of the arguments presented in this book will cease to have any relevance or, indeed, any meaning. The Stockholm International Peace Research Institute (SIPRI, 1978) notes that, if even a fraction of the world's nuclear arsenal were to be actively employed, 'the consequences would be unimaginable ... Most of the cities in the Northern Hemisphere would be destroyed in a flash, and the bulk of their inhabitants would be killed instantly' (p. 15). If the holocaust scenario is viewed as likely then there is little we can do at present to assess the strategies for progress that might emerge from the ruins. This task might be left to the odd economist who manages to escape.

Leaving aside the ultimate disaster, it nevertheless seems probable that limited warfare will continue to play an important role in determining future economic outcomes. In such a case, the history of mankind could easily be rewritten overnight. Although wars have multitudinous causes, competition for scarce resources must be a significant factor. We have already seen that the distribution of world income is heavily inegalitarian and the same can be said for the distribution of mineral wealth. OECD (1979) notes that many mineral supplies essential to industrial production are monopolized by only a handful of countries. Guinea, Australia and Brazil, for example, together possess over 50 per cent of the known reserves of aluminium, whilst the Soviet Union alone owns 75 per cent of the world's vanadium reserves. China possesses one-half of known tungsten deposits. Throughout the 1970s, world interest was largely focused on the monopolized market in oil. In his analysis of the 'geo-political economy' of West Asian oil, Bose (1977) suggested that the use of 'gunboat diplomacy' would prove to be the eventual Western response to the use of the 'oil weapon' by Middle Eastern countries. As technology changes and industrial demands vary, there seems no reason in principle why, in the future, we might not witness the emergence of, say, the 'manganese weapon'. The Soviet Union and South Africa together own over 80 per cent of known reserves in this particular case. The response, by economies that have not been so fortunate in their resource endowments, to the use of all such 'weapons' could conceivably follow the pattern suggested by Bose.

Next on our list of wider issues is the question of social decision making. In many respects, the modern world is truly 'dynamic'. Compared with earlier epochs, population has grown rapidly, material output has risen sharply, mass communications and transport networks have proliferated world-wide, knowledge and technology have developed, specialization and urbanization have spread. In short, the way of life of many inhabitants of the world has altered radically. It therefore seems paradoxical that, compared with this economic dynamism, political procedures are better characterized as conservative. In terms of fundamental nature and principles, the decision-making processes of many economies have resisted noticeable change. Now it is quite possible that the British, German, American or Soviet constitutions, drawn up many decades or even centuries ago, could embody 'eternal truths' that are totally unaffected by socio-economic change. However, just as the invention of the steam engine completely transformed the previously established nature of production, so perhaps recent socio-economic or ideological transitions could give rise to a perceived need to transform the political process.

As far as the Western democracies are concerned, there are two main areas of contemporary debate on the political reform issue. First, it has been suggested that the traditional 'one person, one vote' system employing the simple majority principle, a system that remains a norm in the West, generates outcomes that are logically 'inferior' to those resulting from a preference intensity voting system or proportional representation; some of the arguments were rehearsed in Chapter 4. The Swedish electoral reform of 1971 moved that country some way away from the traditional system but, to date, few other economies have expressed any desire to follow. We could, in fact, go further with the critique of contemporary voting methods by suggesting that developments in technology have now made George Orwell's *1984* vision of instant two-way communication between government and individual into a reality. In certain Western countries, a system of day-to-day direct democracy might be technically feasible in the not too distant future, and liberal ideology would presumably support this as being desirable. Second, there is growing evidence (e.g. Nordhaus, 1975) to support the Downsian hypothesis that, under the existing political structures, governments pursue short-term rather than long-term policies, in order to enhance their re-election chances. Government myopia might therefore rule out otherwise desirable long-run solutions to economic problems. Although such governments might be willing to secure short-run gains at the expense of long-run costs, the long term, unfortunately, eventually arrives. Even if it were to be accepted by all that some form of political reform was necessary, we should naturally anticipate inertia on the part of existing governments. Assuming, as seems reasonable, that politicians actually wish to be elected into office, we should hardly expect them to change the rules of a game that has, in the past, successfully secured their election.

A noticeable feature of all national governments, however elected, is simply that they are all *national* governments, usually making central-ized decisions at an aggregate level. Because of this national orientation, it is quite possible for the subnational problems of a particular region or economic sector to be overlooked. Other things remaining equal, we should expect the likelihood of this occurring to rise with the scale of the society in question. This being the case, we might anticipate that one consequence of a centralized political structure, unresponsive to socio-economic changes, is the alienation of individuals or groups who begin to find that alternative forms of political activity are more attractive. Labour, for example, might discover that organized trade union pressure is a far more effective way of influencing economic policy than voting. *In extremis*, groups might find that political violence, terrorism or even overt revolution represent the only ways of making an impression upon a political system that they believe to be unresponsive to their demands. It goes without saying that the other dimension that a purely national government might overlook is the supranational, the one concerned with global rather than national problems.

Finally, let us consider another issue of particular relevance to the fortunes of Western industrial societies, namely the impact of technical change. Invention and innovations in production have occurred throughout human history, although we are perhaps most aware of the structural changes engendered by technological developments during the past two centuries. Technical change was, after all, a fundamental ingredient of the industrial revolution in Western Europe during the eighteenth and nineteenth centuries. Consider the experience of the British textile industry. Throughout the eighteenth century, a series of innovations took place that led to the mechanization of cotton produc-tion. In most of the central processes – weaving, spinning, carding – machines replaced human labour and the output/labour ratio rose dramatically. Between 1800 and 1860, for example, employment in the cotton industry rose by some 60 per cent, but the volume of raw cotton processed rose more than twenty-fold. Exports of cotton piece-goods in-creased ten-fold between 1815 and 1859. Naturally, the move towards capital-intensive production entailed a change in the composition of employment. In 1806, two-thirds of the individuals employed in the cotton industry were hand-loom weavers; by 1862, their numbers had fallen to 3000 out of a total workforce of 455 000.

Although invention and innovation were not the sole determinants of the phenomenal growth of the British textile industry during the industrial revolution, this example serves to demonstrate the general effects that technical change has had in the past. Broadly speaking, technical change alters the consumption pattern of a society, for example by giving rise to new products or by increasing exports to permit more imports. It also alters the production pattern by changing the demand for capital equipment and labour, both quantitatively and qualitatively.

The occurrence of inventions in the future is particularly hard to predict. Although there might be some superficial correlation between the amount of resources devoted to research and project development and some eventual discovery, scientific breakthroughs still rely upon individual intuition and genius. Even when a discovery has been made, further development or complementary inventions may be required before that discovery can be incorporated into production. Lord Rutherford, for example, discovered the principles of atomic structure and fission in 1911, but the generation of energy from atomic sources did not become a feasible proposition until the 1940s and 1950s.

A reasonable forecast can be made, however, once the process of invention and innovation in a specific area is under way. Of the innovations of the past few decades, one that is likely to have an extremely significant impact on the human future results from developments in electronics and computing. The 1970s witnessed the arrival of the industrial robot, capable of being programmed to replicate a wide variety of human functions. Most modern automobile plants currently employ such robots to perform specific tasks, such as paint-spraying and welding. In certain cases, entire production lines have been automated and require only minimal human supervision. Similarly, warehousing and stock control in many large corporations have been turned over to computer management. There seems every reason to believe that this automation trend will continue. Such machines, after all, can assimilate and process information rapidly, tend not to make mistakes (if properly programmed), do not go out on strike, and do not complain when presented with tedious, repetitive tasks. They can be made to operate in physical environments unsuitable for humans. With the appropriate maintenance, they can also work 24-hour shifts.

In several respects, this trend must be regarded as highly desirable. Many Western consumers appear to enjoy the new products resulting from the new technology – digital watches, colour television sets and home computers. Economies that have gone the furthest in employing such technology find that their trading prospects are enhanced. Furthermore, the very fact that wages are positive in industrial societies would seem to imply that the act of labour *per se* represents a source of disutility. People have to be compensated in order to induce them to work. By replacing man by machine we are therefore abolishing a particular source of disutility.

Unfortunately, the issue is not quite so simple because of the relationship between work and wages. As far as the individual worker is concerned, his replacement by a machine means that he is unable to sell his labour power and he therefore receives no income. As automation continues, it seems probable that Western societies will experience the increasing technological unemployment of workers, who will become the twentieth century's equivalent to the hand-loom weavers.

We suggested earlier (Chapter 11) that the welfare state is unlikely to view unemployment and relative deprivation in a favourable light.

It will therefore be faced with finding a solution to the unemployment problem. There are a number of alternatives. First, we might suggest that no problem really exists because redundant workers will be free to find employment elsewhere in the economy. Here we encounter a particular obstacle. If one worker's particular job has been automated in one industry then it seems probable that it will also have been automated in others. A robot-welder, for example, will be employable in all industries where welding takes place. If this is indeed the case then it is not the worker who is redundant; rather it is the particular skill that is no longer necessary for production. *All* human welders will find themselves in exactly the same position. Thus the individual's ability to find employment will be contingent upon his ability to acquire new skills for which a demand still exists. Second, society might be willing to support the unemployed worker by a form of social security; unemployment benefits are paid in all Western countries. Social security benefits, however, are simply transfer payments from those who own productive resources and who remain in employment. The extent to which the unemployed can be subsidized therefore depends upon the extent to which the employed are willing to be taxed. Third, unemployment might be solved by the restructuring of work practices. Put crudely, if one half of the population is presently working an eight-hour day and the other half is unemployed, all might agree to work a four-hour day. Unless their total wages were to be guaranteed, we might expect the already employed to resist work-sharing of this nature. However, if wages were to be guaranteed in such a manner, the labour costs of production would rise. Entrepreneurs would therefore have a further incentive to innovate with labour-saving technology. Finally, an industrial economy might deliberately fly in the face of history by adopting labour-intensive industrial technology. Although this might prove feasible in certain sectors, the reasons why this is an unlikely alternative in general terms are precisely the reasons why the Western economies evolved as they did.

OECD (1979) has suggested that the electronics revolution, bringing with it developments in automation, will 'change the face of advanced industrial societies' (p. 114). Of this, there seems little doubt. It remains debatable, however, whether Western capitalist societies will be able to accommodate the change within their existing socio-economic structures. In order to reabsorb the labour made redundant by rapid technological change, a high and sustained rate of economic growth will be required. An increased responsibility for the direction of economic activity on the part of the government must be an important supplement to this requirement. In the short term, at least, the unemployed will have to be supported by public expenditure. Retraining schemes will have to be provided, to give workers the new skills necessary for new employment. Institutional labour practices may require statutory reform, either to guarantee production efficiency or to ensure that work opportunities are shared out 'fairly'. At the widest level, we might expect that the citizens of a 'world of leisure' will make considerable demands on educational and recreational facilities. We might note that such features – high real growth rates, an increasing commitment to, and responsibility for, economic direction on the part of governments, and major institutional reform – have not been amongst the more obvious characteristics of Western economies in recent years. Marxists would point out that the growth of unemployment in the form described above is an inevitable consequence of the specific historical conditions of capitalism, in particular the private ownership of the means of production. Indeed, the likelihood of large-scale unemployment resulting from technical change was foreseen by Marx over a century ago. The continued reduction of the labour input into production was, Marx believed, a necessary precondition for economic revolution.

Although we have so far confined our remarks about technological change to the Western economies, there is no reason to believe that the structures of the advanced socialist economies, such as the Soviet Union, are any better, or any worse, equipped to meet the challenge. Nove (1977) notes that the USSR Party congresses of the 1970s laid great stress on the problems that technical change might bring. He suggests, however, that the inherent conservatism and inertia of the centralized planning apparatus will make it as slow to react as the allocation systems of the West. His conclusions in this respect are well in keeping with the overall tenor of the present discussion:

Twenty or even ten years ago it was common to see, and to write, such phrases as that 'the Soviet Union is unsuitable and inappropriate for a modern industrial society'. One's confidence in the validity of the above judgement is affected by a growing feeling that the Western system is not so appropriate either. Perhaps a future historian (if the human race has a future) might conclude that the development of technique, computers, weapons, etc., far outran the capacity of human beings and institutions to handle them (p. 371).

To repeat the question, therefore – where do we stand? From the point of view of a simple extrapolation it seems hard to avoid the conclusion reached in 1945 by the popular visionary, H. G. Wells, that the world is 'at the end of its tether'. Throughout a writing career spanning half a century, Wells had attempted to demonstrate the progressive potential of the application of science to industry, international cooperation, the restructuring of economic organization and the abolition of war. In his last work, however, Wells consigned his optimistic visions to the 'laboratory sink'. Towards the end of his life, Wells had come to recognize a 'jaded world devoid of recuperative power'. He suggested that man 'must go steeply up or down and the odds seem all in favour of his going down and out'.

The problems for progress that confront us in the 1980s are not so different, in qualitative terms, from those foreseen by Wells some 40 years ago, although their quantitative magnitudes are surely far greater. It might therefore be considered strange that the pessimistic prognosis appears to be no longer fashionable. Contrast, for example, the Wellsian conclusions with those of Rostow (1978) – 'it is also possible that the benign side of the scientific revolution will flourish' (p. 657) – or those of Kahn (1979) – 'barring bad management or bad luck or both, the next two or three decades should be good if not great ones for the majority of the world – and great ones for many' (p. 428). In order to make such statements about the possibilities of progress at a world level it is clearly necessary to have a certain degree of faith in human adaptability, and especially in adaptability towards some transnational form of economic structure. As we have seen, many global issues – the threat of war, the expansion of trade, resource depletion, pollution – are games in which the only mutually beneficial solution is the cooperative one. The transnational strategy is, however, still in its infancy and a great deal must therefore be expected of it in a relatively short space of time. Possibly the greatest obstacle to cooperation is highlighted by the following quotation from the Soviet journal, *Pravda*: 'In the field of ideology there is, and there can be, no peaceful coexistence' (in Wilczynski, 1970, p. 218).

Revolutionists, on the other hand, inspired by the works of Karl Marx and his successors, might argue that the apparently rigid structure that is forcing mankind along its downward path should be, and indeed eventually will be, broken down by revolutionary change, both political and economic, both national and international. Belief in the beneficial potential of revolution is as much an act of faith as the belief that the rationality of global cooperation will ultimately prevail. It is also unfortunate that, in itself, the act of revolution cannot guarantee the replacement of villains by heroes.

Perhaps we might conclude our study by reflecting on the fact that the problems facing the economies of the world at present are not, in principle, new at all. They might be immeasurably complex but they remain the latest and specific manifestation of the fundamental economic problem of the competition between individuals and between societies for the enjoyment of scarce resources. In the analysis of all stages of human history, from Stone Age to Nuclear Age, we find ourselves making use of the same types of concept – collective action, competition, conflict, coercion, collusion, external effects, exchange, inequality – in our interpretations of human behaviour. In abstract terms, therefore, the questions we ask about ourselves seem to remain the same. Indeed, people are fond of saying that history repeats itself. If it does, perhaps it is because man has so far proved himself incapable of learning from his mistakes.

Further reading

Data on levels of official development assistance come from McNamara (1980), Annexes 1 and 2. Data on mineral reserves are derived from OECD (1979), Table 15. OECD (1979) itself is a thought-provoking study concerned with 'the future development of advanced industrial societies in harmony with that of the developing countries' (p. 1). Data for the British cotton industry are taken from Mitchell (1962), pp. 179–87. Wellsian quotations are from Wells (1945).

References

ADAM, J. (1980). The Present Soviet Incentive System. *Soviet Studies* **32**, 349–365

ADELMAN, I. and MORRIS, C. T. (1973). *Economic Growth and Social Equity in Developing Countries*. Stanford, Stanford University Press

ADY, P. (ed.) (1971). *Private Foreign Investment and the Developing World*. New York, Praeger

ALCHIAN, A. and DEMSETZ, H. (1972). Production Costs and Economic Organisation. *American Economic Review* **62**, 777–795

AMANN, R., COOPER, J. and DAVIES, R. W. (eds) (1977). *The Techological Level of Soviet Industry*. New Haven, Yale University Press

AMIN, S. (1973). *Accumulation on a World Scale: A Critique of the Theory of Underdevelopment*. New York, Monthly Review Press

ARNOLD, G. (1979). *Aid in Africa*. New York, Kogan Page

ARON, R. (1968). *Progress and Disillusion*. London, Pall Mall

ATKINSON, A. B. and STIGLITZ, J. E. (1980). *Lectures on Public Economics*. Maidenhead, McGraw-Hill

AVINERI, S. (1968). *The Social and Political Thought of Karl Marx*. London, Cambridge University Press

AZIZ, S. (1978). *Rural Development; Learning from China*. London, Macmillan

BACON, R. and ELTIS, W. (1978). *Britain's Economic Problem: Too Few Producers*, 2nd edn. London, Macmillan

BAGCHI, A. K. (1976). De-industrialisation in India in the Nineteenth Century: Some Theoretical Implications. *Journal of Development Studies* **12**, 135–164

BANKS, F. E. (1976). *The Economics of Natural Resources*. New York, Plenum

BARAN, P. A. (1973). *The Political Economy of Growth*. Harmondsworth, Penguin

BARAN, P. A. and SWEEZY, P. (1966). *Monopoly Capital*. Harmondsworth, Penguin

BARBER, W. J. (1967). *A History of Economic Thought*. Harmondsworth, Penguin

BARBERA, H. (1973). *Rich Nations and Poor in Peace and War*. Lexington, Heath

BARDHAN, P. K. (1978). On Measuring Rural Unemployment. *Journal of Development Studies* **14**, 342–352

BARDHAN, P. K. (1979). Agricultural Development and Land Tenancy in a Peasant Economy: A Theoretical and Empirical Analysis. *American Journal of Agricultural Economics* **61**, 48–57

BARDHAN, P. K. and ASHOK, A. (1980). Terms and Conditions of Sharecropping Contracts: An Analysis of Village Survey Data in India. *Journal of Development Studies* **16**, 287–302

BARKER, E. (1951). *Principles of Social and Political Theory*. Oxford, Clarendon Press

319

BARLOWE, R. (1953). Land Reform and Economic Development. *Journal of Farm Economics* **35**, 173–187

BARRATT BROWN, M. (1974). *The Economics of Imperialism*. Harmondsworth, Penguin

BARRAZA ALLENDE, L. (1974). Regional Agricultural Growth and Economic Development. In *Agricultural Policy in Developing Countries* (ed. by N. Islam). London, Macmillan

BARRY, B. (1970). *Sociologists, Economists and Democracy*. London, Collier-Macmillan

BARTHOLOMEW, D. J. (ed.) (1976). *Manpower Planning*. Harmondsworth, Penguin

BATRA, R. N. (1978). *The Downfall of Capitalism and Communism*. London, Macmillan

BECKER, G. S. (1964). *Human Capital*. New York, National Bureau of Economic Research

BECKER, G. S. (1968). Crime and Punishment: An Economic Approach. *Journal of Political Economy* **76**, 169–217

BECKER, G. S. and LANDES, W. M. (eds) (1974). *Essays in the Economics of Crime and Punishment*. New York, National Bureau of Economic Research

BECKER, L. C. (1977). *Property Rights*. London, Routledge and Kegan Paul

BEHRMAN, J. R. (1976). *Foreign Trade Regimes and Economic Development: Chile*. New York, Columbia University Press

BELLANTE, D. and JACKSON, M. (1979). *Labor Economics*. New York, McGraw-Hill

BENNETT, M. K. (1951). International Disparities of Consumption Levels. *American Economic Review* **41**, 632–649

BERELSON, B. (1971). The Present State of Family Planning Programs. In SINGER (1971). 336–363

BERGSTEN, C. F. (1975). *Toward a New World Trade Policy: The Maidenhead Papers*. Lexington, Heath

BHAGWATI, J. N. (ed.) (1972). *Economics and World Order: From the 1970s to the 1990s*. New York, Macmillan

BHAGWATI, J. N. and ECKAUS, R. (eds) (1970). *Foreign Aid*. Harmondsworth, Penguin

BIRNBER, T. B. and RESNICK, S. A. (1975). *Colonial Development: An Econometric Study*. New Haven, Yale University Press

BLAUG, M. (1968). *Economic Theory in Retrospect*, 2nd edn. London, Heinemann

BLAUG, M. (1972). *An Introduction to the Economics of Education*. Harmondsworth, Penguin

BLAUG, M. (1976). The Empirical Status of Human Capital Theory: A Slightly Jaundiced Survey. *Journal of Economic Literature* **14**, 827–855

BLEANEY, M. F. (1976). *Underconsumption Theories*. London, Lawrence and Wishart

BLUHM, W. T. (1974). *Ideologies and Attitudes: Modern Political Culture*. Englewood Cliffs, Prentice-Hall

BONAR, J. (1922). *Philosophy and Political Economy*. London, Allen and Unwin. First published 1893

BORCHERDING, T. E. (ed.) (1977). *Budgets and Bureaucrats: The Sources of Government Growth*. Durham, N. Carolina, Duke University Press

BOS, H. C., SANDERS, M. and SECCHI, C. (1974). *Private Foreign Investment in Developing Countries*. Dordrecht, Holland, Reidel

BOSE, A. (1977). *Political Paradoxes and Puzzles*. Oxford, Clarendon Press

BOSERUP, E. (1981). *Population and Technology*. Oxford, Basil Blackwell

BOWLES, R. A. and WHYNES, D. K. (1979). *Macroeconomic Planning*. London, Allen and Unwin

BRACEWELL-MILNES, B. (1976). *Economic Integration in East and West*. London, Croom Helm

BRETON, A. (1974). *The Economic Theory of Representative Government*. Chicago, Aldine

BROMLEY, R. and GERRY, C. (eds) (1979). *Casual Work and Poverty in Third World Cities*. Chichester, Wiley

BROOME, J. H. (1963). *Rousseau: A Study of his Thought*. London, Edward Arnold

BROWN, C. V. and JACKSON, P. M. (1978). *Public Sector Economics*. Oxford, Martin Robertson

BURK, M. C. (1968). *Consumption Economics: A Multidisciplinary Approach.* New York, Wiley

CÁCERES, L. R. (1979). Economic Integration and Export Instability in Central America: A Portfolio Model. *Journal of Development Studies* **15**, 141–153
CAIRNCROSS, A. K. (1962). *Factors in Economic Development.* London, Allen and Unwin
CARLOS MÉNDEZ, J. (1980). *Chilean Socioeconomic Overview.* Santiago, Matte & Méndez
CARR, E. H. (1961). *What is History?* London, Macmillan
CARR, E. H. and DAVIES, R .W. (1974). *Foundations of a Planned Economy, 1926–1929.* Vol. 1. Harmondsworth, Penguin
CARRINGTON, R. (1963). *A Million Years of Man.* London, Weidenfeld and Nicolson
CASSEN, R. H. (1978). *India: Population, Economy and Society.* London, Macmillan
CAUTE, D. (1970). *Fanon.* London, Collins
CENTRAL STATISTICAL OFFICE (1980). *National Income and Expenditure.* London, HMSO
CHAMPERNOWNE, D. G. (1974). A Comparison of Measures of Inequality of Income Distribution. *Economic Journal* **84**, 787–816
CHAPLIN, D. (ed.) (1971a). *Population Policies and Growth in Latin America.* Lexington, Heath
CHAPLIN, D. (1971b). Some Institutional Determinants of Fertility in Peru. In CHAPLIN (1971a), 223–230
CHENERY, H. B. *et al.* (1974). *Redistribution with Growth.* London, Oxford University Press
CHIPLIN, B. and COYNE, J. (1977). Property Rights and Industrial Democracy. In *Can Workers Manage?* (B. Chiplin, J. Coyne and L. Sirc), 13–48. London, Institute of Economic Affairs
CID (Commission on International Development) (1969). *Partners in Development.* London, Pall Mall
CIPOLLA, C. M. (1965). *The Economic History of World Population,* 3rd edn. Harmondsworth, Penguin
CLARK, C. (1951). *Conditions of Economic Progress.* London, Macmillan
CLARK, W. E. L-G. (1978). *The Fossil Evidence for Human Evolution,* 3rd edn. Chicago, University Press
CLARKSON, S. (1979). *The Soviet Theory of Development: India and the Third World in Marxist–Leninist Scholarship.* London, Macmillan
CLAYTON, E. S. (1970). Agrarian Reform, Agricultural Planning and Employment in Kenya. *International Labour Review* **102**, 431–456
CLEMENCE, R. V. and DOODY, F. S. (1950). *The Schumpeterian System.* Cambridge, Mass., Addison-Wesley Press
CLINE, W. R. (1970). *Economic Consequences of a Land Reform in Brazil.* Amsterdam, North-Holland
COBBAN, A. (1964). *Rousseau and the Modern State.* London, Allen and Unwin
COBBAN, A. (1969). *The Nation State and Self-Determination.* London, Collins
COHEN, A. S. (1975). *Theories of Revolution: An Introduction.* London, Nelson
COLE, J. P. (1981). *The Development Gap.* Chichester, Wiley
CONNELL, J. and LIPTON, M. (1977). *Assessing Village Labour Situations in Developing Countries.* Delhi, Oxford University Press
COON, C. S. (1972). *The Hunting Peoples.* London, Jonathan Cape
CORBET, H. (1975). *Raw Materials: Beyond the Rhetoric of Commodity Power.* London, Trade Policy Research Centre
CORREA, H. (1963). *The Economics of Human Resources.* Amsterdam, North-Holland
CULBERTSON, J. M. (1971). *Economic Development: An Ecological Approach.* New York, Knopf
CULLIS, J. G. and WEST, P. A. (1979). *The Economics of Health: An Introduction.* Oxford, Martin Robertson
CULYER, A. J. (1976). *Need and the National Health Service.* Oxford, Martin Robertson

CULYER, A. J. (1980). *The Political Economy of Social Policy*. Oxford, Martin Robertson

DAHL, R. A. (1956). *A Preface to Democratic Theory*. Chicago, Chicago University Press
DAHL, R. A. (1961). *Who Governs?* New Haven, Yale University Press
DASGUPTA, B. (1977). *Agrarian Change and the New Technology in India*. Geneva, United Nations Research Institute for Social Development
DASGUPTA, B. *et al.* (1977). *Village Society and Labour Use*. Delhi, Oxford University Press
DATAR, A. L. (1972). *India's Economic Relations with the USSR and Eastern Europe, 1953 to 1969*. London, Cambridge University Press
DAVENPORT, M. (1970). The Allocation of Foreign Aid. *Yorkshire Bulletin of Economic Research* **22**, 26–38
DAVIES, D. (1930). *The Problem of the Twentieth Century*. London, Benn
DEANE, P. (1965). *The First Industrial Revolution*. London, Cambridge University Press
DEANE, P. and COLE, W. A. (1967). *British Economic Growth, 1688–1959*, 2nd edn. London, Cambridge University Press
DEATON, A. and MUELLBAUER, J. (1980). *Economics and Consumer Behavior*. Cambridge, Cambridge University Press
DEMSETZ, H. (1967). Toward a Theory of Property Rights. *American Economic Review* **57**, 347–359
DENISON, E. (1964). Measuring the Contribution of Education (and the Residual) to Economic Growth. In *The Residual Factor in Economic Growth*. Study Group in the Economics of Education, Paris, OECD
DENISON, E. (1967). *Why Growth Rates Differ: Post-War Experience in Nine Western Countries*. Washington, Brookings Institution
DENISON, E. (1968). Economic Growth. In *Britain's Economic Prospects* (R. E. Caves *et al.*). London, Allen and Unwin
DENTON, G. (ed.) (1974). *Economic and Monetary Union in Europe*. London, Croom Helm
D'ENTRÈVES, A. P. (1967). *The Notion of the State*. Oxford, Clarendon Press
DEPARTMENT OF EMPLOYMENT (1980). *Family Expenditure Survey 1979*. London, HMSO
DESAI, M. and MAZUMDAR, D. (1970). A Test of the Hypothesis of Disguised Unemployment. *Economica* **37**, 39–53
DIXIT, A. (1968). The Optimal Development in the Labour Surplus Economy. *Review of Economic Studies* **35**, 25–34
DIXIT, A. (1971). Short-run Equilibrium and Shadow Prices in the Dual Economy. *Oxford Economic Papers* **23**, 384–399
DOBB, M. (1946). *Studies in the Development of Capitalism*. London, Routledge
DOBB, M. (1975). *Theories of Value and Distribution since Adam Smith*. London, Cambridge University Press
DORNER, P. (1972). *Land Reform and Economic Development*. Harmondsworth, Penguin
DOWNS, A. (1957). *An Economic Theory of Democracy*. New York, Harper and Row
DOXEY, M. P. (1971). *Economic Sanctions and International Enforcement*. Oxford, Oxford University Press
DREWNOWSKI, J. (1974). *On Measuring and Planning the Quality of Life*. International Institute of Social Studies, The Hague, Mouton
DUNNING, J. H. (ed.) (1972). *International Investment*. Harmondsworth, Penguin
DWORKIN, R. M. (ed.) (1977a). *The Philosophy of Law*. London, Oxford University Press
DWORKIN, R. M. (1977b). *Taking Rights Seriously*. London, Duckworth

EASON, W. W. (1963). Labor Force. In *Economic Trends in the Soviet Union* (ed. by A. Bergson and S. Kuznets), 38–95. Cambrige, Mass., Harvard University Press
EASTERLIN, R. A. (ed.) (1980). *Population and Economic Change in Developing Countries*. Chicago, Chicago University Press

ECKSTEIN, A. (1977). *China's Economic Revolution*. Cambridge, Cambridge University Press

EHRLICH, I. (1974). Participation in Illegitimate Activities: An Economic Analysis. In BECKER and LANDES (1974), 68–134

ELDRIDGE, P. J. (1969). *The Politics of Foreign Aid in India*. London, Weidenfeld and Nicolson

ELLMAN, M. (1973). *Planning Problems in the USSR*. Cambridge, Cambridge University Press

ELLMAN, M. (1979). *Socialist Planning*. Cambridge, Cambridge University Press

EMMANUEL, A. (1972). *Unequal Exchange: A Study of the Imperialism of Trade*. New York, Monthly Review Press

ENGELS, F. (1847). *Draft of a Communist Confession of Faith*. Presented to the First Congress of the Communist League in London. Quotations from K. Marx and F. Engels (1976), *Collected Works*. London, Lawrence and Wishart, Vol. 6, 96–103

FAALAND, J. (ed.) (1981). *Aid and Influence: the Case of Bangladesh*. London, Macmillan

FANON, F. (1961). *Les Damnés de la terre*. Paris, F. Maspero

FEDER, G. (1980). Economic Growth, Foreign Loans and Debt-Servicing Capacity of Developing Countries. *Journal of Development Studies* **16**, 352–368

FEI, J. C. and RANIS, G. (1964). *Development of the Labor Surplus Economy: Theory and Policy*. Homewood, Irwin

FERBER, R. (1973). Consumer Economics – A Survey. *Journal of Economic Literature* **11**, 1303–1342

FIELDS, G. S. (1980). *Poverty, Inequality and Development*. Cambridge, Cambridge University Press

FINE, B. (1975). *Marx's Capital*. London, Macmillan

FITZGERALD, E. V. K. (1978). *Public Sector Investment Planning in Developing Countries*. London, Macmillan

FRANK, A. G. (1966). The Development of Underdevelopment. *Monthly Review*, September, 17–31

FRANK, A. G. (1967). *Capitalism and Underdevelopment in Latin America*. New York, Monthly Review Press

FRANKEL, F. R. (1971). *India's Green Revolution: Economic Gains and Political Costs*. New Jersey, Princeton University Press

FREYHOLD, M. von (1979). *Ujamaa Villages in Tanzania*. London, Heinemann

FRY, J. (1979a). *Employment and Income Distribution in the African Economy*. London, Croom Helm

FRY, J. (ed.) (1979b). *Limits of the Welfare State*. Farnborough, Saxon House

FURUBOTN, E. and PEJOVICH, S. (1972). Property Rights and Economic Theory: A Survey of Recent Literature. *Journal of Economic Literature* **10**, 1137–1162

FURUBOTN, E. and PEJOVICH, S. (eds) (1974). *The Economics of Property Rights*. Cambridge, Mass., Ballinger

GALBRAITH, J. K. (1964). *Economic Development*. London, Oxford University Press

GALLIE, W. B. (1978). *Philosophers of Peace and War*. London, Cambridge University Press

GALTUNG, J. (1971). A Structural Theory of Imperialism. *Journal of Peace Research* **13**, 81–118

GATT (General Agreement on Tariffs and Trade) (1980). *International Trade 1979/1980*. Geneva

GELLNER, E. (1964). *Thought and Change*. London, Weidenfeld and Nicolson

GERSCHENKRON, A. (1952). Economic Backwardness in Historical Perspective. In *The Progress of Underdeveloped Areas* (ed. by B. F. Hoselitz), 3–29. Chicago, Chicago University Press

GERSOVITZ, M. (1976). Land Reform: Some Theoretical Considerations. *Journal of Development Studies* **13**, 79–91

GHATAK, S. (1978). *Development Economics*. London, Longman

GILBERT, B. B. (1966). *The Evolution of National Insurance in Great Britain*. London, Michael Joseph

GILBERT, M. *et al.* (1958). *Comparative National Products and Price Levels*. Paris, OECD

GLEASON, A. H. (1961). The Social Adequacy Method of International Levels of Living Comparisons. *Journal of Economic Behaviour* **1**, 3–20

GLUCKMAN, M. (1965). *Politics, Law and Ritual in Tribal Society*. Oxford, Basil Blackwell

GORDON, B. (1975). *Economic Analysis before Adam Smith*. London, Macmillan

GRAHAM, R. (1978). *Iran: The Illusion of Power*. London, Croom Helm

GRAY, C. M. (ed.) (1979). *The Costs of Crime*. Beverly Hills, Sage

GREEN, H. A. J. (1976). *Consumer Theory*, 2nd edn. London, Macmillan

GREGORY, P. (1980). An Assessment of Changes in Employment Conditions in Less Developed Countries. *Economic Development and Cultural Change* **28**, 673–700

GRIBBIN, J. (1981). The Politics of Carbon Dioxide. *New Scientist* **86**, 9 April, 82–84

GRIFFIN, K. (1969). *Underdevelopment in Spanish America*. London, Allen and Unwin

GRIFFIN, K. (1979). *The Political Economy of Agrarian Change*, 2nd edn. London, Macmillan

GROSSMAN, M. (1972). *The Demand for Health: A Theoretical and Empirical Investigation*. New York, Columbia University Press

GROTH, A. J. (1971). *Major Ideologies: An Interpretive Survey of Democracy, Socialism and Nationalism*. New York, Wiley

HACKETT, J. and HACKETT, A-M. (1963). *Economic Planning in France*. London, Allen and Unwin

HAHN, F. H. and MATTHEWS, R. C. O. (1964). The Theory of Economic Growth: A Survey. *Economic Journal* **74**, 779–902

HALLIDAY, J. (1975). *A Political History of Japanese Capitalism*. New York, Pantheon

HALLWOOD, P. and SINCLAIR, S. (1981). *Oil, Debt and Development: OPEC in the Third World*. London, Allen and Unwin

HAMERMESH, D. S. (1971). *Economic Aspects of Manpower Training Programs*. Lexington, Heath

HANSEN, F. (1972). *Consumer Choice Behavior*. New York, Free Press

HANSON, A. H. (1966). *The Process of Planning*. London, Oxford University Press

HARCOURT, G. C. (1972). *Some Cambridge Controversies in the Theory of Capital*. London, Cambridge University Press

HARCOURT, G. C. and LAING, N. F. (eds) (1971). *Capital and Growth*. Harmondsworth, Penguin

HARRIS, M. (1978). *Cannibals and Kings: The Origins of Cultures*. London, Collins

HARRIS, N. (1968). *Beliefs in Society*. London, Watts

HART, H. L. A. (1961). *The Concept of Law*, Oxford, Clarendon Press

HARTLEY, S. F. (1972). *Population: Quantity vs. Quality*. Englewood Cliffs, Prentice-Hall

HAYEK, F. A. von (ed.) (1935). *Collectivist Economic Planning: Critical Studies on the Possibilities of Socialism*. London, Routledge

HAYTER, T. (1971). *Aid as Imperialism*. Harmondsworth, Penguin

HEALEY, D. T. (1972). Development Policy: New Thinking about an Interpretation. *Journal of Economic Literature* **10**, 757–797

HERFINDAHL, O. C. and KNEESE, A. V. (1974). *The Economic Theory of Natural Resources*. Columbus, Merrill

HEYER, J., ROBERTS, P. and WILLIAMS, G. (eds) (1981). *Rural Development in Tropical Africa*. London, Macmillan

HILTON, R. (1973). *Bond Men Made Free: Medieval Peasant Movements and the English Rising of 1381*. London, Maurice Temple Smith

HIRSCH, F. (1977). *Social Limits to Growth*. London, Routledge and Kegan Paul

HIRSCHLEIFER, J. (1976). *Price Theory and Applications.* Englewood Cliffs, Prentice-Hall

HO, Y-M. (1972). Development with Surplus-Labour Population – The Case Study of Taiwan: A Critique of the Classical Two-Sector Model à la Lewis. *Economic Development and Cultural Change.* **20**, 210–234

HOBHOUSE, L. T., WHEELER, G. C. and GINSBERG, M. (1930). *The Material Culture and Social Institutions of the Simpler Peoples.* London, Chapman and Hall

HOLDEN, B. (1974). *The Nature of Democracy.* London, Nelson

HOLESOVSKY, V. (1977). *Economic Systems: Analysis and Comparison.* Tokyo, McGraw-Hill, Kogakusha

HOLLANDER, S. (1973). *The Economics of Adam Smith.* London, Heinemann

HOLLANDER, S. (1979). *The Economics of David Ricardo.* Toronto, Toronto University Press

HOPKIN, B. *et al.* (1970). Aid and the Balance of Payments. *Economic Journal* **80**, 1–23

HUNT, E. K. (1972). *Property and Profits.* New York, Harper and Row

HUNTER, G., BUNTING, A. H. and BOTTRAL, A. (eds) (1976). *Policy and Practice in Rural Development.* London, Croom Helm

HYDEN, G. (1979). 'We-must-run-while-others-walk'; Policy-making for Socialist Development in the Tanzania-type of Polities. In *Papers on the Political Economy of Tanzania* (ed. by K. S. Kim, R. B. Mabele and M. J. Schultheis), 5–13. Nairobi, Heinemann

ICIDI (Independent Commission on International Development Issues) (1980). *North–South: A Programme for Survival.* London, Pan Books

IEA (Institute of Economic Affairs) (1977). *The State of Taxation.* London

IEA (1979). *Tax Avoision.* London

IISS (International Institute for Strategic Studies) (1978). *The Military Balance 1977–1978.* London

ILO (International Labour Organization) (1976). *The Impact of Multi-national Enterprises on Employment and Training.* Geneva

ILO (1980). *Yearbook of Labour Statistics.* Geneva

IMF (International Monetary Fund) (1981). *External Indebtedness of Developing Countries.* Washington

IONESCU, G. (ed.) (1979). *The European Alternatives: An Inquiry into the Policies of the European Community.* Alphen aan den Rijn, Sijthoff and Noordhoff

ISLAM, N. (1977). *Development Planning in Bangladesh.* London, Hurst

JENKINS, R. (1970). *Exploitation.* London, Paladin

JOLLY, R. *et al.* (eds) (1973). *Third World Employment; Problems and Strategy.* Harmondsworth, Penguin

JONES, D. (1977). *Aid and Development in Southern Africa.* London, Croom Helm

JORGENSON, D. W. (1961). The Development of a Dual Economy. *Economic Journal* **71**, 309–334

KAHN, H. (1979). *World Economic Development.* London, Croom Helm

KALDOR, N. (1966). *Causes of the Slow Rate of Economic Growth of the United Kingdom.* Cambridge, Cambridge University Press

KEDOURIE, E. (1960). *Nationalism.* London, Hutchinson

KELLEY, A. C. *et al.* (1972). *Dualistic Economic Development: Theory and History.* Chicago, Chicago University Press

KELLEY, A. C. and WILLIAMSON, J. G. (1974). *Lessons from Japanese Development: An Analytical Economic History.* Chicago, Chicago University Press

KENNEDY, G. (1974). *The Military in the Third World.* London, Duckworth

KEYNES, J. M. (1964). *The General Theory of Employment, Interest and Money.* London, Macmillan. First published 1936

KINDLEBERGER, C. P. (ed.) (1970). *The International Corporation*. Cambridge, MIT Press

KING, R. (1977). *Land Reform: A World Survey*. London, Bell

KNEESE, A. V. (1977). *Economics and the Environment*. Harmondsworth, Penguin

KOHN, H. (1961). *The Idea of Nationalism*. New York, Macmillan

KRAUSE, W. and MATHIS, F. J. (1970). *Latin America and Economic Integration*. Iowa City, University of Iowa Press

KRAVIS, I. B. (1960). International Difference in the Distribution of Income. *Review of Economics and Statistics* **42**, 408–416

KRAVIS, I. B., HESTON, A. W. and SUMMERS, R. (1978). Real GDP per capita for more than One Hundred Countries. *Economic Journal* **88**, 215–242

KUO, L. T. C. (1976). *Agriculture in the People's Republic of China*. New York, Praeger

LAL, D. (1975). *Appraising Foreign Investment in Developing Countries*. London, Heinemann

LANE, D. (1981). *Leninism: A Sociological Interpretation*. Cambridge, Cambridge University Press

LEACOMBER, R. (1979). *The Economics of Natural Resources*. London, Macmillan

LEFF, G. (1969). *History and Social Theory*. London, Merlin Press

LEHMANN, D. (ed.) (1974). *Agrarian Reform and Agrarian Reformism*. London, Faber and Faber

LEIBENSTEIN, H. (1954). *A Theory of Economic–Demographic Development*. Princeton, Princeton University Press

LEIBENSTEIN, H. (1963). *Economic Backwardness and Economic Growth*. New York, Science Editions

LEWIS, W. A. (1954). Economic Development with Unlimited Supplies of Labour. *Manchester School of Economic and Social Studies* **22**, 139–191

LEWIS, W. A. (1955). *Theory of Economic Growth*. London, Allen and Unwin

LIDER, J. (1977). *On the Nature of War*. Farnborough, Saxon House

LIDER, J. (1981). *Military Force*. Farnborough, Gower

LINDBECK, A. (1975). *Swedish Economic Policy*. London, Macmillan

LINDERT, P. and KINDLEBERGER, C. P. (1981). *International Economics*. Homewood, Irwin

LIPSEY, R. G. (1957). The Theory of Customs Unions: Trade Diversion and Welfare. *Economica* **24**, 40–46

LITTLE, I. M. D. and MIRRLEES, J. A. (1974). *Project Appraisal and Planning for Developing Countries*. London, Heinemann. This is a later edition of *Manual of Industrial Project Analysis for Developing Countries*. Paris, OECD, 1968

LLUCH, C., POWELL, A. and WILLIAMS, R. A. (1977). *Patterns in Household Demand and Saving*. New York, Oxford University Press

LOKEN, R. D. (1969). *Manpower Development in Africa*. New York, Praeger

LUNDBERG, I. C. (1964). *Turgot's Unknown Translator*. The Hague, Martinus Nijholf

MABRO, R. (1967). Industrial Growth, Agricultural Under-employment and the Lewis Model: The Egyptian Case, 1937–1965. *Journal of Development Studies* **3**, 322–351

MCAULEY, A. (1979). *Economic Welfare in the Soviet Union*. Madison, University of Wisconsin Press

MACFARLANE, L. (1974). *Violence and the State*. London, Nelson

MACHLUP, F. (1969). Liberalism and the Choice of Freedoms. In *Roads to Freedom: Essays in Honour of Friedrich von Hayek* (ed. by E. Streissler). London, Routledge and Kegan Paul

MCLACHLAN, G. (ed.) (1980). *The Planning of Health Services*. Copenhagen, WHO

MCNAMARA, R. S. (1980). *Address to the Board of Governers*. World Bank Presidential Address, 30 September 1980. Washington, World Bank

MACPHERSON, C. B. (1962). *The Political Theory of Possessive Individualism*. Oxford, Oxford University Press

MADDISON, A. (1970). *Economic Progress and Policy in Developing Countries*. London, Allen and Unwin

MAINA, J. W. and MACARTHUR, J. D. (1970). Land Settlement in Kenya. In *Change in Agriculture* (ed. by A. H. Bunting), 427–435. London, Duckworth

MALTHUS, T. R. (1895). *Parallel Chapters from the First and Second Editions of An Essay on the Principle of Population*. New York, Macmillan

MAO-TSE-TUNG (1966). *Quotations from Chairman Mao Tse-Tung*. Peking, Foreign Languages Press

MARCUSE, H. (1972). *One Dimensional Man*. London, Abacus

MARGLIN, S. A. (1976). *Value and Price in the Labour Surplus Economy*. London, Oxford University Press

MARX, K. (1844). *Economic and Philosophic Manuscripts*. Quotations from K. Marx and F. Engels (1975), *Collected Works*. London, Lawrence and Wishart, Vol. 3

MASNATA, A. (1974). *East–West Economic Cooperation*. Lexington, Heath

MATHUR, A. (1964). The Anatomy of Disguised Unemployment. *Oxford Economic Papers* **16**, 161–193

MAYNARD, A. K. (1975). *Health Care in the European Community*. London, Croom Helm

MEADE, J. E. (1972). The Theory of Labour-Managed Firms and Profit Sharing. *Economic Journal* **82**, 402–428

MEADOWS, D. H. *et al.* (1972). *The Limits to Growth*. New York, Universal Books

MEEK, R. L. (ed.) (1973). *Turgot on Progress, Sociology and Economics*. London, Cambridge University Press

MEEK, R. L. (1977). *Smith, Marx and After*. London, Chapman and Hall

MEIER, G. M. (1980). *International Economics: The Theory of Policy*. New York, Oxford University Press

MELLOR, J. W. (1976). *The New Economics of Growth*. Ithaca, Cornell University Press

MINCER, J. (1970). The Distribution of Labor Incomes: A Survey. *Journal of Economic Literature* **8**, 1–26

MITCHELL, B. R. (1962). *Abstract of British Historical Statistics*. Cambridge, Cambridge University Press

MOORE, J. H. (1980). *Growth with Self-Management*. Stanford, Hoover Institution

MORAWETZ, D. (1974). Employment Implications of Industrialisation in Developing Countries – A Survey. *Economic Journal* **84**, 491–542

MOULY, J. and COSTA, E. (1974). *Employment in Developing Countries*. London, Allen and Unwin

MUELLER, D. C. (1976). Public Choice – A Survey. *Journal of Economic Literature* **14**, 395–433

MUELLER, D. C. (1979). *Public Choice*. New York, Cambridge University Press

MUELLER, M. W. (1970). Changing Patterns of Agricultural Output and Productivity in the Private and Land Reform Sectors in Mexico, 1940–60. *Economic Development and Cultural Change* **18**, 252–260

MYRDAL, G. (1965). *Beyond the Welfare State*. London, Methuen

MYRDAL, G. (1968). *Asian Drama: An Inquiry into the Poverty of Nations*, 3 vols. Harmondsworth, Penguin

NATIONAL ACADEMY OF SCIENCES (1971). *Rapid Population Growth: Consequences and Policy Implications*. Baltimore, Johns Hopkins University Press

NAYYAR, D. (ed.) (1977). *Economic Relations between Socialist Countries and the Third World*. London, Macmillan

NELLIS, J. R. (1972). *A Theory of Ideology: The Tanzanian Example*. Nairobi, Oxford University Press

NELSON, R. R. (1956). A Theory of the Low-Level Equilibrium Trap in Underdeveloped Economies. *American Economic Review* **46**, 894–908

NEUBERGER, E. and DUFFY, W. (1976). *Comparative Economic Systems: A Decision-making Approach*. Boston, Allyn and Bacon

NEWBERRY, D. (1974). The Robustness of Equilibrium Analysis in the Dual Economy. *Oxford Economic Papers* **26**, 32–44

NEWHOUSE, J. P. (1977). Medical Care Expenditure: A Cross-National Survey. *Journal of Human Resources* **12**, 115–125

NEWHOUSE, J. P. (1978). *The Economics of Medical Care: A Policy Perspective*. Reading, Mass., Addison-Wesley

NEWLYN, W. T. (1977). *The Financing of Economic Development*. Oxford, Clarendon Press

NISBET, R. (1980). *History of the Idea of Progress*. London, Heinemann

NISKANEN, W. (1968). The Peculiar Economics of Bureaucracy. *American Economic Review* **58**, 293–305

NISKANEN, W. (1971). *Bureaucracy and Representative Government*. Chicago, Aldine-Atherton

NISKANEN, W. (1973). *Bureaucracy – Servant or Master?* London, Institute of Economic Affairs

NORDHAUS, W. D. (1975). The Political Business Cycle. *Review of Economic Studies* **42**, 169–190

NORDHAUS, W. and TOBIN, J. (1972). Is Growth Obsolete? In *Economic Growth*. National Bureau of Economic Research, Fifteenth Anniversary Colloquium, New York

NORMANN, G. and SÖDERSTEN, J. (1979). Perspectives on Tax Developments in Sweden. In *Measurement and Economic Theory* (Institute for Economic and Social Research). Stockholm, 101

NOVE, A. (1972). *An Economic History of the USSR*. Harmondsworth, Penguin

NOVE, A. (1977). *The Soviet Economic System*. London, Allen and Unwin

NULTY, L. (1972). *The Green Revolution in West Pakistan*. New York, Praeger

O'DRISCOLL, G. P. (ed.) (1979). *Adam Smith and Modern Political Economy*. Ames, Iowa State University Press

OECD (Organization for Economic Cooperation and Development) (1976). *Measuring Social Well-Being*. Paris

OECD (1977). *Public Expenditure on Health*. Paris

OECD (1979). *Interfutures: Facing the Future*. Paris

OECD (1980a). *Development Cooperation*. Paris

OECD (1980b). *OECD Economic Surveys: Japan*. Paris

OECD (1980c). *OECD Economic Surveys: France*. Paris

OECD (1980d). *OECD Economic Surveys: United States*. Paris

OHKAWA, K. and ROSOVSKY, H. (1973). *Japanese Economic Growth*. Stanford, Stanford University Press

OKWUOSA, E. A. (1976). *New Direction for Economic Development in Africa*. London, Africa Books

OVERBEEK, J. (1974). *History of Population Theories*. Rotterdam, Rotterdam University Press

PACK, H. (1974). The Employment–Output Trade-off in LDCs – A Microeconomic Approach. *Oxford Economic Papers* **26**, 388–404

PAPANEK, G. (1973). Aid, Foreign Private Investment, Savings and Growth in Less Developed Countries. *Journal of Political Economy* **81**, 120–130

PARSONS, J. (1977). *Population Fallacies*. London, Elek/Pemberton

PAUKERT, F. (1973). Income Distribution at Different Levels of Development: A Survey of Evidence. *International Labour Review* **108**, 97–125

PAXTON, J. (1976). *The Developing Common Market*. London, Macmillan

PEAKER, A. (1974). *Economic Growth in Modern Britain*. London, Macmillan

PEARSE, A. (1975). *The Latin American Peasant*. London, Cass

PEN, J. (1971). *Income Distribution*. London, Allen Lane

PETERSEN, W. (1975). *Population*, 3rd edn. New York, Macmillan

PICKLES, D. (1965). *The Fifth French Republic*, 3rd edn. London, Methuen

PLAMENATZ, J. (1970). *Ideology*. London, Pall Mall

POLLARD, S. (1971). *The Idea of Progress*. Harmondsworth, Penguin

POSNER, R. A. (1977). *Economic Analysis of Law*, 2nd edn. Boston, Little, Brown and Co.

POWELL, A. A. (1974). *Empirical Analysis of Demand Systems*. Lexington, Heath

PREBISCH, R. (1964). *Towards a New Trade Policy for Development*. New York, UN

PREOBRAZHENSKY, E. A. (1964). *The New Economics*. Oxford, Clarendon Press. First published in the USSR in the 1920s

PRYOR, F. L. (1977). *The Origins of the Economy*. London, Academic Press

PSACHAROPOULOS, G. (1973). *Returns to Education: An International Comparison*. Amsterdam, Elsevier Scientific

PSACHAROPOULOS, G. and LAYARD, R. (1979). Human Capital and Earnings: British Evidence and a Critique. *Review of Economic Studies* **46**, 485–504

RAJARAMAN, I. (1975). Poverty, Inequality and Economic Growth: Rural Punjab 1960/61 – 1970/71. *Journal of Development Studies* **11**, 278–290

RAWLS, J. (1972). *A Theory of Justice*. London, Oxford University Press

REDDAWAY, W. B. (1939). *The Economics of a Declining Population*. London, Allen and Unwin

REMPEL, H. and HOUSE, W. J. (1978). *The Kenya Employment Problem*. Nairobi, Oxford University Press

REUBER, G. L. *et al.* (1973). *Private Foreign Investment in Development*. Oxford, Clarendon Press

REYNOLDS, L. G. (1977). *Image and Reality in Economic Development*. New Haven, Yale University Press

RICHARDS, J. H. (1970). *International Economic Institutions*. London, Holt, Rinehart and Winston

RIDKER, R. G. (ed.) (1976). *Population and Development*. Baltimore, John Hopkins University Press

RIX, A. (1980). *Japan's Economic Aid: Policy Making and Politics*. London, Croom Helm

ROBINSON, J. (1964). *Economic Philosophy*. Harmondsworth, Penguin

ROBSON, P. (ed.) (1972). *International Economic Integration*. Harmondsworth, Penguin

ROBSON, P. (1980). *The Economics of International Integration*. London, Allen and Unwin

ROSEN, S. J. and KURTH, J. R. (eds) (1974). *Testing Theories of Economic Imperialism*. Lexington, Heath

ROSENSTEIN-RODAN, P. N. (1964). *Capital Formation and Economic Development*. London, Allen and Unwin

ROSTOW, W. W. (1960). *The Stages of Economic Growth*. London, Cambridge University Press

ROSTOW, W. W. (1978). *The World Economy: History and Prospect*. Austin, University of Texas Press

ROWLEY, C. K. and PEACOCK, A. T. (1975). *Welfare Economics: A Liberal Restatement*. Oxford, Martin Robertson

RWEYEMAMU, A. H. and MWANSASU, B. U. (eds) (1974). *Planning in Tanzania: Background to Decentralisation*. Nairobi, East Africa Literature Bureau

SAHLINS, M. (1974). *Stone Age Economics*. London, Tavistock

SAHOTA, G. S. (1978). Theories of Personal Income Distribution: A Survey. *Journal of Economic Literature* **16**, 1–55

SANCHEZ, N. and WATERS, A. R. (1974). Controlling Corruption in Africa and Latin America. In FURUBOTN and PEJOVICH (1974), 279–295

SARTORI, G. (1965). *Democratic Theory*. New York, Praeger

SCHAPIRO, L. and GODSON, J. (eds) (1981). *The Soviet Worker*. London, Macmillan

SCHMIDT, A. (1971). *The Concept of Nature in Marx*. London, New Left Books

SCHNITZER, M. (1970). *The Economy of Sweden*. New York, Praeger

SCHULTZ, T. P. (1971). An Economic Perspective on Population Growth. In NATIONAL ACADEMY OF SCIENCES (1971), 148–174

SCHULTZ, T. W. (1964). *Transforming Traditional Agriculture*. New Haven, Yale University Press

SCHUMPETER, J. A. (1934). *The Theory of Economic Development*. Cambridge, Mass., Harvard University Press

SCHUMPETER, J. A. (1954a). *Capitalism, Socialism and Democracy*, 4th edn. London, Allen and Unwin

SCHUMPETER, J. A. (1954b). *History of Economic Analysis*. New York, Oxford University Press

SCITOVSKY, T. (1976). *The Joyless Economy: An Inquiry into Human Satisfaction and Consumer Dissatisfaction*. New York, Oxford University Press

SCOTCH, N. A. (1963). Sociocultural Factors in the Epidemiology of Zulu Hypertension. *American Journal of Public Health* **53**, 1205–1213

SEERS, D. (1971). Rich Countries and Poor. In *Development in a Divided World* (ed. by D. Seers and L. Joy), 13–33. Harmondsworth, Penguin

SEN, A. K. (1968). *Choice of Techniques*, 3rd edn. Oxford, Basil Blackwell

SEN, A. K. (1975). *Employment, Technology and Development*. Oxford, Clarendon Press

SHEN, T. Y. (1977). Macro Development Planning in Tropical Africa: Technocratic and Non-Technocratic Causes of Failure. *Journal of Development Studies* **13**, 413–427

SHENOY, S. R. (1971). *India: Progress or Poverty?* London, Institute of Economic Affairs

SIEVERS, A. M. (1962). *Revolution, Evolution and the Economic Order*. Englewood Cliffs, Prentice-Hall

SIGMUND, P. E. (1980). *Multinationals in Latin America: The Politics of Nationalisation*. Wisconsin, Wisconsin University Press

SIMON, J. L. (1981). *The Ultimate Resource*. Oxford, Martin Robertson

SINGER, S. F. (1971). *Is There an Optimum Level of Population?* New York, McGraw-Hill

SINGH, T. (1974). *India's Development Experience*. New York, St. Martin's Press

SIPRI (Stockholm International Peace Research Institute) (1978). *World Armaments and Disarmaments: SIPRI Yearbook 1978*. London, Taylor and Francis

SKIDMORE, D. (1974). The Chilean Experience of Change: The Primacy of the Political. In *South Africa: Economic Growth and Social Change* (ed. by A. Leftwich). London, Allison and Busby

SKINNER, A. S. (1979). *A System of Social Science*. Oxford, Clarendon Press

SKLAIR, L. (1970). *The Sociology of Progress*. London, Routledge and Kegan Paul

SMITH, A. (1873). *An Inquiry into the Nature and Causes of the Wealth of Nations*. London, Nelson. First published 1776

SPANIER, J. (1972). *Games Nations Play*. New York, Praeger

SPENGLER, O. (1926–8). *The Decline of the West*. New York, Knopf

STANDING, G. (1978). *Labour Force Participation and Development*. Geneva, ILO

STERN, E. and TIMS, W. (1975). The Relative Bargaining Strengths of the Developing Countries. *American Journal of Agricultural Economics* **57**, 225–236

STEWART, F. (ed.) (1975). *Employment, Income Distribution and Development*. London, Cass

STIGLER, G. J. (1970). The Optimum Enforcement of Laws. *Journal of Political Economy* **78**, 526–536

STREETEN, P. and LIPTON, M. (eds) (1968). *The Crisis of Indian Planning*. London, Oxford University Press

STYCOS, J. M. (1971). Opinion, Ideology and Population Problems – Some Sources of Domestic and Foreign Opposition to Birth Control. In NATIONAL ACADEMY OF SCIENCES (1971), 533–566

STYS, W. (1957). The Influence of Economic Conditions on the Fertility of Peasant Women. *Population Studies* **11**, 136–148

SWANN, D. (1975). *The Economics of the Common Market*, 3rd edn. Harmondsworth, Penguin

SZENTES, T. (1976). *The Political Economy of Underdevelopment*, 3rd edn. Budapest, Akademiai Kiado

TAYLOR, C. (1975). *Hegel*. London, Cambridge University Press

TAYLOR, M. C. (ed.) (1970). *Taxation for African Economic Development*. London, Hutchinson

THIRLWALL, A. P. (1978). *Growth and Development*, 2nd edn. London, Macmillan

THOMAS, D. (ed.) (1970). *The Mind of Economic Man*. Chislehurst, Quadrangle

THOMPSON, K. (1976). *Auguste Comte: The Foundation of Sociology*. London, Nelson

TODARO, M. P. (1969). A Model of Labor Migration and Urban Unemployment in Less Developed Countries. *American Economic Review* **59**, 138–148

TODARO, M. P. (1976). *Internal Migration and Economic Development: A Review of Theory, Evidence, Methodology and Research Priorities*. Geneva, ILO

TOWNSEND, J. R. (1967). *Political Participation in Communist China*. Berkeley, University of California Press

TSOUKALIS, L. (1981). *The European Community and its Mediterranean Enlargement*. London, Allen and Unwin

TUCKER, D. F. B. (1980). *Marxism and Individualism*. Oxford, Basil Blackwell

TUCKER, R. C. (1961). *Philosophy and Myth in Karl Marx*. London, Cambridge University Press

TULLOCK, G. A. (1976). *The Vote Motive*. London, Institute of Economic Affairs

TURNER, R. K. and COLLINS, C. (1977). *The Economics of Planning*. London, Macmillan

TWITCHETT, C. C. (1981). *A Framework for Development: The EEC and the ACP*. London, Allen and Unwin

TWITCHETT, K. J. (ed.) (1980). *European Cooperation Today*. London, Europa

TYLER, W. G. (1974). Labour Absorption with Import-Substituting Industrialisation: An Examination of Elasticities of Substitution in the Brazilian Manufacturing Sector. *Oxford Economic Papers* **26**, 93–103

UCHUMI EDITORIAL BOARD (ed.) (1972). *Towards Socialist Planning*. Dar es Salaam, Tanzania Publishing House

ULAM, A. B. (1974). *Stalin*. London, Allen Lane

UN (United Nations) (1945). *Documents of the United Nations Conference on International Organisation, San Francisco 1945*. New York

UN (1975a). *Multinational Corporations in World Development*. New York

UN (1975b). *The Population Debate: Dimensions and Perspectives*, 2 vols. New York

UN (1979). *Statistical Yearbook 1978*. New York

UN (1980a). *Yearbook of National Accounts Statistics 1979*. New York

UN (1980b). *Compendium of Social Statistics 1977*. New York

UN (1981). *World Statistics in Brief*. New York

UNIDO (United Nations Industrial Development Organization) (1972). *Guidelines for Project Evaluation*. New York, UN

USHER, D. (1968). *The Price Mechanism and the Meaning of National Income Statistics*. Oxford, Clarendon Press

USHER, D. (1980). *The Measurement of Economic Growth*. Oxford, Basil Blackwell

VAN DEN DOEL, H. (1979). *Democracy and Welfare Economics*. Cambridge, Cambridge University Press

VAN DOREN, C. (1967). *The Idea of Progress*. New York, Praeger

VANEK, J. (1970). *The General Theory of Labor-Managed Market Economies*. Ithaca, Cornell University Press

VANEK, J. (ed.) (1975). *Self-Management: Economic Liberation of Man*. Harmondsworth, Penguin

VARMA, B. N. (1980). *The Sociology and Politics of Development*. London, Routledge and Kegan Paul

VILJOEN, S. (1936). *The Economics of Primitive Peoples*. London, King

VINER, J. (1950). *The Customs Union Issue*. New York, Carnegie Endowment for International Peace

WALZER, M. (1977). *Just and Unjust Wars*. New York, Basic Books

WATT, K. E. F. (1978). The Structure of Post-Industrial Economies. *Journal of Social and Biological Structures* **1**, 53–70

WEINER, J. S. (1971). *Man's Natural History*. London, Weidenfeld and Nicolson

WELLS, H. G. (1945). *Mind at the End of Its Tether*. London, Heinemann

WERTHEIM, W. F. (1974). *Evolution and Revolution*. Harmondsworth, Penguin

WHITE, L. J. (1978). The Evidence on Appropriate Factor Proportions for Manufacturing in Less Developed Economies: A Survey. *Economic Development and Cultural Change* **27**, 27–59

WHYNES, D. K. (1976). South African Military Expenditures – Causes and Consequences. University of Nottingham, Department of Economics Discussion Paper 5

WHYNES, D. K. (1979). *The Economics of Third World Military Expenditure*. London, Macmillan

WHYNES, D. K. and BOWLES, R. A. (1981). *The Economic Theory of the State*. Oxford, Martin Robertson

WILCZYNSKI, J. (1970). *The Economics of Socialism*. London, Allen and Unwin

WILCZYNSKI, J. (1973). *Profit, Risk and Incentive under Socialist Economic Planning*. London, Macmillan

WILES, P. J. D. (ed.) (1971). *The Prediction of Communist Economic Performance*. London, Cambridge University Press

WILES, P. J. D. (1974). *Distribution of Income: East and West*. Amsterdam, North-Holland

WILES, P. J. D. (1977). *Economic Institutions Compared*. Oxford, Basil Blackwell

WILSON, D. (ed.) (1977). *Mao Tse-Tung in the Scales of History*. Cambridge, Cambridge University Press

WILSON, D. (1979). *The Welfare State in Sweden*. London, Heinemann

WINCH, D. (1978). *Adam Smith's Politics*. Cambridge, Cambridge University Press

WINTER, J. M. (ed.) (1975). *War and Economic Development*. Cambridge, Cambridge University Press

WITTFOGEL, K. A. (1957). *Oriental Despotism: A Comparative Study of Total Power*. New Haven, Yale University Press

WOLF-PHILLIPS, L. (ed.) (1968). *Constitutions of Modern States*. London, Pall Mall

YOUNGSON, A. J. (1967). *Overhead Capital*. Edinburgh, Edinburgh University Press

Index

Accumulation,
  primitive capitalist, 224
  primitive socialist, 224
Addiction, 127
Agriculture, 53, 154–156, 211, 249, 274,
    308–309
  in Brazil, 119–120
  in China, 271–273
  in India, 266–269
  in Mexico, 117–119
  in USSR, 222, 224–226, 230
  origins, 5–7
  trade, 193–195, 237
Alienation, 45, 57
Arms race, 293, 299
Assistance, 265, 278, 280, 287, 308–309
  informal, 208
  Official Development (ODA), 200–201, 205–
    209, 297–298.
  tied, 207, 297–298
Automation, 314–315

Balance of payments, 245–246, 278, 299
Bargaining strength, 44, 46, 233, 288–290, 294,
    299–300
Birth rate, 7, 48–49, 130–132, 134, 136, 258
Brandt Commission, 299–300
Bureaucracy, 89, 110–113, 228

Capital, 9–10, 27, 38, 41–42, 44, 49, 166–167,
    200–201, 226, 265–266
  human, 145–150, 163, 244
  sources of, 172–178
  trade in, 193–195
Cheating, 211, 284, 300
Coalitions, political, 82–84
Coercion, 78, 85–86, 90, 99–100, 138, 149, 236,
    271, 282–295, 300
Collectivization, 116, 224–225, 270–272
Collusion, 105, 170, 284, 295, 299–300
Common access, 171
Communism, 28, 42, 87–89, 222
Competition, 53, 110–111, 119, 238–239, 284
  international, 9, 210, 234, 239, 288
  political, 83–84, 89, 94
Constitutions,
  political, 24–25, 27, 80, 101, 232
  psychological, 122–123

Consumption, 5, 9–10, 22, 34, 52, 65, 122–141,
    148, 249, 314
  Scitovsky on, 127–128
Contracts, 19–20, 27
Control, 13, 33–34, 109, 217–218, 229, 245, 260,
    266
Cooperation, 12, 32, 77–78, 82, 93, 116
  international, 95–96, 209–212, 279–280, 284,
    295, 299–300
Cooperative production, 108–109, 113, 247, 274
Corruption, 114, 266
  and kleptocracies, 275–276
Credit, international, 200–202, 299
Crime, conditions for, 102–105
Critical minimum effort, 51, 154
Cycles, 45–46, 54–57

Death rate, 7, 11–12, 49, 130–133, 136, 138
Debt, international, 201–202, 296, 298–299
Defence, expenditure on, 20, 70–71, 77, 226,
    232, 237, 292, 300
Democracy, 43
  direct, 78–82, 312
  industrial, 113–114, 218
  people's, 86–89, 91–92, 94
  representative, 81–86, 90–92, 140, 243, 312
Demographic transition, 132, 138
Demonstration effect, 11, 128
Distribution,
  income, 31, 52, 106–108, 123, 127, 177–178,
      219, 236, 242, 247–248, 251–252, 254,
      269, 298, 306, 309
    criteria for, 26–28
    measures of, 67–70
    trends in, 68–69
  land, 115–120, 272–273
Dual economy, 150–157, 231

Economic growth, 9, 38–42, 44, 145, 153, 218–
    219, 251, 253
  costs of, 236, 238–239, 273
  in Japan, 221, 230–236, 238
  in USSR, 221–230
Economics, 13–14
Economies, classification of, 217–220
Education, 30, 70–71, 144–150, 196, 203, 209,
    226–227, 242, 246–247, 274, 315
  contribution to growth, 145